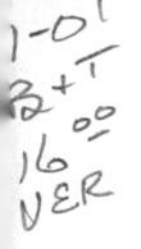

D0840585

THE END OF IDEOLOGY

DANIEL BELL

THE END OF IDEOLOGY

On the Exhaustion of Political Ideas in the Fifties

with "The Resumption of History in the New Century"

HARVARD UNIVERSITY PRESS
Cambridge, Massachusetts, and London, England

Printed in the United States of America

Originally published by The Free Press

Library of Congress Cataloging-in-Publication Data

Bell, Daniel.
The end of ideology : on the exhaustion of political ideas in the fifties / Daniel Bell.
p. cm.
Originally published: Rev. ed., Cambridge, Mass : Harvard University Press, New York : Free Press, 1965, c1962.
Includes bibliographical references and index.
ISBN 0-674-00426-4 (pbk.)
1. United States—Social conditions—1945- 2. Social classes—United States. 3. United States—Economic conditions—1945- I. Title.

HN58 .B424 2000
306′.0973—dc21 00-057523

For Sidney Hook

Contents

II. America: The Complexities of Life

III. The Exhaustion of Utopia

The Resumption of History in the New Century

The End of Ideology was first published in 1960. The essays, a number written in the decade before, dealt with the vicissitudes of the concept of ideology as derived from Marx and elaborated by Karl Mannheim; the exhaustion of Marxism as a political—but not intellectual—doctrine; and the diminishing utility of the use of class in explaining many conflicts, particularly in American life.[1]

Ideology, as I used the term, was not simply a *weltanschauung*, a cultural worldview, or a mask for interests, but an historically located belief system that fused ideas with passion, sought to convert ideas into social levers, and in transforming ideas transformed people as well. When it becomes a striking force, ideology looks at the world with eyes wide shut, a closed system which prefabricates answers to any questions that might be asked.

This is true of many creeds that mobilize individuals—which is why I said, specifically, that ideologies of color and nationalism would appear in the last half of the century. My discussion was focused on Marxism as a creed that, because of its moral failures, had lost its appeal for intellectuals and the masses of people, and why the Marxist political systems, having lost their legitimacy, would fail. (See in particular Chapter 14, on theories of Soviet behavior, especially the section on totalitarianism.)

The immediate context of this argument was the political debates that arose after the war. To that extent this book followed the argument of Albert Camus, who was the first person to use the phrase "the end of ideology"; the volume edited by R. H. Crossman, *The God That Failed,* especially the essays of Arthur Koestler and Ignazio Silone; and the devastating book by Raymond Aron, *The Opium of the Intellectuals.* (That context is elaborated in the Afterword to this volume, added to the Harvard University Press 1988 edition.)

This essay is an effort to present the underlying historical per-

1. An alternative conception of "status politics," presented in Chapter 6, was amplified by Richard Hofstadter, Seymour Martin Lipset, and myself in the volume *The Radical Right* (republished by Transaction Books, 2001).

spective, which had been obscured by the political debates over the title and the theme, and to see where we stand today in the post–Cold War world, a situation that I call "the resumption of history."

The end of the twentieth century has been marked ironically by the declaration of two ends, *the end of ideology* and *the end of history.* Though the two would seem to be similar, they are, in fact, far apart. The end of ideology, as an historical review, is not the end of history, and the end of history, to complete the paralogism, is not the end of ideology.

This book had a fundamental thesis, its underlying framework, namely, that from the seventeenth to the twentieth centuries, there was a great historical crossover in the nature of political discourse and social identifications, a crossover from religion to ideology in the language and rhetoric of the warring belief systems, the great meta-narratives, so to speak, of revolutionary movements and creeds.

An age of revolution had begun in the seventeenth century, a revolution not of an endless rotation of the past, but the overthrow of the existing social order, to turn the world upside-down and bring forth a new heaven on earth, and redeem sin in the souls of men.

The source was the re-introduction of the idea of faith in the conscience of men during the Protestant Reformation. That Reformation, however, divided Christians also by the political allegiances within the various German principalities. The sixteenth and seventeenth centuries were dominated by wars of religion. This came to a surcease, for a time, in the Peace of Augsburg of 1555, with the doctrine of *Cuius regio, eius religio;* the territorial princes determined the religion of their lands, and those who held a different belief would have to migrate (which few could do), convert (which many feared), or corrupt their consciences. It was not until a century later, with the Peace of Westphalia, at the end of the Thirty Years War in 1648, that a policy of toleration was possible for rulers who wanted it.

The millenarian tensions created by the Reformation encouraged the belief in the dissolution of all things secular. Nowhere was this more evident than in the English Revolution of the 1650s, the first sustained effort to realize the kingdom of God on Earth, in the vision given its purest form by the Fifth Monarchy Men. Their source was the Bible: the prophecies in the book of Daniel had long given rise to millennial hopes and expectations. The apocalyptic augury was the image of the four beasts—originally four kings, but after the Reformation, the depiction of four world empires: Babylon, the Medes and the Persians, Greece, and Rome. The last beast had ten horns (or kings) and a little horn, which destroyed the last of them. After that destruction would come the Fifth Monarchy, the kingdom of the saints forever. History, thus, had a divinely ordained conclusion.

The Fifth Monarchy Men was a sect organized to bring about the kingdom of God on Earth. They believed that existing society was the creation of the anti-Christian Fourth Monarchy, and demanded that "all the unGodly be killed and that the wicked have no propriety in their estates." Society was to be remodeled along the pattern laid down in the book of Daniel—a set of precepts, however, so loose that no common program ever emerged.

The conviction that God's saints were engaged in a millenarian struggle in England gave rise to the theory of the elect nation. John Milton, in 1641, wrote of the "*Precedencie* which GOD gave this *Iland,* to be the first *Restorer* of *buried Truth.*"

And the rhetoric of the Fifth Monarchy Men left a deep imprint on the English Revolution. Oliver Cromwell in his early years was a sympathizer, if not a member of a Fifth Monarchy congregation. But their loose resort to arms brought them into disrepute. What followed was Puritanism, the idea of "new men," the saints; new organizations, congregations, and covenants; and the idea of a new society, the holy commonwealth. The rulers, until the return of Christ, would be a small minority, the elect, who would rule as the godly over the unregenerate. The New Model Army that Cromwell created was unique in the history of the military, living under a rigorous self-discipline, avoiding the plunder and pillage typical of almost all armies, because they were in the service of the Lord.

The political struggle was of country against court, parliament against the monarchy. Economic interests were surely at stake, but the language and rhetoric in which the justifications were clothed were in the only terms they knew, the religious terms. What they hoped to do, as Blake wrote later in his *Milton,* was to build Jerusalem in England's green and pleasant land. Yet John Milton himself, who in his *Tenure of Kings and Magistrates* had justified the death of an unworthy king, and had become Latin Secretary for Foreign Affairs in Cromwell's government, was also one of the first to express his disillusionment with one-man rule in his pamphlet *The Ready and Easy Way to Establish a Free Commonwealth.* He was among the first, but not the last.[2]

The great crossover came with the French Revolution. The lan-

2. For this period, see B. S. Capp, *The Fifth Monarchy Men* (London: Faber & Faber, 1972), and Michael Walzer, *The Revolution of the Saints: A Study in the Origins of Radical Politics* (Cambridge, Mass.: Harvard University Press, 1965).

The crossover had ended. That was the thesis of "the end of ideology."

The "end of history," as fashioned by Hegel, was a metaphysical doctrine. The philosophy of history was a parallel (if not replacement) for the theological direction of history. In Christian doctrine, man was separated from God by the Fall. As Augustine formulated the Church's view, the end of time would come with the *parousia,* the Second Coming, when man would be reunited with God. That would be the end of history, of man's time on earth.

In the Hegelian view, there was an original cosmic consciousness that was dirempted by the emergence of self-consciousness. Man was divided into subject and object, the I and the Me, and the distinction between appearance and reality. Through time, this division proceeds through the inner levels of consciousness by the *begriff,* the cunning of reason, while on the manifest level, the divisions of history are realized by world-historical figures such as Alexander, Caesar, and Napoleon, who are the instruments of the sweep to universalism. The end of history, in the Hegelian scheme, becomes the realm of the transcendental.

Marx had taken the Hegelian drama and given it a social location. The original unity of species-being *(wesen)* and primitive communal living became divided by mental and physical labor, town and country living, and, most important of all, the propertied and the propertyless (the proletariat). The end of history on the social level was the end of these divisions under full communism. And on the level of consciousness, as Engels said, there would be an "end of ideology," for ideology, the deceptive images of "false consciousness," would be fused with the material world, the structural source of reality.[5] In both doctrines, the fusion of appearance and reality meant that men would no longer be ruled by ghosts, spirits, fetishes—i.e., religion—but, in the words of Shelley's *Prometheus Unbound,* would become "equal, unclassed, tribeless, and nationless, / Exempt from awe . . . the king / Over himself . . ."

The end of history, as the term was used by Francis Fukuyama, despite its resounding echo, is a far different, even prosaic use of the Hegelian phrase. For Mr. Fukuyama, the end of the Cold War was the victory of democracy and the market, and of a universalist creed that had no other rivals. Islam and Catholicism make

5. I have explored the textual sources of these arguments in my essay "The Misreading of Ideology: The Social Determination of Ideas in Marx's Thought," in the *Berkeley Journal of Sociology,* 1990.

universalist religious claims, and while Islam once tried to conquer the world by the sword, and Catholicism, up until the modern period, through the arms of the secular monarchs, they are incapable of becoming universal today—Islam in particular, since its theocratic view joins economics, politics, and religion into one doctrine (as did communism). To assume, however, that democracy will command the allegiance of the world's peoples is to assume that "ideas" drive history. But, more, it is to stand in the lineage of a single-minded view that "History" has a direction, if not a *telos,* and to obscure the very complexities of history with which we live. What, then, of the post–Cold War, after the "end of ideology"?

We are all embedded in history. The present is not the past, in the obvious sense that while there may be continuities over time—for example, the great historical religions, perhaps the most enduring of human institutions—even these continuities take different form and differentiation over time. In the past four hundred years, science and technology have created not only new modes of thinking, but new instruments to remake nature, if not ourselves.

But how do we characterize history or, since history is not a *thing* but a set of changing relationships, how do we delineate historical inquiry, the ways of identifying the significant patterns of change? Conventionally, we speak of ancient, medieval, and modern history, though, on reflection, this is largely a sequence of Western history. Adam Smith and colleagues of the Scottish Enlightenment had described a four-stages theory through which society passed, based on the modes of subsistence: hunting, pastoral, agricultural, and commercial. Marx, bypassing this, had made the modes of production the fulcrum of social evolution, that of slavery, feudalism, and capitalism.

Apart from the difficulties of establishing a universal frame of reference, there are good sociological reasons why it is difficult to posit *unified periodizations* as a set of frames to understand history. Society is composed, I would argue, of three different realms, each of which follows different "logics" of organization: the techno-economic, the polity, and the culture.

The techno-economic realm is a system in that it consists of loosely interrelated units in which changes in the magnitudes of one set of variables have a more or less determinate outcome among the others in the decisions of the relevant economic actors. Change is "linear" in that if a new product or service is cheaper or more productive than the previous one, then, subject to cost, it is used. It is a process of substitution. The system moves, more or less, through markets, to equilibrium.

The polity is *not* a system, but a social order, a set of rules, by coercion or consent, that regulates the competition of disparate actors, the "ins" and the "outs" for political place and privilege in the society. The polity is also a set of rules for the administration of justice (as defined at the time), the protection of individuals and the punishment of malefactors. The state, as Max Weber famously observed, is the only social unit with a legitimate monopoly in the use of force. There is no "linear" movement, but more often alternations in the constellation of actors—most usually, various elites.

Culture has two dimensions: the styles of the expressive arts, and the modes of meaning, historically the religious. At times the two have fused, as in the liturgy, litany, music, and architecture of the Catholic Church. More often, as in "modern" times, they have been separate. In the expressive arts, there is no principle of substitution. Boulez does not "replace" Bach. The newer tonalities or use of perspective for the picture widen the aesthetic repertoire of mankind. Among the great historic religions, Buddhism, Confucianism, Judaism, Christianity, Islam, despite all the changes in form, the *core* doctrines of karma and transmigration, of monotheism and the covenant, of the Koran and the prophet, are still recognizable today.

Tradition guards the portals of change, and syncretism (as in Augustan Rome or modern times) provides a permeability for culture to pass through national or historical boundaries. Yet though economic systems have crumbled and political empires have disappeared, the great historical religions and the great expressive forms of culture, from Egyptian reliefs and Chinese scrolls through all the myriad works that fill our museums to overflowing, retain their power for appreciation and renewal.

How, then, can one think of unified periods of historical time, which jumble economics, politics, and culture into a single configuration,[6] as being consistent?

How, then, should we look at history? For Clausewitz, history

6. Marx was once asked how it was that, if each mode of production has a qualitatively different form from previous ones, we could still appreciate the artistic and dramatic works of the Greeks. He never responded publicly, but in his *nachlasse,* some posthumous notes, he replied that the Greeks represented "the childhood of the human race, and that we respond to it as we do to all the charming works of children." But Antigone, defying Creon in order to demand the bodies of her brothers to give them a decent burial, is not a child; nor was Nadezhda Mandelstam, seeking the body of her husband Osip, murdered by Stalin, to give him a decent burial. Burial, with monuments, is one of the transcendental markers of a civilized society.

was driven by the interplay of Reason, Passion, and Chance, made manifest by the state, people, and war. For historians of a grand sweep, there are the meta-narratives, *Enlightenment, Progress,* now *Globalization,* that encompass the modalities of philosophical or economic currents. Each of these has its attraction, but for a sociologist they fly too far above the empirical terrain and lack any lenses to identify significant changes in the patterns of social relationships, and to understand the impact on everyday life—what Husserl called the *lebenswelt,* or lived experience.

I would propose three prisms, which are not necessarily congruent, for sociological inquiry:

Contingent turning points: Events, technological or political, that re-orient the course of history in totally unexpected directions.
Institutional structures, which establish set relationships over time for individuals in the positions and roles, of status and class, in the stratification systems of society.
The primordial identities of peoples: The communal entities sharing language or religion, united by what the sociologist Franklin Henry Giddings called "the consciousness of kind," and expressing that unity in a common life both in the polity and in the culture.

Contingent events, by their nature, are unpredictable, for they are not determined, and emerge from the vicissitudes of chance. The February Revolution in Russia was the outcome of a long chain of circumstances that resulted from the breakdown of existing structures, but the October seizure of power by the Bolsheviks was a gamble that paid off. Equally, the choice of Hitler for chancellor by Hindenberg, at a time when the Nazi Party had begun to lose votes, may have been prompted by the belief that Hitler could be controlled by von Papen and General Schleicher. He destroyed both.

Yet the events, though prompted by chance, also produce what Michael Oakeshott, in a stunning phrase, called "interlocking contingencies." The turn itself is uncertain, but what follows is a train of events whose consequences reconfigure history.

Institutional structures have been the major frameworks of history since the beginning of civilization. Technologically, there have been pre-industrial, industrial, and post-industrial societies. Feudalism, capitalism, and socialism have been regnant social systems. But politically, the most enduring institutions have been empires, those vast territorial conglomerates held together most often by armed force. What has been the most fateful fact of the twentieth century, a fact overshadowed by communism and fascism, has been the breakup of empire.

World War I saw the shattering of the Habsburg and Romanov dynasties, of Wilhelminian Germany and the Ottoman Empire, lineages which, in the case of the Habsburgs, had lasted for more than a thousand years, beginning as the Holy Roman Empire. No such large-scale political earthquake had been seen since the breakup of the Roman empire and the existence of Byzantium for a thousand years.

After World War I, the map of Europe was redrawn, with countries such as Poland, Czechoslovakia, Hungary, and the Baltic states becoming national states. In the Middle East, Syria, Lebanon, Palestine, Jordan, and Saudi Arabia emerged, with Syria alone having an historic identity. The others, created by the British, sought uneasily to find out who they were.

World War II saw the end of the English, French, Dutch, Belgian, and Portuguese empires, and more than a hundred new states arising from the ruins, but, in almost all cases, the old natural boundaries of tribes and peoples were crossed by the new entities.

In 1989, the Soviet empire dissolved and Yugoslavia disintegrated, with dozens of peoples coming out of the shadows and seeking to assert a new singularity. The Soviet experiment had been a "revolution from above." Now these peoples were turning to the past, trying to become, in Herder's sense, a *volk.* It is that effort, once more, to become a *people,* which characterizes the end of the twentieth century. That is the resumption of history that stamps itself on our time.

The idea of a "people" is an amorphous concept, yet other than tribe or clan, it is one of the oldest and most powerful feelings in history. History most often has been the subjection of "peoples" by marauding armies. While whole peoples have disappeared, through extermination or assimilation, what is so extraordinary has been the persistence of peoples, and their efforts to achieve self-determination on some territorial ground.

In the nineteenth century, the phrase most commonly used for peoples was race, a term that denoted a common ancestry. One of those who had first used this term was an extraordinary man, now almost forgotten, who was the third man with Marx and Engels (after all, the dialectic is a triad)—Moses Hess. Hess was an early Hegelian who introduced Marx to social and economic problems (when Marx was still wound up in philosophy) and converted Engels to communism. Hess collaborated with Marx on sections of *The German Ideology,* and even participated in the early discussions of *The Communist Manifesto.* The break with Marx came over Judaism. The generation of German Jews who had been emancipated by Napoleon was threatened by the reversion to the ghetto with the return of the German princes. Many Jews, such as Marx's father, converted. Hess's father did not. Nor did Hess. Marx, like Fichte before him, considered the Jews to be a "huckster people" and retrograde. Hess considered the Jews to be "a world-historic civilized people," who, moreover, could never live peacefully in a Europe where Jew-hatred was endemic and would not be eradicated. The only solution for Jews, wrote Hess in 1862, would be to achieve a nationality and a state of their own.

Hess came to his views in sharp disagreement with Marx. "Social institutions," he wrote, "like spiritual outlooks, are racial creations." All of past history was concerned with the struggle of races and classes. "Race struggle is primary; class struggle is secondary. When racial antagonism ceases, class struggle also ceases. Equality of all social classes follows on the heels of equality of all races and finally remains merely a question of sociology."[7]

For those who think of history as irony, Marx's name remains in defeat, though Hess's has not. As a proto-Zionist, he had voiced the need of a people, maintained by history and a vision, to realize an aspiration. The creation of Israel as a Jewish national state, after a diaspora of almost two millennia, is one of the most extraordinary episodes in the history of peoples.

Hess was a nineteenth-century thinker. Yet, as Lionel Trilling observed in his study of Matthew Arnold (who had used race as a way of explaining how "people's habits . . . determine its modes of life, institutions and government") racial theory "was almost undisputed in the nineteenth century." And, he continued, "Stendhal, Meredith, Mme. de Stael, Carlyle, J. A. Froude, Kingsley, J. R. Green, Taine, Renan [from whom Arnold got much of his interest in the Celts], Sainte-Beuve—all built the racial hypothesis into their work. Indeed the list could be made to include nearly every writer of the time who generalized about human affairs."[8]

7. Moses Hess, *Rome and Jerusalem* (New York: Philosophical Library, 1958). At the conclusion of the Foreword, no pagination. About his views of the fate of Jews in Europe, Hess notes that in 1840, after the Damascus Affair, a savage attack on Jews, ". . . the Germans, after their war of Liberation, not only repudiated the Jews who fought with them against France but moreover even persecuted them with the cry of 'Hep-Hep.' . . . What the German patrioteer loves in his fatherland is not the State but racial domination." Ibid., p. 33.

Needless to say, Marx, who could never brook any opposition, damned Hess in vituperative and scatological terms ("someone excreted from a dung factory"), and as a Jew.

8. Lionel Trilling, *Matthew Arnold* (New York, Meridian Books, 1955), pp. 214–215. The study was originally published in 1939.

Race today is a tarnished word, defiled by the Nazis or, even if one seeks for a more neutral use, identified strongly with color. *Ein Volk,* despite its origins with Herder, has eerie echoes of a disturbing kind. The nation comprises a unity of peoples but it is largely a political term, tied up inextricably with State, and conflicted with the question of citizenship. (Are those who "merely" happened to be born on a nation's territory "citizens" despite other origins or kin, as in the United States but not in Germany?)

If the "resumption of history" is the breakup of nations and states, and the re-emergence of "peoples" as a singular social entity, some other word is needed to reduce the amorphousness. I would adopt here the neologism *ethnie,* as used by the French sociologist Dominique Schnapper. *Ethnie* designates the peoples who share an emotional bond and language, whose deepest instincts are to assert themselves as a community that lives a common life, and that declares, in its legends and poetry and song, a common destiny—to the death.[9]

The breakup of any coercive empire multiplies not only the number of new states but the number of *ethnie* within those new states. That is the new situation everywhere. The end of the old Soviet Union resulted in the creation—or rather, the resumption—of fifteen states, including a new, much smaller Russia.[10] Yet about 25 million Russians were now left in these new states. Previously, they had usually held privileged positions, as part of the control apparatus; now they had become ethnic minorities, situations for which they were never prepared. Although ethnic Russians constitute a vast majority in the new Russian Federation (about 80 percent of the population), many non-Russian nationalities have their own republics based on ethno-territorial recognition, and occupy about 53 percent of the whole land mass of the Russian Federation. Such small ethnic nationalities as Tatarstan, Bashkortostan, Udmurtia, Bujryatia, Tuva, Komi, and Yakutia, all claim in their constitutions a desire to secede, or to achieve preferential status as *ethnie* in their republics.[11]

Even the independent states have their difficulties in creating

9. Dominique Schnapper, *Community of Citizens: On the Modern Idea of Nationality* (New Brunswick: Transaction Publishers, 1998.)

10. These are Estonia, Latvia, and Lithuania in the Baltic region; Belarus, Ukraine, and Moldavia in eastern Europe; Armenia, Azerbaijan, and Georgia in the Caucasus; and Kazakhstan, Kyrgyzstan, Uzbekistan, Tajikstan, and Turkmenistan in Central Asia.

11. See Anatoly M. Khazanov, "Ethnic Nationalism in the Russian Federation," *Daedalus,* Summer 1997, p. 135.

"national identification." Tajikstan—a Persian-speaking population descended from the earliest known inhabitants of Central Asia—has slightly more than 5 million people, but only about 60 percent of them are Tajiks. Uzbeks make up almost 25 percent of the population, but there are some 14 million more Uzbeks across the border in neighboring Uzbekistan. And a large number of Tajiks live in Uzbekistan and a roughly equal number in Afghanistan. The Russians, less than 10 percent of the population of Tajikstan, occupied the important positions in industry, the professions, the political police, and the military. In 1992, civil war broke out when the Uzbek minority, aided by Russia, took control of the capital. Negotiations brokered by the United Nations created an uneasy settlement. Here was a tiny center of the Eurasian heartland, once the home of the old Silk Route and the Haushofer doctrine of world military power. But how many persons knew of these ethnic difficulties in the resumption of history?

The world has known of Chechnya because of the brutal Russian campaign to suppress the independence movement of a group of stubborn peoples who, during World War II, had been uprooted by Stalin (for fear of their secession) and deported wholesale into Asia, until their return. But the Caucasus, as readers of Mikhail Lermontov's great romantic collection of stories, *A Hero of Our Time,* know, is a setting of great mountain wilderness and beauty, of stories of passion and brutality. The Caucasus seems almost to have been made for war. Fifty ethnic groups live along the 900-mile-long mountain range that gives the region its name. In the south are Georgia, Armenia, and Azerbaijan, the first two Orthodox Christian cultures, the third Turkified and Islamicized descendants of Caucasian Albania. Four distinct civilizations intersect and overlap: that of the Turkish steppe, the Middle East, eastern Europe, and the Caucasus itself, the home of a resourceful warrior tradition that is millennia old. Ninety years of communist rule could not erase these deep-creviced differences. They have been resumed in our time.

Such is the situation as well in the Balkans. The victory of Tito in 1945 brought an uneasy peace within the region. The new Yugoslavia was made up of six republics—Serbia, Croatia, Bosnia-Herzegovina, Montenegro, Macedonia, and Slovenia—and two autonomous regions, Kosovo and Vojvodina. But the situation was anomalous. Yugoslavia itself was not a single nation-state, and even the distinction between the two was blurred. Only in Slovenia were nation and state coterminous. Yugoslavia was to be a union of communist *peoples.* But while Yugoslavia was to be a union of peoples, the fact remained that out of a population of 20 million persons, 4 million had been displaced or moved away from their original homelands, and now were minorities in other republics.

Yet what was most striking about this tangled set of relations was the depth of feeling of each people as *ethnie,* often going back and retainting their emotions, for as much as a thousand years. Under the successive regimes of dozens of different rulers, the one thing that could hold them together was the legends of the past.

Slovenia "had been trampled on by just about everyone who mattered in Europe," as *The Economist* once wrote. Their longest-standing masters were the Austrian Habsburgs, who had ruled Slovenia for most of the last half-millennium. The French, under Napoleon, conquered Slovenia in the early nineteenth century. In fascist times, its capital, Ljubliana, lay on the fault line between Hitler's Reich and Mussolini's Italy. After the Russians took charge, the Serbs dominated Slovenia from Belgrade. Yet in 1991, it emerged as a nation and a people. The Slovenes had been part of the great Slavic migrations from the Vistula and Oder basins in the sixth century, and under the Austrians had become Roman Catholic. But their national consciousness took a special turn in the nineteenth century, as it did for so many peoples in Europe when Napoleon sought to include them in his "province of Illyria." In resistance, their poets developed a literary collection of legends and folklore about the past. It is possible that such stories were contrived or elaborated, but the essential fact was that they were believed and became the emotional bond that re-fashioned the people as an *ethnie.*

For the Serbs, a Slavic people who came to the Balkans in the seventh century, ousting the Thracians, Illyrians, and Dacians among others, legends have been the scarlet thread that runs through their history. The defining moment came when the Ottoman Turks defeated the Serbs at Kosovo Poljie, the Field of Blackbirds, and presumably beheaded the Serb leader, Prince Lazar. His storied statement, "It is better to die in battle than live in shame"—choosing death rather than surrender—became the founding myth of national consciousness.

Throughout the long bloody history of wars and rebellions, the Serbs kept together. Here we return to Prince Lazar, whose legends were written down by church scribes and canonized in repeated cycles of folk poetry. Lazar's body was placed in a monastery in 1401 or 1402, a monastery he had founded in Ravanica, his body dressed in a coat adorned with lions rampant and covered with a red shroud. In commemoration of the 600th anniversary of the great battle, his bones were taken around Serbia from monastery to monastery. Today Lazar's shriveled bones lie once more in Ravanica. On Sundays, the coffin is opened, but only his brown and withered hands peek out from under the shroud. Should one be cynical? Is all this just a maneuver by the ruling regime? Perhaps. But the fact remains that the legends, and the past, are there for the people to believe. And as one can say of another icon: Prince Lazar has lived, Prince Lazar lives. Prince Lazar will (may) live.[12]

Before World War II, 80 percent of the land mass of the world, and 80 percent of the world's peoples, were under the rule of Western powers. With a rapidity that will astonish the historian of the twenty-first century, colonialism ended with a speed that is unique in political history. Fifty-three sovereign nations (and a few dependencies) emerged from the British Empire. Twenty countries emerged from French rule, sixteen of these in Africa, two in North Africa, and two—Vietnam and Cambodia—in Asia. In all, an astonishing 120 new nations emerged from the wreckages of empire.

But all that adds to the most salient social fact in the world today, that almost *every* nation in the world is a plural nation, a polysemic admixture of majority and minority groups, of linguistic or ethnic groups asserting multicultural rights. No nation today is homogeneous. Japan, which had once asserted that fact, now has large knots of Koreans, and even Chinese and Pakistani workers, living in enclaves in Tokyo and Osaka; and it faces the question of openly admitting immigrants as its working-age population shrinks in ratio to the retired, longer-living workers. Sweden, which had claimed to be culturally unified, has had to deal with clusters of Gypsies and Turks who have become problems for the authorities. Singapore admits large numbers of Pakistanis and other foreign workers, but deports them regularly after five years, in order to maintain control of the city.

Few countries seem to be immune to the issue. Devolution (to

12. Is it only a question of power? I think, for example, of the story of Mihalo Markovic, a courageous dissident during the Tito regime, an editor then of the liberal Marxist magazine *Praxis,* which had the cooperation of Jürgen Habermas and the political theorist Seyla Benhabib. During the Tito regime he was in exile, teaching at the University of Pennsylvania. Today, as a Serb patriot, he is vice-president of Milosevic's Serbian Socialist Party, defending Serbia's actions against Croatia and Bosnia by invoking Abraham Lincoln's effort to save the Union in the American Civil War.

I have written in detail on the Yugoslav civil conflicts in *Correspondence,* no. 4, the periodical of the Committee on Intellectual Correspondence. On the history of Serbia, I have drawn from Tim Judah's excellent volume, *The Serbs* (New Haven: Yale University Press, 1997).

rhyme with evolution, not revolution) has become the accepted policy in the United Kingdom: Scotland now has its own parliament and control of aspects of its cultural life, such as education; Wales has its own assembly; and Northern Ireland may yet become free of Whitehall. There is even a question whether the United Kingdom may not break up in the next decade. Belgium is so completely divided between the Flemish and the Walloons as to be, effectively, two nations. Czechoslovakia has broken apart as the Czech Republic and Slovakia. In Romania and Slovakia there are large Hungarian minorities. Spain has Catalonia and the Basques. Checkerboard patterns exist within Armenia and Azerbaijan. And there are the Kurds, spilled across Turkey, Iraq, and Iran, who still seek a national state of their own.

While such people's movements have existed throughout history, is there some explanation for the present widespread eruptions? In nineteenth-century Europe, it was nationalism, a movement fueled by romanticism, the songs and poetry of writers, and the role of flamboyant red-shirt leaders like Garibaldi, but given an institutional foundation by the growth of industry and trade out of local regions onto a national scale, and therefore needing national political governance such as tariffs or import-export controls, let alone national armies.

In a paradoxical sense, it may be nationalism again, but for the reverse reason, which may be the cause today. The tectonic forces are economic globalization, as capital, currencies, and commodities stream across national boundaries—and people seek to follow. Many states have lost control of their national currencies and are monitored by the International Monetary Fund, or resort to "dollarization" by substituting dollars for their own currencies as the source of their credit and exchange rates.

The national state was an adaptive instrument to meet the new scale of economic activity and confront other national states. But no longer. Increasingly, the national states begin to combine into regional forces such as the European Community (and the Euro currency), and NAFTA, the North American Free Trade Alliance, which combines Mexico, the United States, and Canada as a single production and trading bloc. And the capital investment strength of Japan exercises a net of Asian power.

With economic integration, then, has come political fragmentation, all given an extra spin by the breakup of Western imperialism on the one hand, and the communist bloc on the other.

Is there a new shape to world society, then, after the Cold War? If I leave out the emerging great-power roles of China, and possibly India, on one side, and the intractable economic difficulties of the sub-Saharan states, decimated by ethnic conflict and the inability to move from their resource base to a post-industrial world, on the other, there may yet be a benign view. It would be of a global *economic* society, with a redistribution of production and technology,[13] a set of regional *political* blocs, with uniform budget and welfare rules, and *cultural* autonomy within the national states and regions.

In one respect, the United States, as a continental society, is a model for such a hopeful view. Despite the tensions of race, it has brought the black community into the political system, as witnessed by the fact that almost every major American city (with the exception of Boston) has had a black mayor, plus many hundreds of local black officials. The economic disparities, however, remain. And much depends upon the continuing economic vitality and technological initiatives the United States has demonstrated.

In Europe, other than the Balkans and the Caucusus, the spillovers of empire breakup, ethnic conflicts have not erupted (though violence against immigrants has been ominous in some countries). Catalonia has been an example of viable cultural autonomy, and the tolerance of Turkish communities in Germany indicates a notable political maturity.

This is the benign view, if not hope. The central fact in viewing history as the history of *peoples* (not just of institutions or structures) is the increasing demand for cultural (if not political) autonomy by peoples throughout the world, such as the Québécois, Chiapans, Basques, Lombards, Corsicans, Kosovars, Kurds, Chechens, Kashmiris, Tamils, Tibetans, Palestinians, East Timorese, and a half dozen or more in the Indonesian archipelago.[14] Can this be achieved? The European Charter for Regional or Minority Languages adopted by the forty-member Council of Europe, which went into effect in March 1998, decrees the "inalienable right" to use a regional or minority language in private and public life, defining these as those "traditionally used" by nationals in a state numerically smaller than the rest of the state's population. Yet though fine in theory, only eight countries have ratified the treaty, while France has balked on the ground of alleged dangers to the sanctity of the mother tongue. These are not the clashes of civilization, which may be history writ large, but

13. I have dealt with that problem at length in the new Foreword 2000, in the republication of *The Coming of Post-Industrial Society* (New York: Basic Books, 2000).

14. See Hurst Hannum, *Autonomy, Sovereignty, and Self-Determination* rev. ed. (Philadelphia: University of Pennsylvania Press, 1996).

the conflict of rights within states and nations, which is history writ small, yet closer to the passions of peoples.

But I conclude: the "end of ideology," as the great historic cross-over of beliefs, has run its course, I think. It is now the resumption of history that has begun.

Introduction:

The Restless Vanity

The future belongs to the masses, or to the men who can explain things simply to them.—Jacob Burckhardt

THESE ESSAYS, IN the main, deal with the social changes in the America of the fifties. It was a decade marked by extraordinary changes in the class structure, particularly in the growth of the white-collar class and the spread of suburbia; by the "forced" expansion of the economy, which belied earlier predictions of stagnation; by the creation of a permanent military establishment and a bedrock defense economy; and by the heightening tensions of the Cold War. In consequence, we have had the problem, abroad, of defining ourselves to Indians, Africans, Arabs, *et al.*, and, at home, a preoccupation with "self" and "status" that has brought to the fore not only psychoanalysis but the mirror of popular sociology. The "restless vanity" of which de Tocqueville spoke, which made the American, in his intercourse with strangers, "impatient of the slightest censure and insatiable of praise," has been replaced by an anxious inferiority, fearful of censure and desperately eager to please.

I have not attempted one more contribution to the character structure of the American. Nor have I a thesis about the uniqueness of the American experience or the genius of American politics. I doubt, as I expressed it in the essay on the "refractions of the American past," that any single set of mirrors can focus and capture the glancing ambiguities and complexities of American life. What I seek to emphasize here is the falsity of simplification and the ideological pitfalls into which such simplifications lead; and such efforts are necessarily critical. The critic, said John Stuart Mill in an essay on Bentham, is among the lowest order of the potentates of the mind. I begin, then, at the bottom rung.

The inadequacy of many social theories about America, I argue in Part I, is due in large measure to the uncritical application of ambient ideas from European sociology to the vastly different experiences of American life. This is most evident in the theory of the mass society, a concept that has become the leitmotif of the radical and aristocratic disparage-

way of becoming sophisticated about the world. It is at one with academic sociology in using similar concepts (group, status, social mobility), and with literary analysis in the interest in the moral component of social action.

The focus of sociology is different from literary analysis, and its methods and exploration lead in different directions. Both may be concerned, say, with how the plays of Tennessee Williams and William Inge reflect the changing social and sexual responses of the American male. But literary analysis (as practiced, say, by Lionel Trilling in the older, and by Robert Brustein in the younger, generation) seeks the *prototypical,* or the root ideas of the experience. Sociological analysis, accepting this, looks for the *typical,* or the relevance of one set of ideas to other social mores. A literary analysis is *textual;* it takes the "work" as its world. A sociological analysis is *contextual;* it seeks the wider setting, in order to relate its distinctions to the society as a whole.

I would hope that these essays, by dealing with sociological problems from a critical standpoint, but free from jargon, might bridge the gap between the social sciences and the humanistic world.

An author is not exempt, particularly in essays in social analysis, from making explicit his own values. The perspective I adopt is anti-ideological, but not conservative. In the last decade, we have witnessed an exhaustion of the nineteenth-century ideologies, particularly Marxism, as intellectual systems that could claim *truth* for their views of the world. In reaction to these ideologies—and their compulsions to total commitment of intellect and feeling—many intellectuals have begun to fear "the masses," or any form of social action. This is the basis of neo-conservatism and the new empiricism. Inevitably one shares some of these fears. But a repudiation of ideology, to be meaningful, must mean not only a criticism of the utopian order but of existing society as well. (One is reminded of the dialectical definition, by the wry Polish intellectual, of capitalism and communism. Capitalism, it is said, is a system wherein man exploits man. And communism—is vice versa.) What is left for the critic is the hardness of alienation, the sense of otherness. The claims of doubt are prior to the claims of faith. One's commitment is to one's vocation.

Alienation is not nihilism but a positive role, a detachment, which guards one against being submerged in any cause, or accepting any particular embodiment of community as final. Nor is alienation deracination, a denial of one's roots or country. Some unofficial ideologues fear that a critical view of America would influence intellectuals in Asia and Africa to be anti-American, or to reject democratic values. This is a parochial view of the intellectual life. A society is most vigorous, and appealing, when both partisan and critic are legitimate voices in the permanent dialogue that is the testing of ideas and experience. One can be a critic of one's country without being an enemy of its promise.

For this edition, I have considerably enlarged the concluding essay on "The End of Ideology in the West," in order to trace the historical development of the term "ideology," and to clarify its many, varied usages. In this respect, my own usage is not just of "ideology" as denoting *any* "belief-system," but as a special complex of ideas and passions that arose in the nineteenth century. I am aware, as Fritz Stern has noted in his book, *The Politics of Cultural Despair,* that I have applied the term largely to left-wing thought, and so restrict its scope. This is true. Yet, while there are "ideologies" of the "right" as well as of the "left,"—as there are now "ideologies" of economic development—one's historical contexts defines one's usage; and the word *ideology* was a product of the "left" and gained a distinctive resonance in that context. And this was the focus of my discussion. I have also added some sections on the new "rhetoric of revolution" which some members of the "new left" have adopted in order to justify the suppression of liberties in the new states.

One essay, "Interest and Ideology: on the Role of Public Opinion in Industrial Disputes," an essay on the background of the Taft-Hartley law, and the manipulation of public opinion in that debate, has been eliminated because of its lesser historical interest.

DANIEL BELL

Columbia University
March 1961

PART I

America: The Ambiguities of Theory

Chapter 1

America as a Mass Society: A Critique

> . . . a sombre melancholy weighed on people's souls. . . . It would sometimes seem as if this period had been particularly unhappy, as if it had left behind only the memory of violence, of covetousness and moral hatred. . . . The feeling of general insecurity [was heightened] by the chronic form wars were apt to take, by the constant menace of the dangerous classes, by the mistrust of justice. . . . It was, so to say, bad form to praise the world and life openly. It was fashionable to see only its suffering and misery, to discover everywhere the signs of decadence and the near end—in short to condemn the times or to despise them.
>
> —J. H. Huizinga, *The Waning of the Middle Ages*

THE SENSE OF a radical dehumanization of life which has accompanied events of the past few decades has given rise to the theory of "mass society." One can say that, Marxism apart, it is probably the most influential social theory in the Western world today. While no single individual has stamped his name on it—to the extent that Marx is associated with the transformation of personal relations under capitalism into commodity values, or Freud with the role of the irrational and unconscious in behavior—the theory is central to the thinking of the principal aristocratic, Catholic, or Existentialist critics of modern society. These critics—Ortega y Gasset, Paul Tillich, Karl Jaspers, Gabriel Marcel, Emil Lederer, Hannah Arendt, and others — have been concerned less with the general conditions of freedom in society than with the freedom of the *person* and with the possibility, for some few persons, of achieving a sense of individual self in our mechanized society. And this is the source of their appeal.

The conception of the "mass society" can be summarized as follows: The revolutions in transport and communications have brought men into closer contact with each other and bound them in new ways; the division of labor has made them more interdependent; tremors in one part of society affect all others. Despite this greater interdependence, however, individuals have grown more estranged from one another. The old primary group ties of family and local community have been shattered; ancient parochial faiths are questioned; few unifying values have taken their place. Most important, the critical standards of an educated elite no longer shape opinion or taste. As a result, mores and morals are in constant flux, relations between individuals are tangential or compartmentalized, rather than organic. At the same time, greater mobility, spatial and social, intensifies concern over status. Instead of a fixed or known status, symbolized by dress or title, each person assumes a multiplicity of roles and constantly has to prove himself in a succession of new situations. Because of all this, the individual loses a coherent sense of self. His anxieties increase. There ensues a search for new faiths. The stage is thus set for the charismatic leader, the secular messiah, who, by bestowing upon each person the semblance of necessary grace and of fullness of personality, supplies a substitute for the older unifying belief that the mass society has destroyed.

In a world of lonely crowds seeking individual distinction, where values are constantly translated into economic calculabilities, where in extreme situations shame and conscience can no longer restrain the most dreadful excesses of terror, the theory of the mass society seems a forceful, realistic description of contemporary society, an accurate reflection of the *quality* and *feeling* of modern life. But when one seeks to apply the theory of mass society, analytically, it becomes very slippery. Ideal types, like the shadows in Plato's cave, generally never give us more than a silhouette. So, too, with the theory of "mass society." Each of the statements making up the theory, as set forth in the second paragraph above, might be true, but they do not follow necessarily from one another. Nor can we say that all the conditions described are present at any one time or place. More than that, there is no organizing principle—other than the general concept of a "breakdown of values"—that puts the individual elements of theory together in a logical, meaningful—let alone historical—manner. And when we examine the way the "theory" is used by those who employ it, we find ourselves even more at a loss.

In trying to sort out the ambiguities in the use of the phrase, we can distinguish perhaps five different, and sometimes contradictory, usages:

1. *Mass as undifferentiated number.* As commonly used in the term "mass media," "mass" implies that standardized material is transmitted to "all groups of the population uniformly."[1] As understood generally by sociologists, a *mass* is a heterogeneous and undifferentiated audience, as opposed to a *class,* or any parochial and relatively homogeneous segment. Some sociologists have been tempted to go further and make

"mass" a rather pejorative term. Because the mass media subject a diverse audience to a common set of cultural materials, it is argued that these experiences must necessarily lie outside the personal — and therefore meaningful — experiences to which the individual responds directly. A movie audience, for example, is a "mass" because the individuals looking at the screen are, in the words of the American sociologist Herbert Blumer, "separate, detached and anonymous." The mass "has no social organization, no body of custom and tradition, no established set of rules or rituals, no organized group of sentiments, no structure of status roles and no established leadership."[2]

To become part of the mass is to be divorced—or "alienated"—from oneself. And the instruments which project the dominant social values that men (and women and children) choose as their *imago,* or ideal image and desire—television, radio, and the movies—impose a mass response on their audience.

2. *Mass as the judgment by the incompetent.* As first introduced by the late Ortega y Gasset in 1931, in his famous *Revolt of the Masses,* the terms "masses" and "mass" had a far different meaning than the usage implied by the term "mass media" and its invidious connotations. For Ortega, the word "mass" did not designate a group of persons—the masses were not the workers, even though the revolutionary movements of the time had equated the two—but the low *quality* of modern civilization, resulting from the loss of a commanding position by the "gentlemen" who once made up the educated elite. Modern taste, for Ortega, represents the judgment of the unqualified. Modern life "makes a *tabula rasa* of all classicism." Nothing that is in the past can be "any possible model or standard." Even "the famous Renaissance reveals itself as a period of narrow provincialism—why not use the word?—ordinary." Modern culture, since it disowns the past, seeks a "free expression of its vital desires"; it becomes, therefore, an unrestrained "spoiled child" with no controlling standards, "no limit to its caprice."[3] In Ortega, one finds the most sweeping attack against all "modernity." His is the disdain of the humanist for the vulgar.

3. *Mass as the mechanized society.* In German romanticism, in its idealization of nature and the pastoral, one finds the source of much of the protest against modern life. For these writers—and the poets and critics Ernst and Friedrich George Juenger can be taken as typical—the dehumanizing

element is technology.[4] The mass society is a mechanical society. Society has become an "apparatus." The machine impresses its style on man, makes life mathematical and precise; existence takes on a masklike character: the steel helmet and the welder's face-guard symbolize the individual's disappearance into his technical function. The regulated, functional man emerges as a new type, hard and ruthless, a cog in the technological press.

4. *The mass as the bureaucratized society*. Less romantic, but equally critical, are those theorists who see extreme rationalization and extreme bureaucratization—the *over-organization* of life—as the salient features of the mass society. The idea of "rationalization" goes back to Hegel and Marx and along with it the notions of "estrangement" or "alienation," "reification," and the "fetishism of commodities"—all of which express the thought that in modern society man has become a "thing," an object manipulated by society, rather than a subject who can remake life in accordance with his own desires. In our time, Georg Simmel, Max Weber, and Karl Mannheim have developed and elaborated these concepts. In Mannheim's work—notably in his *Man and Society in an Age of Reconstruction*—the diverse strands are all brought together.

Mannheim's argument, put schematically, runs as follows: modern large-scale organization, oriented exclusively to efficiency, creates hierarchies that concentrate all decisions at the top. Even technical decisions are removed from the shop floor and centered in specialized bodies that have no direct contact with work. Since the concern is solely with efficiency, rather than human satisfactions, all solutions to problems are defined in relation to this single value. Mannheim calls this "functional rationality," or direct means-ends relationships, in contrast to "substantial rationality," which is the application of Reason to human affairs.[5]

This concentration of decision-making not only creates conformity but stunts the initiative of subordinates and leaves them unsatisfied in their personal needs for gratification and esteem. (In effect, the demand for submission to extreme rationality deprives the individual of the power to act rationally; i.e., in accordance with reason. This frustration seeks release in irrational ways.) Normally, the routinization of one's job dulls the edge of frustration and provides some security. But when unemployment looms, the helplessness becomes sharpened, and self-esteem is threatened. Since individuals cannot rationally locate the source of their frustration (i.e., the impersonal bureaucratic system itself), they will, under these circumstances, seek scapegoats and turn to fascism.

5. *The mass as mob.* While for Mannheim, and the neo-Marxists, mass society is equated with monolithic bureaucratization, for Emil Lederer and Hannah Arendt it is defined by the elimination of difference, by uniformity, aimlessness, alienation, and the failure of integration.

In Lederer's view, society is made up of many social groups united by function or self-interest, some rational in purpose, some irrational. So long as society is stratified, these groups can impose only partial control, and irrational emotions are restricted. But when the lines dividing social groups break down, the people become volatile and febrile "masses," ready to be manipulated by a leader.[6]

Hannah Arendt, perhaps because she writes a decade later, sees the masses as already overspilling the bounds. The masses are those who, because of indifference or simply sheer number, do not belong to "political parties or municipal governments or professional organizations or trade-unions" — in short, organizations that exist to satisfy a common interest—and they "form the majority of those large numbers of neutral, politically indifferent people who never join a party or hardly ever go to the polls."

Such people already stand "outside" of society. The revolt of the masses is a revolt against the "loss of social status along with which [is] lost the whole sector of communal relationships in whose framework common sense makes sense. . . . The masses [become] obsessed by a desire to escape from reality because in their essential homelessness they can no longer bear its accidental incomprehensible aspects."[7]

And so, because modern life sunders all social bonds, and because the techniques of modern communication have perfected the means whereby propaganda can manipulate the masses, the "age of the masses" is now upon us.

What strikes one first about these varied uses of the concept of mass society is how little they reflect or relate to the complex, richly striated social relations of the real world. Take Blumer's example of the movie audience as "separate, detached, and anonymous." Presumably, a large number of individuals, because they have been subjected to similar experiences, now share some common psychological reality in which the differences between individual and individual become blurred; accordingly we get the sociological assumption that each person is now of "equal weight," and therefore a sampling of what such disparate individuals say they think constitutes "*mass* opinion." But is this so? Individuals are not *tabulae rasae*. They bring varying social conceptions to the same experience and go away with dissimilar responses. They may be silent, separate, detached, and anonymous while watching the movie, but afterward they talk about it with friends and exchange opinions and judgments. They are once again members of particular social groups. Would one say that several hundred or a thousand individuals home alone at night, but all reading the same book, constitute a "mass"?

Because romantic feeling colors critical judgment, the attacks on modern life often have an unduly strong emotional charge. The image of "facelessness," for example, is given a metaphysical twist by Gabriel Marcel: "The individual, in order to belong to the mass . . . has had to . . . divest himself of that substantial reality which was linked to his initial individuality. . . . The incredibly sinister role of the press, the cinema, the radio has consisted in passing that original reality through a pair of flattening rollers to substitute for it a superimposed pattern of ideas, an image with no real roots in the deep being of the subject of this experiment."[8] Perhaps terms like "original reality" and "real roots in the deep being" have a meaning that escapes an empiricist temper, but without the press, the radio, etc., etc.—and they are not monolithic—in what way, short of being everywhere at once, can one learn of events that take place elsewhere? Or should one go back to the happy ignorance of earlier days?

Some of the images of life in the mass society, as presented by its critics, border on caricature. According to Ernst Juenger, traffic demands traffic regulations, and so the public becomes conditioned to automatism. Karl Jaspers has written that in the "technical mass order" the home is transformed "into a lair or sleeping place." Even more puzzling is the complaint against modern medicine. "In medical practice . . . patients are now dealt with in the mass according to the principle of rationalization, being sent to institutes for technical treatment, the sick being classified in groups and referred to this or that specialized department. . . . The supposition is that, like everything else, medical treatment has become a sort of manufactured article."[9]

The attack on the mass society sometimes widens into an attack on science itself. For Ortega, "the scientific man is the prototype of the mass-man," because science, by encouraging specialization, has made the scientist "hermetic and self-satisfied within his limitations." Ortega draws from this the sweeping conclusion that "the most immediate result of this unbalanced specialization has been that today, when there are more 'scientists' than ever, there are much less 'cultured' men than, for example, about 1750."[10] But how is one to verify such a comparison between 1750 and the present? Even if we could establish comparable categories, surely Ortega would have been the first to shy away from statistical comparisons. Moreover, can we assume that because a man specializes in his work, he is unable, in his leisure and in reflection, to appreciate culture? And what is "culture"? Would not Ortega admit that we have more knowledge of the world than in 1750—knowledge not only of nature but of the inner life of man? Is knowledge to be divorced from culture, or is "true culture" a narrow area of classical learning in which eternal truths reside?

One could argue, of course, that reading a book, to cite my previous example, is a qualitatively different experience from going to a movie. But this leads precisely to the first damaging ambiguity in the theory of the mass society. Two things are mixed up in that theory: a judgment regarding the *quality* of modern experience—with much of which any sensitive individual might agree—and a presumed scientific statement concerning the disorganization of society created by industrialization and by the demand of the masses for equality. It is the second of these statements with which this essay quarrels.

Behind the theory of social disorganization lies a romantic—and somewhat false—notion of the past, which sees society as having once been made up of small, "organic," close-knit communities (called *Gemeinschaften* in the terminology of the sociologists) that were shattered by industrialism and modern life, and replaced by a large, impersonal, "atomistic" society (called *Gesellschaft*) that is unable to provide the basic gratifications, and call forth the loyalties, that the older communities knew.[11] These distinctions are, however, completely riddled by value judgments. Everyone is against atomism and for "organic living." But if we substitute, with good logic, the term "total" for "organic," and "individualistic" for "atomistic," the whole argument looks quite different. In any case, a great weakness in the theory is its lack of history-mindedness. The transition to a mass society, if it be such, was not effected suddenly, explosively, within a single lifetime, but took generations to mature. In its sociological determinism, the hypothesis overlooks the human capacity for adaptiveness and creativeness, for ingenuity in shaping new social forms. Such new forms may be trade unions whose leaders rise from the ranks—there are 50,000 trade-union locals in this country that form little worlds of their own—or the persistence under new conditions of ethnic groups and solidarities.

But more than mere contradictions in usage, ambiguities in terminology, and a lack of historical sense are involved in the theory of the mass society. It is at heart a defense of an aristocratic cultural tradition—a tradition that does carry with it an important but neglected conception of liberty — and a doubt that the large mass of mankind can ever become truly educated or acquire an appreciation of culture. Thus, the theory often becomes a conservative defense of privilege. This defense is at times so extreme as to pose a conflict between "culture" and "social justice." The argument (reminiscent of the title of Matthew Arnold's book *Culture and Anarchy*) is made that any attempts of social betterment must harm culture. And, while mainly directed against "bourgeois" society, the theory also strikes at radicalism and its egalitarian notions.

The fear of the "mass" has its roots in the dominant conservative tradition of Western political thought, which in large measure still shapes many of the political and sociological categories of social theory—i.e., in authoritarian definitions of leadership and in the image of the "mindless masses." The picture of the "mass" as capable only of violence and excess originates with Aristotle's *Politics*. In his threefold typology, democracy is equated with the rule of *hoi polloi*—who are easily swayed by demagogues—and which must degenerate into tyranny. This notion of the masses, developed in Hellenistic times, was deepened by the struggles between plebes and aristocracy in the Roman republic, and by the efforts of the Caesars to exploit mob support; and the image of the insensate mob fed by "bread and circuses" became deeply imprinted on history. (From Plutarch, for example, came the description of the fickle masses and the wily tribunes that was drawn upon so directly by Shakespeare in his tragedy *Coriolanus*.) Early Christian theory justified its fear of the masses with a theory about human nature. In the religious terms of Augustine—as, later, in the secularized version of Hobbes—

the Earthly City bore an ineradicable stain of blood: in Paradise there was neither private property nor government; property and police were the consequence of the Fall of Man; property and police were signs, therefore, not of man's civilization but of his corruption; they were necessary means of keeping man in check.

But it was the French Revolution that transplanted the image of the "mindless masses" into modern consciousness. The destruction of the *ancien régime* and the rallying cry of "equality" sharpened the fear of conservative, and especially Catholic, critics that traditional values (meaning political, social, and religious dogma) would be destroyed.[12] For a Tocqueville and an Acton, there was an irreducible conflict between liberty and equality; liberty guaranteed each man the right to be different, whereas equality meant a "leveling" of tastes to the lowest common denominator. For a Max Scheler, as well as an Ortega, the mass society meant a "democracy of the emotions," which could unleash only irrational forces. For the Catholic de Maistre, as for the Anglican T. S. Eliot, the equality of men meant the destruction of the harmony and authority so necessary to a healthy, integrated society.[13] From this traditionalist point of view, Nazism has been characterized not as a reaction against, but the inevitable end-product of, democracy. Hitler is seen as a replica of the classical demagogue swaying the mindless masses and leading them in nihilistic revolt against the traditional culture of Europe.

Important as these conceptions are, as reminders of the meaning of liberty, and of excellence, they reflect a narrow conception of human potentialities. The question of social change has to be seen against the large political canvas. The starting point of modern politics, as Karl Mannheim has pointed out, came after the Reformation, when chiliasm, or religiously inspired millennial striving to bring about heaven on earth, became an expression of the demands for social and economic betterment of the lower strata of society.[14] Blind resentment of things as they were was thereby given principle, reason, and eschatological force, and directed to definite political goals. The equality of all souls became the equality of all individuals and the right of everyone, as enlightened by progressive revelation, to make a judgment on society.

Comte, the father of modern sociology, expressed great horror at the idea of this universal right to one's own opinion. No community could exist, he wrote, unless its members had a cetrain degree of confidence in one another, and this, he said, was incompatible with the right of everyone to submit the very foundations of society to discussion whenever he felt like it. In calling attention to the dangers of free criticism, Comte pointed to the decline in public morals as evidenced by the increase of divorces, the effacement of traditional class distinctions, and the ensuing impudence of individual ambitions. It was part of the function of government, he thought, to prevent the diffusion of ideas and the anarchic spread of intellectual freedom.[15]

Modern society, apparently, does not bear Comte out: though the foundations of privilege go on being challenged in the name of justice, society does not collapse. Few moralists would now uphold the bleak view once expressed by Malthus, that "from the inevitable laws of human nature some human beings will be exposed to want. These are the unhappy persons who in the great lottery of life have drawn a blank."[16] The most salient fact about modern life—capitalist and communist—is the ideological commitment to social change. And by change is meant the striving for material, economic betterment, greater opportunity for individuals to exercise their talents, and an appreciation of culture by wider masses of people. Can any society deny these aspirations?

It is curious that in these "aristocratic" critiques of modern society, refracted as they are through the glass of an idealized feudal past, democracy is identified with equality alone. The role of constitutionalism and of the rule of law, which, with universal suffrage, are constituent elements of the Western democratic structure, are overlooked. The picture of modern culture as debauched by concessions to popular taste—a picture that leaves out the great rise in the general appreciation of culture—is equally overdrawn. If it is granted that mass society is compartmentalized, superficial in personal relations, anonymous, transitory, specialized, utilitarian, competitive, acquisitive, mobile, and status-hungry, the obverse side of the coin must be shown, too—the right to privacy, to free choice of friends and occupation, status on the basis of achievement rather than of ascription, a plurality of norms and standards, rather than the exclusive and monopolistic social controls of a single dominant group. For if, as Sir Henry Maine once put it, the movement of modern society has been from status to contract, then it has been, in that light, a movement from a fixed place in the world to possible freedom.

The early theorists of the mass society (Ortega, Marcel) focused attention on the "deterioration of excellence," while the later theorists (Mannheim, Lederer, Arendt) called attention to the way in which the over-organization and, at the same time, the disruption of the social fabric facilitated the rise of fascism. Recently, in the light of Communist successes, the argument has been advanced that the mass society, because it cannot provide for the individual's real participation in effective social groups, is particularly vulnerable to Communist penetration, and that the mass organization, because it is so unwieldy, is peculiarly susceptible to Communist penetration and manipulation.[17] Certainly, the Communists have scored enormous successes in infiltration, and their "front organization" may be counted as one of the great political inventions of our century. But without discounting Communist techniques, the real problem here lies less with the "mass society" as such (aside from the excuse it affords disaffected intellectuals for attacks on modern culture) than with the capacity or incapacity of the given social order to satisfy the demands for social mobility and higher standards of living that arise once social change is under way. This is the key to any radical appeal.

It is not poverty *per se* that leads people to revolt; poverty most often induces fatalism and despair, and a reliance, embodied in ritual and superstitious practices, on supernatural help. *Social tensions are an expression of unfulfilled expectations.* It is only when expectations are aroused that radicalism can take hold. Radical strength is greatest (and here the appeal of communism must be seen as a variant of the general appeal of radicalism) in societies where awareness of class differences runs deep, expectations of social advancement outstrip possibilities, and the establishments of culture fail to make room for aspiring intellectuals.

It is among industrial workers rather than apathetic peasants (in Milan rather than Calabria), among frustrated intellectuals rather than workers long unionized (e.g., India), that radicalism spreads. Resentment, as Max Scheler once noted, is among the most potent of human motives; it is certainly that in politics. It is in the advanced industrial countries, principally the United States, Britain, and northwestern Europe, where national income *has* been rising, where mass expectations of an equitable share in that increase are relatively fulfilled, and where social mobility affects ever greater numbers, that extremist politics have the least hold. It may be, as the late Joseph Schumpeter pessimistically believed,[18] that in newly awakened societies, like Asia's, the impatient expectations of key social strata, particularly the intellectuals, may so exceed the actual possibilities of economic expansion that communism will come to look like the only plausible solution to the majority.[19] Whether this will happen in India and Indonesia is one of the crucial political questions of the next decade. But at any rate it is not the mass society, but the inability, pure and simple, of any society to meet impatient popular expectations that makes for a strong response to radical appeals.

From the viewpoint of the mass-society hypothesis, the United States ought to be exceptionally vulnerable to the politics of disaffection. In our country, urbanization, industrialization, and democratization have eroded older primary and community ties on a scale unprecedented in social history. Yet, though large-scale unemployment during the depression was more prolonged and more severe here than in any country in Western Europe, the Communist movement never gained a real foothold in the United States, nor has any fascist movement on a European model arisen. How does one explain this?

It is asserted that the United States is an "atomized" society composed of lonely, isolated individuals. One forgets the truism, expressed sometimes as a jeer, that Americans are a nation of joiners. There are in the United States today at least 200,000 voluntary organizations, associations, clubs, societies, lodges, and fraternities, with an aggregate (but obviously overlapping) membership of close to 80 million men and women. In no other country in the world, probably, is there such a high degree of voluntary communal activity, expressed sometimes in absurd rituals, yet often providing real satisfactions for real needs.[20]

"It is natural for the ordinary American," wrote Gunnar Myrdal, "when he sees something that is wrong to feel not only that there should be a law against it, but also that an organization should be formed to combat it."[21] Some of these voluntary organizations are pressure groups—business, farm, labor, veterans, trade associations, the aged, etc.—but thousands more are like the National Association for the Advancement of Colored People, the American Civil Liberties Union, the League of Women Voters, the American Jewish Committee, the Parent-Teachers Associations, local community-improvement groups, and so on, each of which affords hundreds of individuals concrete, emotionally shared activities.

Equally astonishing are the number of ethnic group organizations in this country carrying on varied cultural, social, and political activities. The number of Irish, Italian, Jewish, Polish, Czech, Finnish, Bulgarian, Bessarabian, and other national groups, their hundreds of fraternal, communal, and political groups, each playing a role in the life of America, is staggering.[22]

Even in urban neighborhoods, where anonymity is presumed to flourish, the extent of local ties is astounding. Within the city limits of Chicago, for example, there are 82 community newspapers with a total weekly circulation of almost one million; within Chicago's larger metropolitan area, there are 181. According to standard sociological theory, these local papers providing news and gossip about neighbors should slowly decline under the pressure of the national media. Yet the reverse is true. In Chicago, the number of such newspapers has increased 165 per cent since 1910; in those forty years, circulation has jumped 770 per cent. As sociologist Morris Janowitz, who studied these community newspapers, observed: "If society were as impersonal, as self-centered and barren as described by some who are preoccupied with the one-way trend from '*Gemeinschaft*' to '*Gesellschaft*' seem to believe, the levels of criminality, social disorganization and psychopathology which social science seeks to account for would have to be viewed as very low rather than (as viewed now) alarmingly high."[23]

It may be argued that the existence of such a large network of voluntary associations says little about the cultural level of the country concerned. It may well be, as Ortega maintains, that cultural standards throughout the world have declined (in everything?—in architecture, dress, design?), but nonetheless a greater proportion of the population today participates in worthwhile cultural activities. This has been almost an inevitable concomitant of the doubling—*literally*—of the American standard of living over the last fifty years.[24]

The rising levels of education have meant a rising appreciation of culture. In the United States, more dollars are spent on concerts of classical music than on baseball. Sales of books have doubled in a decade.[25] There are over a thousand symphony orchestras, and several hundred museums, institutes and colleges are purchasing art in the United States today. Various other indexes can be cited to show the growth of a vast middlebrow society. And in coming years, with steadily increasing productivity and leisure, the United States will become an even more active "consumer" of culture.*

It has been argued that the American mass society imposes an excessive conformity upon its members. But it is hard to discern who is conforming to what. The *New Republic* cries that "hucksters are sugarcoating the culture." The *National Review*, organ of the "radical right," raises the banner of iconoclasm against the domination of opinion-making in our society by "the liberals." *Fortune* decries the growth of "organization man." Each of these tendencies exists, yet in historical perspective there is probably less conformity to an over-all mode of conduct today than at any time within the last half century in America. True, there is less bohemianism than in the twenties (though increased sexual tolerance) and less political radicalism than in the thirties (though the New Deal enacted sweeping reforms). But does the arrival at a political dead center mean the establishment, too, of a dead norm? I do not think so. One would be hard put to find today the "conformity" *Main Street* exacted of Carol Kennicott thirty years ago. With rising educational levels, more individuals are able to indulge a wider variety of interests. ("Twenty years ago you couldn't sell Beethoven out of New York," reports a record salesman. "Today we sell Palestrina, Monte-

* Some further ambiguity in the use of the mass-society concept derives from the confusions in the use of the anthropological and the humanist meanings of the word "culture." Thus some critics point to the "breakdown" of local folk or regional practices—speech differences, cooking, songs, dances, humor—and their replacement by uniform national patterns as an indication of the leveling of the mass society and of the decline of culture. These changes, which are real, are meaningful, however, only in anthropological usage, as a change from parochial to more universal cultural forms. But such changes are not *necessarily* a judgment about the humanist quality of the culture. (It is curious that in the past the breakdown of rustic forms was seen as a necessary prelude to the growth of a "high culture." Today the breakdown of the rustic forms is seen as part of the destruction of humanist culture.) The distinctions should be made clear. The anthropological concept of culture is relativistic. It implies no judgment of any one culture and cannot be used as a stick to criticize "high culture." The fact that the nature of satisfactions has changed from country dances and folksy humor to Brazilian sambas and Broadway flippancy is analytically a different question than that of the character of the culture. As these criticisms are made, one deals with the presumed disorganization of society, the other with the quality of the culture. Again, it is the purpose of this essay to point out that the invocation of the notion of tradition (*Gemeinschaft*, etc.) to make a judgment about the disorganization of the society is scientifically spurious and conceals a value. The other criticism, which is serious, lies outside the scope of this essay. (For a discussion of the issues of "high" vs. "middlebrow" culture, see Clement Greenberg, "The Plight of Our Culture," *Commentary*, June and July, 1953. See also, Mary McCarthy, "America the Beautiful," *Commentary*, September, 1947.)

verdi, Gabrielli, and Renaissance and Baroque music in large quantities.")

The curious fact, perhaps, is that no one in the United States defends conformity. Everyone is against it, and probably everyone always was. Thirty-five years ago, you could easily rattle any middle-class American by charging him with being a "Babbitt." Today you can do so by accusing him of conformity. The problem is to know who is accusing whom. In December, 1958, the *Reader's Digest* (circulation twelve million) reprinted an article from *Woman's Day* (circulation five million) with the title, "The Danger of Being Too Well-Adjusted." The point of the article is that great men were not adjusted, and the article quotes a psychiatrist who says that "we've made conformity into a religion"; we ought to remember, however, that each child is different "and ought to be."

Such citation is no proof that there is not "conformity" in the middle class; but if there is, there is also a great deal of anxiety and finger-pointing about it. Certainly those who live on the margin of society—the Upper Bohemians, whose manners soon become the style for the culture—seek frantically to find different ways of emphasizing their non-conformity. In Hollywood, where Pickfair society in the twenties counterfeited a European monarchy (and whose homes crossed Louis XIV with Barnum & Bailey), "non-conformity," according to *Life* magazine (in its jumbo Entertainment issue of December 22, 1958—readership twenty-five million), "is now the key to social importance and that Angry Middle-Aged man, Frank Sinatra, is its prophet and reigning social monarch." The Sinatra set, *Life* points out, deliberately mocks the old Hollywood taboos and is imitated by a host of other sets that eagerly want to be non-conformist as well. Significantly—a fact *Life* failed to mention—the reigning social set and its leaders, Sinatra, Dean Martin, Sammy Davis, Jr., are all from minority groups and from the wrong side of the tracks. Sinatra and Martin are Italian, Davis a Negro. In earlier times in American life, a minority group, having bulled its way to the top, would usually ape the style and manners of the established status community. In Hollywood, the old status hierarchies have been fragmented, the new sets celebrate their triumph by jeering at the pompous ways of the old.

At the margins of the literary life, and a different social phenomenon, are the Beatniks, a hopped-up, jazzed-up, souped-up, self-proclaimed group of outcasts who are rebelling against the "highly organized academic and literary movement employment agency of the Neoanti-reconstructionist [who form] a dense crust of custom over American cultural life." But the singular fact is, as Delmore Schwartz recently argued, that these beatniks are imaginary rebels, "since the substance of their work is a violent advocacy of a nonconformism which they already possess . . . since nonconformism of almost every variety had become acceptable and respectable and available to everyone. Unlike the Bohemianism of the past, which had to attack the dominant Puritanism and Victorianism of respectable society in a variety of forms, including the censorship of books, Prohibition and a prudery enforced by the police, the new nonconformism has no genuine enemy . . . hence the new rebel bears a great deal of resemblance to a prize fighter trying to knock out an antagonist who is not in the ring with him."[26] The additional sardonic fact is that the man in the gray flannel suit, the presumed target of the Beatniks, is, as Russel Lynes pointed out, especially if he is in advertising, or the entertainment media, an Upper Bohemian himself. The job is accepted as a means of obtaining an income in order to sport and flaunt his presumed, idiosyncratic tastes in dress, food, travel, and the like.* The problem for all these multiple sets is not conformity but added novelty.

To add one more paradox, the early theorists of mass society (e.g., Simmel) condemned it because in the vast metropolitan honeycombs people were isolated, transient, anonymous to each other. Americans, sensitive as they are to the criticism of others, took the charge to heart and, in building the postwar suburbs, sought to create fraternity, communality, togetherness, only to find themselves accused of conformity. In the new, recent trend of people returning to the city, it is clear that, in recoil, people will once again

* "In the richly appointed Lake Shore Drive apartment of Chicago Financier Albert Newman, the guests chatted animatedly, gazed at the original Picasso on the wall, and the Monet, the Jackson Pollock. On tables and shelves stood Peruvian fertility symbols, jade bracelets, sculptures that looked like the superstructure of a Japanese battleship. . . . [The guests] had come to meet 32-year old Allen Ginsberg of Paterson, N. J., author of a celebrated, chock-full catalogue called *Howl* ("I saw the best minds of my generation destroyed by madness, starving hysterical naked."). . . . At length Poet Ginsberg arrived wearing blue jeans and a checked black-and-red lumberjacking shirt with black patches. . . . With the crashing madness of a Marx Brothers scene run in reverse, the Beatniks [Ginsberg and two friends] read their poetry, made their pitch for money for a new Beatnik magazine, *The Big Table,* and then stalked out. . . . The trio was an instant hit with the literary upper crust. . . . [The next evening] at the Sherman Hotel, the Beatniks read more poetry for a curious crowd of 700 (who paid $1 and up) . . ." (*Time,* February 9, 1959).

establish barriers and will thus bring on the charge, in the next inspection by European sociology, of anonymity, isolation and soullessness, and *anomie*.

One hears the complaint that divorce, crime, and violence demonstrate a widespread social disorganization in the country. But the rising number of divorces may indicate not the disruption of the family but a freer, more individualistic basis of choice and the emergence of the "companionship" marriage. And as regards crime, I have sought to demonstrate (see Chapter 10) that there is actually much *less* crime and violence (though more vicarious violence through movies and TV, and more "windows" onto crime, through the press) than was the case twenty-five and fifty years ago. Certainly Chicago, San Francisco, and New York were much rougher and tougher cities in those years. But violent crime, which is usually a lower-class phenomenon, was then contained within the ecological boundaries of the slum; hence one can recall quiet, tree-lined, crime-free areas and feel that the tenor of life was more even in the past. But a cursory look at the accounts of those days—the descriptions of the gang wars, bordellos, and street-fighting in San Francisco's Barbary Coast, New York's Five Points, or Chicago's First Ward—would show how much more violent the actual life of those cities was in the past.

At this point, it becomes quite apparent that such large-scale abstractions as "the mass society," with the implicit diagnosis of social disorganization and decay that derive from them, are rather meaningless without standards of comparison. Social and cultural change is probably greater and more rapid today in the United States than in any other country, but the assumption that social disorder and *anomie* inevitably attend such change is not borne out in this case.

This may be due to the singular fact that the United States is probably the first large society in history to have change and innovation "built into" its culture. Almost all human societies, traditionalist and habit-ridden as they have been and still are, tend to resist change. The great efforts to industrialize underdeveloped countries, increase worker mobility in Europe, and broaden markets—so necessary to the raising of productivity and standards of living — are again and again frustrated by ingrained resistance to change. Thus, in the Soviet Union, change has been introduced only by dint of wholesale coercion. In the United States—a culture with no feudal tradition, with a pragmatic ethos, as expressed by Jef-

to him, but to his heirs. This "fiction," as Sir Henry Maine called it, regarding the ownership of property, was necessary to preserve its "inalienability," i.e., the fact that it could not be freely disposed of at will. The effort to freely dispose of land—to make it alienable—to rid it of all entails, strict settlements, primogenitures, and the like, was part of the effort to make property a free commodity. In English law, it was not until 1925, in fact, that all impediments to the alienability of property were completely removed.

In philosophical terms, the *linked* institutions of property and family were always seen as a necessary precondition to established society. When Godwin and Condorcet, at the turn of the nineteenth century, insisted that progress and freedom lay only in striking the bonds of marriage and sharing all property, they were answered for all bourgeois society by Parson Malthus, who insisted that without the restraints of family and property the "natural" instincts to lust and licentiousness would assert themselves so freely that population would break all bounds, outstrip the growth of resources, and result in privation and misery for the multitude rather than happiness. The Essay on Population, in fact, was not an exercise in demography, but a sermon in morals.

But more than economic or moral considerations were involved in the linkage of the family and property systems. Through the fusion of the two institutions, a class system was maintained: people met at the same social levels, were educated in common schools appropriate to their wealth, shared the same manners and morals, read the same books and held similar prejudices, mingled in the same milieus—in short, created and shared a distinctive style of life.

The singular fact is that in the last seventy-five years the old relation between the two institutions of property and family, which, Malthus maintained, represented the "fundamental laws" of society, has broken down. The specific reasons for this breakdown are too complex for a short sketch, but the process is clear. In bourgeois society, marriage was a means of keeping sex relations within bounds; in bourgeois marriage, as Denis de Rougement wittily observed, every woman had a husband and desired a lover; the great Continental novels of the nineteenth century, Tolstoy's *Anna Karenina,* Flaubert's *Madame Bovary,* with their geometry of adultery, pointed up this paradox. The growth of romanticism, the high premium on individual attachment and free choice, the translation of passion into secular and carnal terms

—all worked against the system of "dynastic" marriage. The emancipation of women meant, in one sense, the disappearance of one of the stable aspects of bourgeois society. If women could marry freely, crossing class lines if they so desired, then the economic enterprise with which the "dynastic" marriage was intertwined would lose some of its staying power.

But there are also reasons more indigenous to the nature of the economic system why the mode of family capitalism has given way. Some are general: the decline of the extended family or clan narrowed the choice of heirs competent to manage the enterprise; the increasing importance of professional techniques placed a high premium on skill rather than blood relationships. These reasons apply largely to the United States, and principally to those corporate areas where managerial and technical skill refuse simply to be agencies of family domination and want to lead in their own right. Yet in Europe, as studies by David Landes, for example, have shown, the continuity of family enterprise has been remarkable.[27] And the continuing existence of such family enterprises, with its caution, conservatism, and fear of allowing outside capital to enter into its affairs, argues Landes, is one of the chief reasons, until now, for the slow rate of economic growth on the Continent.

The situation in America, from the start, has been somewhat different. One important reason is that title to almost all land in the United States has been held in fee simple, rather than entail as in Europe, and family founders have been comparatively unable to impose their wishes regarding the conservation of property upon successive generations. Another is that there has been in the United States, for a variety of complex reasons, a tradition—or at least a myth—whereby the son does not succeed the father but strikes out for himself. These two factors, historical and socio-psychological, have been distinctive elements which hindered the development of a full system of family capitalism in the United States.

Yet efforts to create such a system were constantly being made. As Bernard Bailyn has pointed out in his study of American merchants in the seventeenth century, the rise of business enterprise in the United States was due not to individual initiative but to family solidarity.[28] The family was the source of initial capital, and from the extended family one could draw a variety of skills for the growth of the enterprise. Family enterprises were quite common along the eastern seaboard—particularly in the major cities of Boston, Philadelphia, and New York—in the post-colonial period, and "society" was made up of these leading family clans. The constant movement westward, the vast speculations, the wild economic swings, all acted as disruptive factors.[29]

With the rapid industrialization after the Civil War, the new enterprises often began as family groups. In a capitalist society, control of money and credit, the sources of capital formation, is the fulcrum of power. Few of the companies that began were public corporations. They drew capital from family holdings and expanded by "self-financing." Most of the large "middle-sized" industries in the country have been typical family enterprises. This has been most true of textiles and brewing, but equally of others. International banking, characteristically, has been a "family" affair because of the "secret" nature of much of the business and the need for people one could trust to be placed in different parts of the world. The same reasons apply to shipping. Packing, for historical reasons, has been a closely-held family set of enterprises, as have chemicals, soap, and newspapers. The big "names" in American industry began as "family" names: du Pont, Swift, Armour, Grace, Ford, Olin chemical, Dow, etc. Even today, most major newspapers are family-owned, rather than being public corporations on the market.

The family system had a social counterpart as well: the domination, by the leading family, of the towns in which the family enterprise resided; and, since most industrial enterprise, at least in the late nineteenth and early twentieth century were located in river-valley areas, the stratification had a topographical correlate as well: the workers lived in the valley because the factory was located there, and the family owners lived "on the hill" because it had the commanding view.

However much family capitalism has entrenched itself in many middle-sized enterprises and left its mark on so many cities, it never succeeded in establishing its hegemony in the area of large-scale capital industries. For this, one has to look to the peculiar set of economic events which mark the crucial period of American capitalism, the period from 1890-1910.

The breakup of family capitalism began, roughly, around the turn of the century, when American industry, having overextended itself, underwent a succession of crises. At this point, the bankers, with their control of the money and credit market, stepped in and reorganized and took control of many of the country's leading enterprises. The great mergers at the turn of the century, typified by the formation of United States Steel, marked the emergence of "finance capitalism" in this country.

By their intervention, the investment bankers, in effect, tore up the social roots of the capitalist order. By installing professional managers—with no proprietary stakes themselves in the enterprise, unable therefore to pass along their power automatically to their sons, and accountable to outside controllers—the bankers effected a radical separation of property and family.

The men who made the "modern" corporation were not family enterprisers. Nor were they just bureaucratic managers administering a finished set of routines. The "corporate organizers" were a special breed, often engineers, whose self-conscious task was to build a new economic form, and whose rewards were not primarily money—few accumulated the large fortunes made by a Carnegie, a Rockefeller, a Harriman, or a Ford—but status achievements and, ultimately, some independent power of their own. Thus, T. N. Vail, who created American Telephone & Telegraph, Elbert Gary, who became the public relations face of U. S. Steel ("he never saw a blast furnace until he died," said Ben Stolberg once, bitterly), Alfred P. Sloan, who fashioned the decentralized structure of General Motors, Gerard Swope, who held together General Electric, Walter Teagle, who rationalized Standard Oil, left no personal dynasties, nor do the corporations bear their names; but their imprint on American society is indelible. Following them, the "young men from the provinces," passing through the classrooms of the Harvard Business School, now had an avenue by which to ascend to high social as well as economic positions. Thus family capitalism gave way to social mobility.

In time, however, the power of the bankers, too, declined as the managers became able, especially in the last twenty years, to detach themselves from financial controls and win independent power in their enterprises. In some cases they were able to do this because they, the corporate engineers, were strong individuals; even more important was the enforced separation, by the New Deal measures, of investment and banking functions, which limited the investment bankers' control of the money market; but, most important of all, perhaps, was the fact that the tremendous growth of American corporations enabled them to finance their expansion from their own profits rather than by borrowing on the money market.

The breakup of family capitalism may explain, in part, the "dynamic" nature of modern American capitalism, for the establishment of independent managerial controls has produced a new impetus and new incentives. Unable to withdraw enormous sums of wealth from their corporations, as, say, Andrew Carnegie did from his steel company, the chief status drives of the managers have been performance and growth. Such aims, combined with the changed tax laws, have stimulated a high and constant degree of reinvestment of profits. Whereas only 30 per cent of corporate profits in 1929 were reinvested, about 70 per cent of corporate profits in the postwar years were plowed back for expansion.

The fact that the new managers have lacked a class position buttressed by tradition has given rise to a need on their part for an ideology to justify their power and prestige. In no other capitalist order, as in the American, has this drive for an ideology been pressed so compulsively. In other orders it was less needed. Private property was always linked, philosophically, to a system of natural rights; thus, property itself provided a moral justification. But private productive property, especially in the United States, is largely a fiction, and rarely does one hear it invoked any longer as the moral source of the corporate executive's power. As we have had in the corporation the classic shift from ownership to managerial control, so, on the symbolic level, we have the shift from "private property" to "enterprise" as the justification of power. And, as with any ideology, the symbol itself sometimes becomes a propelling force, and "performance" for its own sake has become a driving motive of the American corporate head.

Sociologically, the breakup of family capitalism is linked to a series of shifts in power in Western society as a whole. No longer are there America's "Sixty Families" (or even France's "Two Hundred"). Family capitalism meant social and political as well as economic dominance. It does so no longer. Many middle-sized enterprises are still family-owned, with son succeeding father (e.g., breweries), and many towns, like St. Louis and Cincinnati, still reveal the marks of the old dominance by families, but by and large the system of family control is finished—so much so, that a classic study of American life like R. S. Lynd's *Middletown in Transition,* with its picture of the "X" family dominating the town, has in less than twenty years become a picture of the past rather than of contemporary society.

Two "silent" revolutions in the relations between power and class position in modern society seem to be in process. One is a change in the *mode of access* to power insofar as inheritance alone is no longer all-determining; the other is a change in the *nature of power-holding itself* insofar as technical skill rather than property, and political position rather than wealth, have become the basis on which power is wielded.

The two "revolutions" proceed simultaneously.* The chief consequence, politically, is the breakup of the "ruling class." A ruling class may be defined as a power-holding group which has both an established *community* of interest and a *continuity* of interest. Today, there is an "upper class" and a "ruling group." Being a member of the "upper class" (i.e., having differential privileges and being able to pass those privileges along to one's designees) no longer means that one is a member of the ruling group, for rule is now based on other than the traditional criteria of property; the modern ruling groups are essentially coalitions, and the means of passing on the power they possess, or the institutionalization of any specific modes of access to power (the political route, or military advancement), is not yet fully demarked and established.

* One of the great problems for the social analysis of power is the "foreshortening" of time as regards the stable organization of power. The ownership of private property as a basic *mode* of power held constant, in Western law, for nearly two thousand years; and within that time, property as land, was long a dominant form. Within that mode of power, specific family groups might retain power over a span of as many as ten generations. Even where new means of access to power was introduced, such as the *condottieri* of Italy, who simply seized booty, the legitimation of power involved property. In the last hundred and fifty years we have witnessed a rapid breakdown both of the *mode* of power itself and the stability of family and social groups whose power is based on that mode. Hence the difficulty in locating viable time periods for the measurement of power.

Chapter 3

Is There a Ruling Class in America?

The Power Elite Reconsidered

POWER IS A difficult subject. Its effects are more observable than its causes; even the power-wielders often do not know what factors shaped their decisions. Its consequences are more refractory to control—and prediction—than any other form of human behavior. C. Wright Mills' *The Power Elite,* because it seeks to locate the sources of power in an identifiable constellation of elites, is one of those rare books in contemporary sociology that deal with the "world of causality" rather than mere description of methodological discussion. It is, in addition, something else: a political book whose loose texture and power rhetoric have allowed different people to read their own emotions into it: for the young neo-Marxists in England (*vide* the group around the *Universities and Left Review*) and the old orthodox Marxists in Poland (*vide* the reception by Adam Schaff, the Party's official philosopher), it has become a primer for the understanding of American policy and motives. This is curious, since Mills is not a Marxist, and if anything, his method and conclusions are anti-Marxist. But because it is tough-minded and "unmasks" the naive, populist illusions about power, it has won a ready response among radicals.

The Mood and the Intent

The mood that pervades Mills' book—and most of his work —provides some clue to the response. In writing about labor (*The New Men of Power*), the white-collar class, and now the power elite—the range of classes in society—Mills is modeling himself on Balzac and writing what Balzac called the *étude de moeurs,* the "comedy" of morals. Some of the Balzac method is there: Balzac sought to reconcile the discoveries of science with poetry and to build up visual effects by the massing of factual detail. Mills takes statistic after statistic and clothes them with angry metaphors.

But more than stylistic analogy is involved. Balzac lived at a time very much like ours: a time of upheaval, when old mores were called into question, a time of class change, when individual social mobility was becoming possible for the first time. Balzac's heroes, Louis Lambert, Rastignac, and most of all Vautrin (a collateral descendent of Macheath, of John Gay's *Beggar's Opera*), begin as mobile men, men seeking a place in society, but end by hating the bourgeois society they find. Their stance is that of the outsider, and their world (Vautrin's underworld is a *counter*-society to the upper world, as is Bertolt Brecht's underworld in *Three-penny Opera*) is built on the premise that the public morality, its manners and ideals, is all a fraud. It is interesting that Mills quotes with approval Balzac's dictum, "Behind every fortune is a crime," and sees it as a judgment which applies equally today. For Mills, too, is an outsider.

But whatever its initial emotional impulse, Mills' book is molded by more direct intellectual progenitors. These are: Veblen, from whom the rhetoric and irony are copied; Weber, for the picture of social structure, not, however, of classes, but of vertical orders, or *Standen;* and, most crucially, Pareto, but not for the definition of elite, which is much different from Mills', but the method. While the debts to Veblen and Weber are conscious, that to Pareto is probably not so. Yet there is the same scorn for ideas, and the denial that ideology has any operative meaning in the exercise of power. And by seeing power as an underlying "combination of orders," Mills parallels, in method, what Pareto was doing in seeing social groups as "combinations of residues." This leads, I think, despite the dynamism in the rhetoric, to a static, ahistorical approach.* For *The Power Elite* is not an empirical analysis of power in the United States, though many readers have mistaken its illustrations for such an analysis, but a *scheme* for the analysis of power; and a close reading of its argument will show, I think, how confusing and unsatisfactory this scheme is.

* My own masters, in this respect, are Dewey and Marx. Dewey, for his insistence on beginning not with structure (habit) but with problems: with the question of why something is called into question, why things are in change and what people did; Marx, for the interplay of ideology and power: for the emphasis on history, on crises as transforming moments, on politics as an activity rooted in concrete interests and played out in determinable strategies.

The Argument

One can examine Mills' book by an alternate scheme,* but as a prior necessity one must write a textual analysis: identify the key terms, see how consistently they are used, and relate evidence to propositions in order to test the coherence of the argument. This, then, is an exercise in hermeneutics.

The argument, as it unfolds in Mills' opening chapter (the others are largely uneven illustrations rather than development or demonstration of the thesis), shuttles perplexingly back and forth on the key problem of how power is wielded. One can show this only by some detailed quotation, a difficult but necessary burden for exposition.†

Within American society, says Mills, major national power "now resides in the economic, political and military domains."

> The way to understand the power of the American elite lies neither solely in recognizing the historical scale of events, nor in accepting the personal awareness reported by men of apparent decision. Behind such men and behind the events of history, linking the two, are the major institutions of modern society. These hierarchies of state and corporation and army constitute the means of power; as such, they are now of a consequence not before equalled in human history—and at their summits, there are now those command posts of modern society which offer us the sociological key to an understanding of the role of the higher circles in America [p. 5].

Thus power, to be power, apparently means control over the *institutions* of power:

> By the powerful, we mean, of course, *those who are able to realize their will, even if others resist it.* No one, accordingly, can be truly powerful unless he has access to the command of major institutions, for it is over these institutional means of power that the truly powerful are, in the first instance, powerful [p. 9].

* For one such alternate scheme, see Talcott Parsons' essay-review "The Distribution of Power in American Society," World Politics, October 1957, Vol. X, No. 1. Parsons argues that Mills sees power as a secondary "distributive" concept in a zero-sum game, where the focus is on who has power. Parsons organizes his analysis on the functional, or integrative purpose of power in the ordering of society. Another view, which sees power as a positive force in securing social values for the benefit of society, is advanced by Robert S. Lynd in the symposium edited by Arthur Kornhauser, *Problems of Power in American Democracy,* Wayne State Press, 1958.

† All italics, unless otherwise indicated, are mine. They are intended to underline key statements. All citations are from C. Wright Mills' *The Power Elite,* New York, Oxford University Press, 1956.

It is shared by only a few persons:

By the power elite, we refer to those political and economic and military *circles* which as an intricate set of overlapping cliques *share decisions having at least national consequences. Insofar as national events are decided, the power elite are those who decide them* [p. 18].

But although these people make the key decisions, they are not the "history makers" of the time. The "power elite" is not, Mills says (p. 20), a theory of history; history is a complex net of intended and unintended decisions.

The idea of the power elite implies *nothing about the process of decision-making as such:* it is an attempt to delimit social areas within which that process, *whatever its character,* goes on. It is a conception of *who* is involved in the process [p. 21].

But historical decisions are made:

In our time the pivotal moment does arise, and at that moment small circles do decide or fail to decide. In either case, they are an elite of power. . . . [p. 22].

Does then the elite make history? Sometimes it is role-determined, sometimes role-determining (pp. 22-25). Mills is obviously wrestling with a contradictory position. For if the power elite are not the history makers, why worry much about them? If they are, it seems to lead to a simple-minded theory of history. Finally Mills resolves the problem:

It was no "historical necessity," but a man named Truman who, with a few other men, decided to drop a bomb on Hiroshima. It was no historical necessity, but an argument within a small circle of men that defeated Admiral Radford's proposal to send troops to Indochina before Dienbienphu fell [p. 24].

If we extract a residue from all this backing and filing, it is that a smaller number of men than ever before holding top positions in government, economic life, and the military, have a set of responsibilities and decision-making powers that are more consequential than ever before in United States history—which, in itself, does not tell us very much.

But it is less the argument than the rhetoric which found an echo, and crucial to Mills' book are a set of operative terms —*institutions* (with which are interchanged freely, *domains, higher circles, top cliques*), *power, command posts,* and *big decisions*—the political use of which gives the book its persuasiveness. These are the key modifiers of the term "elite." What do they mean?

The Terms

(a) *Elite.* Throughout the book, the term elite is used in a variety of ways. Sometimes the term denotes "membership in clique-like sets of people," or "the morality of certain personality types," or "statistics of selected values" such as wealth, political position, etc. In only one place, in a long footnote on page 366, among the notes, Mills explicitly tries to straighten out the confusion created by the profuse interchange of terms. He says that he defines elites primarily on the basis of "institutional position." But what does this mean?

(b) *Institutions, Domains, etc.* Behind men and behind events, linking the two, says Mills, are the major institutions of society: The military, the political, and the economic. But, actually, the military, the economic, the political, as Mills uses these terms, are not institutions but sectors, or what Weber calls *orders,* or vertical hierarchies—each with their enclosed strata—in society. To say that this sector, or order, is more important than that—that in some societies, for example, the religious orders are more important than the political—is to give us large-scale boundaries of knowledge. But surely we want and need more than that.

Such usage as "the military," "the political directorate," etc., is extraordinarily loose. It would be hard to characterize these as institutions. Institutions derive from *particular, established* codes of conduct, which shape the behavior of *particular* groups of men who implicitly or otherwise have a loyalty to that code and are subject to certain controls (anxiety, guilt, shame, expulsion, etc.) if they violate the norms. If the important consideration of power is *where people draw their power from,* then we have to have more particularized ways of identifying the groupings than "institutionalized orders," "domains," "circles," etc.

(c) *Power.* Throughout the book, there is a curious lack of definition of the word power. Only twice, really, does one find a set of limits to the word:

By the powerful we mean, of course, those who are able to realize their will, even if others resist it [p. 9].

All politics is a struggle for power: the ultimate kind of power is violence [p. 171].

It is quite true that violence, as Weber has said, is the ultimate sanction of power, and in extreme situations (e.g., the Spanish Civil War, Iraq, etc.) control of the means of violence may be decisive in seizing or holding power. But power is not the inexorable, implacable, granitic force that Mills and others make it to be. (Merriam once said: "Rape is not evidence of irresistable power, either in politics or sex.") And is it true to say that *all* politics is a struggle for power? Are there not ideals as a goal? And if ideals are realizable through power—though not always—do they not temper the violence of politics?

Power in Mills' terms is domination. But we do not need an elaborate discussion to see that this view of power avoids more problems than it answers, and particularly once one moves away from the outer boundary of *power as violence to institutionalized power,* with which Mills is concerned. For in society, particularly constitutional regimes, and *within* associations, where violence is not the rule, we are in the realm of norms, values, traditions, legitimacy, consensus, leadership, and identification—all the models and mechanisms of command and authority, their acceptance or denial, which shape action in the day-to-day world, *without violence.* And these aspects of power Mills has eschewed.

(d) *The Command Posts.* It is rather striking, too, given Mills' image of power, and politics, as violence, that the metaphor to describe the people of power is a military one. We can take this as a clue to Mills' implicit scheme. But, being little more than a metaphor, it tells us almost nothing about *who* has the power. The men who hold power, he says, are those who run the *organizations* or *domains* which have power. But how do we know they have power, or what power they have? Mills simply takes as postulates: (1) the organization or instituton has power; (2) *position in it gives power.* How do we know? Actually, we can only know if power exists by what people *do* with their power.

What powers people have, what decisions they make, how they make them, what factors they have to take into account in making them—all these enter into the question of whether position *can* be transferred into power. But Mills has said:

"The idea of the power elite implies nothing about the process of decision-making as such—it is an attempt to delimit the social areas within which that process, *whatever its character,* goes on. It is a conception of who is involved in the process" (p. 21). Thus, we find ourselves stymied. *Who* depends upon positions? But position, as I have argued, is only meaningful if one can define the character of the decisions made with such power. And this problem Mills eschews.*

Mills says, further, that he wants to avoid the problem of the self-awareness of the power holders, or the role of such self-awareness in decisions. ("The way to understand the power of the elite lies neither in recognizing the historic scale of events or the personal awareness reported by men of apparent decision behind the men and the institutions" [p. 15].) But if the power elite is *not* the history-maker (p. 20), as Mills sometimes implies, *then what is the meaning of their position as members of the power elite?* Either they can make effective decisions or not. It is true that many men, like Chanticleer the Cock, crow and believe that they have caused the sun to rise, but if such power is only self-deception, that is an aspect, too, of the meaning of power.

(e) *The Big Decisions.* The power elite comes into its own on the "big decisions." In fact, this is an implicit definition of the power of the elite: only they can effect the "big decisions." Those who talk of a new social balance, or pluralism, or the rise of labor, are talking, if at all correctly, says Mills, about the "middle levels" of power. They fail to see the big decisions.

But, curiously, except in a few instances, Mills fails to specify what the big decisions are. The few, never analyzed with regard to how the decisions were actually made or who

* In his extraordinary story of policy conflicts between the Army, Air Force and Navy on strategic concepts—policy issues such as reliance on heavy military bombers and all-out retaliation, against tactical nuclear weapons and conventional ground forces for limited wars, issues which deeply affect the balance of power within the military establishment—General James Gavin provides a striking example of the helplessness of some of the top Army brass against the entrenched bureaucracy within the Defense Department. "With the establishment of the Department of Defense in 1947," he writes, "an additional layer of civilian management was placed above the services. Furthermore, by the law, military officers were forbidden to hold executive positions in the Department of Defense. As a result the Assistant Secretaries of Defense relied heavily on hundreds of civil service employees, who probably have more impact on decision-making in the Department of Defense than any other group of individuals, military or civilian." From *War and Peace in the Space Age* (Harper and Brothers), reprinted in *Life,* August 4, 1958, pp. 81-82.

made them, are five in number: the steps leading to intervention in World War II; the decision to drop the atom bomb over Hiroshima and Nagasaki; the declaration of war in Korea; the indecisions over Quemoy and Matsu in 1955; the hesitation regarding intervention in Indochina when Dien Bien Phu was on the verge of falling.

It is quite striking (and it is in line with Mills' conception of politics) that all the decisions he singles out as the "big decisions" are connected with *violence*. These are, it is true, the ultimate decisions a society can make: the commitment or refusal to go to war. And in this regard Mills is right. They *are* big decisions. But what is equally striking in his almost cursory discussion of these decisions is the failure to see that they are not made by the power elite. They are the decisions which, in our system, are vested constitutionally in the individual who must bear the responsibility for the choices—the president. And, rather than being a usurpation of the power of the people, so to speak, this is one of the few instances in the Constitution where such responsibility is specifically defined and where accountability is clear. Naturally, a president will consult with others. And in the instances Mills has cited, the president did. Richard Rovere has written a detailed analysis (in the *Progressive,* June, 1956) of the decisions that Mills has cited and, as Mills defines this elite, has broadly refuted the notion that a "power elite" was really involved. Few persons, other than the president, were involved in these decisions: on the atom bomb, Stimson, Churchill, and a few physicists; on Korea, a small group of men whose counsel was divided, like Acheson and Bradley; on Quemoy and Matsu, specifically by Eisenhower; and on Dien Bien Phu, a broader group, the military and the Cabinet: but in this instance, "the" power elite, narrowly defined, was for intervention, while Eisenhower alone was against the intervention and decided against sending in troops, principally, says Rovere, because of the weight of public opinion.

Now it may well be that crucial decisions of such importance should not be in the hands of a few men. But short of a system of national initiative and referendum, such as was proposed in 1938-39 in the Ludlow amendment, or short of reorganizing the political structure of the country to insist on party responsibility for decision, it is difficult to see what Mills' shouting is about. To say that the leaders of a country have a constitutional responsibility to make crucial decisions is a fairly commonplace statement. To say that the power elite makes such decisions is to invest the statement with a weight and emotional charge that is quite impressive, but of little meaning.

The Question of Interests

So far we have been accepting the terms "command posts" and "power elite" in Mills' own usage. But now a difficulty enters: the question not only of *who* constitutes the power elite but how *cohesive* they are. Although Mills contends that he does not believe in a conspiracy theory, his loose account of the centralization of power among the elite comes suspiciously close to it. (It is much like Jack London's *The Iron Heel*—the picture of the American oligarchs—which so influenced socialist imagery and thought before World War I.)

Yet we can only evaluate the meaning of any centralization of power on the basis of what people do with their power. What *unites* them? What *divides* them? And this involves a definition of *interests*. To say, as Mills does: "*All* means of power tend to become *ends* to an elite that is in command of them. And that is why we may define the power elite in terms of power—as those who occupy the command posts" (p. 23)—is circular.

What does it mean to say that power is an end in itself for the power elite? If the elite is cohesive and is facing another power group, the maintenance of power may be an end in itself. But is the elite cohesive? We do not know without first coming back to the question of interests. And the nature of interests implies a selection of values by a group, or part of a group, over against others, and this leads to a definition of particular privileges, and so on.

Certainly, one cannot have a power elite, or a ruling class, without *community of interests*. Mills implies one: the interest of the elite is in the maintenance of the capitalist system as a *system*. But this is never really discussed or analyzed in terms of the meaning of capitalism, the impact of political controls on the society, or the changes in capitalism in the last twenty-five years.

But even if the interest be as broad as Mills implies, one still has the responsibility of identifying the conditions for the maintenance of the system, and the issues and interests involved. Further, one has to see whether there is or has been a *continuity of interests*, in order to chart the cohesiveness or the rise and fall of particular groups.

One of the main arguments about the importance of the

command posts is the growing centralization of power, which would imply something about the nature of interests. Yet there is almost no sustained discussion of the forces leading to centralization. These are somewhat assumed, and hover over the book, but are never made explicit. Yet only a sustained discussion of these tendencies would, it seems to me, uncover the *locales* of power and their shifts. For example: the role of technology and increasing capital costs as major factors in the size of enterprise; forces in the federalization of power, such as the need for regulation and planning on a national scale because of increased communication, complexity of living, social and military services, and the managing of the economy; the role of foreign affairs. Curiously, Soviet Russia is not even mentioned in the book, although so much of our posture has been dictated by Russian behavior.

Since his focus is on *who* has power, Mills spends considerable effort in tracing the social origins of the men at the top. But, in a disclaimer toward the end of the book (pp. 280-87) he says that the conception of the power elite does not rest upon common social origins (a theme which underlies, say, Schumpeter's notion of the rise and fall of classes) or upon personal friendship, but (although the presumption is not made explicit) upon their "institutional position." But such a statement begs the most important question of all: *the mechanisms of co-ordination among the power holders.* One can say obliquely, as Mills does, that they "meet each other," but this tells us little. If there are "built-in" situations whereby each position merges into another, what are they? One can say, as Mills does, that the new requirements of government require increased recruitment to policy positions from outside groups.* But then, what groups—and what do they do?

At one point Mills says that the Democrats recruited from Dillon, Read, and the Republicans from Kuhn, Loeb. But the point is never developed, and it is hard to know what he

* One key theoretical point, for Marxists, which Mills, surprisingly, never comes to is the question of the ultimate source of power. Is the political directorate autonomous? Is the military independent? If so, why? What is the relation of economic power to the other two? Mills writes: "Insofar as the structural clue to the power elite today lies in the enlarged and military state, that clue becomes evident in the military ascendency. The warlords have gained decisive political relevance, and the military structure is now in considerable part a political structure." (p. 275) If so, what is one to say then about the other crucial proposition by Mills that the capitalist system in the U.S. is essentially unchanged? [See section below on "The Continuity of Power."]

means. One could equally say that in the recruitment of science advisors the Democrats took from Chicago and Los Alamos, and the Republicans from Livermore; but if this means anything, and I think it does, one has to trace out the consequences of this different recruitment in the *actions* of the different people. Mills constantly brings the story to the point where analysis has to begin—and stops.

The most extraordinary fact about American foreign policy—the most crucial area of power—has been the lack of co-ordination between the military and foreign-policy officials, and the failure of both to think in political terms. This is exemplified in the lack of liaison in the final days of World War II, and the non-political decisions made by the U.S. generals which have had incalculable consequences for the balance of power in postwar Europe. Unlike the Soviet Union, the United States subordinated all political questions to immediate military objectives. The British, fearful of a postwar Europe dominated by the Soviet Union, were anxious in the final months of the war to push the Allied armies as fast as possible across the North German plain to Berlin—either to beat the Russians or to participate in its capture. But for the U.S. chiefs of staff, Berlin was of secondary importance.

Said General Marshall, chairman of the Joint Chiefs of Staff: "Such psychological and political advantages as would result from the possible capture of Berlin ahead of the Russians should not override the imperative military consideration which, in our opinion, is the destruction and dismemberment of the German armed forces."

And Ray S. Cline in *Washington Command Post: The Operations Division,* a volume in the official army history of World War II, notes the lack of "systematic co-ordination of foreign policy with military planning" and the uncertainty—even in the fall of 1944—of State Department officials "about American foreign policy as applied to the surrender and occupation of Germany." And the Pentagon, which usually is seen as the cold political brains of U.S. foreign policy, in the negotiation on the occupation of Berlin, rejected a British suggestion for a full land corridor from West Germany to Berlin on the ground that the Soviet Union was an ally and that such a corridor was therefore unnecessary.

The European Image

How explain this image of power and policy in terms of the

intents of self-conscious groups of men having fixed places in society? The peculiar fact is that while all the illustrations Mills uses are drawn from American life, the key concepts are drawn from European experiences; and this accounts, I believe, for the exotic attractiveness—and astigmatism—of the power elite idea.*

For example: having defined politics and power in terms of the ultimate sanction of violence, Mills raises the provocative question: Why have the possessors of the means of violence—the military—not established themselves in power more than they have done in the West? Why is not military distatorship the more normal form of government?

Mills' answer is to point to the role of status. "Prestige to the point of honor, and all that this implies, has, as it were, been the pay-off for the military renunciations of power . . ." (p. 174).

Now, to the extent that this is true, this fact applies primarily to the *European* scene. On the Continent, the military did create and seek to live by a code of honor. Many European works deal with this code, and many European plays, particularly those of Schnitzler, satirize it. But does the concept apply in the United States? Where in the United States has the military (the Navy apart) been kept in check by honor? The military has not had the power—or status—in American life for a variety of vastly different reasons: the original concept of the Army as a people's militia; the populist image of the Army man—often as a "hero"; the "democratic" recruitment to West Point; the reluctance to accept conscription; the low esteem of soldiering as against money-making; the tradition of civil life, etc.

All this Mills sees and knows. But if "honor" and "violence" are not meaningful in our past, why conceptualize the problem of the military in terms of violence and honor as

* This is a refractory problem which has distorted much of American sociological thinking. Throughout the 1930's, American intellectuals always expected that U.S. social development would inevitably follow that of Europe, particularly in the emergence of fascism. To a great extent these expectations were a product of a mechanical Marxism which saw all politics as a reflex of economic crises, and which postulated common stages of social evolution that each country would pass through. Even as late as 1948, Harold Laski could write that "the history of the United States would, despite everything, follow the general pattern of capitalist democracy in Europe" (Harold Laski, *The American Democracy,* New York, 1948, p. 17). And even so brilliant an observer as Joseph Schumpeter, in his *Capitalism, Socialism and Democracy,* could, with sleight of hand, mix American experiences with European concepts to achieve his gloomy predictions.

a general category, when the problem does not derive from the American scene in those terms? Unless Mills assumes, as many intellectuals did in the thirties, that we shall yet follow the European experience.

A similar pitfall can be found in the treatment of prestige. Mills says: "All those who succeed in America—no matter what their circle of origin or their sphere of action—are likely to become involved in the world of the celebrity." And further, "With the incorporation of the economy, the ascendency of the military establishment, and the centralization of the enlarged state, there have arisen the national elite, who, in occupying the command posts, have taken the spotlight of publicity and become subjects of the intensive build-up. *Members of the power elite are celebrated because of the positions they occupy and the decisions they command*" (p. 71).

Now by celebrities, Mills means *those names that need no further identification.* But are the relationships of celebrity, prestige, status, and power as direct as Mills makes them out to be? Certainly celebrities and glamor exist in American life, but these are the concomitants or the necessary components, *not* of an elite, but of a *mass consumption* society. A society engaged in selling requires such a system of lure and appeal. But why assume that positions of power involve one in this system of glamor? And could even a sophisticated reader quickly identify the president and board chairman of the top ten corporations on the *Fortune* magazine list of 500 largest corporations, e.g., Standard Oil of New Jersey, A.T.&T., General Motors, etc.; the top-ranking members of military staffs, e.g., the Chairman of the Joint Chiefs of Staff, the head of the Army, the Naval Chief of Operations, Air Chief of Staff, General of S.A.C., etc., and name the members of the cabinet?

Again the confusion arises from Mills' unthinking use of older, European conceptions of prestige. In such feudal-like hierarchies, prestige was identified with *honor* and with *deference.* Those who held power could claim honor and deference. This was true in Europe. But has it been so in the United States? When Harold Lasswell first attempted in the late thirties to use deference as a key symbol, it already had a false ring. Mills, in effect, substitutes glamor or celebrity for deference, but toward the same end. But does power today carry the immediate glorification and celebration of name? It is doubtful if, in the mass consumption society, the notions of celebrity, glamor, prestige, and power have the kind of connotations, or are linked, as Mills suggests.

History and Ideas

Now, if one is concerned with the question about changes in the source and style of power, or in the synchronization and centralization of power, one would have to examine the problem historically. Yet except in one or two instances, Mills ignores the historical dimensions. In one place he speaks of a periodization of American history wherein political power has replaced economic power. But this is too loose to be meaningful. In another place—the only concrete discussion of social change in historical terms—he cites an interesting statistic:

> In the middle of the nineteenth century—between 1865 and 1881—only 19 per cent of the men at the top of government began their political career at the national level; but from 1905 to 1953 about one-third of the political elite began there, and in the Eisenhower administration some 40 per cent started in politics at the national level—a high for the entire political history of the U.S. [p. 229].

Even in its own terms, it is hard to figure out the exact meaning of the argument, other than the fact that more problems are centered in Washington than in the states and, for this reason, more persons are drawn directly to the national capital than before. Surely there is a simple explanation for much of this. During World War II, with a great need for both national unity and for specialists, more outsiders were coopted for cabinet posts and the executive branch than before. And, in 1952, since the Republicans had been out of top office for twenty years and would have fewer persons who had a career in government, they would bring in a high proportion of outsiders.

What is interesting in the use of this kind of data is the methodological bias it reveals. In using such data—and variables like lower or national levels—there is a presumption that in the different kind of recruitment one can chart differences in the character of the men at top, and that therefore the *character of their politics* would be different too. (Mills seems to imply this but never develops the point other than to say that, today, the *political outsider* has come into the ascendant. But as a counter-methodology, it would seem to me that one would start not with recruitment or social origins but with the *character of the politics*. Has something changed, and if so, what and why? Is the change due to differences in recruitment (differential class and ethnic backgrounds) or to some other reason? But if one asks these questions, one has to begin with an examination of *ideas and issues,* not social origins.

But Mills, at least here, is almost completely uninterested in ideas and issues. The questions in politics that interest him are: In what way have strategic positions changed, and which positions have come to the fore? Changes in power then are for Mills largely a succession of different positions. As different structural or institutional positions (i.e., military, economic, political) combine, different degrees of power are possible. The circulation of the elite—by which Pareto meant the change in the composition of groups with different "residues"—is transformed here into the succession of institutional positions.

But how does this apply to people? Are people—character, ideas, values—determined by their *positions*? And if so, in what way? More than that, to see political history as a shift in the power position of "institutions" rather than, say, of concrete interest groups, or classes, is to read politics in an extraordinarily abstract fashion. It is to ignore the changes in ideas and interests. This is one of the reasons why Mills can minimize, in the striking way he does, the entire twenty-year history of the New Deal and Fair Deal. For him these twenty years were notable *only* because they fostered the centralizing tendencies of the major "institutions" of society, notably the political.

In this neglect, or even dismissal of ideas and ideologies, one finds a striking parallel in Pareto's explanation of social changes in Italy. For Pareto, the rise of socialism in Italy was a mere change in the "derivations" (i.e., the masks or ideologies) while the basic combination of residues remained (No. 1704).[30]

In effect, the shifts of temper from nationalism to liberalism to socialism reflected shifts in the distribution of class II residues (i.e., the residues of group peristence). Thus changes in the political class meant simply the circulation of socio-psychological types. All ideologies, all philosophical claims, were masks "for mere purposes of partisan convenience in debate. [They are] neither true nor false; [but] simply devoid of meaning" (No. 1708).

Similarity, for Mills, changes in power are changes in combinations of constitutional position; and this alone, presumably, is the only meaningful reality.

> Except for the unsuccessful Civil War, changes in the power system of the United States have not involved important challenges to basic legitimations. . . . Changes in the American structure of power have generally come about by institutional shifts in the relative positions of the political, the economic and the military orders [p. 269].

Thus the extraordinary changes in American life, changes in the concepts of property, managerial control, responsibility of government, the changes in moral temper created by the New Deal, will become "reduced" to institutional shifts. But have there been no challenges to basic legitimations in American life? How continuous has been the system of power in the United States?

The Continuity of Power

If in his analysis of politics Mills draws from Pareto, in his image of economic power he becomes a "vulgar" Marxist. Mills notes:

> The recent social history of American capitalism does not reveal any distinct break in the continuity of the higher capitalist class. . . . Over the last half-century in the economy as in the political order, there has been a remarkable *continuity of interests*, vested in the *types* of higher economic men who guard and advance them . . . [p. 147].

Although the language is vague, one can only say that an answer to this proposition rests not on logical or methodological arguments but on empirical grounds, and in Chapter Two, on the breakup of family capitalism in America, I have sought to indicate an answer. For the singular fact is that in the last seventy-five years the established relations between the system of property and family, which, Malthus maintained, represented the "fundamental laws" of society, have broken down. And this has meant too the breakup of "family capitalism," which has been the social cement of the bourgeois class system.

In his summation of economic control, Mills paints an even more extraordinary picture:

The top corporations are not a set of splendidly isolated giants. They have been knitted together by explicit associations within their respective industries and regions and in supra-associations such as the NAM. These associations organize a unity among the managerial elite and other members of the corporate rich. They translate narrow economic powers into industry-wide and class-wide power; and they use these powers, first, on the economic front, for example, with reference to labor and its organizations; and second, on the political front, for example in their large role in the political sphere. And they infuse into the ranks of smaller businessmen the views of big business [p. 122].

This is a breath-taking statement more sweeping than anything in the old TNEC reports or of Robert Brady's theory of *Spitzenverbande* (or peak associations) in his *Business as a System of Power*. That there is some co-ordination is obvious; but unity of this scope — and smoothness — is almost fanciful. Mills cites no evidence for these assertions. The facts, actually, point to the other direction. Trade associations in the United States have declined; they were primarily important during wartime as a means of representing industry on government boards. The NAM has become increasingly feckless, and there has been a decline in member interest and contributions. And industry has divided on a wide variety of issues including labor policy (e.g., the large steel and auto companies have been attacked by General Electric and other firms for accepting s.u.b. — supplementary unemployment benefits).

Mills speaks of "their large role in the political sphere." But against whom are the members of the power elite united, and what kinds of issues unite them in the political sphere? I can think of only one issue on which the top corporations would be united: tax policy. In almost all others, they divide. They are divided somewhat on labor. There are major clashes in areas of self-interest, such as those between railroads, truckers, and the railroads and the airlines; or between coal and oil, and coal and natural gas interests. Except in a vague, ideological sense, there are relatively few political issues on which the managerial elite is united.

The problem of *who unites with whom on what* is an empirical one, and this consideration is missing from Mills' work. If such co-ordination as Mills depicts does exist, a further question is raised as to how it comes about. We know, for example, that as a consequence of bureaucratization, career lines within corporations become lengthened and, as a consequence, there is shorter tenure of office for those who reach the top. Within a ten-year period, A.T.&T. has had three executive officers, all of whom had spent thirty to forty years *within* the corporation. If men spend so much time *within* their corporate shells, how do members of the "elite" get acquainted?

In this preoccupation with elite manipulation, Mills becomes indifferent to the problems of what constitutes problems of power in the everyday life of the country. This is quite evident in the way he summarily dismisses all other questions, short of the "big decisions," as "middle level" and, presumably, without much *real* meaning. *Yet are these not the stuff of politics,* the issues which divide men and create the interest conflicts that involve people in a sense of ongoing reality: labor issues, race problems, tax policy, and the like? Is this not the meaning of power to people as it touches their lives?

The use of the term elite poses another question about the utility of its limits for discussing powers. Why use the word *elite* rather than *decision-makers,* or even *rulers?* To talk of *decision-making,* one would have to discuss policy formulation, pressures, etc. To talk of *rule,* one would have to discuss the nature of rule. But if one talks of an elite, one need only discuss institutional position, and one can do so only if, as Mills assumes, the fundamental nature of the system is unchanged, so that one's problem is to chart the circulation at the top. The argument that the fundamental nature of the system—i.e., that of basic legitimations, of continuity of the capitalist class—is unchanged is a curious one, for if power has become so centralized and synchronized, as Mills now assumes, is this not a fundamental change in the system?

Yet, even if one wants to talk in terms of elites, there have been key shifts in power in American society: the breakup of family capitalism (and this is linked to a series of shifts in power in Western society as a whole), but most importantly —and obviously—the decisive role of the political arena.

From Economics to Politics

In the decade before World War I, the growing power of the trusts, the direct influence of the bankers in the economy, the ideological rise of socialism all tended to focus attention on the class system as the hidden but actually decisive element in shaping society and social change. A group of "realistic" historians, notably J. Allen Smith and, most importantly, Charles A. Beard, began the task of reinterpreting the early colonial and constitutional struggles in economic terms. The Beard interpretation schematically, was roughly this:

The earliest struggles in American history were direct class struggles between the merchant group, represented by the Federalists, and the agrarians, represented by the Democrats. Society was split fairly cleanly between the two groups with antagonistic interests (tariff, cheap money, etc.). The unadorned way in which class conflict was discussed by the "founding fathers" could be strikingly documented in the Federalist papers. As in the later struggle between the English landed gentry and the manufacturing class over the protectionist corn laws, a decisive victory for either would have decided the basic character of the society. But that early American plutocracy, the Eastern merchants, proved to be an unstable social group that was incapable of maintaining the political initiative. So the Federalists lost. Yet the Democrats —in the face of the economic facts of life of a burgeoning capitalism—could not really win, and the "Jeffersonian revolution" was something that Jefferson found easier to promise than to execute.

But later historiography has considerably modified this crude chiaroscuro and has drawn in many subtle tones between the black and the white. As Dixon Ryan Fox, for one, in his study of politics within one state in the first four decades of the nineteenth century, *Yankees and Yorkers,* has written:

"Because of rivalries between English and Dutch, Presbyterian and Anglican, merchants and farmers, and others, party spirit early appeared in New York and persisted in changing manifestations. Yet the party lines were not closely drawn between rich and poor. So assured were the aristocrats of their social place and so various their backgrounds that they did not move as one interest; families faced each other as Capulets and Montagues. As Henry Adams has remarked, 'All these Jays, Schuylers, Livingstones, Clintons, Burrs, had they lived in New England would probably have united, or abandoned the country; but being citizens of New York they quarreled.' When the Tories were removed the Whigs soon split into factions, not merely two, but several, each ready for trade and compromise."

It is at this point that we find the seeds of the peculiarly American party system. The mutual defeat of attempts to establish exclusive domination left the social system undefined from the very start. It was not predominantly mercantile, slave, free, agrarian, industrial, or proletarian. The wealthy families, having lost direct political control, sought to work indirectly through the politician. But in a rapidly shifting society, whose very hugeness casts up a variety of conflicting interests, a politician can succeed only if he is a broker and the party system an agency of mediation.

This is not to deny the existence of classes or the nature of a class system. *But one cannot, unless the society is highly stratified, use the class structure for direct political analysis.* A class system defines the *mode* of gaining wealth and privilege in a society. (This mode can be land [real property], corporate title ["fictitious" property], skill [technical or managerial], mercenaries [*condottieri*], or direct political allocation [party, bureaucracy, or army], and this class system has to be legitimated, in legal forms, in order to assure its continuity. Often this wealth and privilege carries with it power and prestige, but there is no direct correlation.) But most important, whatever the mode, class analysis does not tell us directly *who* exercises the power, nor does it tell us much about the competition within that mode for power. Unless that mode and its legitimations are directly challenged, one rarely sees a class acting as a class in unified fashion. Once a specific mode is established, competition for privilege within the system is high, and various and different interests develop. The growing complexity of society necessarily multiplies those interests, regional or functional, and in an open society the political arena—unless there is a conflict to overthrow the system—is a place where different interests fight it out for advantage. That is why, usually, the prism of "class" is too crude to follow the swift play of diverse political groups.

In European society, the *political* issues, especially after the French Revolution, tended to fall along class lines, but even then, any detailed analysis risked falsification of events simply by focusing the issues in gross class terms. Such a classic of Marxist political analysis as *The Eighteenth Brumaire of Louis Bonaparte* comes alive only because Marx depicts so skillfully the play of diverse group interests, as these are manipulated so imperiously by Louis Napoleon, beneath the larger façade of class interests. In the United States, so heterogeneous from the start, and striated even further by diverse ethnic, national, and religious differences, it is difficult to read the political order—which after all became an independent road to privilege for the leaders of minority groups—as a reflection of the economic order. But even where there was some rough correspondence, the play of diverse interests was immense. As late as 1892, Marx's co-worker, Friedrich Engels, wrote in a letter to his friend Sorge: "There is no place yet in America for a *third* party, I believe. The divergence of interests even in the *same* class group is so great in that tremendous area that wholly different groups and interests are represented in each of the two big parties, depending upon the locality, and almost each particular section of the possessing class has its representatives in each of the two parties to a very large degree, though *today* big industry forms the core of the Republicans on the whole, just as the big landowners of the South form that of the Democrats. The apparent haphazardness of this jumbling together is what provides the splendid soil for the corruption and the plundering of the government that flourishes there so beautifully."[31]

At one point in later American history, the dominant business class—the plutocracy, rather than any landed squirearchy—came close to imprinting a clear mark on American politics. By the turn of the twentieth century the growing industrial class had scored a smashing economic victory. With that victory came some efforts to dissolve the structure of group interests by developing a pervasive political ideology which could also serve the emergent national feeling. One such attempt was the doctrine of imperialism in the "manifest destiny" of Beveridge and the "Americanism" of Franklin Giddings. This was alien to a heterogeneous people, or at least premature. The second and more successful effort was in the identification of capitalism with democracy. The early commercial class had feared democracy as a *political* instrument whereby the "swinish multitude" (Burke) would prepare the way for a radical despotism. The ideology of victorious industrial capitalism defined democracy almost completely in agreeable *economic* terms, as liberty of contract.

If the dominant business class was unable to exercise direct political control of the society, it could establish its ideological hegemony. While in the period from 1880 to 1912 the middle class (small farmers and businessmen, and many professionals) had supported the sporadic antitrust and antimonopoly outbursts, such opinions and movements were dissolved by the subsequent two decades of war, prosperity, and propaganda.

This unity burst with the bubble of prosperity because the

ideologists of free enterprise, rugged or otherwise, did not understand the realities of the "socialized" economy that had come into being. They had failed to grasp the degree to which this market economy imposes a particular type of dependency upon everyone.

In a pure market society, as Marx once phrased it, each man thinks for himself and no one plans for all. Today it is no longer individual men who are in the market but particular collectivities, each of which tries—by administered prices, farm supports, uniform wage patterns and the like—to exempt itself from the risks of the market; inevitably, the measures each group resorts to for protection provoke governmental concern that the entire economy not be overturned in the anarchic stampede to safety.

De Tocqueville once wrote that historians who live in aristocratic ages are inclined to read all events through the will and character of heroic individuals, whereas historians of democratic times deal perforce with general causes. The dazzling aristocratic glamor of Franklin D. Roosevelt has often confused the efforts to put the New Deal period in historical perspective, and even now we lack an adequate political characterization of the era. There have been many historical analogies inspired by the flavor and verve of Roosevelt himself: e.g., Roosevelt was a temporizing Solon whose political reforms sought to stave off the revolution of propertyless masses; Roosevelt was a Tiberius Gracchus, a patrician who deserted his class to become the people's tribune; Roosevelt was a Louis Napoleon, an ambitious politician manipulating first one class and then another, while straddling them all, to maintain his personal rule. Certainly, they shed little light on the way government action gives rise to new combinations of interests and the operation of these shifting coalitions.

The public face of the New Deal was a set of sweeping social reforms, and, quite naively, some writers, and indeed, Roosevelt himself, have called the New Deal an assertion of human rights over property rights. But such terms carry little meaning, either philosophically or pragmatically. Are "support prices" for farmers a property right or a human right? In effect, what the New Deal did was to *legitimate* the idea of *group* rights, and the claim of groups, as groups, rather than individuals, for government support. Thus unions won the right to bargain collectively and, through the union shop, to enforce a group decision over individuals; the aged won pen-sions, the farmers gained subsidies; the veterans received benefits; the minority groups received legal protections, etc. None of these items, in themselves, were unique. Together, they added up to an extraordinary social change. Similarly, the government has always had some role in directing the economy. But the permanently enlarged role, dictated on the one hand by the necessity to maintain full employment, and, on the other, by the expanded military establishment, created a vastly different set of powers in Washington than ever before in our history.

What is amazing, in retrospect, is that while the commitment to a politically managed economy could have been foreseen, we were quite badly deficient in organizing our economic thinking for it. A managed economy requires not only that we have a housekeeping budget for the government as the large spending unit, but also an economic budget that states the major magnitudes of economic interaction for society as a whole—the total amount of goods and services produced in a year's time and the total amount of income paid out. Through these figures we can chart the gaps in consumer spending and in investment and, if necessary, make up the differences by appropriate fiscal measures. Yet it was only in 1936 that the Department of Commerce brought out its first report on national income, and only in 1942 that the other side of the economic balance sheet, the gross national product, was first estimated by government. The two indexes as the pulse beat of economic health were only first combined and published together in President Roosevelt's budget message in 1945.

In the emergence of the political economy, a new kind of decision-making has taken place. In the market society, peoples' wants are registered by their "dollar votes," as part of the automatic interaction of supply and demand. The sum total of individual dollars-and-cents decisions, operating independently of each other, added up, as Bentham thought, to a social decision, e.g., the general consensus. Thus, when decisions on the allocation of resources operated through the market, dollars, not ideology, determined what was to be produced. In this sense, economics was the key to social power, and politics its pale reflection.

But politics, operating through the government, has more and more become the means of registering a social and economic decision. Here, instead of acting independently as in a market, the individual is forced to work through particular collectivities to enforce his will. Since in a managed economy, "politics," not dollars, determines major production, the intervention of the government not only sharpens pressure-group identifications but forces each to adopt an ideology which can justify its claims and which can square with some concept of "national interest."

The Types of Decisions

Ultimately, if one wants to discuss power, it is more fruitful to discuss it in terms of *types of decisions* rather than elites. And curiously, Mills, I would argue, ultimately agrees, for the real heart of the book is a polemic against those who say that decisions are made democratically in the United States. Mills writes:

> More and more of the fundamental issues never came to any point of decision before Congress . . . much less before the electorate [p. 255].

> Insofar as the structural clue to the power elite today lies in the political order, that clue is the decline of politics as genuine and public debates of alternative decisions . . . America is now in considerable part more a formal political democracy [p. 224].

Now, to some extent this is true, but not, it seems to me, with the invidious aspect with which Mills invests the judgment.

In many instances, even the "interested public" feels itself "trapped," so to speak, by its inability to affect events. Much of this arises out of the *security* nature of problems, so that issues are often fought out in a bureaucratic labyrinth. The decision on the H-bomb was one such issue. Here we had groups of scientists versus a section of the military, particularly SAC. Unless one assumes that everyone ever involved in decision-making is a member of the power elite—which is circular—*we have to locate the source of such decisions, for these are the central problems of a sociology of power.*

But another, equally important reason for being unable to affect events is the onset of what one can only call, inaptly, "technical decision making": the fact that once a policy decision is made, or once a technological change comes to the fore, or once some long crescive change has become manifest, a number of other consequences, if one is being "functionally rational," almost inevitably follow. Thus, shifts of power become "technical" concomitants of such "decisions," and a sociology of power must identify the kinds of consequences which follow the different kinds of decisions.

Three short examples may illustrate the point:

(1) *The federal budget as an economic gyroscope.* From 1931 to 1935, in the depth of the depression years, total federal budget expenditures of all kinds averaged 5.2 billion dollars. In the next four years, 1936 to 1940, it reached a new high of 8 billion dollars. (Income during this period was about 60 per cent of expenditures.) Four years later, the federal government was spending, yearly, a staggering total of over 95 billion dollars and accumulating a national debt which more than quintupled the debt of the previous decade. The figures are in constant dollars.

More importantly, these expenditures have to be compared with gross national product (g.n.p.), the sum total of goods and services produced during a year. During the depresssion decade, despite the then relatively high government spending, the federal budget "consumed" and pumped back between 5 to 10 per cent of g.n.p. During the war, the figure mounted to over 40 per cent. But while this represented an "abnormally" high figure, in the decade and a half since the end of the war, the government has become the "consumer" of nearly one-fourth of the total g.n.p. Except for one year, 1948, the one "peacetime" year in postwar history, when the federal budget reached a "low" of 33 billion dollars (against a g.n.p. of 257 billion), the expenditures in the Korean campaign and the sums required to maintain the arms pace of the cold war has kept the federal budget at record highs. In the last half of the 1950 decade it averaged about 70 billion dollars, with g.n.p. about 325 billion dollars. In 1960, the federal budget will reach over 80 billion (estimated), and g.n.p. over 400 billion. In the 1950's, the yearly interest alone on the public debt, over 7.2 billion dollars, was greater than the *total* federal government expenditures each year during the depression.

The fact is that this enormous rise in the expenditures of the federal government was not "willed" by any one man or group of men, but arose, inevitably, as a necessary outcome of the war and its effects. And the permanent role of the federal government as the economic gyroscope of the country is due to that fact.

(2) *The "dual economy" of 1950-55.* When the Korean war broke out in 1950, the government was faced with the

immediate choice of either converting existing machinery production to war goods or encouraging new plants. The decision rested on an estimate of the type of war. If it seemed as if the Korean war might spread into a general war, then the order to convert civilian facilities could be constructed to build large stockpiles of arms. The decision, based on political-military estimates, was to build a "dual economy." The chief consequence, economically speaking, was the decision to speed new capital expansion by allowing firms to write off the costs of new facilities in five years, as against the normal twenty-five years. (Thus firms could deduct 20 per cent of the new costs from profits and thus gain a considerable tax benefit.) This five-year tax amortization scheme encouraged an extraordinarily high rate of capital investment, undoubtedly spurred the prosperity boom of the mid-fifties, and was responsible for the overexpansion of capacity which was a contributing element to the recession of 1958-59.

(3) *Weapons technology.* The rapid emergence of new weapons decisively affects the relative weight of power and influence within the military, and within each arm of the military, of the different branches. Thus the rise of missiles reduces the importance of the battleship, once the mainstay of the navy, and of the army itself. In the new technology, for example, the missile-carrying submarine becomes a key arm of striking power, while the extension of the range of the missile makes the manned airplane obsolete. These changes in the composition of the armed forces, the requirements of new skill groups, of technicians and of technologists, mean a change in the profile of military power. Research and Development become more important than Operations, and the power of the scientist, the engineer, and the technologist grows accordingly.

All of these consequences grow out of the "big decisions" that Mills has talked about. But the fundamental policy issues which Mills mentions are primarily, as I pointed out before, decisions to be involved in war or not—or, more broadly, the question of foreign policy. And how can one discuss this question, which Mills completely evades, without discussing the cold war, *and the extent to which our posture is shaped by the Russians!* United States foreign policy since 1946—or, more specifically, since Byrnes' Stuttgart speech, which reversed our position on weakening Germany—was not a reflex of any *internal* social divisions or class issues in the United States but was *based on an estimate of Russia's intentions.*

Nor was this estimate made, in the first instance, by "the power elite." It was an estimate made by American scholarly experts, most notably by George Kennan and the policy-planning staff of the State Department. It was a judgment that Stalinism as an ideoligical phenomenon, and Russia as a geopolitical power, were aggressively, militarily, and ideologically expansionist, and that a policy of containment, including a rapid military build-up was necessary in order to implement that containment. This underlay Truman's Greco-Turkish policy, and it underlay the Marshall Plan and the desire to aid the rebuilding of the European economy. These policies were not a reflex of power constellations within the U.S. They were estimates of national interest and of national survival.

From the first decision, many others followed: the creation of a long-distance striking arm in the air (SAC), the establishment of a West European Defense Community (EDC, and following its failure, NATO, etc.). This is not to say that every strategic step followed inexorably from the first decision (after France rejected EDC, one had to rely more on Germany for military support), *but that the broad imperatives were clear.*

Once these broad lines were laid down, interest groups were affected, and Congress was used—often disastrously—to pass acts which gave pressure groups larger allocations of aid money (e.g., the Bland Act, pressured both by the unions and maritime industry, which provided that 50 per cent of all Marshall Plan aid had to be carried in American bottoms) or to hinder the flexibility of the State Department (e.g., the Battle Act, which forbade trade with the Soviet bloc and, in effect, crippled Ceylon, when it was our ally, by threatening to stop aid if Ceylon sold rubber to China).

To ignore the problems of this type of "imperative" decision-making is, it seems to me, to ignore the stuff of politics as well as the new nature of power in contemporary society. The theory of the "power elite" implies a unity of purpose and community of interest among the elite that is not proven or demonstrated. It is simply asserted.

Coda

Much of Mills' work is motivated by his enormous anger at the growing bureaucratization of life—this is his theory of history—and its abettors; and this gives the book its appeal and pathos. Many people do feel helpless and ignorant and react in anger. But the sources of helplessness ought to be made clear, lest one engage, as I think Mills does, in a form of "romantic protest" against modern life. (The Sorelian tones of power as violence, and the populist imagery of power as closed conspiracy, find disturbing echo in Mills' book.)

Complexity and specialization are inevitable in the multiplication of knowledge, the organization of production, and the co-ordination of large areas of political society. That these should lead to "bureaucratization" of life is not necessarily inevitable, particularly in a society of growing education, rising incomes, and multipilicity of tastes. More importantly, such ambiguous use of terms like "bureaucratization" and "power elites" often reinforces a sense of helplessness and belies the resources of a free society: the variety of interest conflicts, the growth of public responsibility, the weight of traditional freedoms (*vide* the Supreme Court, an institution that Mills fails to discuss), the role of volunteer and community groups, etc., etc. Like the indiscriminate use by the Communists of the term "bourgeois democracy" in the thirties, or by Burnham of "managerial society" in the forties, or the term "totalitarianism" in the fifties, *particular and crucial* differences between societies are obscured. This amorphousness leads, as in the case of *The Power Elite* with its emphasis on "big" decisions, to a book which discusses power, but rarely politics. And this is curious, indeed.

Chapter 4

The Prospects of American Capitalism:

On Keynes, Schumpeter, and Galbraith

I

IT IS A striking cultural phenomenon, especially for anyone with a memory of the thirties, that American capitalism has obtained grudging regard and a new theoretical definition from critics, especially Keynesian ones, who once were hostile. The term "American capitalism" points to a necessary distinction, for neo-classical economics, which marked out the ground rules for capitalism in general, has never lacked competent intellectual spokesmen. The case for the free market propounded most sharply in our time by Frank Knight —the proposition that a competitive society is the indispensable *model* to obtain both efficient allocation of resources and free consumer choice—has proved itself a compelling one. It was accepted even by socialist theoreticians like Oskar Lange and A. P. Lerner, who, turning the table, argued that only a socialist society, by removing the structural rigidities inherent in a large corporate economy, could restore the free market.

Who, however, was prepared to justify the American capitalist reality, the salient feature of which was an (apparently) paralyzing corporate giantism? By 1940, the majority of the younger economists were convinced that our economy was entering a phase of "secular (in the sense of long-term or permanent) stagnation." The prophet of this new creed was Alvin Hansen of Harvard, but its patristic source was clearly John Maynard Kenyes. Although for decades a chorus of Marxian economists had chanted a requiem for the aging capitalist system, in less apocalyptic fashion Keynes located the reasons for degeneration. The system was not functioning, he said, because savings (meaning, on the whole, profits) were not passing over smoothly into investment (particularly in producer's goods), so that the total demand for goods and services would fall short of the capacity of the economy to produce them, resulting thus in unemployment.

Classical economics, it will be remembered, could not admit of crises under capitalism. It repeated Say's Law that every amount of production meant exactly the same amount of consumption, i.e., the money paid out for the production of goods would eventually be used for consumption, so that there could be neither "overproduction" nor "underconsumption." Unemployment, therefore, represented only a temporary dislocation until production and consumption came into balance. (Imbalances would be corrected if prices fell, inducing the consumer to buy, and unemployment would be reduced if wages were lowered, inducing employers to hire. It was all a matter of a free market—and time.)

Almost every strand of unorthodox economics, from Sismondi and Marx to Hobson, has been based on their rejection of Say's Law. But the refutation had never been stated so elegantly before. Marx never fully worked out a complete theory of crises, and several theories are intertwined in his analyses. Elaborating the underconsumption thesis of Malthus and others, Marx pointed to the unequal distribution of income between the share of labor and of capital (the "surplus value"). Yet such inequality, while leading to underconsumption, could only be a crude and partial explanation; for any economy that wants to expand, including a socialist one, needs some "surplus value" as investment capital. Marx found a second explanation in the disproportionate development of different lines of production, especially in the expanding stage of capitalism, so that unequal rates of demand are generated, particularly between capital goods and consumption goods. But even this does not necessarily indicate a long-run or secular decline in the system. Marx went beyond these notions, conventional already in his own time, and propounded two others. Because of the nature of the impersonal market, he said, capitalism is forced to expand production without reference to consumption, so that periods of overproduction arise in which capital values have to be destroyed to bring the two into harmony. Finally, Marx suggested a law of the falling rate of profit, which he felt to be the "law of motion" of a capitalist economy. Because of competition or the desire for low labor costs, the capitalist introduces technological equipment into his plant and thus has to invest more capital per worker. In turn, the profit per unit declines as less labor is embodied in the product (assuming that profit arises only from the extraction of "surplus value"), so that the capitalist is forced to expand into wider and wider areas in order to maintain the volume of profit. This pressure for expansion Marx saw as the crucial long-range problem of capitalism. Yet it is important to note that nowhere in Marx's writing is there a prediction of the *breakdown* of capitalist economic production; we have rather the generalized statement that as the rate of capital accumulation, the key to capitalism, slows down, the crises may grow more severe. Marx as an economist was more tentative than many of his disciples who have sought to translate what he described as tendencies into iron laws.

Keynes had foreshadowed the outlines of the modern "stagnation theory" in his famous *Economic Consequences of the Peace,* written in 1919. The argument, novel then, is familiar now. The compelling social myth that held society together, said Keynes in a metaphor, was the "non-consumption of the cake." Workers were "cajoled by custom, convention, authority" into accepting a small share of the increasing production of the nineteenth century, while the capitalist, free to consume it, made "the duty of 'saving' nine-tenths of virtue, and the growth of the cake the object of true religion." Thus a huge share of production was saved for investment. This tied in with the reality of the nineteenth century: a growing population, which needed food, clothing, shelter, and employment; new sources of foods and raw materials, which demanded exploitation; the development of technology, which permitted new industries. Under these circumstances the entrepreneur could go on baking cakes in order not to eat them.

But this was, after all, said Keynes, only an extraordinary episodic period in economic history. By the 1920's, population growth had slowed down, investment opportunities were vanishing, the spirit of the entrepreneur was flagging. And, perhaps most important of all, savings were losing their social function. The habitual holding-back of large sums from consumption no longer had the useful effect of increasing production; rather it led to economic crises—and stagnation. (Thus Keynes was not concerned with the productivity-increasing aspects of investment: that is something his followers took up. His prognosis was that the economy was close to saturation, and the problem which only the government could undertake was to maintain *effective demand* by spending.)

Keynes's writings in the next fifteen years were a detailed effort to document his analysis. The root evil was the bourgeois "virtue" of thrift ("the penny wisdom of Gladstonian finance"), and the necessary intellectual task of the generation was to exorcise that ghost. Keynes's great work on *The*

General Theory of Employment, Interest and Money was not only an economic tract but equally a savage sociological polemic against the "puritanism . . . which has neglected the arts of production as well as those of enjoyment."

His aim was the "euthanasia of the *rentier,*" enjoying a free and unhampered consumption in a "quasi-stationary" community which, because it had no desire or need to grow, also had little use for savings. But since this psychological revolution against saving was difficult to effect, only one force could effectively guarantee the movement of stored, useless capital into channels that would revive economic activity—and that was the state. With one bold stroke, thus Keynes reintroduced the study of *political* economy, which for him meant a statement of human aims to be defined consciously by an organized consensus (the social interest), as against "*pure* economics" or the "natural laws" of distribution, as determined through the market by the sum total of individual decisions. The political problem of how to reach a consensus, and apply its decisions, which for us raises many difficult questions of bureaucratization and power, did not trouble Keynes. Writing in the full stream of English political thought, with its sense of homogeneity and the image of a "common will embodied in the policy of the State," he felt such problems could be solved simply and rationally. His program, "moderately conservative in its implications," as he put it, excluded any question of the ownership of the instruments of production; all that it required, he wrote blandly, was a "somewhat comprehensive socialization of investment" in order to assure full employment.*

The theory of "oversavings," which Keynes had formulated as the key to depression, was picked up enthusiastically by the younger American economists and became the guiding

* The socialists in the 1930's, it should be noted, were more dogmatic than Keynes. Because of the "all-or-none" nature of socialist economic doctrine, the socialist parties never felt that they could really "tinker" with capitalism and stabilize its economic functioning. Hence, when for political reasons the socialists in Germany and England were forced to assume power, their economic policies were completely orthodox. Laborite prime minister Ramsay Macdonald foundered on the rocks of the 1931 economic crisis because he was convinced, by the Bank of England, that it was more important to balance the budget and halt the outflow of capital than to increase aid to the unemployed. In Germany, socialist economic policy adhered rigidly to the gold standard. But in 1933, Franklin D. Roosevelt took the U.S. off the gold standard and embargoed the flight of capital, while in Germany Hjalamar Schacht showed Hitler how large state intervention in the economy, through public works and deficit financing, could erase unemployment. (For a discussion of this problem, see Adolf Sturmthal's *The Tragedy of European Labor,* New York, 1943).

conception of the Temporary National Economic Committee investigations and monographs of the late thirties. Where Keynes's *General Theory* had been analytical, the American school sought to add a historical dimension as further proof of the impending "secular stagnation." The lead was taken principally by Alvin Hansen, and the materials summarized in Hansen's major work, *Fiscal Policies and Business Cycles,* in 1941.

His theory, built largely on the statistical investigations of the German economist Spiethoff and the Russian Kondratieff, stated that the nineteenth century was a unique era wherein a fateful combination of factors had combined to create an industrial explosion. We were, said Hansen, beached at the end of a series of "long waves" whose force was not spent. Mid-nineteenth-century America (1840 to 1870) had been propelled by the age of the railroad; the first part of the twentieth century (1890 to 1930) had been the age of electrification and the automobile. But we cannot now "take for granted," Hansen wrote, "the rapid emergence of new industries as rich in investment opportunities . . ." Other factors also tended to create stagnation: chief of these was a decline in population growth, the disappearance of new territory, and the growth of monopoly and imperfect competition, which, by protecting prices, inhibited the introduction of new machinery which a competitive process would have stimulated.

Within the operational machinery of the capitalist system itself certain internal forces worked to calcify the society. Keynes had not been concerned with industrial organization. Hansen was. He argued that "bigness" was a cause of depression because large corporations tended to accumulate huge depreciation reserves for replacement of plant and equipment, reserves which remained unspent and also reduced the need for outside money. In addition, the growth of "capital-saving" (as opposed to labor-saving) machinery, which meant a long-term tendency to lower the ratio of capital to output, added to the piling-up of idle capital. Hansen's conclusions provided a rationale for New Deal policies: state intervention to move the idle capital, attempts to break up "monopolies," and a shift to a high-consumption, low-growth economy.

This then was the image of capitalism in the early forties: the capitalist was an old miser sitting on his pile of sterile bullion, which weighed down the economy. Since *he* found it impossible to inject the money into an economy which needed it, if that economy was to provide jobs and the standard of living it was technologically capable of producing, the government would have to force him to disgorge it—or tax it away and spend it on useful projects.

II

The conservative counterattack arose on the question of "politicalizing" the economy. The lead-off book was Frederick Hayek's *The Road to Serfdom.* Hayek argued that laissez-faire economies tended to equilibrium, but that crises arose primarily because of the arbitrary tampering with the economic system by the State. Governments and banks, in their desire to pay off debts cheaply and to make money, have inflationary proclivities, said Hayek. The result is an over-expansion of credit, while the interest rate is deflected from its true purpose of allocating savings either into investment or consumption. The State, in Hayek's view, was not an executive committee of a ruling class, but (in a view derived from Schmoller and Max Weber) an independent bureaucratic force which, by its Leviathan nature, was coercive and against freedom. Any policy that strengthened the role of the state negated liberalism.

The business community hailed the Hayek volume with alacrity. But the appreciation was more for its catch-phrase title than for its prescriptions. After all, what businessman was prepared for the complete elimination of tariffs, "fair-trade" pricing, price "umbrellas," and similar devices to eliminate competition? On the other hand, the liberals, while sensitive in the abstract to the dangers of "statism," could see in Hayek only some stale Liberty League clichés and refused the challenge to measure governmental "welfare" steps against the dangers of concentrated power. Because of the ideological use to which his book was put, it soon became apparent that Hayek could never become a convincing adversary of Keynesian thought. In short, except as an ideology, no one really wanted "economic liberalism."

If there was one conservative theoretician who could take the measure of Keynes, and possibly even of Marx, it was Joseph Schumpeter. Schumpeter's *Capitalism, Socialism and Democracy,* published in 1942, received notice only in a small circle. Only in 1946, with a new edition and under the cumulative weight of four years' critical appreciation, did the volume gain wider attention. By the time of his death in 1950, a stream of exegetical writing had already begun to appear and a number of Schumpeter's early works and collected essays were being issued in book form.

The outline of Schumpeter's main theoretical statements had already been firmly laid down in a major work, *The Theory of Economic Development,* written in 1912 at the young age of twenty-seven. Thirty years later the time was ripe for these ideas to gain acceptance. On the one hand, U.S. business, as a result of its prodigious production effort during the war, was experiencing a tremendous surge of self-confidence. Through writers like Peter Drucker and the editors of *Fortune,* it was gaining a new rationale based first on its sense of social responsibility and second on the discovery that, unlike its avuncular European kin, American capitalism had still untapped dynamism and drive. On the other hand, the intellectuals, now frightened by the implications of statism, which they once accepted uncritically, and impressed by the lack of the recession every Keynesian economist had so confidently predicted would follow the war ("sixty million jobs" was reached in 1947), were increasingly silent or disoriented.

Schumpeter was important as an intellectual lodestar because he posed his arguments on the very grounds that American Keynesians (and Marxists) had set as the conditions of the debate: he spoke not of the problems of maximum production under the perfectly equilibrated competitive balances of classical economics, but of the concrete social institution, capitalism, operating in historical time. His purpose was to understand the capitalist social organism by examining sociologically and historically the conditions of its emergence, growth and decline. For this reason among others he was disdainful of Keynes, who, for all the radical implications of his work, operated fundamentally within the framework of a static economics abstracted from concrete history. Keynes dealt with "phenomena whose range is limited by his assumption that techniques of production remained unchanged." But it was just the fact that techniques of production, under capitalism, do change rapidly that was decisive for Schumpeter.

Schumpeter's defense of capitalism took, as the crucial starting point, the fact that capitalist society was characterized by interrupted but high productive expansion. The contemporary "rediscovery" of productivity (and the consequent ideological use of this concept as a distinguishing element of "American" from static "European" capitalism) is due in great measure to the primary emphasis on productivity in Schumpeter's book. "The capitalist achievement does not typically consist in providing more silk stockings for queens but in bringing them within the reach of factory girls in return for steadily decreasing effort." Using rough computations, Schumpeter pointed out that U.S. national income had been increasing at a compound rate of more than 2 per cent a year. But increase in productivity was possible only through the activity of entrepreneurs, the engineers of social change. By cutting costs, opening new markets, creating new types of production, in short through innovation, the entrepreneur is able to achieve a temporary monopoly position which is the source of *his* profit. Capitalism can continue only if it maintains entrepreneurial rewards whose "short-run inequity" is the price that the masses must pay for the long-run rising living standards that capitalism can achieve.

Schumpeter's iconoclasm extended also to the defense of "bigness." Bigness was a virtue because only big companies could afford the huge and sometimes fruitless outlays for research which were necessary for technical change. Bigness, in that sense, represented the social price for technical change.

But what of the Great Depression? Schumpeter denied that the period from 1929 to 1932 represented a decisive break in the propelling mechanism of capitalist production, as he described it. Contrary to the views of most economists, classical or Keynesian, he calmly accepted depressions as natural, inevitable, and even therapeutic for the growth of the economy. Technological revolutions periodically reshape the existing structure of industry. "The capitalist process, not by coincidence but by virtue of its mechanism, progressively raises the standards of life of the masses. *It does so through a sequence of vicissitudes, the severity of which is proportional to the speed of the advance.*" Any process of change provides disruption; a depression is a normal process of readjustment and displacement, a shaking out" of the antiquated, the marginal, and inefficient. The depression of 1929 remained for him a special case (because of the "speed of advance" in the twenties and because it capped a "long wave" of economic growth), matched only in relative severity by the depression of 1873-79. Recovery was slower in the U.S. than, say, France because a new social atmosphere and new fiscal policies in the thirties held down private investment. The effort of economic policy to redistribute income and increase consumption had, according to Schumpeter, only inhibited progress.

Against the pessimism of Hansen and Keynes regarding the

possibilities of an expanding economy, Schumpeter projected a vision of new frontiers. "Technological possibilities," he wrote, "are an uncharted sea." It might take the form of great innovations through a new "age of chemicals," which would succeed electricity as a source of investment, or it might be a multiplicity of new products no single one of which might match the impact of, say, the automobile, but which collectively could provide the stimulus toward new growth.

The future, however, rested on the entrepreneur. In his theory of the entrepreneur Schumpeter confronted Marx and Keynes and, in fact, the entire classical school of economics. For Marx, economic growth was a product of the accumulation of capital ever seeking new outlets; Keynes saw that the desire to save became excessive, and he saw effective demand as falling in the absence of government intervention. Schumpeter denied the theoretical basis for chronic oversavings, and his answer to Marx and Keynes rested on a historical foundation. For him, the expansion of industry arises not from the "push" of capital but the "pull" of the entrepreneur. For Schumpeter, industry is financed typically by banks and by the expansion of credit. The entrepreneur works with "other people's money." To collect money from old and unproductive channels, and to command resources, he pays interest. His reward is profit. Economic advance, therefore, is not slowed by oversavings, or lack of savings, or even the inability of entrepreneurs to tap savings, but simply the lack of opportunities for the entrepreneur to come forth and break new ground—for profit. The function of government, therefore, is not to direct investment, as Keynes saw it, but to encourage the entrepreneur.

And yet, said Schumpeter paradoxically, the *vision* of Marx was correct; capitalism is indeed doomed, but not for the reasons Marx advanced. Capitalism decomposes because its mentality creates a social atmosphere hostile to its functioning, and because, at the same time, the bureaucratization of business atrophies its driving force, the entrepreneurial function.

Paradoxically, capitalism is destroyed by its success. The creation of an open society arouses greater wants and expectations than even capitalism can fulfil. After all, even in the ideal circumstances of America it is still not possible to increase productivity by more than 2 to 3 per cent a year. If the case for capitalism rests on its long-run achievements, in the short run it is the profits and inefficiencies that dominate the picture, and these continually offer ammunition for its critics.

And capitalism itself fosters the criticism that threatens it. "The capitalist process," writes Schumpeter, "rationalizes behavior and ideas, and by so doing chases from our minds, along with metaphysical belief, mystic and romantic ideas of all sorts . . ." The critical turn of mind that such rationality creates knows no bounds, and it turns against all institutions, against all accepted tradition and custom, against all authority; it culminates logically in the creation of the "intellectual." The intellectual is both critic and utopian: he needs a hero. The capitalist unheroically estimates rather than gambles, appraises rather than acts. "The stock exchange," as Schumpeter says wryly, "is a poor substitute for the Holy Grail." And so the intellectual, the product of capitalist rationalism, turns his back on the system and infects the rest of the society with his disappointment. Similarly, the state, responsive to the anticapitalist temper of the society, enacts legislation which is restrictive of the entrepreneurial spirit.

Not only is it menaced from without; the capitalist system is also menaced from within. The entrepreneur, the man who broke "the cake of custom," is replaced by the "executive," and innovation is routinized as technology becomes the business of a team of specialists; thus economic progress tends to become depersonalized and automatized and, without *élan*, must "inevitably" run down. The bureaucratization of capitalism is its undoing.

Schumpeter's appeal for the old "left" intellectual is apparent. Here was a rarity: an economist with a tragic sense of life. Moreover, his doctrine allowed capitalism's critics to have their cake and eat it too: capitalism *was* good, but it had now become depersonalized and bureaucratized—the very charges they had themselves levied against the system. And yet, for the plain and prosaic tasks of understanding the specific problems ahead, Schumpeter's insights are of limited help. In his brilliant book, Schumpeter talks of "capitalism" rather than, like Keynes, of "economies." *He does not talk, however, of concrete capitalist societies.* It was thus not easy to notice that in his analyses he selected the economics of American industry and the sociology of European society and derived his justifications for capitalism from the first and his apocalyptic visions as to its fate from the second.

In a curious way, Schumpeter identified capitalism with "family capitalism" and saw its drive as part of the effort of a new class to win power and place in society. Similarly, he identified American capitalism with the "new men" of the nineteenth century and thus refused to believe, first, that the modern corporation could provide its own incentives for growth, and second, that the government, for a variety of reasons (i.e., defense, social responsibility, etc.) would necessarily underwrite economic expansion. Schumpeter was too much of a European to believe that government ever could be an auxiliary or mediating body. For him, the State would be an autonomous force taking over the direction of society for its own bureaucratic impulses. To that extent his prediction of the decline of "capitalism" hinges on the definitions employed. Equally, Schumpeter saw democracy and the hostility of the intellectuals and the workers within the framework of the European philosophical tradition. To that extent, while he approved of the rationalism of capitalism, he also shared the aristocratic image of the mass society. American democracy, with its philosophical roots in Jeffersonianism and its development into a multi-group society, may have very different consequences for capitalism from those of European democracy. But this Schumpeter did not see, or rather did not care to see.

III

If we are to obtain a realistic picture of what is happening to capitalist society, the inherent contradictions between the visions of Keynes and Schumpeter will have to be resolved. For while both agree that traditional capitalism is giving way, their theories concerning the reasons for the change are so divergent as to give rise to directly contradictory proposals for policies that might save it. It is one of the virtues of J. K. Galbraith's *American Capitalism* that the problems common to Schumpeter and Keynes are posed in more prosaic yet more manageable terms and some implicit attempt at reconciliation is made.*

Galbraith's starting point was the remarkable "failure of nerve" by all strata of American society regarding the future of capitalism at a time when the productive apparatus is actually expanding at a rate as fast as any previous period in

* Since the Keynesian economic model is essentially static, and the Schumpeterian economic model primarily historic, an exact reconciliation is extremely difficult. Schumpeter thought of Keynesian "oversaving" as a "special case" within his own system. In recent years, a number of English economists, particularly J. R. Hicks and Roy Harrod, have sought to extend a dynamic system from the staples of Keynesian concerns. A synthesis of the two systems would have to unite the Keynesian problems of income, output, and employment, with the Schumpeterian emphasis on entrepreneur, innovation, and equilibrium. A full one is still to be written.

United States history. The business community seems almost to have been mesmerized by Marx into believing that capitalism was inherently unstable. The industrial managers, no less than the liberal economists, expected a sharp economic collapse on V-J day and each year thereafter; hence, the policy of low inventory, limited dividends, and building of huge financial reserves; all this, said Galbraith, in the "face of record income and yields." The farmer and Congress revealed similar concerns. "These were bonanza years such as few had ever dreamed of," yet for five years following the war Congress was tinkering with price supports and crop guarantees. Meanwhile, the liberals were bemoaning the increasing concentration of economic power which World War II allegedly accelerated, the conservatives were conjuring up ghastly visions of the Omnipotent State which would reduce their freedom and install an oppressive bureaucracy. Yet if all these dire predictions were true, Galbraith observes, the conservative after twenty years of Democratic rule would have long since been dispossessed, the liberal become a "mere puppet" in the business society.

The truth is that none of these pictures even closely approximates present reality. Then why these strong *idées fixes;* why this high degree of illusion and insecurity? The answer, says Galbraith, is that both camps are *"captives of ideas which cause them to view the world with misgivings or alarm."* These ideas derive from the system of classical economics and its theory of power.

Classical economists rooted their system in a fear of concentrated power. A liberal society, therefore, was one that diffused power. In the economic realm, no single individual or group should be able to dictate what was to be produced and who would do it. They envisaged a market society in which prices fluctuated readily in response to supply and demand, where producers were free to enter or depart from business, etc. The corollary assumption, operating from economic deterministic premises, is that free markets make free men. If economic power were fragmented, then political power would be atomized as well.

The fact is, of course, that in the major industrial areas of production, oligopoly, i.e., the dominance of a few, is the prevailing feature of the society. Prices are "administered" rather than set in the market; other firms follow this "price leadership," entry into the business is exceedingly difficult, etc. The liberal, seeing this concentration of economic power, believes it to be dangerous and seeks to break it up.

The singular point that Galbraith makes, following the lead of Schumpeter, is that while oligopoly does exist, few of the consequences the liberals fear actually eventuate. The pattern of oligopoly is natural and almost inevitable in a high-investment economy, and turns out to be not the product of any conspiratorial plot, as the early Money Trust investigations and later Pecora and TNEC investigations thought, but of the market itself. As an industry grows, the firms already in operation grow, realizing the technical efficiencies gained by large-scale production. The established firms also gain from "the economics of experience." A new firm, when it can mobilize the capital, faces the additional handicaps of lack of personnel, untried executives, etc. So new competition is difficult. Oligopoly in any industry is likely to be achieved in the short space of a few years, and once equilibrium has been achieved the degree of concentration remains remarkably stable, as M. A. Adelman points out in a revealing study of industrial concentration (*Review of Economic Statistics*, November, 1951). "If there has been any strong and continuing tendency to a greater concentration in manufacturing . . . these statistics do not show it."

Against the yardstick of a pure theory of price, the result may be some distortions and inefficiencies in the allocation of resources. But the compensation lies in the technological progress fostered by the large corporation. "It is admirably equipped for financing technical development. Its organization provides strong incentives for undertaking development and for putting it into use . . . The power that enables the firm to have some influence on price insures that the resulting gains will not be passed on to the public by imitators (who have stood none of the costs of development) before the outlay for development can be recouped. *In this way market power protects the incentive to technical development.*" In agriculture, the principal area where the competitive model still obtains, the farmer does almost no research on his own behalf; the job is left to the state experiment stations and the U.S. Department of Agriculture.

Here is a strong and sophisticated defense of bigness on the criteria of *performance*. But—and this is where Galbraith seeks to explain why businessmen and liberals are captives to the old phantoms—the businessman cannot admit he exercises tremendous power. "This is partly a matter of tradition; it is also an invitation for attention from the public and from the anti-trust section of the Justice Department. Hence, in order to justify his unwillingness to accept federal regulation, he has to deny his exercise of economic power altogether, and maintain the ideology of competition."

The other side of the coin is the phantasm of the liberal: the specter of untrammeled corporate power standing firm on the "commanding heights of the economy." It is against the liberal view, actually, that Galbraith develops his theory of "countervailing powers," a phrase which in its imaginative simplicity crystallizes a feeling a number of observers have had about the society.

In general this feeling was summed up in the image of "functional blocs," such as industry, labor, farmers, that confront and check each other. Galbraith's view is more subtle in its characterization. "Dogmatically stated . . . private economic power is held in check by the counter-vailing power of those who are subject to it. The first begets the second. The long trend toward concentration of industrial enterprise in the hands of a relatively few firms has brought into existence not only strong sellers, as the economists have supposed, but also strong buyers, as they have failed to see." The self-regulation of the market in America today comes not from the competition of producers, where oligopoly prevails, but the self-generating counter-power of buyers and sellers.

The theory is most evident in the labor-relations field, where strong unions have arisen to check the power of corporations in wage determination. But it operates in other areas as well: great buying chains like Sears Roebuck were able to avoid the oligopolistic domination of rubber prices because of their bulk purchases; A&P, by threatening to go into the processing business, could bring down the price of food supplies. "There are no consumer cooperatives of any importance in the United States," Galbraith writes, "because the chain stores preempted the gains of counter-vailing power first." The power of the auto companies curbed steel. (Until the practice was outlawed by the Supreme Court, Detroit was the only city in the United States not subject to the discriminatory basing-point pricing in steel.) In some instances, e.g., the building trades, the powers that should oppose each other have entered into collusion, with a consequent loss of economic efficiency.

These economic valences developed in the twenties when

buyer combined against seller. Where groups like farmers and workers were unable to generate such balances, the state was forced to step in and help. In the case of the farmers, the effort was begun by Hoover, whose Federal Farm Board undertook to sponsor a system of national co-operatives. In general, however, the New Deal established the countervailing power of the disadvantaged groups. From this theory, the substitution of countervailing power for competition as the regulator of private economic power, Galbraith seeks to establish a yardstick for state action, not for regulation, or even "trust-busting," but for the development, where needed, of countervailing power.

In all this, Galbraith has skilfully developed a realistic theory of political economy, more suitable than the old competitive one to a world of economic behemoths. And yet, Galbraith is enough of a Keynesian to know this is not enough. "We have within the economy no mechanism which acts autonomously to insure proper performance; it is sadly evident from experience as well as from theory that the peacetime norm of the American economy is not necessarily stability at a high level of production and employment." The need, therefore, is for some form of centralized government decision, namely, in the area of fiscal policy so as to influence the total demand for goods through taxation or government spending. "If the Keynesian formula is workable, then the last of the major reasons for alarm over American capitalism dissolves."

Yet Galbraith's book fails in a crucial sociological instance. It never answers its own question: *why* are the business community and the Left captives to a description of reality that no longer exists; *why*, in effect, is the myth more compelling than the reality? To reply, as Galbraith does, by supplying a truer picture of the reality is merely like telling a neurotic that his fears are groundless; they may be, but the answer cannot convince the neurotic of the fact until the sources of the fear are laid bare.

Perhaps the most important fact, sociologically, about the American business community today is the *insecurity* of the managerial class. The corporation may have an assured continuity; its administrators have not. This is a consequence of the swift and remarkable breakdown of "family capitalism" and the transformation to corporate capitalism. The new class of managers, recruited from the general grab bag of middle-class life, lacks the assured sense of justification which the older class-rooted system provided. They have no property stake in the system; nor can they pass their power to their heirs. Hence the growing need of achievement as a sign of success and the importance of ideology as a means of justification. Ideology serves as a social cement, binding the business class together.

Since the new managers are insecure and defensive about their status, the need to retain the older justifications of capitalism—based on private property—is strong. These are, in a sense, the only justifications the managers have known. Only recently, with the emphasis on productivity and performance, are new justifications appearing. Parallel to the movement from "ownership" to "control" in business organization, there has been a shift in the symbolism from "property" to "enterprise." At the same time, the shift in power from the economic realm to the political also strengthens the need to retain a system of justifications—the competitive model of capitalism—which emphasizes the system of decentralized power and minimizes the role of the interventionist state. For if the government, either for welfare reasons or defense, emphasizes its role as central for the society, then the claims of the corporation for social priorities (e.g., tax relief, subsidies) have to take second place.

These reasons would apply primarily to the managers. Among the middle-sized business concerns—more of which are predominantly family enterprises—other factors enter. The very amorphousness of society, the rise of new and threatening interest groups, the emergence of social movements and of ideologies, heighten the anxieties of people who, within their small ponds, once had power and now find themselves in the currents of swift-moving streams. It is among this group that one finds the fierce Taft partisans, the crabbed "small-town" mind.

The amorphousness of society poses a problem, too, for the liberal. For the past decade, or more precisely since the beginning of the war economy, the liberal, too, has not shared power, at least not to the degree he once did in the early days of the New Deal. The polity has become like a Calder mobile, in rough and uneven balance as different parts swing around to the winds of war mobilization. More often than not, the crucial decisions, e.g., the distribution of government contracts and the allocation of metals, are *technical* decisions, motivated by the simple need of commanding available resources with the greatest speed. But the sense behind technical decisions is not generally known, and it is easier to see or hunt for some hidden reason or power source behind the decision.

Hence the social compulsions among different groups to deny the new reality of "countervailing power."

But the countervailing system of modern society, both in its political and economic aspects, is itself in the process of being shattered by inflation and war. *Countervailing power operates within a framework of relative scarcity of demand*—that is, where the buyer calls the tune. Under inflation, where a seller's market prevails, the buyer is helpless, and the seller's price is passed along to the market. The threat of inflation itself arises, principally, from war. And the combination of the two provides the greatest danger to a present-day capitalism defined and justified as a system of decentralized economic decisions. For inflation and war tend to centralize power in the *state* to compensate for the disappearance of countervailing power in the society. Administrative decision by the state or the large corporation rather than "rationing by purse" becomes the chief means of allocating resources and making the production and consumption decisions in the economy.

Curiously, the problems caused by a permanent war economy Galbraith avoids almost completely. The "creeping socialism" of which the Republicans complain so bitterly is the product not of any willed, ideological plan, but the hardly conscious response of the society to the challenge of war. The most important change in the American economy in the last decade has been the growth of the federal budget. Of every dollar spent in 1953 by the U.S. government, eighty-eight cents went for defense and payment of past wars; social security, health and welfare, education, and housing comprised 4 per cent of the budget. A Republican administration cannot affect appreciably the total magnitude of spending; it can, through tax policy, only effect the distribution of the burden. Thus, the key economic decision—the size of the budget—is, in a cold-war economy, out of the full reach of the business community or of any other single group in the country.

The degree of freedom in a capitalist economy—and the working-out of countervailing power—depends on the degree of mobilization necessary to meet the needs of war. For while individual companies and powerful groups may be able to gain special advantage, the main organizing features of the system impose a technical logic that can only be ignored at peril.

A total war economy involves a detailed co-ordination of diverse items which can only be achieved by requisitioning. It means not only the allocation of basic metals, for example, but the detailed scheduling which controls the literal day-to-day operations of the company. In a modern industrial economy the whole society turns, as the nursery rhyme, on the "want of a nail." So detailed are the technical requirements of direct planning that in the case of nickel, one of the critical "nails" during the Korean war, the NPA was forced to allot the precise quantity of nickel necessary for each ingot which the manufacturer produced.

The "total" war economy itself may be a myth. We know, for example, how inefficient and haphazard the German war economy was; and our planning engendered tremendous waste. But a defense economy does require a considerable degree of planning and direction—masked as they may be. And the "readiness economy" which has now become a bedrock feature of the society makes moot the question that agitated liberals for many years: whether the marvelous productivity of the American economy can be utilized to the full without war orders. The fact is that, for the foreseeable future, "defense" and its large budgets will be with us.

But the defense bedrock apart, the experiences since the end of World War II have demonstrated the increased resilience of the economy to shock. The immediate postwar experience is instructive. From a peak of 135 billions in 1944, government expenditures dropped to only 25 billion dollars in 1946; despite this major contraction of demand, total output in the economy fell only 15 per cent. A large backlog of consumer demand, steady rebuilding of depleted inventories, and new plant expansion had taken up the slack. In early 1947, the economists were again pessimistic, as consumption goods (textiles, shoes, clothing) began to slump. The export market that had held up also began to slip. But the Marshall Plan and a boom in home building created counter-pressures.

The sources of this resilience are fairly clear. Firm farm-price supports plus a limited redistribution of income (through veterans' payments, social security, and the like) provide a minimum planking. Structural changes in the corporation are significant: during 1946-48, corporations reinvested 62 per cent of their profits after taxes, as compared with 31 per cent in 1929 and 41 per cent three years before the war. Contrary to the gloomy predictions of the demographers, the American birth rate began rising steadily, and one of the chief factors behind the steady expansion of late nineteenth-century economy has been re-established. (Alvin Hansen based his theory of secular stagnation principally on the falling birthrate.)

These are structural facts on the plus side of the ledger. On the minus side, new instabilities are being introduced into the economy mostly by political countervailing forces. Antiquated industries, like Northern textiles, utilize political pressure to maintain outmoded and dilapidated plants. Wage rates tend to be "sticky," so that prices cannot fall or readjust easily and an employer will tend to cut production instead. The pressure for spending creates a long-run inflationary swell which strands, in the side waters, significant salaried and *rentier* segments of the society.

But the balance, inevitably, will be maintained by government. We seem to be reaching a point where about 20 per cent of gross national product and national income is absorbed and spent by the government. By fairly simple fiscal (i.e., tax and subsidy) payments the government has direct mechanisms to pump money into the economy and (though politically it is more difficult) to suck excess money out of the economic stream. This high federal budget is fixed—for the foreseeable future—by the nature of international tensions and by the indebtedness of the past. It is hard to see how any administration can cut the federal budget below the 20 per cent floor which the permanent mobilization entails.

The striking advances in economic understanding by Keynes and Schumpeter, and the partial synthesis by Galbraith, gives us a more comprehensive picture of contemporary society. But extraordinary as these achievements are as intellectual feats, they are bound, too, coming as they do out of the rigors of economic logic, to the specific analytic framework of economic variables (i.e., the postulates of investment and consumption), and as part of the theory (though not in practical awareness) they are forced to neglect the *political* side of the economy. But these political issues are now the crucial ones.

The key question remains one of *political* economy. On a technical level, economic answers to the organization of production, control of inflation, maintenance of full employment, etc., are available. Political answers, in an interest-group soci-

reviewers have, but against the book which consciously or otherwise Lerner was trying to take the measure of, Harold Laski's *The American Democracy,* which was published just ten years ago.

The surface similarities are striking: both are big books; Lerner's is 1,036 pages, Laski's, in smaller type, 783 pages. There is an extraordinary congruence in topic: Laski begins with the traditions of America, deals with education, culture, business enterprise, the political system, America as a world power, and ends with Americanism as a principle of civilization. Lerner, too, begins with tradition, continues with the idea of America as a civilization, covering the same ground as Laski, but in deference to newer concerns adds two chapters on parent-child relations and on American character, and ends, almost like Laski, with America as a world power.

Politically and temperamentally the two have had much in common. Both are prolific writers whose signatures are primarily in the phrases they formulated for the liberal middle-class intelligentsia of the thirties and forties ("the revolution of our time," "ideas are weapons"). Both were pipers of the "popular front" ideology, although Lerner became more astringently anti-Stalinist. Both have been open, gregarious, buoyant, academic yet *engagé,* interested in influencing the young and shaping the political culture, yet eschewing office or organizational commitment. Laski could easily have become a Labour M.P.; Lerner has shied away from positions in A.D.A.

Both as Jews were aware of their distance from the established idols of society. Both have been highly self-conscious of their varied aspirations and roles (Laski more so, as we can see from his posturings in his letters to Holmes). Both felt that they were summing up a generation. Both books were a decade in the writing, and were published a decade apart.

And it is that decade which marks the difference.

Laski was trying to write a Marxist analysis of America. For all his awareness of the complexities of the American past, his picture of the contemporary scene was cast in a rigid frame: America was a political democracy, but only of the middle class "which assumes though it does not announce, the authority of wealth," and is careful not to "jeopardize the claims that the men of property invariably put forward as the boundaries beyond which democracy may not pass." Nor could the political democracy "conceal the facts that [its forms] were based on an economic foundation which was growing oligarchical in character," while the courts served to "act as a brake on the democratic habits of the legislature." His conclusion was dark. "The spirit of America in the nineteen forties . . . [with] a growth of anti-semitism and of bitter hostility to the Negro advance" must give any "honest observer . . . some hesitation about its outcome."

This was Laski in 1947, after fourteen years of the New Deal and Fair Deal. He could hold these views, knowing as much as he did about the details of life in the United States, because of the conviction, shaped by a Marxist view of social evolution, "that the history of the United States, would, *despite everything,* follow the general pattern of capitalist democracy in Europe."

How reckless the unqualified phrase, "despite everything," yet this conviction was held in unwavering form by most of the left-wing intelligentsia in the thirties and forties, and is one of the reasons why the "left" so consistently misinterpreted American political developments.

In reading Lerner, one is struck immediately by the difference in key terms: the language is no longer Marx, but cultural anthropology *cum* a Jungian and nervous sociological idiom. Where for Laski the U.S. comes into perspective only through *socio-economic forces, vested interests, and power,* in Lerner there are *myth, norms, character, culture and personality*. Where Laski felt that we would recapitulate the fate of Europe, for Lerner there was the "psychic necessity for rejecting Europe" arising out of (with reference to *The Golden Bough*) "the symbolic slaying of the father." Frustration for Laski was a socio-political problem because "the ruling class of the United States employed the traditional American spirit to prevent the adaptation of American life to the facts it encountered" (i.e., the need for a socialist solution to economic difficulties). For Lerner, frustration is a socio-psychological drama induced by success, the conflicts in values and the inability of individuals rising in status to learn new styles of life.

The contrasts are most extreme in their key image of Americanism. There is a malaise in America, said Laski, which was responsible for the "European escapism" of Henry James, the "religious escapism" of Willa Cather, and the "provocative defiance" of Tate and Ransom (i.e., the Southern agrarians). That malaise, he said, arose out of *Americanism,* a chauvinistic doctrine fostered by the industrial oligarchy to hide if not corrupt "the failure [in America] of the historic drive towards the egalitarian society."

The American, says Lerner in a rapturous paragraph, is the modern man par excellence, restless, mobile, a man of energy, mastery, and power. Above all he is the man for whom the walls have broken down. "He is the double figure in Marlowe of Tamerlane and Dr. Faustus, the one sweeping like a footloose barbarian across the plains to overleap the barriers of early civilization, the other breaking the taboos against knowledge and experience, even at the cost of his soul . . . Thus the great themes of the Renaissance and Reformation are fulfilled in the American as the archetypical modern man—the discovery of new areas, the charting of skies, the lure of power, the realization of self in works, the magic of science, the consciousness of the individual, the sense of the unity of history." These promises, says Lerner (following Wyndham Lewis), together with the "logic" of its geography and history, will make America "the epitome of all societies."

The images are only a decade apart. Wherein lies the reality?

Clearly the picture sketched by Laski is out of focus today. Business is less pecuniary and acquisitive, although more manipulative and security-conscious; it has achieved a certain social-mindedness and become decent, at least to its "exempt" personnel (a curious legal term signifying those who are exempt from unions under the Taft-Hartley law, or to whom the overtime provisions of the Walsh-Healey act do not apply). The social strains of the last ten years have *not* been over property but over status: McCarthy was backed not by corporate big business but by a curious mixture of the new rich and various ethnic groups whose unity lay in a hate of intellectualism, while the traditional conservatives proved to be the strongest bulwark against McCarthy. The courts, which in the past struck down social legislation, this time upheld the constitutional spirit against the "democratic" legislatures.

But whether the U.S. will, in Lerner's dithyramb, "epitomize" all other societies is a moot point. What is true—and has to be explained—is the remarkable fact that the United States is probably the first large-scale society to have built change and innovation into the culture. This constant "creative destruction" reworks continually the topography of the society, allowing new social groups to claim a place in the social order. Older societies which, much later, entered this process of change have almost been overwhelmed by the breakdown of the traditional structures. And it is significant that the major theorists of mass society—Karl Mannheim, Emil Lederer, Hannah Arendt—have been European, and derived their concept from European experience.

What is startling is that in the next half century a common technological foundation will underlie all cultures for the first time in human history. Yet this does not mean that all societies will be alike. Despite certain "logics" which follow from the fact of industrialization (technical education, new professional classes, the increase in white-collar occupations), each society is sufficiently singular in its cultural traditions for the profiles of these countries to remain markedly different. And it is this cultural "superstructure," in fact, which belied Laski's gloomy predictions. Any attempt, then, to encompass the variety which is America, must not only describe such changes, but find some scheme or method which gives coherence to the impulses which are responsible for this fluidity and change.

In looking at a society or an epoch, what marks a work as great is either a new vision (such as Tocqueville's), a sense of tragedy (as Henry Adams' *Education*), or, failing these, some new image of the inner unity of a civilization, that is, an answer to the crucial problem first posed by Montesquieu: how does this all hang together? Older moralists thought that God or chance ruled the world. (Descartes, as Isaiah Berlin reminds us, spoke of history "as a tissue of idle gossip and travelers' tales suitable only for whiling away an idle hour.") But for Montesquieu, the first sociologist, societies were not fortuitous collections of heterogeneous elements or artificial constructions, but natural growths which obtain a definable character out of "climate, religion, law, the maxims of government, the examples of past things, customs, manners; and from the combination of such influences a general spirit is produced."

But each society combines these factors in different ways; each society has its own inner structure and "general spirit." What is that of America? Laski tried to narrow the problem by insisting on the tensions between the egalitarian aspirations of the masses and the power of the industrial oligarchy as the foundation for all other behavior; and the superstructure came toppling down upon him. Others—and Lerner lists twenty of the more serious efforts—have tried to capture the "uniqueness" of America in some *distinctive* aspect of our development: e.g., the lack of a feudal past, the refusal to accept authority, the multiplicity of ethnic groups, etc. The search is an endless one.

Like all of us, Lerner is trapped by sheer inability to capture a definition which will not fall apart on close analysis. One can see him, year after year, desperately mulling over the question, reading all the previous answers, spotlighting their deficiencies; yet, in the end, like a mountain climber unable to gain a foothold on the slippery rock face, he suddenly lets go, and says: "there is no single talisman to the secret of American civilization," there is no single organizing principle. And, in defense of this argument, Lerner invokes the social sciences. "Causation," he says of its newer methodologies, "is giving way to relation and inter-action." For every yea, there is a nay. And the failure becomes the problem to be studied. "The study of American civilization," Lerner says, "becomes the study of the polar pattern itself, not a search for some single key that will unlock causation."

In the end, there is no answer, but process. Lerner is forced to say that analysis consists only of "an inter-play of the material world and the moral-psychological." And so while he has talked bravely of America as a "civilization"—and has defined the term as a "distinctively etched style of life, historically shaped and recognized by self and others as a new design for living"—in the end the "interplay" dissolves all coherence, and there is no unifying vision.

What remains is problematic: a new set of labels, drawn from the contemporary social sciences. In reaction to the deterministic efforts of his predecessors — and most likely Laski—Lerner wanted to emphasize the variety and complexity of life in America. But he ends up by sacrificing theory and method for description. In hoping to apply the language of cultural anthropology to contemporary history, Lerner was, I think, seduced by the social sciences. The concepts of anthropology are "holistic," that is to say they seek to grasp the totality of a culture. But even the most successful attempts at understanding a primitive society, let alone a modern one, have foundered on the problem of description, and, as with Ruth Benedict's descriptions of cultures as Apollonian or Dionysian, have had to resort to metaphors. But metaphors, at best, are only suggestive, and at worst, dissolve all history into cloudy abstractions. One must go back, I think, to history, and the attempts to find causal chains, while always partial, can give us, perhaps, a better sense of the involved skein of society than the dissolution of causation into the "interplay of the material and moral-psychological worlds."

It may well be that Lerner's is the last of such synoptic efforts to encompass the entire range of American experience, not only because that experience, and its documented materials, are becoming too vast to be treated by a single person, but because of the realization that the rubric itself is at fault, that the ambiguity lies really in the term *America,* which is a cluster of many meanings. To ask, What is the secret of America? is to pose a metaphysical question whose purpose is either ideological or mythopoeic. And unfortunately the emphasis on seeing America in such terms is reinforced by the postwar emergence of "American Studies" programs, which finds its justification—an effort to "prove" to the rest of the world that America has a culture too—in such metaphorical, or pseudo-Hegelian, idiom. But to ask why and how particular configurations of character and institutions have emerged in the United States is to ask questions which fall within what Robert Merton has called the middle range, and which are susceptible, through empirical check, to controlled generalizations.

One area, and one which will come into increasing prominence in future years, is the comparative question. Why, for example, could McCarthyism flourish in the United States but not in Britain? Edward Shils, in his *Torment of Secrecy,* has provided some answers: the different elite structures, and more, the tradition of civility in Britain, with its emphasis on privacy and social distance, in contrast to that of populism in the United States with its insistence on disclosure and leveling. Surely, in an age when the image of America becomes reflected against the other peoples of the world, no inquiry into the American character can neglect comparative questions.

A second area is that, not of "inter-play," but of the "functional" relationship of institutions, or, how behavior in one area is shaped by or grows out of behavior in others. For example, Eric Erikson, in his *Childhood and Society,* seeks to relate the family to the political structure. The American family, he says, in contrast to that of Europe, is not divided into unequal partners (adults over children; husbands over wives; older sibs over younger ones), but one in which each person has equal rights and where one gains privileges by making concessions. The American family is thus "a training

Rights party, Prohibition party, Socialist Labor party, Union Labor party, Farmer-Labor party, Socialist party. None has succeeded; few have lasted long.

One important reason is the constraining role of the electoral system. Take the curious situation in the midwest of the United States and Canada. The wheat farmers of the north central plains have a homogeneity of cultural outlook and a common set of economic problems which national boundary lines cannot bisect. Yet in Canada the wheat farmers formed a Social Credit party in Alberta and a Cooperative Commonwealth Federation in Saskatchewan, movements outside the "party structure," while their brothers in North Dakota could only, at best, form a Non-Partisan League—within the Republican party—after finding that the Socialist party wouldn't do.

These factors of rigid electoral structure have set definite limits on the role of protest movements, left and right, in American life. ("Let me make the deals, and I care not who makes the ideals," an American politician has said.) They account in significant measure for the failure of the right-wing Lemke-Coughlin movement in 1936, and of the left-wing Wallace-Progressive party in 1948. They account for the new basic alliance between the unions and the Democratic party. Whatever lingering hopes some trade-unionists may have had for a labor party in the United States, they were dispelled by Walter Reuther at the CIO convention in November, 1954, when, in answering transport leader Mike Quill, he pointed out that a third party was impossible within the nature of the U.S. electoral system. This is a lesson that every social movement has learned. And any social movement which hopes to effect or resist social change in the U.S. is forced now to operate within one or the other of the two parties. This itself places an enormous strain on these parties.

The democratic tradition, the second of the conventional categories, has played an important role in shaping American poltical forms. The distinctive aspect of the political tradition in the United States is that politics is the arena of the *hoi polloi*. The "common man" is the source of ultimate appeal, if not authority. This was not so at the beginning. The "founding fathers," with the Roman Republic, let alone the Articles of Confederation, in mind, feared the "democratic excesses" which the poor and propertyless classes could wreak against those with property. Whatever the substantive inadequacies of the Beardian interpretation of American history, it is still clear that in 1787 self-consciousness of property, and a desire to limit the electoral role of the people, was uppermost in the minds of those who framed the Constitution, and was reflected in the erection of such institutions as a non-popular Senate, selected by the states; an appointive judiciary holding office for life; and a president elected through the indirect and cumbersome means of an electoral college.

But the barriers soon broke down. The victory of the Jeffersonians was the first step in the establishment of a "populist" character in American democracy. The Federalists, seeing the success of the Jeffersonian methods, realized the necessity of imitating those "popular, convivial, and charitable techniques." As early as 1802, Hamilton, in a letter to Bayard, outlined a plan for a "Christian Constitutional Society" which would appeal to the masses "through the development of a 'cult' of Washington and his benevolent activities." A Washington Benevolent Society was formed in 1808, but it was too late; the Federalists had already lost. Thirty years later, however, their spiritual descendants, the Whigs, beat the Democrats at their own game. Casting aside Henry Clay, whose "Hamiltonian" views were too well established, the Whigs nominated General William Henry Harrison, the hero of the battle of Tippecanoe, against Andrew Jackson's successor, Martin Van Buren.

The campaign tactics, so strangely modern, were set down by Nicholas Biddle, Jackson's antagonist and the former head of the National Bank. "If General Harrison is taken up as a candidate," he said, "it will be on account of the past. . . . Let him say not one single word about his principles, or his creed —let him say nothing—promise nothing. Let no Committee, no convention—no town meeting ever extract from him a single word about what he thinks or will do hereafter. Let the use of pen and ink be wholly forbidden."

The "cider election" of 1840 was a turning point in American political life. Harrison traveled from place to place in a large wagon with a log cabin on top, and a barrel of hard cider on tap for the crowds. Daniel Webster, with the fustian of the demagogue, lamented that he had not been born in a log cabin, although he pointed out that his elder brothers had begun their lives in a humble abode. In shameless fashion, Whig orators berated Van Buren for living in a lordly manner, accused him of putting cologne on his whiskers, of eating from gold plate, and of being "laced up in corsets such as women in town wear and if possible tighter than the best of them."

Harrison won, and the lesson was clear. Politics as a skill in manipulating masses became the established feature of political life, and the politician, sometimes a front-man for the moneyed interests, but sometimes the manipulator in his own right, came to the fore. Increasingly, the upper classes withdrew from direct participation in politics. The lawyer, the journalist, the drifter, finding politics an open ladder for advancement, came bounding up from the lower middle classes. The tradition of equality had been established. The politician had to speak to "the people" and in democratic terms.

If the politician spoke to the people, he acted for "interests." The awareness of the interest-group basis of politics, the third of the conventional categories, goes far back to the early days of the Republic. Madison, in the oft-quoted Number Ten of the Federalist Papers, had written, "the most common and durable source of factions has been the various and unequal distribution of property. Those who hold and those who are without property have ever formed distinct interests in society." James Harrington's maxim that "power follows property" was regarded by John Adams, the outstanding conservative of the time, "to be as infallible a maxim in politics, as that action and reaction are equal in mechanics."

The threat to property on the part of the small farmer and the landless formed the basis of the first disquiet in American politics. The supporters of the Shay Rebellion in Massachusetts and other insurgents, General Henry Knox complained to George Washington, "believe that the property of the United States has been protected from the confiscations of Britain by the joint exertions of all." Madison, looking to the future, anticipated that "a great majority of the people will not only be without land, but any other sort of property." When this has occurred, he predicted, the propertyless masses will "either combine under the influence of their common situation; in which case the rights of property and the public liberty will not be secure in their hands; or what is more probable," he continued, with the lessons of the Roman demagogues in mind, "they will become tools of opulence and ambition, in which case there will be equal danger to the other side."

The early factional struggles in American political life, rustic in form because of the agrarian weight of the population, soon become sectional. This was inevitable, since the different regions developed different interests: the rice, tobacco, and cotton of the South; the fishing, lumbering, commerce, of New England. National parties came into being when the Federalists succeeded at first in combating the large planters of the upper and lower South with the commercial interests of the North Atlantic region, and when Jefferson challenged this combination by uniting the grain growers and other small farmers both north and south into a rival party.

Since then the national parties have been strange alliances of heterogeneous sectional groups: Midwest farmers with Eastern financiers; Northern urban immigrants with racists and nativists in the South. Ethnic and functional groups have often flowed into one of the two parties by historic accident: the Negroes, because of the Civil War, for sixty years or so voted Republican; the Irish, because of their original relation to Tammany Hall, became Democrats; the Germans, settling in the Midwest, became Republican; the urban Italians, in reaction to being excluded from city politics by the Irish, at first were Republicans.

Within the sectionalism of American political life arose the narrower, more flexible tactic of the pressure group standing outside the particular party, committed to neither, giving support or winning support on the basis of allegiance to the single issue alone. One of the first skillful innovators of this tactic was George Henry Evans, a confrere of Robert Owen and a leading figure for a time in the reform politics of the 1830's and 40's. Evans had been one of the leaders of the Workingman's party in 1829, a New York party that began with moderate success but which faded when ideological differences inflamed a latent factionalism and when the Democrats "stole their thunder" by adopting some of their immediate demands. Evans, who believed that free land would solve the class tensions and plight of the propertyless workers, organized an Agrarian League in the 1840's. His experience had taught him that a minority party could not win by its own votes and that politicians, interested primarily in "deals not ideals" would endorse any measure advocated by a group that could hold the balance of power. Evans therefore asked all candidates to support his "sliding measures." In exchange for such a pledge, the candidate would receive the votes of the workingmen behind him. While the Agrarian League itself met with only middling success, its agitation—and tactics—paid later in the passage of the Homestead Acts.

In 1933, heralded by the New Deal, the feeling arose that a new era was emerging. In a widely quoted book, *The New Party Politics,* Professor Arthur N. Holcombe of Harvard wrote: "The old party politics is visibly passing away. The character of the new party politics will be determined chiefly by the interests and attitudes of the urban population . . . there will be less sectional politics and more class politics."

The emergence of "functional" groups, particularly labor, and the growing assertion by ethnic groups, seemed to underscore the shift. The fact that Franklin Roosevelt was able to weave together these groups, some of whom like the farmers had been allied with the Republican party, seemed to indicate that some historic realignments were taking place. Some realignments have, but not so dramatic as once thought. The trade-union movement, politically articulate for the first time, is outspokenly Democratic; but the working-class vote usually has been Democrat. Ethnic groups which came to the fore have, by and large, retained their loyalty to the Democratic party; but there are many indications that, as a result of rising prosperity and higher social status, significant numbers of these nationality and minority groups are beginning to shift their allegiance. The farmers, despite the enormous financial aid granted them by the New Deal, have returned to the Republican fold.

But while sectional politics has somewhat diminished, class politics has not taken its place. Instead, there has been the spectacular rise of pressure groups and lobbies, part sectional, part class, part ideological. The most dramatic use of this kind of pressure-group tactic was made by the Anti-Saloon League, which, starting in 1895, was able in less than a decade and a half to push through a Constitutional amendment prohibiting the manufacture and sale of liquor in the U.S. Since then, the pressure-group device has been adopted by thousands of organizations, whether it be with regard to tariff-reform opposition to federal medical programs or political aid to the state of Israel. In 1949 the Department of Commerce estimated that there were 4,000 national trade, professional, civic, and other associations. Including local and branch chapters there were probably 16,000 businessmen's organizations, 70,000 local labor unions, 100,000 women's clubs, and 15,000 civic groups carrying on some political activity. The enormous multiplication of such groups obviously cancels out many of the threats made to candidates defying one or the other of the interests. But it makes it possible, too, for small interests to exercise great political leverage. Thus, when peanuts were eliminated from a farm subsidy program in 1955, over one hundred Southern congressmen held up a crop-support bill until the subsidy was restored—although Georgia peanuts account for less than one half of 1 per cent of farm income. (Subsidizing peanuts has cost the U.S. government over one hundred million dollars in the past decade.)

The multiplication of interests and the fractioning of groups, occurring simultaneously with the breakup of the older family capitalism and the rise of new managerial groups to power within business enterprises, make it difficult to locate the sources of political power in the United States. More than ever, government in the U.S. has become, in John Chamberlain's early phrase, "the broker state." To say that this is a broker state does not mean, however, that all interests have equal power. This is a business society. But within the general acceptance of corporate capitalism, modified by union power and checked by government control, the deals and interest-group trading proceeds.

Granting the viability of these conventional lines of political analysis—the role of the two-party system in limiting social movements and social clashes, the political tradition of direct appeal to the people, and the force of interest-groups in shaping and modifying legislative policy—they nevertheless leave us somewhat ill-equipped to understand the issues which have dominated the politics of the 1950's decade. These lines of thought do not help us, for example, to understand the Communist issue, the forces behind the new nationalism of, say, Senators Bricker and Knowland, and the momentary range of support and the intense emotional heat generated by Senator McCarthy. In short, what has traditionally been called "interest-group" politics does not help to explain the emergence of the new American right wing, the group that S. M. Lipset has dubbed the "radical right"—radical because it opposes traditional conservatism, with its respect for individual rights, and because it sought to impose new patterns in American life. All this is dramatized by the issue of McCarthy and the Communists.

For Europeans, particularly, the Communist issue must be a puzzle. After all, there is no mass Communist party in the United States such as one finds in France and Italy; the Communist party in the U.S. never, at any single moment, had more than 100,000 members. In the last five years, when

of prosperity "status" issues emerge. But these issues, usually "patriotic" in character, are amorphous and ideological.

These political forces, by their very nature, are unstable. McCarthy himself, by the logic of his own political position, and by the nature of his personality, had to go to an extreme. And he ended, finally, by challenging Eisenhower. It was McCarthy's great gamble. And he lost, for the challenge to a Republican president by a Republican minority could only have split the party. Faced with this threat, the party rallied behind Eisenhower, and McCarthy himself was isolated. In this respect, the events prove the soundness of the thesis of Walter Lippmann and the Alsops in 1952 that only a Republican president could provide the necessary continuity of foreign and domestic policy initiated and maintained by the Fair Deal. A Democratic president might have polarized the parties and given the extreme Republican wing the license to lead the attack; the administration of a moderate Republican could act as a damper on the extreme right.

The lessening of international tensions after the settlement in Korea confirmed McCarthy's defeat. Yet McCarthy has to be understood in relation to the people behind him and the changed political temper which these groups have brought. He was the catalyst, not the explosive force. These forces still remain.

There are several consequences to the changed political temper in American life, most notably the introduction on a large scale of "moral issues" into political debate. By and large, this is new. Throughout their history, Americans have had an extraordinary talent for compromise in politics and extremism in morality.

The saving grace, so to speak, of American politics, was that all sorts of groups were tolerated, and the system of the "deal" became the pragmatic counterpart of the philosophic principle of toleration. But in matters of manners, morals, and conduct—particularly in the small towns—there has been a ferocity of blue-nose attitudes unmatched by other countries.

The sources of this moralism are varied. This has been a middle-class culture, and there is much truth to the generalization of Max Scheler that moral indignation is a disguised form of repressed envy and a peculiar fact of middle-class psychology. In aristocratic cultures, with their free-and-easy ways, with their search for pleasure and their concentration on aestheticism, one rarely finds moral indignation an aspect of their temper. Some Catholic cultures, wordly in their wisdom and tolerant of human frailties, do not look with horror at gambling, drink, or even easy sexual conduct; disapproval is tempered with a sense of the inevitability of sin, and salvation is of the other world, not this; theft after all is a venial disgrace, but pride bears the strain of the mortal sin.

Moral indignation—and moralism—are characteristic of religions that have abandoned otherwordly preoccupations and concentrate on thiswordly concerns. In Protestantism, such a displacement finds piety giving way to moralism, and theology to ethics. Becoming respectable represents "moral" advancement, and regulating conduct, i.e., being "moral" about it, has been a great concern of the Protestant churches of America.

This moralism, itself not unique to America, is linked to an evangelicism that is unique. There has long been a legend, fostered for the most part by literary people, and compounded by sociologists, that America's has been a "puritan" culture. For the sociologists this has arisen out of a mistaken identification of the Protestant ethic with the Puritan code. Puritanism and the "New England mind" have played a large intellectual role in American life. But in the habits and mores of the masses of the people, the peculiar evangelicism of Methodism and Baptism, with its high emotionalism, its fervor, enthusiasm, and excitement, its revivalism, its excesses of sinning and of high-voltage confessing, has played a much more important role. Baptism and Methodism have been the favorite American religious creeds, because they were the rustic and frontier religions. In his page on "Why Americans Manifest a Sort of Fanatical Spiritualism," Alexis de Tocqueville observed: "In all states of the Union, but especially in the half-peopled country of the Far West, itinerant preachers may be met with who hawk about the word of God from place to place. Whole families, old men, women and children, cross rough passes and untrodden wilds, coming from a great distance, to join a camp-meeting, where, in listening to these discourses, they totally forget for several days and nights the cares of business and even the most urgent wants of the body."

The Baptist and Methodist churches grew, while the more "respectable" Protestant bodies remained static, precisely because their preachers moved with the advancing frontier and reflected its spirit. "In the camp-meeting and in the political gathering logical discourse was of no avail, while the 'language of excitement' called forth an enthusiastic response," H. Richard Niebuhr has observed.

The revivalist spirit was egalitarian and anti-intellectual. It shook off the vestments and the formal liturgies and preached instead the gospel and roaring hymn. This evangelicism was reflected in the moralism of a William Jennings Bryan, a religious as well as an economic champion of the West, and in the urban revivalism of a Dwight Moody and the Y.M.C.A. movement that grew out of his gospel fervor. The evangelical churches wanted to "improve" man, whereas the liberals wanted to reform institutions. The former were the supreme champions of prohibition legislation and Sabbath observance. *Reform in their terms meant not a belief in welfare legislation but in the redemption of those who had fallen prey to sin*—and sin meant drink, loose women, and gambling.

This moralism, so characteristic of the American temper, had a peculiar schizoid character: it would be imposed with vehemence in areas of culture and conduct—in the censorship of books, the attacks on "immoral art," etc., and in the realm of private habits; yet it rarely was heard regarding the depredations of business or the corruption of politics. On this the churches were largely silent.

The moralizing temper had another consequence: the reinforcement of the "populist" character of American society. Long ago, travelers to these shores noticed the extreme egalitarianism of American manners and customs and warned of the "leveling" consequence of the glorification of the common, rather than the uncommon, man: for if one holds that each man is as good as the next, it is easy to say, as has often been the case, that no man can claim to be better than the next. Unfortunately, good and better are never defined. That no man should claim birth alone as the inherent possessor of a status is understandable; in that respect each man is as good as the next. But populism goes further: that some are more qualified than others to assert opinions is vehemently denied.

The populist imprint on American life has had its positive as well as negative sides. The idea of the "right of the people to know" is an underpinning of the guarantees of free press, of unrestrained inquiry, and of unhampered discussion. But in a populist setting, it operates without a sense of limits and often becomes an invasion of privacy. For what is it that "the people" have a right to know? One's morals and habits? One's political views? The earlier "reformers," self-appointed guardians of morals, insisted on the right of scrutiny of private conduct in the name of public decency. Later Congressional investigators have insisted that the right to inquire is not bounded by legislative purpose but is an inherent aspect of the process of becoming the "public watchdog."

All these, in itself, would be less injurious to privacy—and freedom—if moralism and the populist conceptions of democracy were not also tied to a distinctive aspect of social control: the control of conduct, and the operation of sanctions against individuals through "public opinion" rather than law. Law, at least in the past, because it is tradition-bound and restrictive, is inhibitive of change and often has not squared with the experiences and needs of a people. But as the hard-won residue of human encounter with injustice, it sets up a strict set of procedures and a strict set of rules in admitting evidence and determining guilt. Americans, as an impatient people, however, have often been impatient with law, and the quicker sanctions of vigilantism and shaming through opinion have predominated. Moreover, the small-town character of much of the American temper derives its strength from the whispered play of gossip, from regulating conduct through public opinion rather than law. This was the exercise of conformity that was attacked so savagely by Sinclair Lewis in his *Main Street,* and the attack on the American small town was the leitmotif of the social criticism and literature of the twenties.

While in American culture the small town has been "defeated" (although in popular culture it has merged with the brassier tones of Hollywood), in American politics it has still held sway. A disproportionate percentage of the Congress, because of the gerrymandering of districts by rural-dominated legislatures, comes from small towns; these men usually have longer tenure and seniority, and the temper of the Congress, as an ideology, reflects the pseudo-egalitarian attitudes of the small town. So long as world-experiences could be assimilated into the perceptions of the small town, i.e., so long as one translated all problems into the small-town setting, the dichotomy of politics and moralism could prevail. Business was business, and the church was church; and politics was a business. But with the growth of international ideologies, the breakdown of market mechanisms, the bewildering complexities of economic decisions, the rise of submerged groups, the anxieties of decision-making became overwhelming.

American political attitudes towards China and the defeat of Chiang Kai-shek is probably the clearest case in point. As Denis Brogan has pointed out, Americans, in their extraordinary optimism, find it hard to stand defeat; it is a sickening thrust at the omnipotence which, as an unconscious self-image, underlies American power. Hence, if Chiang Kai-shek's regime came toppling down, it was easier to ascribe the reason to betrayal—by the State Department or by intellectuals—than to recognize the complex reasons involving an understanding of the breakdown of Chinese institutions since the Republic of 1911, and the failure, because of civil war and invasion, to create a viable political structure in China.

The cry of betrayal and the charge of conspiracy is an old one in American politics. One of its chief roots is in the political Populist movement, which, in its grievances against the industrial order, found its devils among those who symbolized the monetary and credit system. Populism arose, after the Civil War, among the poor farmers of the South and West. It was a protest movement against the railroads, which by freely manipulating freight rates were able to "tax" the farmer unduly, and against the bankers, who by tightening money and credit and raising the interest rates made it difficult for the farmer to buy seed or pay off mortgages. While the grievances were real, and often legitimate, what the Populists could not perceive was that a system, and not individuals, was to blame. But politics is rarely won by attacking a system. The case of Tom Watson of Georgia is one in point. Watson, who ran for vice-president on the Populist ticket in 1896, was a pioneer muckraker whose "Watson's Jeffersonian Weekly" made pungent analyses of the system of tenant land tenure, of credit manipulation, and other evils in American life. But after the turn of the century, the Populist movement became fragmented, with large chunks of it following Bryan into the Democratic party, while other elements went over to the socialists. Watson became more rancorous. He attacked Wall Street, the international bankers, and finally the Jews. The identification of Jews with money power was an old one. Ignatius Donnelley, the spokesman for Midwestern populism, had made this a central theme of his widely read novel *Caesar's Column* years earlier. Donnelley, however, had regarded the Jews as victims, since by virtue of medieval exclusions money-lending was one of the few trades open to them. Watson made the Jews the active agents of a closed conspiracy for world control. Watson was elected to the U.S. Senate, from Georgia, in 1920. He became the prototype of the new crop of Southern demagogues, Alabama's Tom Heflin, Mississippi's Theodore Bilbo, and Georgia's Eugene Talmadge. And yet, when he died, he could still be mourned by Eugene Debs as one who had fought for the people during his life.

In the twisted strands of Populism[34] one finds other, strange tales which on the surface seem metamorphoses, but which at bottom represent the workings out of the underlying Populist temper. William Lemke and Gerald Nye came out of the vigorous North Dakota Non-Partisan League, an independent grouping of radical farmers which, finding itself unable to operate outside the two-party system, had captured the Republican party of the state. North Dakota progressivism was one of the spearheads of reform and social legislation of the twenties and thirties; public power, anti-injunction laws, regulation of child labor, etc., etc. Nye led the famous investigation of the munitions makers during the thirties which, to the sorrow of the historian, made the overly simple identification of the causes of war coterminous with the hunger for profits of the "merchants of death."

These men were "terrible simplifiers." All politics was a conspiracy, and at the center of the web were the "international bankers" and the "money changers." Thus, when war loomed in the late thirties, the suspicion of the bankers which was the root of the crabbed Populist mentality became focused on the Jews, and one found the strange spectacle of William Lemke running for president of the United States in 1936 on a ticket organized by Father Coughlin and his Social Justice Movement. (The candidacy was supported by Dr. Francis Townsend, whose old-age scheme featured a device to increase the circulation of money, while Father Coughlin, who became a national figure because of his radio sermons in the mid-thirties, had started out as a money reformer with the nickname of "Silver Charlie.") These simplifications, now somewhat attenuated, still formed a backdrop for more recent events. But other forces were at work, too.

An unsettled society is always an anxious one, and nowhere has this been truer than in the United States. In an egalitarian society, where status is not fixed, and people are not known or immediately recognizable by birth or dress, or speech or manners, the acquisition of status becomes all-important, and the threats to one's status anxiety-provoking. Gunnar Myrdal, in his investigation of the Negro problem in America, pointed out that class antagonisms are strongest between "adjacent" classes rather than between the very bottom and the top. Thus, in the South, the deepest emotional resentment of the Negro has come from the poor whites, and particularly from those once-poor whites who, having risen, sought more than ever to emphasize their distance from those below them. As one once was more royalist than the king, one becomes more traditionalist than even the settled families, and, in the case of nationality groups, more compulsively American than the older families.

The socio-psychological attitude that Myrdal discerned in the South has been equally characteristic of the immigrant pattern in American life. As each successive wave of people came over, they grouped together and viewed the next wave with hostility and fear. In the nineteenth century, the xenophobic strain was one of the deepest currents in American life. Before the Civil War, the Catholic was the chief target. There were riots, lynchings, and the burnings of convents in Boston in the 1820's. In 1832, the anti-Catholic movement was spurred by the publication of a book, *Foreign Conspiracy against the Liberties of the United States,* by Samuel F. B. Morse, who in the popular textbooks is accorded recognition only as a leading portrait painter and as the inventor of the telegraph. Fearing the spread of papal influence in Metternich's Europe, Morse formed the Anti-Popery Union to fight the Church. Out of its agitation grew a political party, the Native Americans, which sought to exclude all foreigners and to extend the naturalization period before citizenship to twenty years. The nativist sentiment elected James Harper mayor of New York in 1843 and was responsible for the nomination of Millard Fillmore—who had succeeded to the presidency in 1850 on the death of President Taylor—for the presidency again in 1856 on the Know-Nothing ticket. Anti-Catholic agitation was pushed into the background by the Civil War, but the tensions have remained to this day. In the East, Catholic political power came to the fore in the large urban cities of Boston, New York, Jersey City, and Chicago. In the Midwest it remained a political issue in the latter half of the nineteenth century through the agitation of the American Protective Association and the fundamentalist Protestant churches.

But what began as religious discrimination turned, in the decades that followed the Civil War, into social distinctions;

these came when the rise of new social classes began to create status demarcations. In the expansion and prosperity of the 1870's and 1880's, Oscar Handlin points out, "Many a man having earned a fortune, even a modest one, thereafter found himself laboring under the burden of complex anxieties. He knew that success was by its nature evanescent. Fortunes were made only to be lost; what was earned in one generation would disappear in the next. Such a man, therefore, wished not only to retain that which he had gained; he was also eager for the social recognition that would permit him to enjoy his possessions; and he sought to extend these on in time through his family. . . . The last decades of the nineteenth century therefore witnessed a succession of attempts to set up areas of exclusiveness that would mark off the favored groups and protect them against excessive contact with outsiders. In imitation of the English model, there was an effort to create a 'high society' with its own protocol and conventions, with suitable residences in suitable districts, with distinctive clubs and media of entertainment, all of which would mark off and preserve the wealth of the fortunate families."

The process of status demarcation, associated largely with wealth in the 1890's, in more recent years has been a problem for the rising ethnic groups which have sought recognition of their new position in American life. But the older means of such distinction have disappeared, because in the mass consumption economy all groups can easily acquire the outward badges of status and erase the visible demarcations. So it is largely through politics that the rising ethnic groups began to assert their new power and social position.

These elements of moralism, populism, Americanism, and status anxieties achieved a peculiar congruence in the fifties because of the changed nature of American politics: the emergence of foreign policy as the chief problem of politics. The politics of the 1930's were almost entirely domestic, and the sharp political conflicts of that decade were around economic issues, and the divisions in interest-group terms. The debate whether or not to go to war, although sharp, was extremely brief, and the war years were characterized by a high degree of national unity. But with the postwar emergence of Soviet Russia as the dominant force on the European continent, the breakup of the old colonial empires, the eruption of Communist challenges in China and southeast Asia, and the war in Korea, the debate on the war from 1930-41 that was interrupted so abruptly by Pearl Harbor was brought back, albeit in disguised form. The attempt to pin a charge of treason on the Democrats, the new nationalism of Bricker and Knowland, the reckless actions of McCarthy, represented, in extreme, aspects of that first debate. Thus the new issues no longer represented old interest-group or internal power divisions, but the playing-out of old frustrations and anxieties.

Few "symbols" are more representative of this change than the role of Dean Acheson. In the early days of the New Deal, Acheson, a young lawyer, resigned as Assistant Secretary of the Treasury in protest against the "tinkering" with the dollar and the departure from orthodox practices; and Acheson was one of the symbols of conservative protest against the New Deal. A decade and a half later, as Truman's Secretary of State, he had become the symbol of the "radical" policies of the Fair Deal. In those terms, of course, the conceptualization was meaningless.

But the fact that the arena of politics was now foreign policy allowed the moralistic strains to come to the fore. One of the unique aspects of American politics is that while domestic issues have been argued in hard-headed, practical terms, with a give-and-take compromise as the outcome, foreign policy has always been phrased in moralistic terms. Perhaps the very nature of our emergence as an independent country forced us to constantly adopt a moral posture in regard to the rest of the world; perhaps being distant from the real centers of interest conflict allowed us to employ pieties, rather than face realities. But since foreign policy has usually been within the frame of moral rather than pragmatic discourse, the debate in the fifties became centered in moral terms. And the singular fact about the Communist problem is that, on a scale rare in American political life, an ideological issue was equated with a moral issue and the attacks on communism were made with all the compulsive moral fervor which was possible because of the equation of communism with sin.

In itself this reflects a curious change in American life. While we gain a more relaxed attitude towards private morals, we are becoming rather more extremist in public life.

The "ideologizing" of politics gains reinforcement from another, independent tendency in American life, the emergence of what may be called the "symbolic groups." These are the inchoate entities known generally in capital letters as "Labor," "Business," the "Farmers," et al. The assumption is made that these entities have a coherent philosophy, a defined purpose, and that they represent tangible forces. This tendency derives from varied sources, but the biggest impetus has come from the changing nature of economic decision-making and the changing mode of opinion-formation in modern society. The fact that major economic decision-making has been centralized in the narrow cockpit of Washington, rather than spread over the impersonal market, leads groups like the National Association of Manufacturers, the Farm Bureau, the American Federation of Labor, etc., to speak for "Business," for "Labor," for the "Farmers." At the same time there is an increased sensitivity to "Public Opinion," heightened by the use of opinion polls in which the "Citizen" (not the specific individual with his specific interests) is asked what "Business" or "Labor" or the "Farmer" should do. In effect, these groups are often forced to assume a unique identity and a greater coherence beyond what they normally do.

Political debate, therefore, moves from specific clashes of interest, in which issues can be identified and possibly compromised, to ideologically tinged conflicts which polarize the various groups and divide the society.

The tendency to convert concrete issues into ideological problems, to invest them with moral color and high emotional charge, is to invite conflicts which can only damage a society. "A nation, divided irreconcilably on 'principle,' each party believing itself pure white and the other pitch black, cannot govern itself," wrote Walter Lippmann many years ago.

It has been one of the glories of the United States that politics has always been a pragmatic give-and-take rather than a series of wars-to-the-death. One ultimately comes to admire the "practical politics" of Theodore Roosevelt and his scorn for the intransigents, like Godkin and Villard, who, refusing to yield to expediency, could never put through their reforms. Politics, as Edmund Wilson has described T.R.'s attitude, "is a matter of adapting oneself to all sorts of people and situations, a game in which one may score but only by accepting the rules and recognizing one's opponents, rather than a moral crusade in which one's stainless standard must mow the enemy down."

Democratic politics means bargaining between legitimate groups and the search for consensus. This is so because the historic contribution of liberalism was to separate law from morality. The thought that the two should be separate often comes as a shock. In the older Catholic societies ruled by the doctrine of "two swords," the state was the secular arm of the Church, and enforced in civil life the moral decrees of the Church. This was possible in political theory, if not in practice, because the society was homogeneous, and everyone accepted the same religious values. But the religious wars that followed the Reformation proved that a plural society could only survive if it respected the principles of toleration. No group, be it Catholic or Protestant, could use the State to impose its moral conceptions on all the people. As the party of the *politiques* put it, the "civil society must not perish for conscience's sake."

These theoretical foundations of modern liberal society were completed by Kant, who, separating legality and morality, defined the former as the "rules of the game," so to speak; law dealt with procedural, not substantive, issues. The latter were primary matters of conscience, with which the State could not interfere.

This distinction has been at the root of the American democracy. For Madison, factions (or divergence of interests), being rooted in liberty, were inevitable, and the function of the Republic was to protect the causes of faction, i.e., liberty and the "diversity in the faculties of men," for "freemen, 'diverse' men, fallible, heterogeneous, heterodox, opinionated, quarrelsome man was the raw material of faction."

Since faction was inevitable, one could only deal with its effects, and not smother its causes. One way, of course, was, as adopted in the federal system, to separate the powers of government, so that no faction could easily secure a monopoly of power. But Madison knew that this was not enough. The threat to liberty would be reduced by representative government, and in this *extensive republic,* as he put it, the larger number of interests would "lessen the insecurity of private rights." But representative government, as John Stuart Mill cogently pointed out, must mean the representation of all interests, "since the interest of the excluded is always in danger of being overlooked." And being overlooked, as Calhoun added, constitutes a threat to civil order.

But representative government is important for the deeper reason that by including all representative interests one can keep alive "the antagonism of influences which is the only real security for continued progress." It is the only way of securing the "concurrent majorities," which, as Calhoun argued, was the solid basis for providing a check on the tyrannical "popular" majority. For only through representative government can one achieve consensus—and conciliation.

This is not to say that the Communist "interest" is a legitimate one, akin to the interest of other groups in the society, or that the Communist issue was completely irrelevant. As a conspiracy, rather than a legitimate dissenting group, the Communist movement remains a threat to democratic society. And by the criteria of "clear and present danger" democratic society may at times have to act against that conspiracy. But these are questions to be handled by law. The tendency to use the Communist issue as a political club against other parties or groups, or the tendency to convert questions of law into issues of morality (and thus shift the source of sanctions from the courts and legitimate authority to private individuals) can only create strains in a liberal society.

In the 170 years since its founding, American democracy has been rent only once by civil war. We have learnt since then, not without strain, to include the "excluded interests," the workers and the small farmers. These have secured a legitimate place in the American political equilibrium. And the ideological conflicts that almost threatened to disrupt the society, in the early years of the New Deal, have been mitigated.

The new divisions, created by the status anxieties of new middle-class groups, pose a new threat. The rancors of McCarthyism were one of its ugly excesses. However, the United States, so huge and complex that no single political boss or any single political group has ever been able to dominate it, will in time undoubtedly diminish these divisions, too. This is an open society, and these anxieties are part of the price we pay for that openness.

PART II

America: The Complexities of Life

Chapter 7

Crime as an American Way of Life:

A Queer Ladder of Social Mobility

IN THE 1890's the Reverend Dr. Charles Parkhurst, shocked at the open police protection afforded New York's bordellos, demanded a state inquiry. In the Lexow investigation that followed, the young and dashing William Travers Jerome staged a set of public hearings that created sensation after sensation. He badgered "Clubber" Williams, First Inspector of the Police Department, to account for wealth and property far greater than could have been saved on his salary; it was earned, the Clubber explained laconically, through land speculation "in Japan." Heavy-set Captain Schmittberger, the "collector" for the "Tenderloin precincts"—Broadway's fabulous concentration of hotels, theaters, restaurants, gaming houses, and saloons—related in detail how protection money was distributed among the police force. Crooks, policemen, public officials, businessmen, all paraded across the stage, each adding his chapter to a sordid story of corruption and crime. The upshot of these revelations was reform — the election of William L. Strong, a stalwart businessman, as mayor, and the naming of Theodore Roosevelt as police commissioner.

It did not last, of course, just as previous reform victories had not lasted. Yet the ritual drama was re-enacted. Thirty years ago the Seabury investigation in New York uncovered the tin-box brigade and the thirty-three little McQuades. Jimmy Walker was ousted as Mayor and in came Fiorello LaGuardia. Tom Dewey became district attorney, broke the industrial rackets, sent Lucky Luciano to jail, and went to the governor's chair in Albany. Then reform was again swallowed up in the insatiable maw of corruption until in 1950 Kefauver and his committee counsel Rudolph Halley threw a new beam of light into the seemingly bottomless pit.

How explain this repetitious cycle? Obviously the simple moralistic distinction between "good guys" and "bad guys," so deep at the root of the reform impulse, bears little relation to the role of organized crime in American society. What, then, does?

The Queer Ladder

Americans have had an extraordinary talent for compromise in politics and extremism in morality. The most shameless political deals (and "steals") have been rationalized as expedient and realistically necessary. Yet in no other country have there been such spectacular attempts to curb human appetites and brand them as illicit, and nowhere else such glaring failures. From the start America was at one and the same time a frontier community where "everything goes," and the fair country of the Blue Laws. At the turn of the century the cleavage developed between the Big City and the small-town conscience. Crime as a growing business was fed by the revenues from prostitution, liquor, and gambling that a wide-open urban society encouraged and that a middle-class Protestant ethos tried to suppress with a ferocity unmatched in any other civilized country. Catholic cultures have rarely imposed such restrictions and have rarely suffered such excesses. Even in prim and proper Anglican England, prostitution is a commonplace of Piccadilly night life, and gambling is one of the largest and most popular industries. In America the enforcement of public morals has been a continuing feature of our history.

Some truth may lie in Max Scheler's generalization that moral indignation is a peculiar fact of middle-class psychology and represents a disguised form of repressed envy. The larger truth lies perhaps in the brawling nature of American development and in the social character of crime. Crime, in many ways, is a Coney Island mirror, caricaturing the morals and manners of a society. The jungle quality of the American business community, particularly at the turn of the century, was reflected in the mode of "business" practiced by the coarse gangster elements, most of them from new immigrant families, who were "getting ahead," just as Horatio Alger had urged. In the older, Protestant tradition the intensive acquisitiveness, such as that of Daniel Drew, was rationalized by a compulsive moral fervor. But the formal obeisance of the ruthless businessman in the workday world to the church-going pieties of the Sabbath was one that the gangster could not make. Moreover, for the young criminal, hunting in the asphalt jungle of the crowded city, it was not the businessman with his wily manipulation of numbers but the "man with the gun" who was the American hero. "No amount of commercial prosperity," once wrote Teddy Roosevelt, "can supply the lack of the heroic virtues." The American was "the hunter, cowboy, frontiersman, the soldier, the naval hero"—and in the crowded slums, the gangster. He was a man with a gun, acquiring by personal merit what was denied him by complex orderings of stratified society. And the duel with the law was the morality play par excellence: the gangster, with whom ride our own illicit desires, and the prosecutor, representing final judgment and the force of the law.

Yet all this was acted out in a wider context. The desires satisfied in extra-legal fashion were more than a hunger for the "forbidden fruits" of conventional morality. They also involved, in the complex and ever shifting structure of group, class, and ethnic stratification, which is the warp and woof of America's "open" society, such "normal" goals as independence through a business of one's own, and such "moral" aspirations as the desire for social advancement and social prestige. For crime, in the language of the sociologists, has a "functional" role in the society, and the urban rackets—the illicit activity organized for continuing profit, rather than individual illegal acts—is one of the queer ladders of social mobility in American life. Indeed, it is not too much to say that the whole question of organized crime in America cannot be understood unless one appreciates (1) the distinctive role of organized gambling as a function of a mass-consumption economy; (2) the specific role of various immigrant groups as they, one after another, became involved in marginal business and crime; and (3) the relation of crime to the changing character of the urban political machines.

Gatsby's Model

As a society changes, so does, in lagging fashion, its type of crime. As American society became more "organized," as the American businessman became more "civilized" and less "buccaneering," so did the American racketeer. And just as there were important changes in the structure of business enterprise, so the "institutionalized" criminal enterprise was transformed too.

In the America of the last fifty years the main drift of society has been toward the rationalization of industry, the domestication of the crude self-made captain of industry into the respectable man of manners, and the emergence of a mass-consumption economy. The most significant transformation in the field of "institutionalized" crime in the 1940's was the increasing importance of gambling as against other kinds of illegal activity. And, as a multi-billion-dollar business, gambling underwent a transition parallel to the changes in American enterprise as a whole. This parallel was exemplified in many ways: in gambling's industrial organization (e.g., the growth of a complex technology such as the national racing-wire service and the minimization of risks by such techniques as lay-off betting); in its respectability, as was evidenced in the opening of smart and popular gambling casinos in resort towns and in "satellite" adjuncts to metropolitan areas; in its functional role in a mass-consumption economy (for sheer volume of money changing hands, nothing has ever surpassed this feverish activity of fifty million American adults); in the social acceptance of the gamblers in the important status world of sport and entertainment, i.e., "café society."

In seeking to "legitimize" itself, gambling had quite often actually become a force against older and more vicious forms of illegal activity. In 1946, for example, when a Chicago mobster, Pat Manno, went down to Dallas, Texas, to take over gambling in the area for the Accardo-Guzik combine, he reassured the sheriff as follows: "Something I'm against, that's dope peddlers, pickpockets, hired killers. That's one thing I can't stomach, and that's one thing the fellows up there—the group won't stand for, things like that. They discourage it, they even go to headquarters and ask them why they don't do something about it."

Jimmy Cannon once reported that when the gambling raids started in Chicago the "combine" protested that, in upsetting existing stable relations, the police were only opening the way for ambitious young punks and hoodlums to start trouble. Nor is there today, as there was twenty or even forty years ago, prostitution of major organized scope in the United States. Aside from the fact that manners and morals have changed, prostitution *as an industry* doesn't pay as well as gambling. Besides, its existence threatened the tacit moral acceptance and quasi-respectability that gamblers and gambling have secured in the American way of life. It was, as any operator in the field might tell you, "bad for business."

The criminal world of the 1940's, its tone set by the captains of the gambling industry, is in startling contrast to the state of affairs in the decade before. If a Kefauver report had been written then, the main "names" would have been Lepke and Gurrah, Dutch Schultz, Jack "Legs" Diamond, Lucky Luciano, and, reaching back a little further, Arnold Rothstein, the czar of the underworld. These men (with the exception of Luciano, who was involved in narcotics and prostitution) were in the main "industrial racketeers." Rothstein, the model for Wolfsheim the gambler in F. Scott Fitzgerald's *The Great Gatsby,* had a larger function: he was, as Frank Costello became later, the finançier of the underword, the pioneer big businessman of crime who, understanding the logic of coordination, sought to *organize* crime as a source of regular income. His main interest in this direction was in industrial racketeering, and his entry was through labor disputes. At one time, employers in the garment trades hired Legs Diamond and his sluggers to break strikes, and the Communists, then in control of the cloakmakers union, hired one Little Orgie to protect the pickets and beat up the scabs; only later did both sides learn that Legs Diamond and Little Orgie were working for the same man, Rothstein.

Rothstein's chief successors, Lepke Buchalter and Gurrah Shapiro, were able, in the early thirties, to dominate sections of the men's and women's clothing industries, of painting, fur dressing, flour trucking, and other fields. In a highly chaotic and cutthroat industry such as clothing, the racketeer, paradoxically, played a stabilizing role by regulating competition and fixing prices. When the NRA came in and assumed this function, the businessman found that what had once been a quasi-economic service was now pure extortion, and he began to demand police action. In other types of racketeering, such as the trucking of perishable foods and waterfront loading, where the racketeers entrenched themselves as middlemen—taking up, by default, a service that neither shippers nor truckers wanted to assume—a pattern of accommodation was roughly worked out, and the rackets assumed a quasi-legal veneer. On the waterfront, old-time racketeers perform the necessary function of loading—but at an exorbitant price—and this monopoly was recognized by both the union and the shippers, and tacitly by the government.

But in the last decade and a half, industrial racketeering has not offered much in the way of opportunity. *Like American capitalism itself, crime shifted its emphasis from production to consumption.* The focus of crime became the direct exploitation of the citizen as consumer, largely through gambling. And while the protection of these huge revenues was inextricably linked to politics, the relation between gambling and "the mobs" became more complicated.

Big-Business Bookies

Although it never showed up in the gross national product, gambling in the last decade was one of the largest industries in the United States. The Kefauver Committee estimated it as a $20 billion business. This figure has been picked up and widely quoted, but in truth no one knows what the gambling "turnover" and "take" actually is, nor how much is bet legally (parimutuel, etc.) and how much illegally. In fact, the figure cited by the committee was arbitrary and was arrived at quite sloppily. As one staff member said: "We had no real idea of the money spent. . . . The California crime commission said twelve billion. Virgil Peterson of Chicago estimated thirty billion. We picked twenty billion as a balance between the two."

If comprehensive data are not available, we do know, from specific instances, the magnitude of many of the operations. Some indication can be seen from these items culled at random:

James Carroll and the M & G syndicate did a $20 million annual business in St. Louis. This was one of the two large books in the city.

The S & G syndicate in Miami did a $26 million volume yearly; the total for all books in the Florida resort reached $40 million.

Slot machines were present in 69,786 establishments in 1951 (each paid $100 for a license to the Bureau of Internal Revenue); the usual average is three machines to a license, which would add up to 210,000 slot machines in operation in the United States. In legalized areas, where the betting is higher and more regular, the average gross "take" per machine is $50 a week.

The largest policy wheel (i.e., "numbers") in Chicago's "Black Belt" reported taxable net profits for the four-year period from 1946 through 1949, after sizable deductions for "overhead," of $3,656,968. One of the large "white" wheels reported in 1947 a gross income of $2,317,000 and a net profit of $205,000. One CIO official estimated that perhaps 15 per cent of his union's lower-echelon officials are involved in the numbers racket (a steward, free to roam a plant, is in a perfect situation for organizing bets).

If one considers the amount of dollars bet on sports alone —an estimated six billion on baseball, a billion on football pools, another billion on basketball, six billion on horse racing —then Elmo Roper's judgment that "only the food, steel, auto, chemical, and machine-tool industries have a greater volume of business" does not seem too farfetched.

While gambling has long flourished in the United States, the influx of the big mobsters into the industry—and its expansion—started in the thirties, when repeal of Prohibition forced them to look about for new avenues of enterprise. (The change, one might say crudely, was in the "democratization" of gambling. In New York of the 1860's, 1870's, and 1880's, one found elegant establishments where the wealthy men of the city, bankers, and sportsmen gambled. The saloon was the home of the worker. The middle class of the time did not gamble. In the changing mores of America, the rise of gambling in the 1930's and 1940's meant the introduction of the middle class to gambling and casinos as a way of life.) Gambling, which had begun to flower under the nourishment of rising incomes, was the most lucrative field in sight. To a large extent the shift from bootlegging to gambling was a mere transfer of business operations. In the East, Frank Costello went into slot machines and the operation of a number of ritzy gambling casinos. He also became the "banker" for the Erickson "book," which "laid off" bets for other bookies. Joe Adonis, similarly, opened up a number of casinos, principally in New Jersey. Across the country, many other mobsters went into bookmaking. As other rackets diminished and gambling, particularly horse-race betting, flourished in the forties, a struggle erupted over the control of racing information.

Horse-race betting requires a peculiar industrial organization. The essential component is time. A bookie can operate only if he can get information on odds up to the very last minute before the race, so that he can "hedge" or "lay off" bets. With racing going on simultaneously on many tracks throughout the country, this information has to be obtained speedily and accurately. Thus, the racing wire is the nerve ganglion of race betting.

The racing-wire news service got started in the twenties through the genius of the late Moe Annenberg, who had made a fearful reputation for himself as Hearst's circulation manager in the rough-and-tough Chicago newspaper wars. Annenberg conceived the idea of a telegraphic news service which would gather information from tracks and shoot it immediately to scratch sheets, horse parlors, and bookie joints. In some instances, track owners gave Annenberg the rights to send news from tracks; more often, the news was simply "stolen" by crews operating inside or near the tracks. So efficient did this news distribution system become, that in 1942, when a plane knocked out a vital telegraph circuit which served an Air Force field as well as the gamblers, the Continental Press managed to get its racing wire service for gamblers resumed in fifteen minutes, while it took the Fourth Army, which was responsible for the defense of the entire West Coast, something like three hours.

Annenberg built up a nationwide racing information chain that not only distributed wire news but controlled sub-outlets as well. In 1939, harassed by the Internal Revenue Bureau on income tax and chivvied by the Justice Department for "monopolistic" control of the wire service, the tired and aging Annenberg simply walked out of the business. He did not sell his interest or even seek to salvage some profit; he simply gave up. Yet, like any established and thriving institution, the enterprise continued, though on a decentralized basis. James Ragen, Annenberg's operation manager and likewise a veteran of the old Chicago circulation wars, took over the national wire service through a dummy friend and renamed it the Continental Press Service.

The salient fact is that in the operation of the Annenberg and Ragen wire service, formally illegal as many of its subsidiary operations may have been (i.e., in "stealing" news, supplying information to bookies, etc.), gangsters played no part. It was a business, illicit, true, but primarily a business. The distinction between gamblers and gangsters, as we shall see, is a relevant one.

In 1946, the Chicago mob, whose main interest was in bookmaking rather than in gambling casinos, began to move in on the wire monopoly. Following repeal, the Capone lieutenants had turned, like Lepke, to labor raketeering. Murray ("The Camel") Humphries muscled in on the teamsters, the operating engineers, and the cleaning-and-dyeing, laundry, and linen-supply industries. Through a small-time punk, Willie Bioff, and union official George Browne, Capone's chief successors, Frank ("The Enforcer") Nitti and Paul Ricca, came into control of the motion-picture union and proceeded to shake down the movie industry for fabulous sums in order to "avert strikes." In 1943, when the government moved in and smashed the industrial rackets, the remaining big shots, Charley Fischetti, Jake Guzik, and Tony Accardo, decided to concentrate on gambling, and in particular began a drive to take over the racing wire.

In Chicago, the Guzik-Accardo gang, controlling a subdistributor of the racing-news service, began tapping Continental's wires. In Los Angeles, the head of the local distribution agency for Continental was beaten up by hoodlums working for Mickey Cohen and Joe Sica. Out of the blue appeared a new and competitive nationwide racing information and distribution service, known as Trans-American Publishing, the money for which was advanced by the Chicago mobs and Bugsy Siegel, who, at the time, held a monopoly of the bookmaking and wire-news service in Las Vegas. Many books pulled out of Continental and bought information from the new outfit; many hedged by buying from both. At the end of a year, however, the Capone mob's wire had lost about $200,000. Ragen felt that violence would erupt and went to the Cook County district attorney and told him that his life had been threatened by his rivals. Ragen knew his competitors. In June, 1946, he was killed by a blast from a shotgun.

Thereafter, the Capone mob abandoned Trans-American and got a "piece" of Continental. Through their new control of the national racing-wire monopoly, the Capone mob began to muscle in on the lucrative Miami gambling business run by the so-called S & G syndicate. For a long time S & G's monopoly over bookmaking had been so complete that when New York gambler Frank Erickson bought a three months' bookmaking concession at the expensive Roney Plaza Hotel, for $45,000, the local police, in a highly publicized raid, swooped down on the hotel; the next year the Roney Plaza was again using local talent. The Capone group, however, was tougher. They demanded an interest in Miami bookmaking and, when refused, began organizing a syndicate of their own, persuading some bookies at the big hotels to join them. Florida Governor Warren's crime investigator appeared—a friend, it seemed, of old Chicago dog-track operator William Johnston, who had contributed $100,000 to the Governor's campaign fund—and began raiding bookie joints, but only those that were affiliated with S & G. Then S & G, which had been buying its racing news from the local distributor of Continental Press, found its service abruptly shut off. For a few days the syndicate sought to bootleg information from

New Orleans, but found itself limping along. After ten days' war of attrition, the five S & G partners found themselves with a sixth partner, who, for a token "investment" of $20,-000, entered a Miami busines that grossed $26,000,000 in one year.

Gamblers and Guys

While Americans made gambling illegal, they did not in their hearts think of it as wicked—even the churches benefited from the bingo and lottery crazes. So they gambled—and gamblers flourished. Against this open canvas, the indignant tones of Senator Wiley and the shocked righteousness of Senator Tobey during the Kefauver investigation rang oddly. Yet it was probably this very tone of surprise that gave the activity of the Kefauver Committee its piquant quality. Here were some senators who seemingly did not know the facts of life, as most Americans did. Here, in the person of Senator Tobey, was the old New England Puritan conscience poking around in industrial America, in a world it had made but never seen. Here was old-fashioned moral indignation, at a time when cynicism was rampant in public life.

Commendable as such moralistic fervor was, it did not make for intelligent discrimination of fact. Throughout the Kefauver hearings, for example, there ran the presumption that all gamblers were invariably gangsters. This was true of Chicago's Accardo-Guzik combine, which in the past had its fingers in many kinds of rackets. It was not nearly so true of many of large gamblers in America, most of whom had the feeling that they were satisfying a basic American urge for sport and looked upon their calling with no greater sense of guilt than did many bootleggers. After all, Sherman Billingsley did start out as a speakeasy proprietor, as did the Kriendlers of the "21" Club; and today the Stork Club and the former Jack and Charlie's are the most fashionable night and dining spots in America (one prominent patron of the Stork Club: J. Edgar Hoover).

The S & G syndicate in Miami, for example (led by Harold Salvey, Jules Levitt, Charles Friedman, Sam Cohen, and Edward [Eddie Luckey] Rosenbaum), was simply a master pool of some two hundred bookies that arranged for telephone service, handled "protection," acted as bankers for those who needed ready cash on hard-hit books, and, in short, functioned somewhat analogously to the large factoring corporations in the textile field or the credit companies in the auto industry. Yet to Kefauver, the S & G men were "slippery and arrogant characters. . . . Salvey, for instance, was an old-time bookie who told us he had done nothing except engage in bookmaking or finance other bookmakers for twenty years." When, as a result of committee publicity and the newly found purity of the Miami police, the S & G syndicate went out of business, it was, as the combine's lawyer told Kefauver, because the "boys" were weary of being painted "the worst monsters in the world." "It is true," Cohen acknowledged, "that they had been law violators." But they had never done anything worse than gambling, and "to fight the world isn't worth it."

Most intriguing of all were the opinions of James J. Carroll, the St. Louis "betting commissioner," who for years had been widely quoted on the sports pages of the country as setting odds on the Kentucky Derby winter book and the baseball pennant races. Senator Wiley, speaking like the prosecutor in Camus's novel, *The Stranger,* became the voice of official morality:

SENATOR WILEY: Have you any children?
MR. CARROLL: Yes, I have a boy.
SENATOR WILEY: How old is he?
MR. CARROLL: Thirty-three.
SENATOR WILEY: Does he gamble?
MR. CARROLL: No.
SENATOR WILEY: Would you like to see him grow up and become a gambler, either professional or amateur?
MR. CARROLL: No. . . .
SENATOR WILEY: All right. Is your son interested in your business?
MR. CARROLL: No, he is a manufacturer.
SENATOR WILEY: Why do you not get him into the business?
MR. CARROLL: Well, psychologically a great many people are unsuited for gambling.

Retreating from this gambit, the Senator sought to pin Carroll down on his contributions to political campaigns:

SENATOR WILEY: Now this morning I asked you whether you contributed any money for political candidates or parties, and you said not more than $200 at one time. I presume that does not indicate the total of your contributions in any one campaign, does it?
MR. CARROLL: Well, it might, might not, Senator. I have been an "againster" in many instances. I am a reader of *The Nation* for

fifty years and they have advertisements calling for contributions for different candidates, different causes. . . . They carried an advertisement for George Norris; I contributed, I think, to that, and to the elder LaFollette.

Carroll, who admitted to having been in the betting business since 1899, was the sophisticated—but not immoral!—counterpoint to moralist Wiley. Here was a man without the stigmata of the underworld or underground; he was worldly, cynical of official rhetoric, jaundiced about people's motives; he was an "againster" who believed that "all gambling legislation originates or stems from some group or some individual seeking special interests for himself or his cause."

Asked why people gamble, Carroll distilled his experiences of fifty years with a remark that deserves a place in American social history: "I really don't know how to answer the question," he said, "I think gambling is a biological necessity for certain types. I think it is the quality that gives substance to their daydreams."

In a sense, the entire Kefauver materials, unintentionally, seem to document that remark. For what the committee revealed time and time again was a picture of gambling as a basic institution in American life, flourishing openly and accepted widely. In many of the small towns, the gambling joint is as open as a liquor establishment. The town of Havana, in Mason County, Illinois, felt miffed when Governor Adlai Stevenson intervened against local gambling. In 1950, the town had raised $15,000 of its $50,000 budget by making friendly raids on the gambling houses every month and having the owners pay fines. "With the gambling fines cut off," grumbled Mayor Clarence Chester, "the next year is going to be tough."

Apart from the gamblers, there were the mobsters. But what Senator Kefauver and company failed to understand was that the mobsters, like the gamblers, and like the entire gangdom generally, were seeking to become quasi-respectable and establish a place for themselves in American life. For the mobsters, by and large, had immigrant roots, and crime, as the pattern showed, was a route of social ascent and place in American life.

The Myth of the Mafia

The mobsters were able, where they wished, to "muscle in" on the gambling business because the established gamblers were wholly vulnerable, not being able to call on the law for protection. The senators, however, refusing to make any distinction between a gambler and a gangster, found it convenient to talk loosely of a nationwide conspiracy of "illegal" elements. Senator Kefauver asserted that a "nationwide crime syndicate does exist in the United States, despite the protestations of a strangely assorted company of criminals, self-serving politicians, plain blind fools, and others who may be honestly misguided, that there is no such combine." The Senate committee report states the matter more dogmatically; "There is a nationwide crime syndicate known as the Mafia. . . . Its leaders are usually found in control of the most lucrative rackets in their cities. There are indications of a centralized direction and control of these rackets. . . . The Mafia is the cement that helps to bind the Costello-Adonis-Lansky syndicate of New York and the Accardo-Guzik-Fischetti syndicate of Chicago. . . . These groups have kept in touch with Luciano since his deportation from the country."

Unfortunately for a good story—and the existence of the Mafia would be a whale of a story—neither the Senate Crime Committee in its testimony, nor Kefauver in his book, presented any real evidence that the Mafia exists as a functioning organization. One finds police officials asserting before the Kefauver committee their *belief* in the Mafia; the Narcotics Bureau *thinks* that a world-wide dope ring allegedly run by Luciano is part of the Mafia; but the only other "evidence" presented—aside from the incredulous responses both of Senator Kefauver and Rudolph Halley when nearly all the Italian gangsters asserted that they didn't know about the Mafia—is that certain crimes bear "the earmarks of the Mafia."

The legend of the Mafia has been fostered in recent years largely by the peephole writing team of Jack Lait and Lee Mortimer. In their *Chicago Confidential,* they rattled off a series of names and titles that made the organization sound like a rival to an Amos and Andy Kingfish society. Few serious reporters, however, give it much credence. Burton Turkus, the Brooklyn prosecutor who broke up the "Murder, Inc." ring, denies the existence of the Mafia. Nor could Senator Kefauver even make out much of a case for his picture of a national crime syndicate. He is forced to admit that "as it exists today [it] is an elusive and furtive but nonetheless tangible thing," and that "its organization and machinations are not always easy to pinpoint."* His "evidence" that many gangsters congregate at certain times of the year in such places as Hot Springs, Arkansas, in itself does not prove much; people "in the trade" usually do, and as the loquacious late Willie Moretti of New Jersey said, in explaining how he had met the late Al Capone at a race track, "Listen, well-charactered people you don't need introductions to; you just meet automatically."

Why did the Senate Crime Committee plump so hard for its theory of a Mafia and a national crime syndicate? In part, they may have been misled by their own hearsay. The Senate committee was not in the position to do original research, and its staff, both legal and investigative, was incredibly small. Senator Kefauver had begun the investigation with the attitude that with so much smoke there must be a raging fire. But smoke can also mean a smoke screen. Mob activities is a field in which busy gossip and exaggeration flourish even more readily than in a radical political sect.

There is, as well, in the American temper, a feeling that "somewhere," "somebody" is pulling all the complicated

* The accidental police discovery of a conference of Italian figures, most of them with underworld and police records, in Apalachin, New York, in November 1957, revived the talk of a Mafia. *Time* magazine assigned a reporter, Serrell Hillman, to check the story, and this is what he reported: "I spent some two weeks in New York, Washington and Chicago running down every clue to the so-called Mafia that I could find. I talked to a large number of Federal, state and local law enforcement authorities; to police, reporters, attorneys, detectives, non-profit civic groups such as the Chicago Crime Commission. Nobody from the F.B.I. and Justice Department officials on down, with the exception of a couple of Hearst crime reporters—always happy for the sake of a street sale to associate the 'Mafia' with the most routine barroom shooting—and the Narcotics Bureau believed that a Mafia exists as such. The Narcotics Bureau, which has to contend with a big problem in dope-trafficking, contends that a working alliance operates between an organized Mafia in Italy and Sicily and a U.S. Mafia. But the Bureau has never been able to submit proof of this, and the F.B.I. is skeptical. The generally held belief is that there is no tightly knit syndicate, but instead a loose "trade association" of criminals in various cities and areas, who run their own shows in their own fields but have matters of mutual interest to take up (as at the Appalachian conference). At any rate, nobody has ever been able to produce specific evidence that a Mafia is functioning."

In early 1959, Fredric Sondern, Jr., an editor of the *Reader's Digest*, published a best-selling book on the Mafia, *Brotherhood of Evil*, but a close reading of Mr. Sondern's text indicates that his sources are largely the files of the Narcotics Bureau, and his findings little more than a rehash of previously publicized material. (For a devastating review of the book, see the *Times Literary Supplement*, London, June 12, 1959, p. 351.) Interestingly enough, in May, 1959, Alvin Goldstein, a former assistant district attorney in New York, who had prosecuted racketeer Johnny Dio, conducted a crime survey of California for Governor Pat Brown and reported that he found no evidence of the existence of a Mafia in California.

strings to which this jumbled world dances. In politics the labor image is "Wall Street" or "Big Business"; while the business stereotype was the "New Dealers." In the field of crime, the side-of-the-mouth low-down was "Costello."

The salient reason, perhaps, why the Kefauver Committee was taken in by its own myth of an omnipotent Mafia and a despotic Costello was its failure to assimilate and understand three of the more relevant sociological facts about institutionalized crime in its relation to the political life of large urban communities in America, namely: (1) the rise of the American Italian community, as part of the inevitable process of ethnic succession, to positions of importance in politics, a process that has been occurring independently but also simultaneously in most cities with large Italian constituencies —New York, Chicago, Kansas City, Los Angeles; (2) the fact that there are individual Italians who play prominent, often leading roles today in gambling and in the mobs; and (3) the fact that Italian gamblers and mobsters often possessed "status" within the Italian community itself and a "pull" in city politics.[35] These three items are indeed related —but not so as to form a "plot."

The Jews . . . the Irish . . . the Italians

The Italian community has achieved wealth and political influence much later and in a harder way than previous immigrant groups. Early Jewish wealth, that of the German Jews of the late nineteenth century, was made largely in banking and merchandising. To that extent, the dominant group in the Jewish community was outside of, and independent of, the urban political machines. Later Jewish wealth, among the East European immigrants, was built in the garment trades, though with some involvement with the Jewish gangster, who was typically an industrial racketeer (Arnold Rothstein, Lepke and Gurrah, etc.). Among Jewish lawyers, a small minority, such as the "Tammany lawyer" (like the protagonist of Sam Ornitz's *Haunch, Paunch and Jowl*), rose through politics and occasionally touched the fringes of crime. Most of the Jewish lawyers, by and large the communal leaders, climbed rapidly, however, in the opportunities that established and legitimate Jewish wealth provided. Irish immigrant wealth in the northern urban centers, concentrated largely in construction, trucking, and the waterfront, has, to a substantial extent, been wealth accumulated

rough and ready contractors, the construction people, trucking entrepreneurs, as well as racketeers, polished up their manners and sought recognition and respectability in their own ethnic as well as in the general community. The "shanty" Irish became the "lace curtain" Irish, and then moved out for wider recognition.[38] Sometimes acceptance came first in established "American" society, and this was a certificate for later recognition by the ethnic community, a process well illustrated by the belated acceptance in established Negro society of such figures as Sugar Ray Robinson and Joe Louis, as well as leading popular entertainers.

Yet, after all, the foundation of many a distinguished older American fortune was laid by sharp practices and morally reprehensible methods. The pioneers of American capitalism were not graduated from Harvard's School of Business Administration. The early settlers and founding fathers, as well as those who "won the West" and built up cattle, mining, and other fortunes, often did so by shady speculations and a not inconsiderable amount of violence. They ignored, circumvented, or stretched the law when it stood in the way of America's destiny and their own—or were themselves the law when it served their purposes. This has not prevented them and their descendants from feeling proper moral outrage when, under the changed circumstances of the crowded urban environments, latecomers pursued equally ruthless tactics.

The Embourgeoisement of Crime

Ironically, the social development which made possible the rise to political influence sounds, too, the knell of the rough Italian gangster. For it is the growing number of Italians with professional training and legitimate business success that both prompts and permits the Italian group to wield increasing political influence; and increasingly it is the professionals and businessmen who provide models for Italian youth today, models that hardly existed twenty years ago. Ironically, the headlines and exposés of "crime" of the Italian "gangsters" came years after the fact. Many of the top "crime" figures had long ago forsworn violence, and even their income, in large part, was derived from legitimate investments (real estate in the case of Costello, motor haulage and auto dealer franchises in the case of Adonis) or from such quasi-legitimate but socially respectable sources as gambling casinos. Hence society's "retribution" in the jail sentences for Costello and Adonis was little more than a trumped-up morality that disguised a social hypocrisy.

Apart from these considerations, what of the larger context of crime and the American way of life? The passing of the Fair Deal signalizes, oddly, the passing of an older pattern of illicit activities. The gambling fever of the past decade and a half was part of the flush and exuberance of rising incomes, and was characteristic largely of new upper-middle-class rich having a first fling at conspicuous consumption. These upper-middle-class rich, a significant new stratum in American life (not rich in the nineteenth-century sense of enormous wealth, but largely middle-sized businessmen and entrepreneurs of the service and luxury trades—the "tertiary economy" in Colin Clark's phrase—who by the tax laws have achieved sizable incomes often much higher than the managers of the super-giant corporations), were the chief patrons of the munificent gambling casinos. During the war decade when travel was difficult, gambling and the lush resorts provided important outlets for this social class. Now they are settling down, learning about Europe and culture. The petty gambling, the betting and bingo which relieve the tedium of small-town life, or the expectation among the urban slum dwellers of winning a sizable sum by a "lucky number" or a "lucky horse," goes on. To quote Bernard Baruch: "You can't stop people from gambling on horses. And why should you prohibit a man from backing his own judgment? It's another form of personal initiative." But the lush profits are passing from gambling as the costs of co-ordination rise. And in the future it is likely that gambling, like prostitution, winning tacit acceptance as a necessary fact, will continue on a decentralized, small entrepreneur basis.

But passing, too, is a political pattern, the system of political "bosses" which in its reciprocal relation provided "protection" for, and was fed revenue from, crime. The collapse of the "boss" system was a product of the Roosevelt era. Twenty years ago Jim Farley's task was simple; he had to work only on some key state bosses. Now there is no longer such an animal. New Jersey Democracy was once ruled by Frank Hague; now there are five or six men each "top dog," for the moment, in his part of the state or faction of the party. Within the urban centers, the old Irish-dominated political machines in New York, Boston, Newark, and Chicago have fallen apart. The decentralization of the metropolitan centers, the growth of suburbs and satellite towns, the breakup of the old ecological patterns of slum and transient belts, the rise of functional groups, the increasing middle-class character of American life, all contribute to this decline.

With the rationalization and absorption of some illicit activities into the structure of the economy, the passing of an older generation that had established a hegemony over crime,[39] the general rise of minority groups to social position, and the breakup of the urban boss system, the pattern of crime we have discussed is passing as well. Crime, of course, remains as long as passion and the desire for gain remain. But the kind of big, organized city crime, as we have known it for the past seventy-five years, was based on more than these universal motives. It was based on certain characteristics of the American economy, American ethnic groups, and American politics. The changes in all these areas mean that, in the form we have known it, it too will change.

Chapter 8

The Myth of Crime Waves:

The Actual Decline of Crime in the United States

IF ONE WERE TO believe the newspapers—and the statistics on crime—every year in the United States seems to show a new and more serious wave of crime. Periodically, newspapers in the large urban cities feature stories of open assaults in the streets, and warn of areas that are unsafe at night. Juvenile delinquency seems to mount steadily, so sharply, in fact, that in California, according to the 1958 report of the State Youth Authority, one out of every four youths aged seventeen was arrested in the state that year. Congressional investigations, from Kefauver to McClellan, uncover sensational stories of graft, corruption, and racketeering.

And yet, a sober look at the problem shows that there is probably less crime today in the United States than existed a hundred, or fifty, or even twenty-five years ago, and that today the United States is a more lawful and safe country than popular opinion imagines. What is the evidence?

For one thing, newspaper accounts, the main source of the public's image, have to be discounted hugely. Long ago, Lincoln Steffens told the classic story in his *Autobiography* of how competition between newspapermen generated a "crime wave" by taking run-of-the-mill burglaries off the police blotter and featuring them in black headlines. The "crime wave" ended when Theodore Roosevelt, the police commissioner at the time, called off the competition. ("The morning newspapers," Steffens recalled, "found the 'fickle' public 'sick of crime' while the monthly magazines and scientific quarterlies had some belated, heavy [*sic*] incorrect analyses of the periodicity of lawlessness.")

Crime stories are, of course, circulation builders: they create alarm, arouse apprehension, and stimulate calls for action—a satisfying, if stereotyped, instance of Aristotle's dramaturgical definition of catharsis. But whether such stories are guides to accuracy is dubious. For crime headlines appear most often when readers are surfeited with stories about East Pakistan and South Vietnam, and the very timing of such crusades casts doubt on the question whether there is more crime or simply more excitement about crime.

What, then, about the statistics? In 1954, for example, J. Edgar Hoover announced that major crimes had increased 8 per cent in a year and that the trend, if unchecked, would mean a new reign of lawlessness in America. The figure was quite specific, even if the conclusion was merely rhetorical. But, unfortunately, crime statistics are as reliable as a woman giving her "correct" age. The annual figures reported by the FBI are based on reports from 6,595 police chiefs and agencies. But there are no uniform definitions of crime—since these are set by the states*—and, more importantly, there are no uniform standards of reporting. Take the startling case of Philadelphia: in 1953 the City of Brotherly Love reported 28,560 major crimes, as against 16,773 in 1951—a sudden jump of over 70 per cent. But there had been no invasion by criminals. Police Commissioner Thomas J. Gibbons, who assumed office in 1952 as part of the reform administration of Mayor Clark, had found that for years crime records, in order to minimize the amount of crime in the city, had been faked. One center-city district, he discovered, had handled 5,000 more complaints than it had recorded. A new central reporting system was installed, and as a result the number of "crimes" went up. An even more fantastic episode occurred in New York. Crime figures, the FBI thought, seemed remarkably low. On checking, it found that in 1950, for example, the number of property crimes reported by the police were about half those reported privately by insurance companies. Local precincts simply held back complaints because detectives feared that the reporting of large numbers of unsolved burglaries would provoke shakeups. Detectives receiving slips regarding burglaries would "paste them in their hats" and wait, usually, until a burglar might be nabbed who would confess to other "unsolved" burglaries. Following a survey by police expert Bruce Smith, a new system of central recording was installed. All precinct numbers, for example, were taken out of the New York telephone book, and any person wishing to report a crime had to call the central sta-

* As Roscoe Pound points out, the number of crimes for which one may be prosecuted in Rhode Island has more than doubled in fifty years, and multiplied by eight in 100 years.

tion, Spring 7-3100. In the one year following the change, assaults rose 200 per cent, robberies 400 per cent, and burglaries 1,300 per cent over 1948 figures. As Smith concluded, "such startling rises . . . do not themselves represent an increase in crime, but rather a vast improvement in crime reporting."

From the statistical side alone, the middle Atlantic states showed startling increases for all major offenses in the years 1950-54. But New York and Philadelphia account for 25 per cent of the urban population (in cities with over 100,000 inhabitants). Do we then have a crime wave or a "crime reporting" wave?*

One startling fact is that every ten years the number of crimes in the United States "automatically" drops—that is to say, each year, for ten years, the number of crimes mounts sharply, but in the tenth year it drops. This is not due to sunspots or some other cyclical theory, but to a simple statistical pitfall.[40] A report on the number of crimes alone is, of course, a crude index, for increases in crime have to be specified in regard to changes in population. The FBI rates relate crime to per 100,000 population, but there is no population-accounting for inter-census years, so that the rates not only reflect the lower population base of ten years before but, more importantly, do not take into account the enormous internal migrations. Thus, in 1949, the murder rate in California was 4.97 per 100,000, robbery was 136.1, theft 2141.6, etc. But from 1940 to 1950 California gained three million new persons, or a population increase of 50 per cent. Because there were no official figures available for the inter-census years, all the crimes committed from 1940 to 1949 (the numerator, so to speak) were attributed to the smaller denominator of 1940. When the new census was taken in 1950, the crime rates were adjusted, and crime "dropped" spectacularly. During the 1940-50 decade the three Pacific coast states increased their population about 40 per cent. But the 1949 crime rates were still computed on the basis of the smaller 1940 population; in effect the larger number of crimes in 1949 were charged to only 60 per cent of the population, thus overstating considerably the amount of criminality. Conversely, where states suffered population losses, the picture was understated.

* One can also point out a converse meaning to increases in reported crimes: many crimes are reported only occasionally—i.e., small larcenies, briberies, prostitution, gambling, etc.—even though they are known to the police. An increasing number of crimes reported could also lead to the paradoxical conclusion that the law is being better enforced.

Even if one granted the adequacy of specific crime rates, what are the criteria of a "crime wave" or of the amount of "real criminality"? In 1957, for example, there were 2,070,-794 arrests, of which 800,000 were for drunkenness and 200,-000 for disorderly conduct. But what do such figures mean? Thefts, assaults, and burglaries have increased in recent years, but murders and homicides have declined. The number of homicides, i.e., killings, the criminal act which attracts the most public attention, is lower today than it was twenty-five years ago. In 1930 there were 8.9 homicides per 100,000 population, and in 1955 there were 4.6. Assuming even that improved hospital and medical techniques have saved more people than before, the drop is almost 48 per cent. Kidnapping, the big bugaboo of the early thirties, has virtually disappeared. How does one weight these valences?

Even taking general "lawlessness"—the thefts of property (burglaries, auto thefts) and crimes against a person (robbery, assault, murder, rape)—the type of activity that we ordinarily associate with crime, and even allowing for statistical peculiarities, has crime been on the rise?

An overview tells us this much: in very small towns (from 2,500 to 10,000 persons), the crime picture, with the exception of homicide, grew darker from 1940 to 1953. But cities between 10,000 and 250,000 population showed decreases in crime. The greatest increases were registered in the largest cities; the enormous increase in the robbery rate, for example, took place almost entirely in cities with more than 250,000 persons, and yet in the cities there are amazing variations. In San Francisco there was no rise except for assaults. In Los Angeles all crime was rising. Portland and Seattle, despite a 21 per cent population growth, showed decreases. In Miami, crime jumped, with larceny and auto thefts leading the way. Cleveland and Chicago showed little change (except for the rise of auto thefts in the latter). In Detroit the rates were climbing. Omaha and Nebraska were down, with Nebraska showing a 50 per cent decline in five years (although authorities expressed skepticism regarding the validity of the figures). Boston, Birmingham, and Memphis showed little change. Houston and Dallas showed large rises; New Orleans, some slight increases, with auto thefts on the rise.

Analysts were hard put to find any meaningful causal explanation of the picture. Explaining rising auto thefts was easy: there were more cars around to be stolen; and 80 per cent of car thefts are committed by juveniles, often on impulse—and there are more youths now too; also, almost all such stolen vehicles are quickly recovered undamaged. But assault crimes rose rapidly—a sign to some of "increasing lawlessness"—yet murder and manslaughter were consistently down. Cities like Atlanta attributed the rise in crime merely to population increase. But a city like Los Angeles, where population since 1949 has risen 12 per cent, saw a 34 per cent increase in Class One crimes (burglary, robbery, etc.) And crimes in such towns as Dallas and Houston have outstripped population increase. The common explanation, such as the one offered by Los Angeles police chief William Parker, is that "some sort of moral degeneration has set in." He also thinks good times breed more crimes than bad times and that the increase of leisure explains the fact that more crimes are committed during leisure-hour periods (but how does this explain the fact that underprivileged Negro groups contribute most heavily to Los Angeles police statistics?).

Perhaps a more meaningful explanation of the rise in crime in Los Angeles—and in a few other places—lies in the nature of the population make-up. Los Angeles has a large transient population. It is a year-round resort town, attracting much money and undesirables in pursuit of it. The other cities with large increases, like Houston and Dallas, also have mushroomed, with large numbers of newcomers and transients. And a simpler explanation of these disparities may be that crime increases are also associated directly with the quality of police enforcement. Where there is a good police force, more arrests are made (and people feeling confident of help report more crimes such as minor burglaries or thefts), and initially there may be more "crime," since more is reported and recorded. But over a period of time, strict enforcement may mean a reduction of crime, since criminals will avoid the city.

But these explanations, while important, really tell us little about the sources and nature of crime; for this we have to turn to two factors which are usually ignored: the role of youths and that of minority groups, principally the Negroes.

Nearly half of all crimes, if we can judge by arrests, are committed by youths under twenty-five. Allowing for the important quibble that youths, being inexperienced, are caught more easily, 19.4 per cent of all robberies, 36.9 per cent of all larcencies, 47.8 per cent of all burglaries, and 52.6 per cent of all auto thefts were committed by the group under eighteen years of age. In 1953, of the 1,110,000 persons charged with crimes, 44 per cent were under twenty-five.

One way, thus, of explaining the fluctuations in crime in the last fifteen years may be related to the simple fact that during war years there was a *decline* in the rate of crime simply because millions of youths were tied down to army posts overseas, whereas in the postwar years, 1946-47, and in the post-Korean years, with millions of youths returning to civilian life, the crime market became more active. The second fact is that, with a rising and a shifting population, there will be more crime, and as the war crop of babies mature and the youth crop becomes a greater proportion of the population, crime will rise.

Beyond the question of youth is the problem of the large role of Negro violators. In Cleveland, more than three-fourths of all major crimes are committed by Negroes, who make up 16.2 per cent of the population. The greatest number of crimes in Chicago is committed in "Bronzeville," the narrow, choked Negro ghetto which runs like a dagger down the south side. In Atlanta, 75 per cent of felonious assaults are committed by Negroes, who make up one-third of the population. In Detroit, where Negroes constitute 17 per cent of the population, the number of Negroes arrested for armed robbery was two and a half times the white rate. In Philadelphia, Negroes, who make up one-fourth of the population, are responsible for two-thirds of the crimes. Similar pictures are reported in Boston and New Orleans.

One must take into account the fact that city police tend to be more strict with Negro offenders and more likely to look for a Negro as the criminal than a white. And, often when the issue is only one man's word against another's, the Negro is at a disadvantage.[41] But even making such allowances, the fact remains that, statistically and sociologically, proportionately more crimes are committed by Negroes than by whites.

In one sense, this is understandable. Crime of this sort represents a form of "unorganized class struggle."[42] And, in a rough sense, it follows the business cycle. Crime is a form of resentment, a desire for gain, an act of violence against a person who has more. These are lower-class crimes, and the Negro makes up the bulk of the lower class. There is nothing racial about this fact. At the turn of the century, the majority of such crimes were committed predominantly by the Irish, later by the Italians, then by the Slavs. Today it is the Negro and to a lesser extent the Puerto Rican who, in marginal position, play this role. In this pattern of group succession, Minneapolis in 1954 was having Indian troubles. As the government began withdrawing from Indian reservations, more and more Indians began streaming into the cities, and drunkenness and assaults began to rise. Although the Indians were only 0.9 per cent of the population of Minneapolis, Indians constituted better than 10 per cent of the inmates at the men's workhouse and 69 per cent of the women's.

Whatever general theory one adduces—moral character or class character—explanations of the variations in crime rates are meaningful if related to the fluctuations in specific crimes and to changes in population. The fact is that the time span of the statistics we have is less than twenty-five years (before 1930, there were no uniform crime reports), and even the data that we have, as has been argued above, is not wholly reliable. For this reason alone, unfortunately, one moralist's guess is as good as any sociologist's.

The Rumble of Youth

If the pattern of crime rates is not too clear, the situation regarding juvenile delinquency is little better. Less is known about the amount of delinquency than is known about adult crime. In "adult crimes," rates are based on "crimes known to the police," that is, on those reported by a complainant. But with juveniles, "arrest" figures must be used, since delinquents must be caught before it can be said in fact that they are juveniles. But the use of arrest figures creates a number of problems. As Professor Sellin puts it, "The police are likelier to arrest juveniles merely on suspicion, to hold them for questioning, than to arrest adults. Also the number of juvenile arrests in any given year includes *repeated* arrests of the same individual—a known member of a juvenile gang may be picked up a dozen times, adding twelve arrests to the total."

This is one reason, for example, why the figure cited at the start of this chapter from the California Youth Authority, that one out of every four of the seventeen-year-old youths in California was "arrested" in 1957, is meaningless. Worse, every time an officer in California stops a teen-ager and takes his name the Bureau of Criminal Statistics in California counts it an arrest. One reason, perhaps, why the California Youth Authority released its reckless statistic is that it hoped,

produce race hatred impair the ethical development of children."

This point of view has been argued most forcefully by the psychiatrist Fredric Wertham in his book *Seduction of the Innocent.* Citing the undeniably gory content of comic books,* Wertham concludes that anybody "who has had much experience with juvenile delinquency in the past ten years knows that brutality in children's play and violence in their delinquent acts have greatly increased."

Considering the fact that ninety million comic books are printed a year, that, in 1954, 95 per cent of the children in the six to eleven age group read about fifteen comic books a month, and that eight of ten children in the older group of twelve to eighteen [43] read about a dozen a month, the judgments, if true, would be cause for grave alarm.

But the judgment is debatable. As Dr. Marie Jahoda of New York University, in a study for the American Book Publishers Council, points out, there is no adequate evidence on the impact of literature to support the theory. Reading itself does not lead to "acting out" one's impulses; more often the comics may simply lead a child to escape from reality and to deaden his feelings about the brutality in the world.

Certainly, however, such things as comic books or horror movies are not causal agents of delinquency; at worst they may trigger some latent impulses. Some other factors are at work. The most exhaustive attempt to uncover the differences between persistent juvenile delinquents and children who never had any conflict with the law is the volume *Unraveling Juvenile Delinquency,* by Sheldon and Eleanor Glueck of the Harvard Law School. The Gluecks "matched" 500 delinquents and 500 "non-delinquents" on the basis of age, intelligence, national origin, school level, etc. The two groups were then given anthropometric (physique and growth) tests, intelligence tests, Rorschach, and psychiatric interviews.

The Gluecks held constant a number of items which sociologists have stressed, such as culture conflict (e.g., immigrant background and different cultural values), large families, ill health, difference in parents' ages, domination of family by mother, overcompetitiveness, and living in a slum area,

* Some front covers: a motor car drags two persons to their death while a gloating face above exults that no one will be able to "identify the meat" after the faces are "erased." In other pictures, a woman is having her eye put out with a needle, a nailed boot smashes in the face of a man, a girl is about to be raped with a red-hot poker.

in order to uncover psychological and temperamental factors. They did find that delinquents came from homes where there is little stability in affection and where parents cannot serve as effective models, that, intellectually, delinquents express themselves in a direct and concrete manner and are less adept at using symbols and abstraction, and that, temperamentally, delinquents are restless, energetic, destructive—factors which the Gluecks say may be related to erratic growth or to biologic maturation patterns. The emphasis on a constitutional or body type is one that sociologists hitherto have slighted. For a variety of reasons, sociologists have preferred to stress environmental factors. In part this is due to the "natural" search for group factors, in part because of "liberal" political bias, since constitutional or hereditary factors, emphasizing the unchanging, have usually been associated with political conservatism.

Using the constitutional types defined by Sheldon (the ectomorph or thin, the endomorph or fat, and the mesomorph or muscular), the Gluecks note the striking incidence of mesomorphic (muscular, solid) dominance in body structure of delinquents, whereas the non-delinquents tend to ectomorphic (linear, thin) dominance. Among the delinquents, they noted delayed growth spurts, and speculate about the possibility that the piling-on of physiological tensions leads to the assertive, impulsive manner. Delinquency, they note, increases steadily from ten to nineteen, remains constant until twenty-seven and twenty-eight, and then declines; this, they speculate, may be associated with "delayed general maturation" and the tendency to abandon criminal behavior with increasing maturity.

None of these factors by themselves "create" delinquency. These are all *predispositional* tendencies which find outlet in the environment. If one looks at many of the factors associated with the delinquent—the high mesomorphic content, the strong aggressive drives, the preference for the direct and concrete rather than the abstract and symbolic—one could almost say that this is the drive-image of the businessman. The question, thus, is how the drive is channeled. And here the psychological element (the way in which the parental image is internalized) and the sociological element (the norms and values of the sub-culture group of the child) become important.

The Gluecks have worked out a prediction technique for spotting future delinquents which is now being tested in New York over a long-range period: a five-factor test—discipline of a boy by the father, supervision by the mother, affection of the father for the boy, affection of the mother, and cohesiveness of family—which has been given to several hundred first-graders in two Bronx schools. A boy who is going to get into trouble begins, usually, the Gluecks have found, at the age of eight. Where a child is rated as having a 50 per cent chance of becoming delinquent, an attempt is made to obtain psychiatric treatment for the child and the family. The experiment will continue three to four years.

Controlled Crime

Whatever the proximate or long-run sociological causes of crime may be, the degree of "lawlessness" in a city, is, first of all, a function of the quality of law enforcement and of the police force itself. And, in 1954, at least, when this survey was made, it might seem that a crime wave, if one existed, was not among the criminals but the police themselves. Some random examples:

In New Orleans, the superintendent of police and the chief of detectives were indicted for malfeasance in their inept handling of the case of two officers accused of burglarizing a drug store. A dozen or more police were under indictment for perjury about their "outside" income, and a grand jury came to the "inescapable conclusion" in March, 1954, that "there is a lack of enforcement of the laws of the city of New Orleans."

In Miami Beach, the chief of police was dismissed for laxness: two officers investigating a robbery were caught stealing, while a detective was arrested for sending two bandits to rob a hotel, after warning the hotel clerk, an ex-convict, not to resist a holdup.

In Detroit, eighteen policemen were under indictment for bribery.

In Chicago, Captain Redmond Gibbons, the chief of the uniformed police (who had reorganized the Berlin police after the war) was suspended when the *Sun-Times* published a "little red book," reputedly in his handwriting, which listed a number of taverns and bars which were making weekly payments for protection.

In Birmingham, police discovered a series of thefts organized by a ring of police over a two-to-three-year period.

New York had a continuing series of police scandals from the disclosures that Brooklyn bookmaker Harry Gross was paying $1,000,000 a year in protection to policemen and that these payments were made in descending scale from captain to patrolman. The situation was so bad that the Brooklyn Grand Jury in 1951 asked the commissioner to discharge all police officers who had been division commanders in the previous ten years, because they had protected bookmakers. (In 1959, New York had another police scandal involving protection of bookmakers.)

Whether the proportion of police involved in corrupt practices is higher or lower than in some other institutions, be they corporations or labor unions, is difficult to tell. In New York it is estimated that no more than 5 per cent of the 18,000 policemen received *regular* protection payments; but these included 400 key supervisors and plain-clothesmen. In this context two things need to be noted: the most serious instances of corruption are to be found, usually, among the undercover squads, who are charged with suppressing gambling, vice, narcotics, and similar chores that require sleuthing; and second, that such laxity inevitably affects the morale of the rest of the force.

Some city police departments, either out of cynicism or inertia, accept the theory of "controlled crime." A certain amount of vice, gambling, etc., is tolerated on the theory that the effort to clamp down tightly would be more costly and would produce more crime and police corruption. Many large cities adopt the theory of keeping the center of the metropolis free and of "dumping" gambling and vice onto the "satellite" towns. Thus Cincinnati, for years, was a tight town, but Newport, Kentucky, across the river was wide open.

Central to the problem of an efficient—let alone, honest—force is that the police are usually loath to bring charges against or to discipline recalcitrant officers. In many cases, political pressure protects the man. "The personnel records of New York police," wrote Bruce Smith, "are replete with examples of the reinstatement and repeated reinstatement of police offenders who have spent a considerable portion of their official lives under suspension. . . . Even though the actual number . . . may not be large in a given city, it is difficult to overestimate the damage to police morale and discipline which accompanies this practice." In an examination of police discipline cases in New York over a twenty-year period, Smith found that 88 per cent of those charged were found guilty, but only 55 per cent of these officers were fined and a mere 2 per cent removed from the force either by dismissal or resignation.

If morale and discipline represent one end of a long continuum of police problems, the establishment of precise lines of relationship between the multifarious levels of police operation is the other. In no other country in the world has local autonomy been carried to such extreme lengths. Almost every local government maintains its own police force, and the relationships between village constable, town police, country sheriff, city police, state patrol, and federal agents (and within the federal government, of immigration and border control, customs patrol, treasury men, narcotics, secret service, postal inspectors, and the FBI) amount to complexity, confusion, and destructive rivalries.

Such duplications and overlaps reflect, of course, the multiple layers of government and, for that reason alone, flourish. Setting aside even the question of higher costs and taxes which result from the duplications of local government, such rivalries simply encourage a competing system of "protection" which allows racketeers to thumb their noses at the law. The growth in the previous decade of "satellite cities" was due to the fact that "protection" was obtained more easily from county sheriffs and local police who were more open to political pressure and to money than the big-city police.

The expansion of "bedroom cities," prompted largely by the rapid growth of suburbs, poses new problems. Boston, proper, for example, has 800,000 residents, but 55 per cent of the population of Massachusetts, or about 2,500,000 persons, live within a twenty-mile radius of the city, and a goodly portion of these come daily into the city, creating not only the usual traffic problems but, in many instances, crime problems as well. About one-third of all persons arrested in Boston for crimes are non-residents, a proportion undoubtedly higher than any other city in the country because of the packed density of the area. The distribution of the tax load, the overlapping of city, county, and town police, all create incredible problems of management.

In many large cities, police organization, archaic and hobbled by tradition, has failed to adopt simple organizational principles common to efficient business. It usually has multiplied particular services and increased specializations in order to keep abreast of new problems, rather than overhaul the force. In New York, for example, as Smith pointed out in his management survey, the "police structure has adhered closely to an arms-and-services plan of organization with no real aid from the general staff principle."

While decentralization has gone to extreme lengths, few

observers would recommend a national police force, although, it should be noted, when the FBI took over the basic responsibility for kidnapping, the crime virtually disappeared. But no national police, as J. Edgar Hoover would be the first to point out, could cope with the multifarious problems raised by the tens of thousands of communities, nor could a highly bureaucratized national police cope with the hundred thousand problems raised by local conditions. Yet some rethinking of police organization on metropolitan and regional lines is necessary; by itself, it cannot be done; it is part and parcel of the rethinking of the political-administrative structure of the states themselves.

The Decline in the Rackets

Thus far, we have been discussing crime as an "unorganized" form of illegal gain. Assault, burglaries, thefts, and the like are usually "freelance" affairs, committed sporadically by individuals or intermittent gangs. But the "big money" in crime—as it has colored American life—has been the attempt to *regularize* gain by organizing a service for the illicit and forbidden desires of the public: prostitution, bootlegging, gambling, and even industrial racketeering. This is crime as an "American Way of Life." What has happened to it?

Forty to fifty years ago, commercialized vice was the major source both of illicit wealth and the corruption of the police. Gaudy houses of ill repute could be found in New York's famed Tenderloin and in the transient belt around the Chicago Loop. The famous exposés in the twentieth century, from Rev. Parkhurst's tour through the vice dens of New York to Tom Dewey's prosecution of Lucky Luciano, the vice-lord of New York, were of prostitution.

Today, there are few major cities in the United States with regularly operating houses of prostitution. San Francisco's famed Barbary Coast is shut down. In 1938, according to police estimates, about 1,600 prostitutes were employed. As late as 1950 a number of establishments were operating openly in San Francisco. But the California Crime Commission published the details, and the lid went down.

The decline in organized prostitution can be ascribed to many causes. Houses of prostitution have to move regularly to avoid exposure, and during the war, because of the housing shortage, it became more difficult to maintain established houses. Revulsion at vice protection particularly after the disclosures in the Luciano trial of the savage exploitation of the girls, made it more difficult for operators to buy police protection. And, simply as a business proposition, the returns, relative to the risks and the money-making possibilities in gambling and other rackets, made vice unattractive to the racketeers.

For a while, vice, driven out of the metropolitan centers, flourished in "satellite cities," where police protection was easier. Cincinnati had Newport and Covington across the river, Chicago had Calumet City to the south, Detroit had Mt. Clemens, St. Louis the roadhouses near Fairmount track across the river. Few of these spots operate today. Many, like Mt. Clemens and the Miami areas, were cleaned up during the war. Newport and the New Orleans parishes shut down after the Kefauver investigations. Phoenix City, Alabama, was shut down by state troopers. Chicago, until recently, according to County Judge Gutknecht, had seventy-eight spots outside the city proper where vice and gambling still flourished, but the election of a new sheriff, Joseph Lohman, a sociologist formerly at the University of Chicago, led to their shutdown.

The changes in moral temper permit freer sexual relations between young people; and the lowering of the marriage age has reduced the demand for commercialized sex. But prostitution has not been completely erased. In many cities "call-houses" operate where a customer, with references, can find a companion. Bars in big cities have "B girls" who solicit drinks from customers. Sleazy motels today serve as houses. In some areas in the Northwest, near the large federal dam and construction projects, some commercial prostitution, operating with trailers, can be found. *But*—as an *organized* business, functioning as a chain operation across the country, with police protection, prostitution has disappeared from American life.

Gambling, which in the forties was the major source of illegal revenue, has declined considerably. Years ago nearly every luxury hotel along the five-mile strip of ocean front at Miami Beach was equipped with a public-address system over which horse-race results blared out so loudly they could be heard in the streets. Tourists in bathing suits would sit around the pools and hand bets to waiters who brought them drinks. If they wanted to gamble, limousines took them to a number of lavishly appointed casinos. A "city hall bookie" regularly covered the municipal offices at Miami Beach. In neighboring Miami, bookmaking was wide open, on street corners, in pool rooms, cigar stands, and in bookie parlors. Today the entire area is shut down tight, the loudspeakers are silent; whatever gambling takes place is behind shuttered doors.

New Orleans, which ranked with Miami as a glittering hot spot, particularly after Huey Long gave the slot-machine and gambling "concessions" to Frank Costello, is even more drab. The Costello-Kastel Beverly Club, a night spot which ranked with any in the country in the brilliance of its shows and the size of its gambling stakes, was darkened in 1951. Where ten years ago you could walk the length of downtown streets and never get out of the hearing of loud-speakers announcing race-horse results, bookmaking is pretty much a small-time business. Nor can one, as one did before, easily find a slot machine in New Orleans or in the neighboring Jefferson and St. Bernard parishes.

In New York, where Brooklyn bookie Harry Gross at one time paid $1,000,000 a year to the police in protection money, and where Frank Erickson ran the biggest lay-off book in the country, a would-be bettor can still find a furtive bookie, but the big regular horse players have to call Montreal, where the large books have found refuge.

Gambling flourished during the war because, in part, hot and black-market money needed a convenient outlet, but more generally it was a substitute excitement for travel. The shift in "consumer" habits has been one force for change. Federal action, following the Kefauver investigation, has also been a factor. In 1952 Congress passed an act forcing gamblers to register and to declare their earnings. With federal agents in the picture, local protection became insufficient. Federal agents began making book-making raids without notifying the local police department. This disrupted the warning system that was the key to protection. Where bookmaking still exists, it is local, small scale, and run by independents.

The Moral Lapses of Labor

The McClellan Committee hearings of 1957-58 revealed an extraordinary range of malfeasance in the labor movement. But a necessary distinction should be kept clear. The pattern that was revealed was *not*—with the exception of the Teamsters and sections of the restaurant workers—of racketeering, but of corruption. In dozens of unions, labor leaders had treated the union as their own property, squandering money for personal use or spending union funds to aid personal investments of their friends or themselves. But if the picture is compared to that of twenty-five to thirty years ago, the amount of industrial racketeering has declined. At one time, mobs dominated the men's and women's clothing industry, cleaning and dyeing trades, the produce markets, and the food industry. A George Browne and Willie Bioff ran the theatrical and Hollywood unions and shook down the studio moguls regularly: Joey Fay dominated construction in the East. George Scalise controlled the Building Service union. The influx into labor came when racketeers, who had been driven, following Prohibition, to search for new sources of revenue, found an entry into the union field. But an important point has to be noted: racketeers were able to enter only into small, unit-sized industries where chaotic competition prevailed. Because no single firm or group of firms could organize or rationalize the industry, the racketeer could enter.

The greatest potential for racketeering is in the Teamsters union, because of its strategic position in controlling deliveries and because of its decentralized control, which allowed individuals to carve out petty dominions. In the Teamsters, the line between stabilization and racketeering is sometimes a thin one. This is best seen in the vending-machine and jukebox industry. In Cleveland, for example, the industry is controlled by the Phonograph Merchants Association and by the Vending Machine Services Employees, Local 410 of the Teamsters. An individual running a one-man business, i.e., leasing a number of jukeboxes, obtaining concessions, and servicing the machines himself, has to join both the association and the union and pay dues to both. Jukebox wholesalers and distributors must sell or lease their wares only to members of the association or be boycotted by the union. In effect, this is a monopoly, run by the union. The union is headed by William Presser, who managed the employer association in 1949 and 1950; in 1951 he became the union president. Presser, a power in the area, is president of the Teamsters District Council of Cleveland and of the Ohio Teamsters Council.

Curiously, with the "rationalization" of the trucking industry under Beck and Hoffa, racketeering is driven to the fringes of the industry. Under the rationalization process, agreements are no longer local, but are made uniform over an eleven- or twelve-state area, thus stabilizing the costs to the employer and his competitors. The "fringes" can be quite lucrative. In one state, for example, every jukebox in a saloon or store has to carry a sticker marked *Teamster* serviced, which is sold to the owner for fifty cents a month. In this area, there are 10,000 machines, or a private income for two Teamster business agents of $5,000 a month, plus their salaries and expenses. When a political machine is built on supporters who have such an easy investment to protect, it is not easy to dislodge the small racketeer.

In some areas, what was once considered racketeering has become institutionalized. This is notably true in the building trades, where often a regular scale of gratuities is paid to the business agent in return for services, in effect, as a "straw boss" for the contractor. A similar accommodation has existed on the waterfront, where the loading racket was accepted as a fact of life and the costs passed on to the public.

More importantly, many old-line racketeers, having started in "business" thirty years ago or more, naturally want to settle down and avoid the more hazardous elements of life (from beatings to murders). These individuals have often invested in "legitimate" businesses which receive special protection or concessions from unions. This has been the case in the garment industry, trucking, breweries, coin-vending, and restaurants. Here the line between the legal and illegal is no longer the question, but only that of the moral and immoral.

What is of serious concern, however, is not so much racketeering as the sharp decline of moral tone in the labor movement and the rise of corruption. This takes many forms. A surprising number of union leaders operate businesses on the side. These are legal enterprises but it is hard to draw the ethical line. The boss of an AFL meatcutters' local ran a well-known steakhouse in New York. A Midwest UAW-CIO official ran a sporting-goods store, which sold equipment to companies (who were under contract to the union) for plant teams. The wives of Hoffa and Brennan, two prominent Teamsters-union officials, received $60,000 in dividends from a dummy trucking corporation set up by a large trucker. A number of labor leaders own shares in a printing company which publishes a "labor paper" that solicits ads, in a heavy "boiler-room operation" from employers all over the country. The harness-racing scandals disclosed that several labor leaders were on track payrolls as labor advisers. And the welfare-fund disclosures showed how hundreds of union officials have taken lush salaries or siphoned off commission money from trust funds.

What such behavior shows is that the labor leader has

sometimes become the parvenu and behaves like one. The union leader is one of the last "self-made" men in America. Few heads of unions have come in from "the outside" as lawyers or experts. Almost all came up from below and, in many a union, in a political rough-and-tumble as fierce as any Jersey ward. These men are often in industries where corners are cut and a "fast buck" is made, and the prevailing cynicism encourages a similar attitude on the part of the union leader.

If racketeering continues, it is because the customer wants a service or because a powerful few gain by the collusion. At root a racketeer can only exist by political protection, whether it be the protection of a union charter or the protection of a political boss. When gambler Joe Adonis and his associate, Willie Moretti, were driven out of New York by Fiorello LaGuardia, they moved across the river to Jersey. A special inquiry in 1953 showed that Moretti had paid $286,000 to an aide of Governor Driscoll for "protection," while Joseph Bozzo, an associate of Longy Zwillman,* had "loaned" the Republican state committee $25,000. Only when this protection is withdrawn can a racket be smashed.

Americans, characteristically, have approached the question of rackets moralistically, and reform movements have threaded their way through political life with rhythmic regularity. But rackets are a form of "marginal business" satisfying certain needs of a society; and as a marginal business it has been performed, as pariah occupations usually are, by marginal groups in the society; hence the high incidence of foreign-born and second-generation Americans among the racketeers.

Illicit desires may always exist, but the definition of what is licit or illicit changes with the moral temper and practices of a society. The problem of crime does not rest upon the truisms about human nature, but on the way the methods of securing gain are *organized.*

The Show of Violence

If the evidence, inconclusive as it is, shows that there is less crime today than at previous periods in United States history, the final problem is to account for the *feeling* that life

* Zwillman, a prohibition bootlegger who became a "respectable" businessman dominating the vending-machine business in New Jersey, committed suicide on February 26, 1959, while under federal indictment for income tax evasion.

today is more *violent* than ever before. The standard cliché of the moralist is that modern life, because it breaks the tenets of community and because its pace is more rapid, creates more tensions, induces greater brutality and sadism, heightens the stress of living, and produces more crack-ups.

One finds it hard to create indices which allow us to look at life a hundred or fifty years ago and to match conditions with those of today. A recent Rand study by Goldhamer and Marshall, *Psychoses and Civilization,* comes up with the startling conclusion that the amount of insanity a hundred years ago was the same as today. Admission rates to Massachusetts hospitals in the 1840's were compared with the present. (Detailed descriptions of the disorders labeled "mania," "melancholia," "monomania of suspicion," indicated that they were similar to modern-day manic-depressive and schizophrenic psychoses, so that equivalences could be made.) By establishing age comparisons, the authors point out that the rates of hospital admissions for mental disease, up to the age of fifty, were generally the same, then as now. The chief difference regarding the over-fifty group is that, a hundred years ago, senile individuals were cared for in the family rather than in mental institutions as at present. In other words, the talk about tensions, mental health, etc., reflects not an increase in insanity but an increasing *concern* about it.

The problem of violence is a different one. While there is a greater "show" of violence—in literature, in movies, plays, etc. (and there is, as one of the sickening aspects of twentieth-century life, a "bureaucratization of violence"—in concentration camps, war, etc.) in the *personal lives* of Americans, in the day-to-day routines of the city, there is *less* violence than a hundred or fifty or even twenty-five years ago. One has only to go, say, to the contemporary accounts of life in New York and San Francisco to verify this conclusion.

A "stone's throw" from Broadway, in the 1850's in New York, was the Five Points, the most notorious place in the city. "Policemen entered the Five Points only in pairs, and never unarmed. Respectable New Yorkers avoided the district in daylight. . . . It was the haunt of murderers, thieves, prostitutes and receivers of stolen goods." The ruler of the Five Points was a "Captain" Isaiah Nynders, who, mobilizing a large gang of thugs, terrorized the polling places during elections and put in as Mayor, Fernando Wood, who gave Nynders legal immunity for the operation of dives, gambling establishments, and the like.

George Templeton Strong, a prominent New York lawyer, whose diaries, kept from 1835 to 1875, comprise one of the great sourcebooks for nineteenth-century social history, records in his diary for 1869: "February 12 . . . Crimes of violence—burglaries, highways, robberies and murders—have been of late many and audacious beyond example . . . tonight's *Post* speaks of 'secret meetings of respectable citizens' and of Vigilance Committees already organized and ready for action in *this* ward and in another. We want a *Vehmgesicht** badly, but even in the best hands it would be a fearful experiment . . ."

And a year later, Strong indignantly records an incident: "January 25, Tuesday. At half-past ten last evening [Franklin Huges] Delano, wending his way home from a dinner at John Astor's was set upon and robbed by three men on the corner of Fifth Avenue and Eleventh St. Of course there was no arrest. Crime was never so bold, so frequent, so safe as it is this winter. Few criminals are caught, and fewer punished. Municipal law is a failure in New York, and we must soon fall back on the law of self-preservation."

Across the country in San Francisco, the accounts were equally sharp. The *Herald* in 1855 complained: "There are certain spots in our city infested by the most abandoned men and women. . . . The upper part of Pacific Street after dark is crowded by thieves, gamblers, low women, drunken sailors," who thronged the thousand saloons and gambling dives of the Barbary Coast. The *Annals* of San Francisco, a compilation of contemporary records of the 1860's, reports that in the downtown wharf sections "no decent man was in safety to walk the street after dark; while at all hours, both night and day, his property was jeopardized by incendiarism and burglary." From 1860 to 1880, there was not one night along the Barbary Coast without at least one murder and innumerable robberies. The "fame" of the Barbary Coast and of its bagnios and "cribs" spread far and wide, and for sixty years, until the clean-up of the city just before World War I, commercialized prostitution and crime enjoyed a quasi-lawful status.

The protection of prostitution, as well as the links with corrupt politicians and police, was one of the chief features of crime for over seventy-five years and the great source of

* The *Vehme,* were secret German courts of the sixteenth century, which organized "people's justice" on malfactors—these were a model for vigilante committees.

street violence in the urban centers. In New York, as the countless reform probes showed, Tammany Hall, the police, and the underworld were in open alliance. Tammany used the mobs to rule the polls, and the underworld got protection from the police. Around 1910 in New York, the two most famous mobs were run by Monk Eastman and Paul Kelly, whose real name was Paul Vaccarelli. Kelly's gang was said to number fifteen hundred members; Eastman's roster was put at twelve hundred. When the two mobs had a falling-out, so relentless was the feud conducted that, one night, after two years of prolonged guerrilla warfare, a pitched battle was fought on Second Avenue and Rivington Street, in which a hundred gangsters were engaged.

However fierce the juvenile gang wars in East Harlem, the intermittent slashings in Bronzeville, or the rumbles along North Beach, it is clear that the score of violence today in no way approaches the open, naked brawling of even thirty or forty years ago.

The assertion that modern life is more violent in its personal dimensions may be largely a literary creation. In a famous essay, which became widely discussed in literary magazines, George Orwell pointed out that the standard character in crime fiction had shifted from Raffles, the gentleman thief, to the sadistic gangster like Popeye in Faulkner's *Sanctuary* or to the thugs in James Hadly Chase's *No Orchids for Miss Blandish.* Orwell felt that this change in fiction reflected a change in society. But was this not, rather, a shift in the historical reality, or, in a sense, "the democratization" of literature? Perhaps it was not that society had changed but that literature had caught up with life.

A hundred and fifty years ago, the lines between classes were delineated socially and ecologically. The "nostalgic" memories of oldsters for quiet, tree-shaded sections of the city are not so much distorted in time as in space. Because the city was marked off by neighborhoods, crime and quiet could coexist, without each section, or class, being immediately aware of each other.

The mores and styles of life of the classes contrasted vividly. Violence was primarily a lower-class phenomenon, restricted generally as in the London of Defoe or in the New York of George Templeton Strong, to the geographical boundaries of lower-class life.

In the last forty years or so, there has been the blurring, culturally and ecologically, of class lines. And in this blurring,

I make a necessary distinction between corruption and industrial racketeering. Corruption involves spoliation of union funds, payoffs, bribes, shakedowns, etc. It is a form of abuse of office or extortion from others for the personal gain of the malefactor. If the cost is not too high, or can be passed along easily to others as in the building trades, it becomes an accepted part of the way of doing business; if too exorbitant it may lead to a demand for government intervention. Industrial racketeering, however, performs the function—at a high price—which other agencies cannot do, of stabilizing a chaotic market and establishing an order and structure in the industry. Industrial racketeering can exist only in a specific type of economic market. It does not exist in steel, auto, chemical, rubber, etc., where a few giant firms, acting in oligopolistic fashion, establish an ordered price structure in the industry. It has existed in small-unit size, highly competitive, local-product markets, such as trucking, garment, baking, cleaning, and dyeing, where no single force other than the industrial racketeer was strong enough to stabilize the industry. This was especially true in the 1920's when industrial racketeering flourished. In the early 1930's, legalized price-fixing by the New Deal, through the NRA, undercut the role of the industrial rackketeer. What hitherto had been a quasi-economic but necessary function now became outright and unnecessary extortion. And in the garment area (dominated by Lepke and Gurrah), in the restaurant field, and in similar industries infested with industrial racketeers, the employers and the union appealed to government for help. And that is how Tom Dewey, as district attorney of New York County in the mid-thirties, first came into prominence as a prosecutor. Following the demise of the NRA, the trade-unions in most of these fields were strong enough to take over the role of stabilizing and policing the industry. On the New York waterfront, the racket pattern continued. Why?

It is the thesis of this paper that the distinctive economic matrix of the port shaped a pattern of accommodation between the shippers and the racketeers and led to the continuation of the system. Without these economic requirements, the system would go under. In our fascination these days with power and manipulation, we often ignore the economic fulcrum underneath. The political intervention of the state and federal agencies and the AFL, in the New York waterfront situation in 1953 and after, was based on the belief that by changing the power relations in the longshore union the conditions which gave rise to racketeering might be eliminated. Certainly this was the justification for the extraordinary intervention by the Eisenhower and Dewey administrations in the waterfront strikes in 1955 and 1956, although the Republicans had previously proclaimed that government should keep its hands out of any labor dispute. The political effort failed. Yet if it had succeeded, it is doubtful whether the pattern of racketeering would have been upset, for without the re-shaping and rationalization of the "technological" environment (using the word in its broadest sense to cover ecological, mechanized handling techniques, and economic aspect of operations), the conditions which gave rise to racketeering would persist. And that is what this paper seeks to show. If what follows, then, is in great measure history, it is history written through sociological perspectives: to explain how racketeering became an integral part of a union and to demonstrate the role of a particular type of market in shaping a set of complex social relations.

The Economic Fulcrum

It is a schoolboy's maxim that New York owes its commanding position as the largest city in the United States to its magnificent port. In the growing commerce of the country, no other city could match its assets: wide and deep channels and ice-free and rarely foggy waters allowed great freighters to sail a few miles inland into a set of vast natural harbors, into protected estuaries curving into the bays, and into long, navigable rivers, which offered numerous and accessible wharfs. It was thus inevitable that shipping would come to New York. The frequency of sailings, the availability of cargo space, the many converging railroad trunk lines, and the ready banking facilities soon made the port attractive both to factors who wanted to move goods from inland to Europe and to importers bringing goods from abroad for sale in the United States. Because of the heavy commerce, the nation's banks made it a practice to keep large reserve deposits on hand, and this accumulation of liquid capital made New York the security trading center of the country. By the turn of the century, New York had become the greatest concentration point of economic and social power in the United States. The spatial counterpoint of downtown financial skyscraper and squat West Side bulkhead became the topographical symbol of this reciprocal genuflection of finance and commerce.

Although the New York harbor curves in a sinuous perimeter of seven hundred miles, the hub of the port is the four to five miles of piers and landings along the west side of Manhattan. Here the ocean-going vessels dock. Here the tremendous amount of cargo and produce which is consumed in the city or shipped inland, and the cargo sent from the industrial East for export abroad, are loaded and unloaded. But Manhattan is an island, and its handicaps are unique. Although much of the general cargo tonnage is handled on narrow Manhattan, the island does not have a single steamship pier with direct track connection to a trunkline railroad. Rail freight has to be delivered to or taken from the ships either by lighters which float across the harbor or by truck. But the width of the slips between piers is insufficient both for the berthing of ocean-going freighters and for the squat lighters which hover alongside the ships to unload or deliver the bulk cargo. Hence, serious congestion and delay create costly shifting expenses. And the narrowness of the piers themselves work havoc on the dock for the trucks. Only a few of New York's piers can accommodate the forty-foot mammoth trucks which carry cargo, so that, for the most part, freight must be handled in the choked marginal streets outside the piers. Congestion is so fierce and waiting-time so high that the large motor carriers publish penalty rates for deliveries to steamship piers within the metropolitan area.

As a result of these antiquated facilities, shore-handling costs, which once were a minor factor in the operation of a boat, in most instances began to exceed the combined costs of vessel depreciation, crew's wages, insurance, supplies, overhead, maintenance, and fuel oil. The biggest single shore expense became longshoring, which accounted for 50 per cent of the ship's total expense in moving cargo. If a shipping company was to have a profitable run, it needed a quick "turn-around," i.e., speedy unloading and loading, and a quick getaway. And for this, it needed a ready and compliant labor force.

THE SHAPE OF THE LABOR SUPPLY

Shipping, by custom, is a "casual" operation. The industry itself is seasonal and cyclical, the volume of business subject to wars, to political blackouts of trade routes, etc. Individual schedules are subject to the vagaries of weather, port delays, the kind of bulk consignments, etc. The demand for labor fluctuates widely, depending upon the number of ships in port. To get a quick "turn-around" the steamship company wants an over-supply of labor which can be readily available, will work long and continuous hours a few feverish days in the week, and will wait patiently over the idle stretches until the next ship comes.

Because their needs are irregular, most of the shipping companies do not hire longshoremen directly, but contract with stevedoring concerns on a tonnage basis for the loading and unloading of their ships. Approximately sixty such stevedoring concerns hire all dock labor, and they, together with the shipping lines, constitute the New York Shipping Association, which negotiates with the union on wages and working conditions.

Historically, the way of maintaining the necessary oversupply was an "open shape," i.e., encouraging all kinds of transients to congregate at the dock and picking the men on a gypsy basis. For a cab driver, an idle teamster—and even a city fireman or policeman off duty!—the system was an easy way to pick up a few extra dollars, particularly on weekends or evenings, when overtime rates prevailed. Thousands of such workers put in small and irregular amount of time on the docks. But for the thousands of workers who sought regular livelihood the conditions of an open shape, and the favoritism it encouraged, were intolerable.

Prior to World War II, all hiring was done by open shape. Twice a day, at 7:55 A.M. and at 1 P.M. (and, when necessary, a third time in the evening), the men "shaped up" in loose semicircle in front of the pier and were picked for a half-day's work by the hiring or "shaping boss." No formal system existed for informing the men where they might be needed from day to day. Some men got the information from bulletin boards on piers, some through gossip, some followed newspapers and trade papers. If a man was not hired at the 7:55 A.M. shape, he had little chance of working during the rest of the day. And not knowing where else in the Port there might be work, he squatted on his pier; even if he did go to some other pier, the chances were that he would be late or that some other transient had gotten the nod. In the absence of any information, men congregated at the piers where they had obtained work in the past. Each pier or group of piers, thus, tended to build up its own labor force. Some longshore locals, such as Local 968, an all-Negro one, had no particular pier, since it had been crowded off its Brooklyn docks by an Italian local, and its members roamed the city or sought to set up their own "labor exchange" in Harlem.

In April, 1942, Rear Admiral Land, then head of the War Shipping Administration, bitterly criticized the shape-up as inefficient and chaotic. Because of the manpower shortage, and for reasons of security, the open shape, i.e., picking a group at random, was modified by the creation of steady or regular gangs who remained intact and had first crack at jobs on the gang's regular pier. (After the war, the regular-gang system remained on most Hudson River docks. The others, along the East River and Brooklyn, reverted to open shapes or to the use of traveling gangs.)

The system of regular gangs did allow new solidarities to form. And it is significant that strikes erupted on the New York waterfront after the war—there were none in the twenties and thirties and during the war—only when some form of regularized employment had arisen.

The shape-up obviously gave the shipping companies the floating labor force they needed. In 1946, the peak postwar year, a total of 60,000 longshoremen were employed on the piers. In 1950, because of the decline of shipping, this had fallen to 40,000. This was the total labor supply—regular workers and transients. Actually, the "full-time" longshore force was between 16,000 to 20,000 men; the rest were floaters. Of the regular group, only between 5 to 8 per cent worked 2,000 hours a year (i.e., a regular forty-hour week for fifty weeks). Between 20 and 25 per cent worked between 1,200 to 2,000 hours a year. And the remaining 35 to 45 per cent worked from 700 to 1,200 hours a year. The simplest indicator of the low and unstable income status of a New York longshoreman is that banks and finance companies do not make personal loans to dockworkers, nor are longshoremen accepted, usually, as low-income tenants in public or private housing projects.

THE PADRONE AND THE PEONS

The system of the shape tended to emphasize the uncertainties and insecurities of the job. Under a brawny leader, pier cliques grew up to assure the pick of the jobs for themselves. Rackets multiplied. By possessing two social security cards a man could work a minimum number of hours on one card and then collect insurance while working regularly on the other. Or the surplus work cards were used to pad the payroll by adding a fictitious work gang to the roster, and the extra money was divided by the hiring boss, the payroll clerk, and the clique. This type of payroll padding, as well as loansharking and any number of other parasitic practices, was possible because of the "brass check,"* a system which had died out almost everywhere else at that time in U.S. industry. The worker collected his pay by turning in the brass check, but so could anyone else who had the check. Longshoremen who went broke before pay day, or needed money in a hurry to pay bills, sold their checks for a percentage of their value. The stevedoring companies blinked at the padding because the sums were petty beside the vaster benefits obtained by a pliant hiring boss who would drive the men for greater productivity.

The key man on the dock was the hiring or "shaping" boss. Although the hiring boss was, in fact, a foreman, and thus a management representative, all the hiring bosses were members of the International Longshoreman's Association, and their choice was dictated by the local union; in few cases could a steamship or stevedore company name a hiring boss. As a key patronage job, the choice fell to the union officer, who traded it to a friend.

It was quite common for the hiring bosses on many of the piers to possess criminal records. A cynical reason was supplied by an official of a large stevedoring concern: "If I have a choice of hiring a tough ex-convict or a man without a criminal record I am more inclined to take the ex-convict. Know why? Because if he is in a boss job he'll keep the men in line and get the maximum work out of them. They would be afraid of him."

THE WORLD OF THE I.L.A.

Why did the union tolerate these conditions? Stated more simply, why didn't the International Longshoremen's Association act like a union? The classic pattern of American unionism, its *raison d'être,* is *job control.* Job control means limiting the number of jobs, or the number of men seeking jobs, and a defined system of seniority, in order to assure equity and security in the title to the job. Few unions in the United States encourage cutthroat competition among men for jobs or tolerate a condition of job insecurity. The ILA did.

The answer was obvious long ago. Msgr. Swanstrom, a

* An old system of paying unskilled labor. A worker was given a brass check for each day worked, and these checks were turned in at the end of the week for cash. Thus bookkeeping was minimized and few records had to be kept. Since prostitutes were once also paid in this manner, the term, particularly among the Wobblies, became one of contempt and was used so by Upton Sinclair as the title of a book on the "kept" press.

Catholic priest who published a study in 1939 entitled "The Waterfront Labor Problem," wrote: "Merely as a statement of fact, [the union's] officers and delegates have a vested interest in keeping the membership at a high level." By encouraging a surplus of labor, the union accommodated the companies; by controlling the shape-up, the union leadership had an effective club over the men.

Actually, the International Longshoremen's Association has been less a trade union than a collection of Chinese warlords, each ruling a great or small province. In the New York region there are about seventy locals, some craft, others geographically based, whose memberships range from ten to fifteen hundred members each. Roughly thirty of these are longshore locals which normally have geographical jurisdiction over one or a small group of adjacent piers. In addition, the ILA also contains craft locals of carpenters, clerks, and checkers, and a large, miscellaneous collection of locals of lumberyard workers, warehousemen, oil handlers, lightermen, tugboat operators, grain-elevator workers, ship caulkers, captains of deck scows, and others with such fancy titles as "Steamship Horse and Cattle Fitters," "Grain Ceilers," "Marine Carpenters," "Sugar Samplers," "Grain Trimmers," "Boom Testing and Rigging Testing" workers, etc.

Within a local, the small membership and the "face-to-face" contact made it possible for small cliques to gain and "enforce" control. A tight machine of loyal followers was built up through the handing-out of regular jobs to a favored few. The rest of the membership was cowed by the discriminatory threats of loss of job. In the postwar years, when for the first time some records were kept, only seven locals, it was shown, held regular elections by secret ballot. The others voted openly, or not at all.

The violations of democracy were widespread not only in the locals but in the district regions as well. In the New York area, the longshore locals were grouped into a District Council which dealt with the problems of the longshoremen, checkers, cargo repairmen, maintenance men, etc. But the area itself was politically gerrymandered. By design, there were far too many longshore locals with a paper membership. Since all actions of any consequence had to be approved by the District Council, dissident locals were easily outvoted. On major strike issues, an archaic system of voting enabled the top officers to manipulate the results. When a poll was to be taken, the prevailing custom was to place ballot boxes in each of the union's locals from Maine to Virginia. The totals were telephoned to the offices of the International where they were tabulated, the results announced, and the letters confirming receipt of the totals forwarded to each local. In the 1951 strike vote, reported the New York State Inquiry board, "testimony discloses that not a single local in the Port of New York confirmed the report by telephone or telegram. The testimony also showed that no permanent record of the result of the balloting was made in the books of the locals examined. . . ."

THE RACKET FULCRUM

On the waterfront, control of a union local means much more than the ordinary prizes of political victory. Control of a union local means control of a pier, and control of the host of rackets that are spawned on the docks. A victorious clique has a number of concessions it can parcel out. These include bookmaking, loansharking, kickbacks for jobs, etc. Hence, the often bitter struggles for control, and the iron suppression of opposition once in power.

But the biggest prize of all was the "loading racket." Control of "loading" and its lucrative revenues was the major prize over which the bloody pier wars were fought on the New York docks for thirty years. The "loading racket" was the key to criminal infiltration and baronial domination of sections of the ILA, and its intricate political and economic accommodations among the power elements in New York waterfront history reveals all the facets.

Public loading arose out of a peculiar situation. When the steamship companies deposited a consignment from the ship onto the pier-shed floor, they took no further responsibility for it. A trucker who arrived to pick up the consignment had to lift the shipment onto the truck himself or get some help. Public loading was simply the act of employing a helper to take the stack of goods stored in the pier shed and to lift it manually or mechanically with a forktruck from the floor of the dock to the tailgate of the waiting truck. A lift of about a foot and a half. That was all.* Yet, for the privilege of controlling the loading "concessions" on different piers, more

* The public loader, therefore, differed from the longshoremen who were hired by the stevedoring companies to load and unload ships. Public loaders were in origin roughly akin to public porters at rail stations who are not allowed through the train gate. They were, in effect, independent "middlemen" between the stevedoring operation and the trucker.

than a score of men were murdered, prominent shipping executives cowed, entire union locals taken over by mobsters, and city officials persuaded to look the other way. How come?

"Time," said Benjamin Franklin, "is money." Time is the answer. During World War I the number of vehicles trucking freight to and from the docks increased enormously. The cobbled streets along the waterfront right-of-way had not been built for such traffic. Nor were the city's narrow piers. The long lines piled up. The most expensive cost item in trucking became waiting time. Rather than pay a driver's helper for snoozing on the truck, the practice arose of sending a driver alone to the pier and having him hire a loader from among the "shenangos" or bar-flies at the nearby saloon.

Gradually, through a process of squatters' rights, various individuals began to assert a monopoly on loading at each pier. At first they offered a service; later they began to enforce compulsory service; and, in classic monopoly fashion, they began to charge, literally, all that the traffic would bear. (Truckers in a special hurry could pay a "hurry-up" fee and go to the head of the line.) So the tollgate was established. Whether you needed a loader or not, you had to pay for the service, and on each ton of goods an extra tax was levied. So the industrial racketeer becomes established; he finds a strategic juncture and proceeds to occupy this point of vantage to his own profit.

When you have a good thing, said the devil, you organize it. And many men tried. "They hold their piers through a process of conquest and military occupation," wrote Alva Johnston in a New York *Tribune* series on loading in 1931. A gangster's crown, however, is like the Golden Bough of the priests of Nemi. One could succeed to the title of king only by slaying his predecessor. In the twenties a dozen members of the waterfront dynasty succeeded one another in rapid fashion.*

In the mid-thirties, however, peace was established. The various loading bosses in the West Side piers pooled their efforts and formed an organization known as Varick Enterprises, Inc., which served as a central collection agency and strong-arm operation for the mobsters. The organization had

* The shortest waterfront reign was that of Eddie McGuire who ruled for five minutes. When the leadership was vacant in 1928 the pier leaders met on the Colombian pier and shook dice for the leadership. Eddie won. Five minutes later everybody left the pier but Eddie. A watchman found him dead, with five bullets in his body.

so efficient an intelligence service that it kept accurate tabs on every shipment, whether by rail or water, arriving in the city. Various loaders, operating through the agency, would go to the terminals, check on weights and names of truckers and consignees, and issue a loading ticket—whether any services were performed or not—setting forth the amount of the charge. Then the collectors made their rounds. If payment was refused, Varick, through its union contacts, could provoke a slowdown or threaten a reluctant shipper with a strike.

Varick Enterprises, which at one time helped elect a leader of Tammany Hall, dissolved in the mid-forties when the District Attorney's office began to investigate its operations. The boss loaders then reverted to the previous policy of controlling territories on an independent basis.

The career of John "Cockeye" Dunn illustrates the ripe rewards and the casual murders that attended the growth of the loading racket. In 1936, Dunn, a man who had served time in two reformatories and a stretch in Sing Sing, turned to the waterfront. In short order, by murdering two men and wounding another, Dunn blasted his way into control of loading on Pier 59. In November, 1936, he and his lieutenants formed a "workers committee" and obtained from the ILA a charter for a union local known as the Terminal Checkers and Platform Men, Local 1346-2. With this local, Dunn planned to control loading not only at the piers but in the inland freight terminals as well. Dunn did not organize workers; he simply went to the employers, "negotiated" a contract, and then told the freight handlers they belonged to his union. The following year, Dunn extended his activities. He dropped his ILA charter and obtained from the national AFL three federal charters under the name of Motor and Bus Terminal Checkers, Platform and Office Workers. The charters were for New York, New Jersey, and Pennsylvania, and Dunn made himself business agent and vice-president of the New York local, while his hired slugger, Andrew "Squint" Sheridan, became organizer for the Jersey local. Through these locals, Dunn became a power in the trucking industry, at the same time maintaining control over a number of piers.

Shortly after the war, in May, 1946, a man named Anthony Hintz was designated as hiring boss on Pier 51. Hintz refused to play ball with Dunn and held out for months, despite efforts at intimidation. On January 8, 1947, as Hintz started down the stairway of his house to go to the dock, three men came up, and one pumped six bullets into him. For three days Hintz wavered on the edge of death; then, while his life was ebbing away, he told police, "Dunn shot me." The reason was simple. As Squint Sheridan, Dunn's partner, told the police: "To control a pier you've got to control the loading . . . Andy [Hintz] was a boss loader"—and he stood in the way. The profits of loading from one pier alone, said Sheridan, were about $900 a week.

For a while it seemed as if Dunn would talk and name others connected with the loading racket. In the end, however, he remained silent, and Dunn and Sheridan went to the chair in July, 1949.

In the postwar years, public loading was grudgingly given a garb of legality and became institutionalized. The process started incongruously when loading shakedowns began to reach outrageous heights. In the fall of 1948, tough, barrel-chested Joseph Adelezzi, managing director of the Motor Carriers Association, was ready to declare war. "We had a belly full of it," he said. "There was no uniformity as to loading rates. . . . There was no system, no regulation, no control of any kind. We told them we had gone as far as we could, and we would go no further, regardless of their guns."

The truckers demanded that the shipping lines, who were the pier lessees, or their stevedoring agents, take over the loading. This would have meant the establishment of regular charges by the shipping companies, and the end of the racket. But the shipping companies refused. Their interest was in a quick turn-around of their ships, and to get it they needed a large labor supply and a tractable labor force. For this, they needed a "cooperative" union local; and by this time, the locals were controlled by the racketeers. Moreover, by the ability to create delay, by slowdown or strike, the pier cliques were able to exert crippling leverage upon the companies. For this reason, it paid the shipping companies to cooperate and buy off the mobsters.

The shipping companies, therefore, refused to handle the loading. Actually, the truckers did not want to handle loading either. What they objected to was the arbitrary and erratic setting of rates which made it difficult to rationalize the extra charges to their customers. All they wanted was stability and order.

ILA president, Joe Ryan, hastily called a conference between the public loaders and truckers. The truckers agreed, in return for a contract setting uniform loading rates, that they would surrender the right to do the loading themselves. The contract was signed, but the abuses continued. Following renewed complaints, Commissioner of Investigation Murtagh asked the steamship companies to take over the loading themselves or to designate in writing the names of the public loaders authorized to operate on their piers. Hitherto, even the official identity of the loaders had been unknown; payments were made in cash, no books or records were kept. The steamship companies, mindful of the power of the loaders, refused to take over the job themselves, and proceeded to name the same persons, many of them men with criminal records, who were already in control of the piers, as the legal designees for the job. The effect of the city's feeble gesture was to give official stamp and recognition to the public loaders on the dock. The public loaders, though in effect independent contractors, became officially members of the longshore union, the loaders negotiated loading rates with the truckmen's association. Loading in New York had become "legitimatized."

The beauty of "loading" was that it provided a bland legal mask for extraordinary gain on almost no investment, other than muscle-men for intimidation, and that it provided a lucrative income, as regular as death and taxes, and subject only to the normal vagaries of the business cycle.[44]

The real significance of the racket, for sociological investigation, is that "loading" is to be found *only* on the New York waterfront. There has never been a loading racket in San Francisco, in New Orleans, in Baltimore or Philadelphia—the other major maritime ports in the U.S. There are many indigenous or historical factors to account for this lack, but the key fact is that the *spatial* arrangements of these other ports is such that loading never had a "functional" significance. In all these ports, other than New York, there are direct railroad connections to the piers, so that transfer of cargoes is easily and quickly accomplished; nor is there in these ports the congested and choking narrow-street patterns which in New York forced the trucks to wait, piled up "time charges," or made for off-pier loading. Here is where a difference in the "economic matrix" helps in part to explain the presence or absence of racketeering.

The History of the ILA

What in the background or nature of the union led it to its parlous state?

The politics and the tactics of "immigrant" unions can be more readily understood if seen against the complicated background of competing ethnic groups in urban politics. Just as the "Jewish" unions in New York — the Ladies' Garment Workers, the Amalgamated Clothing Workers, and the Hatters—were intertwined at birth and at early growth with the Socialist party, so the "Irish" unions in New York—the longshoremen, the teamsters, and the building trades—were inextricably linked with Tammany Hall and its system of privilege. Many of the early builders, contractors, and stevedores were union men who struck out for themselves. They prospered by obtaining city contracts for paving, hauling, construction, etc. In these efforts they were often aided by the union leaders with political pull. Out of these collusive arrangements a complex web of friendships and political alliances arose. Except for a brief period in its early abortive days, the longshoremen's union has been part of this web.

Longshore organization has had a sporadic history on the East Coast. In the 1870's and 1880's a group of workers formed the Longshoremen's Union Protective Association, which sought to stabilize conditions on the docks. A more determined effort was made in the mid-1880's by an Englishman, Edward McHugh, who came to New York as an emissary from the dockworkers of London and Glasgow to organize a longshoremen's union so that simultaneous union action on both sides of the Atlantic would be possible against recalcitrant employers. McHugh organized the American Longshoremen's Union, but like many other unionists at the time, his interest soon turned to politics. In 1886, McHugh and the fledgling longshoremen's union took an active part in the Henry George mayoralty campaign, but in the following year, when the coalition United Labor party fell apart, the union faded and McHugh returned to London.

Longshore organization in New York was revived after the turn of the century by a fabulous West Side character named Dick Butler, who took over the old name and started anew the unaffiliated Longshoremen's Union Protective Association. A longshoreman and construction worker in his youth, Butler soon found the primrose path of politics and the *bon vivant* life of a Broadway blade and saloon keeper more to his taste. But through all these peregrinations, he retained a significant role in the union. A follower of former New York police chief and Tammany insurgent Big Bill Devery, Butler realized that a union was a convenient base for making political deals and getting out—and protecting—the vote during roughhouse Tammany primaries. His method of collective bargaining was primitive. Soon after the LUPA was revived, he won for the men a three cents an hour raise in wages. "I managed this," he recalled later, "by going down and having a heart-to-heart talk with P. A. S. Franklin who is now the head of the International Mercantile Marine." The personal touch was to dominate ILA bargain methods to this day.

Meanwhile, in 1892, a "Lumber Handlers of the Great Lakes" was started in Buffalo, which affiliated with the AFL. A year later, its jurisdiction was extended to all longshore work, and the following year, in 1894, it took the name of the International Longshoremen's Association. The union began its growth in the Great Lakes area under the leadership of T. V. O'Connor, who had started as a dockhand on a Great Lakes tugboat. In 1906, O'Connor became head of the Licensed Tugmen's Protective Association of the Great Lakes, and later, head of the ILA.

In 1912, O'Connor threatened to "muscle in" on the East Coast. To avoid fratricidal warfare, Dick Butler merged his LUPA with the International Longshoremen's Union and became the first Atlantic District president of the ILA. A third man rounded out the triumvirate of early ILA leaders. This was an Italian prize fighter, Paul Vacarelli, who was known better by his *nom de guerre* of Paul Kelly. Vacarelli started out his work career on a garbage scow and soon organized the scow trimmers' union. He stepped ashore and, like Butler, went into the saloon business while retaining union office. Politics was the next natural calling and, under the tutelage of Big Tim Sullivan, Vacarelli became the political *padrone* of the lower East Side. His saloon in Great Jones Street, called "Little Naples," was the hangout for such famous characters of New York lore as Monk Eastman, Six-fingered Murphy, Nine-eyed Donnigan, Yaky Yaky Brady, and Big Jack Zelig.

A triumvirate in power is an unstable combination. In 1917, Dick Butler set out to challenge O'Connor. Naturally he needed some sinews of war, and Butler appealed to his political and underworld friends. All the big gamblers up and down Broadway contributed to Butler's war chest. (Arnold Rothstein, the financier of the underworld, gave fifteen hundred dollars.) Said Butler simply: "The gamblers were grateful because I protected them during the Gaynor regime." Butler also had the support of the Atlantic District and two of its rising powers, Joseph P. Ryan and Al Marinelli.[45] Butler also had the backing of the other member of the *troika,* Paul Vacarelli, but, in classic fashion, Vacarelli double-crossed Butler at the last moment and swung his support to O'Connor. Butler lost in a close fight.

Two years later, at Galveston, in 1919, Butler made another try. He sought to persuade Joe Ryan to run for the presidency, but the latter refused. When Big Dick came to the convention, he found to his surprise that he and confrere Marinelli had been denied seats. Butler attacked O'Connor as a strikebreaker. The latter retorted that Butler and Marinelli had organized a private detective agency which had "shaken down" the workers for "protection." Said Butler, in protest to these allegations: "To support this good work we collected a dollar a year from each man, which is a common practice in organized labor. O'Connor knew all about this but he elected to use it for propaganda against us."

In spectacular fashion, Butler made his big bid for power in the famous general port strike of 1919. During the war, living costs had sky-rocketed, but longshore wages were kept at 65 cents an hour by the government's National Adjustment Commission. The men demanded a dollar an hour straight time and two dollars for overtime; they got instead a "Woolworth raise"—five cents straight and ten cents overtime. The rank and file ignored the leaders, and 25,000 longshoremen walked out, completely paralyzing the port. Unable to control the men, O'Connor declared that the port had been taken over by an "irresponsible mob of longshoremen who have been stampeded into an unauthorized strike by I.W.W. and Bolshevik influences." But the leader of the "subversives" was none other than Dick Butler, supported strangely, or perhaps not so strangely, by New York's Mayor Hylan, a puppet of William Randolph Hearst, and Jersey City's Mayor Hague. In fact, when the shipping companies sought to bring scabs into Jersey docks, Hague's cops stood firm against them. Violence flared throughout the port. For four weeks the men held out firmly. Finally, through the intervention of Secretary of Labor Wilson, a conciliation commission, composed of Mayor Hylan, Vacarelli, and James Hughes, was named. On the promise of a new award, Hylan and Butler brought the striking longshoremen back.

As a reward for his role in the 1919 strike, O'Connor was appointed by President Harding a member of the Shipping Board; made chairman of it by Coolidge; reappointed by Hoover; and ousted by Franklin D. Roosevelt. Butler returned to Tammany politics and was named by Jimmy Walker as superintendent of the "white-elephant" Bronx Terminal. Joe Ryan, who had replaced Vacarelli as vice-president of the union, finally became president of the ILA. Said Butler, lightheartedly: "[Joe Ryan] broke in under me in 1913 and if he hasn't forgotten the tricks I taught him, he ought to get along." He did.

For a quarter of a century Joe Ryan was the paladin of the ILA. At the hale and hearty age of sixty-eight, before the sorrows of a criminal indictment, he looked like the cartoonist's caricature of a Tammany Hall gent: well-tailored clothes draped over a hulking frame, a large diamond glittered from a thick finger of his ham-shaped hands, and a bulbous nose limned a fleshy face. Ryan mixed with the Broadway sporting crowd, lived well, and ate well at a favorite Chelsea restaurant, where he occasionally indulged his taste for caviar—a taste, as he admits, that was developed in the days when boxes of the Russian delicacy often broken open on the docks during unloading.

Life was not always so easy for Joseph Patrick Ryan. He was born in 1884, the son of a landscape gardener who died when young Joe was a few years old. Shortly after, his mother passed away too, and Joe was raised in the tough West Side neighborhood abutting the Hudson. In good Chelsea tradition, he left school at the age of twelve, after completing six grades, and after some sundry jobs he settled down as a streetcar conductor for five and a half years and a car inspector for another two years. Bored with the routine, Joe, in 1912, turned to the casual work of the waterfront, and, soon after, his jovial manner, heavy fists, and lush oratorical manner made him a leader in the union. In his first year on the waterfront, Ryan was partially incapacitated when a heavy sling-weight broke and showered him with dense bits of iron. Ryan's local, Local 791, came to his aid by making him part-time financial secretary. Ryan never did any longshore work after that. In three years, the post had become converted to a full-time job. Ryan, proving himself to be a deft labor politician, became an International vice-president in 1918, and president of the union in 1927. In 1943, a grateful convention elected him president of the union for life. Ten years later, in maudlin sorrow, he left the office under fire.

While Joe Ryan symbolized the "Irish" rule of the longshoremen, actually the union has always had an Italian majority. Ryan remained at the top because he had strong political influence with the Irish leadership of Tammany Hall—and political support was necessary to keep the police from interfering with the pier rackets—because he had "front" and could talk to the shipowners, whereas the Italians, mostly immigrants, had few individuals who could present a public appearance, and because Joe Ryan left the Italians strictly alone.

A rough geographical separation underlay this political division. Almost all the West Side piers, along the Hudson, were controlled by the Irish. These were the first piers that were built, and the Irish, as the earlier immigrants, congregated in these areas. The West Side was a community, with the men living near the piers, in Chelsea and in the brownstone strip between the Tenderloin and the river. The saloons and the parish houses bounded their lives. They rarely moved away. They lived as an isolated mass against other ethnic masses in the city.

When shipping expanded after World War I, the congested Hudson piers were unable to carry the traffic, and new piers and bulkheads were established in Brooklyn, Staten Island, and Hoboken, where the Italian communities, living in the slum areas adjacent to these piers, claimed the jobs. And the Italian mobs, deeply entrenched in bootlegging, gambling, and narcotics, quickly moved onto the piers.

The heart of mob control in Brooklyn was the six so-called Italian locals of the ILA, whose four thousand members worked the South Brooklyn piers from Brooklyn Bridge to Twentieth Street. For twenty years these locals were ruled by the notorious Camarda family and their underworld associates. These included, over the years, Albert Anastasia, Joe Adonis, and other notorious members of Italian gangsterdom. When, in 1939, a rank-and-file leader named Peter Panto protested the extortions and depredations along the waterfront, he was cruelly murdered and his body found, two years later, in a lime pit in New Jersey. Albert Anastasia, the chief executioner for "Murder Inc.," was arrested for the murder, and although a former killer for the mob, Allie Tannenbaun, testified that Anastasia had personally supervised the killing, District Attorney William O'Dwyer unaccountably failed to press the indictments. (It was a case that was to haunt O'Dwyer many years later when he was mayor of New York. The release of Anastasia was a question, raised by the Kefauver Committee, which O'Dwyer was never able to answer satisfactorily). In the investigations that followed the Panto murder, the Brooklyn Grand Jury revealed, in 1940, that the treasuries of the six locals had been looted of several hundred thousand dollars; but, quite mysteriously, the books disappeared or were found burned. Although, after the murder, the ILA announced a reform in the Brooklyn locals, the Camarda family effectively retained control of the six locals, gradually to be replaced by Tony Anastasia, brother of Albert, who, despite the fact that in 1946 he had led a group of strikebreakers for the Phelps-Dodge corporation, became boss of the Erie Basin group of docks and, soon after, of the entire Brooklyn waterfront.

The Pattern of Political Accommodation

Central to any understanding of crime is the political setup of a city. For more than forty years, through reform as well as Tammany administrations, the waterfront was a protected political enclave. It was so because of the singular relationships of the business community, which wanted to keep the waterfront as it was, and of the political machines to which it paid tribute.

Doing business in the Port of New York are 155 steamship lines, a dozen large (and twenty small) stevedoring concerns, a half-dozen major railroad lines, a fleet of tugboat operators, etc. In learning the ropes, the "savvy" businessman had to learn to untie knots, and the biggest knot was the political one. Since the port is a municipal enterprise, a businessman had to negotiate pier leases from the city, get various licenses, and learn his way around the Office of Marine and Aviation. Without some political know-how and political support, he is, literally, sunk.

The exploitative possibilities of pier contracts were developed almost fifty years ago by Charles F. Murphy, the famed leader of Tammany Hall. A contemporary account in the New York *World* of October 1, 1905, reported: "During Mr. Murphy's short career as leader of Tammany Hall his contracting firm has acquired, mainly through manipulation of the Dock Department, contracts aggregating $30,000,000 . . ."

In the early thirties, the Seabury investigation showed that the North German Lloyd line paid the president of the National Democratic Club $50,000 in order to bid for a new pier the city had just acquired; the pier itself, assessed at $633,000, was offered to the city, through the law firm of George Olvany, the leader of Tammany Hall, for $3,000,000. Such history repeats itself in every generation; in 1947, during the O'Dwyer regime, an ex-bootlegger who sought to rent a pier was told to see Clarence Neal, a power in Tammany Hall, and to engage his services for $100,000. As a result of these disclosures, Mr. O'Dwyer's Commissioner of Marine and Aviation and his two chief deputies retired, but in quiet.

Since Tammany has always loomed so important, one of the sources of ILA power in New York has been its influence in Tammany Hall. From 1928 to 1938, Joe Ryan was chairman of the AFL Central-Trades and Labor Council, and in that post spoke for "labor" in the political campaigns. Thus, official political endorsement by labor came, in effect, from Joe Ryan. More tangibly, the longshoremen have long been allied with the teamsters, forming a powerful political bloc which supplies manpower—and money—for Tammany campaigns. Ryan was long a figure in the "West Side" Tammany bloc, largely of Irish leaders, and was instrumental in electing the late Michael J. Kennedy to Congress in 1938. Later, Kennedy was elected leader of Tammany Hall.

Another, and for many years, hidden source of ILA influence was the strange but potent friendship between Joe Ryan and a prominent New York businessman with diverse port and business interests, named William J. McCormack. For a period of thirty years, McCormack was one of the silent powers in Democratic politics. He was one of the organizers and, for many years, executive vice-president of the powerful U.S. Trucking Corporation, whose board chairman was Alfred E. Smith. He was a partner with politically hefty Sam Rosoff in a number of contracting and bus ventures.* He is the owner of Transit-Mix Concrete Company, which has held a number of city contracts and supplies building materials to builders who do. His Morania Oil Company supplies fuel oil to the city. His largest enterprise, Penn Stevedore Company, unloads all the freight brought into the city by the Pennsylvania Railroad, principally all the fruit and vegetables freighted daily into the metropolis. For many years, in effect, McCormack acted as the agent of the Pennsylvania Railroad in New York politics.

McCormack's entente cordiale with Joe Ryan was of long standing. In fact, McCormack was the veteran chairman of the

* The story is told—and perhaps it is apocryphal—that McCormack and Rosoff got their starts in a unique partnership. Rosoff had a New York contract to remove all cinders and ashes from city buildings, including schools. McCormack won a New York City contract to pave city streets. Rosoff would dump the cinders on an empty lot on the West Side, where they would be picked up by McCormack's trucks and used to pave the city's streets.

reception committee of the annual dinner-dance of the Joseph P. Ryan Association, a fraternal club whose yearly affairs used to bring together the weirdest collection of city notables, steamship company officials, and waterfront denizens that ever stepped out of a Damon Runyon story.

Because of his influence in union circles,* teamster as well as longshoreman, and because of his standing in business and his power in politics, silent William McCormack was long regarded as the virtual czar or "Mr. Big" of the port. McCormack's friendship with Ryan seems to have weighed heavily in his own favor in the ILA's dealing with the Penn Stevedore firm, which unloads all the freight cars of the Pennsylvania Railroad that are floated across the harbor. Although the ILA rate for longshore work in 1951 was $2.10 an hour, the men working on McCormack's piers, members of a separate ILA local, received only $1.54 an hour (a saving of 56 cents an hour on 2,000 or more men employed on the piers!). The reason given was that these men were railway "freight handlers" and not longshoremen. But when the question arose as to the eligibility of these men for the multiple welfare benefits under the Railway Retirement Act, it was said that they were longshoremen.

The results of the political accommodation were most evident in the throttling of needed reforms on the waterfront. In 1948, the New York Port Authority† submitted to the city a comprehensive plan for putting the port on a businesslike, non-political basis under Port Authority rule. Its blueprint called for $114 million capital investment for a huge produce terminal to be built over the water (to replace the shoddy and sprawling Washington market area), as well as consolidated railroad car floats, new piers, and a plan for traffic control. Its designs would have allowed greater mechanization of work, the reduction of waiting time, flexible planning to regularize employment — in short, those factors which could "rationalize" a chaotic and crumbling industry and bring the port back to prominence and use. But it also would have spoiled McCormack's control of some piers. The offer was rejected by the city. The excuse was that the financial return

* So fraternal are Mr. McCormack's ties with the ILA that, according to the *New Yorker* profile of restauranteur Toots Shor, McCormack presented the latter's first-born with a silver cargo hook and a lifetime membership card in the ILA!

† An independent agency chartered by the States of New York and New Jersey, which runs the Hudson River bridges and tunnels, the airports in the metropolitan area, and several harbor facilities.

under the old Irish rule, and wanted a larger share of the spoils. The only way they could hit at Ryan was through the shipowners, and they did. The combination of these elements made the postwar period a volatile one indeed. In the years from 1946 to 1951, almost every major agreement reached by Ryan and the shipowners was followed by a wildcat strike which tied up the port. It was the only way open to the dissidents.

Over the years Ryan had worked out a technique to control bargaining. The employers represented only Port of New York shippers and their New York stevedoring contractors. The union group, however, consisted of coastwise delegations, not only of longshoremen but of checkers, cargo repairmen, etc. Each local in the four ILA Atlantic Coast districts from Newfoundland to Cape Hatteras, no matter how small (and many had fewer than fifty members), had one vote, plus additional votes in proportion to their membership. The effect was to discriminate against the large longshore locals in New York. And although the agreement was with the New York shippers, the entire Atlantic Coast district voted on contract provisions which applied principally to New York.

In October, 1945, when contract talks had just concluded, longshoremen working the Grace Line piers, along the lower Hudson, walked off because the union negotiators had failed to press the demand for a limitation of slingloads to two tons. Ryan denounced the walkout as the work of "hotheads." A day later, the Atlantic wage conference voted unanimously to accept the new contract. Despite the "unanimous" conference vote, however, the leading dissident in the port, Local 791, which manned a number of the Hudson River piers, voted not to go back, and 30,000 longshoremen followed its lead.

Ryan sought to drive the men back to work by announcing that he had reopened negotiations with the shipowners and that 75 per cent of the men voting in a referendum favored returning to work. The leadership of Local 791 wavered, but a new element entered the waterfront, a rank-and-file committee in Brooklyn headed by a man named William E. Warren, but guided, actually, by the Communists. There was little question of the Communist role. Strategy was being planned by a Communist party functionary named John Steuben; Harold Cammer of the law firm of Witt and Cammer, which handled chiefly party-line unions, became the legal adviser for the rank-and-file committee. But the grievances were genuine, and the men were motivated by a hatred of Ryan.

On the promise of arbitration, the rank-and-file revolt caved in. The arbitration award, by William H. Davis, confirmed the rank and file. The men won a 25-cent-an-hour wage increase as against the original 10 cents; the elimination of the third shape; and a vacation plan with one week's pay for a man with 1,350 hours of work credit.

Seeking to tighten his control, Ryan moved to "clean house." Warren, the leader of the Brooklyn locals, was expelled from the union (for "non-payment of dues"). Asked if he would be allowed to work, an ILA official said: "Sure he can report, but if he falls and hurts himself it'll be no one's fault." The day after, Warren reported for work at the Columbia Street piers and "fell and hurt himself." Shortly after, Warren announced that he had been duped by the Communists and repudiated the role of Witt and Cammer.

In the next years, restlessness on the docks continued. In 1946 and 1947, Local 791 took the lead in a number of wildcat strikes. Steam was building up, and the boiler finally exploded in 1948. The issue, presumably, was wages. But what scared the steamship operators was an economic issue which subsequently became known as "overtime-on-overtime." Complicated as the issue is, it is the dollars-and-cents problems such as these that are the heart of union problems. And this one, therefore, is worth following in some detail.

Until 1945, the ILA and the New York Shipping Association had designated forty-four hours as the straight-time workweek, and overtime was paid from that point on. However, longshore work which was "out-of-hours"—that is, at night or on Sunday—commanded premium or extra pay. Sometimes a man worked more than forty-four hours, but some portion of those original forty-four hours were evening or Sunday, hours which commanded time-and-a-half premium pay. Was the "overtime" wage (the hours beyond forty-four) to be time-and-a-half of the straight-time wage, or was the time-and-a-half to be based on the average of the straight-time *and* premium pay? In principle: Should overtime only be paid as a function of the straight-time *rate*, or, as time-and-a-half of the *actual earned* (including premium pay) rate? To complicate matters further, the Federal Wage and Hour Law, passed in 1940, set *forty* hours as the regular workweek. The federal law specified overtime as beginning after forty hours, while the longshore contract had set it at forty-four. Were the longshoremen now entitled to back pay for the overtime between forty and forty-four hours?

In 1941, a number of ILA workers filed a legal suit charging that true overtime had not been paid. Their claim was upheld by the Wage and Hour Administrator, by seven different courts (including three U.S. Circuit Courts of Appeals), and finally, in 1948, by the U.S. Supreme Court, which held that the longshore contracts violated the Wage and Hour Law.* The shippers feared that as a result of the decision they would be liable for millions of dollars in back pay. More than that, they would face the further embarrassment of opening their books for the wartime period to determine who was entitled to how much back pay, a procedure which might reveal the extent of payroll padding, duplicate hiring, and other practices which, since the government was paying all bills during this period on a cost-plus basis, could only have been conducted on a collusive basis. The shipping companies demanded, therefore, that the union waive all claims for overtime pay. This became one of the issues in dispute.

In August, 1948, when the parties could not reach an agreement, President Truman stepped in and slapped down an eighty-day Taft-Hartley injunction. The day before the injunction expired, Ryan and the shippers came to an agreement. The union agreed to petition Congress jointly with the steamship companies to exempt the longshore industry from the Wage and Hour Law on premium pay and to wipe out all back suits! Ryan also obtained a ten-cent-an-hour increase, a minimum guarantee of four hours "call-in" work, and the reduction in the eligibility requirement for vacation pay from 1,350 to 1,250 hours. Ryan called it a "good deal" and a "fine agreement." The men thought otherwise. Again they walked off. This time, Ryan turned *volte-face* and accepted the walkout and made the strike legal. *This was the first regularly called strike in the history of the union.* Ryan was sent back to negotiate, and the operators suffered what they themselves called "an old-fashioned shellacking." Still, the "shellacking" was not so bad. Pressure from the union and the shippers resulted in a congressional bill in March, 1949, reversing the Supreme Court. By classifying premium pay as overtime pay, the bill exempted the longshore industry from the Wage and

* The Court's reasoning: the "out of hours" pay was not overtime, but regular pay, and overtime should therefore be calculated on that basis.

Hour act and wiped out all claims to back pay during the 1940 to 1948 period. It was a rare act of "sacrifice" on the part of a union: abandoning several millions of dollars of legally entitled back pay for the workers in order to assure labor-management "harmony."

Restlessness on the waterfront increased in the years following the 1948 strike. The case of "Cockeye" Dunn added to the tension. Sitting in the death house at Sing Sing, he sent word to the District Attorney that he wanted to "talk." Rumors of a statement implicating some "Mr. Big," a higher-up power on the waterfront, circulated freely. Although Dunn went to the chair without making a public statement, the affair itself spurred public curiosity. The waterfront exposés in the New York *Sun* by Malcolm Johnson, which later won the Pulitzer Prize, increased the heat. A valiant crusade by a Jesuit priest, Father John Corridan of the Xavier Labor School, raised embarrassing questions for Ryan. Father Corridan made an economic analysis of the plight of the longshoremen and, for the first time, obtained the release of data indicating the extent of casual employment and low pay. Investigators for the Kefauver Committee asked embarrassing questions, particularly regarding the large financial worth of union officials who earned moderate salaries. A series of biting exposés by New York *Post* columnist Murray Kempton got under Ryan's skin. Finally, the establishment of the New York Anti-Crime Committee, with a division headed by William J. Keating, a former assistant attorney who had specialized on the waterfront, brought together in one place a vast amount of data which was freely used by journalists to spotlight poor labor conditions.

In such an explosive atmosphere, any spark could ignite the harbor. The spark was the 1951 negotiations. The ILA won a ten-cent-an-hour wage increase, the amount permissible then under Wage Stabilization Board rules; one shape a day; and welfare benefits. Paradoxically, it was a good contract, as good as could be gotten—the first good one that Ryan had negotiated. Yet a wildcat strike erupted. Realistically, within the wartime Wage Stabilization Board framework there was little more that the strikers could have obtained. But the impulse behind the walkout was no longer economic; it was purely the reaction of a fed-up group "voting with their feet."

The lead was taken by Local 791 and its business agent, "Gene" Sampson. But this time other elements appeared in the leadership as well. A number of local mobsters, seeing an opportunity to dump Ryan, moved in for the kill. For the first time, Ryan's regime was really in danger. The shipowners, fearing that the ouster of Ryan might lead to a new ferocious war for power, decided to stand by the aging ILA leader and take a long strike. For twenty-five days the strike rolled on. Finally, a face-saving maneuver was worked out by the New York State Board of Mediation. The rank and file had charged that the contract had been signed illegally. Now a fact-finding board would decide whether the contract had been duly ratified. After hearing thirty witnesses fill two thousand pages of testimony, the Board, in Solomon-like judgment, found most of the rank-and-file charges to be true, yet certified the contract as valid.

Intervention

For more than a year the waterfront simmered. Rumors of investigation flew thick and fast. The feuding for control of the Jersey waterfront made news as sluggings, bombings, and beatings continued on the Jersey City docks. In November, 1952, the whole pot slopped over. The waterfront story that hitherto had been spelled out in bits and pieces blazed into headlines as the New York State Crime Commission opened public hearings in December, 1952, and paraded a number of witnesses to the stand to describe the seamy side of waterfront life. In the broad picture, there was little new. But what the Crime Commission did, backed by the data seized by subpoena, was to dot every "i" and cross every "t"—the payoffs of the stevedoring concerns to the union officials, the parceling out of crime concessions, the income from loading, and the like.[47]

Once the documented picture of waterfront corruption was on the record, the American Federation of Labor and the New York State authorities were forced to begin a clean-up. The action was a remarkable tribute to the force of public opinion. Clearly, the shipping industry had wanted the pattern of accommodation to continue. The ILA obviously desired no change. The American Federation of Labor, hobbled by a tradition of non-interference in the internal affairs of its affiliates, had pursued a hands-off policy. And the City of New York, even through the reform administration of Fiorello H. LaGuardia, as well as during the lax regimes of O'Dwyer and Impelliteri, feared to tangle with the entrenched powers. But the situation was too volatile. The intermittent wildcat strikes, the lucrative racket prizes which attracted new gangster elements who used the contract grievances to keep the pot boiling, and the constant drumfire of press and magazine criticism finally forced the authorities to act. Governor Dewey, harassed by concurrent scandals in harness-track trotting which involved high Republican officials, saw the waterfront situation as a providential means of gaining favorable publicity and hurting the Democrats as well. George Meany, more mindful than his predecessor of the harm to the Federation in the continuing publicity about labor corruption, felt compelled to move too.

The mobs sought desperately to hold on. Representatives of the loaders approached state officials and proposed various legal dodges which would have left them effectively in control of the piers; the names of the respectable banking officials who were prepared to "front" for the mobs left the state leaders almost stunned. Tony Anastasia privately approached the AFL and indicated that he would dump the West Side "Irish" mobs if the AFL would leave his barony untouched; the Irish mobs made the same proposals regarding Anastasia. But the situation had gone too far. The point of no return had been reached. In September, 1953, the AFL expelled the ILA and chartered a new union in its stead. And the states of New York and New Jersey set up a bi-state waterfront commission with broad regulatory powers over the longshoremen, the loaders, and the stevedoring concerns. In effect, the harbor was declared a quasi-utility, and a set of controls, as stringent as any imposed on an industry, was established. All pier superintendents and hiring bosses had to obtain licenses, and no ex-convict could be employed in these jobs unless he could prove good conduct over the previous five years. All longshoremen had to register. To maintain registration, a longshoreman had to work steadily or, failing to work nine months, lose his registration. In this fashion, the commission sought to cut the supply of casual or "weekend" laborers, who, by bribing hiring bosses for the lucrative evening and weekend premium-pay hours, had contributed to waterfront disorganization. Ex-convicts were barred from registration unless they obtained clearance from the commission. The shape-up, as such, was abolished, and replaced by employment centers. The stevedoring concerns still maintained control over hiring, however, but they could only employ registered longshoremen. Compulsory public loading was outlawed. Either the steamship companies could provide loaders, or the teamsters could employ their own men. Apart from the licensing and registration provisions, the New York State waterfront act also stipulated that union locals whose officers included convicted felons could not collect dues from registered longshoremen. About 3 per cent of the ILA officers in the New York port, it was estimated, had criminal records.

While these moves were taking place, the collective-bargaining contract between the shippers and the old ILA had expired. The two parties sought to come to a new long-term agreement which would give the ILA exclusive control of the waterfront. But this situation was a difficult one. The old ILA had to make substantial demands to show the longshoremen that it was no longer a tool of the shippers. The steamship companies were unwilling to pay the price. On September 30, 1953, the old ILA, desperately striving to win a new contract, called a strike which effectively shut down the East Coast ports. The fact that it was able to do so against adverse odds testified to its grip on the docks.

In response to various pressures, President Eisenhower set up a Board of Inquiry preliminary to obtaining a Taft-Hartley injunction. The board skirted the issue which it had been called upon to judge. In effect, the question of the injunction was left squarely up to the Administration. And the Administration, guided by Governor Dewey's office, in turn left the issue up to the AFL! So close was the co-operation between the AFL and the state officials that if the AFL had opposed a Taft-Hartley injunction none would have been issued.

The Administration applied to the federal court for an eighty-day injunction. Under the injunction, the ILA would be unable to strike, while presumably the nascent AFL union would be free to exert pressure on the shippers. It was clearly a political move intended to help the AFL. Caught between fires, the shippers appealed to the National Labor Relations Board to hold a representation election, promising to refrain from signing any contract with the ILA until the Board had determined who was the legal bargaining agent. The NLRB, fearful that the expiration of the Taft-Hartley injunction would mean a ruinous waterfront war for which they would be blamed, ordered an election for December 22. When the results were in, the ILA had won. It had received 9,060 votes to 7,568 for the AFL, while 4,399 votes were challenged, principally by the AFL.

How can one explain the victory of the old union in such

an obviously rotten and exploitative situation? When the ILA was first expelled from the AFL, many observers felt that the old union would crumble and that the longshoremen, "emancipated" finally from the grip of the racketeers, would rush joyfully into the ranks of the new union. But they did not. A list of factors indicate the complexity of the problem:

(1) While many of the longshoremen were cowed and exploited, a sizeable core, roughly one-third of the work force, did have considerable privileges because of the system of favoritism. This group worked hard for the ILA.

(2) A number of the wildcat walkouts over the collective-bargaining agreements were not as "spontaneous" as they seemed, but were inspired by dissident racketeer elements who sought to use these walkouts either for shakedowns of shipping concerns or to pry control of some piers from entrenched groups. Hence, the depth of the "spontaneous" support the AFL would get was exaggerated.

(3) Politics is primarily a matter of organization; and organization, particularly in such a rough-and-ready place as the waterfront, is built on the informal and "natural" leaders of the group. Years of racket control, however, had eliminated the independent leadership among the men.

(4) Ethnic considerations were important. The Italians in Brooklyn feared Anastasia, but they knew him as one of their own. The AFL was never able to obtain a foothold in the closely-knit Italian community.

(5) The AFL union imprudently accepted into its ranks several old ILA officials who had mob connections, principally Tony (Cheese) Marchitto of Jersey City. This confirmed a latent cynicism of many longshoremen that both sides were no good.

(6) The ILA itself put on a "reform" face. At a special convention in Philadelphia in mid-November, Joe Ryan, who had been acclaimed president "for life," stepped down with a pension "for life," and Captain William Bradley, head of a small tugboat local, was named president. John L. Lewis, for reasons of power or of pique at the AFL, thereupon announced his backing of the "new" ILA and pledged a loan of $200,000 to aid the union in its fight against the AFL.

(7) The longshoremen resented the close ties of the AFL to the Dewey administration and feared that the AFL support for the licensing and registration features of the Waterfront Act would lead to government hiring-halls.

A second NLRB election, held after Governor Dewey had

"twisted the arm" of the Board, was again won by the ILA, by a count of 9,110 to 8,977, with 1,797 pro-ILA votes challenged. Again the ILA held its ranks and rode out the storm.

For the next three years, from 1953 to 1956, the ILA sought some cover of respectability in the labor movement. In the "public morality" of American society, corruption can be tolerated, if clothed, but naked corruption is unsettling. At first the ILA, under the new "reform" leadership of William Bradley, a former tugboat captain, sought to affiliate with the Miners. But this was not feasible, since the Miners, because Lewis had refused to sign the non-Communist affidavit of the Taft-Hartley Act, could not participate in the NLRB elections. Bradley then worked out a "mutual-aid pact" with Jimmy Hoffa, the fast-moving boss of the Midwest teamsters, who was then seeking to extend his power in the union. There seem to have been private negotiations, too, with Harry Bridges' West Coast longshoremen, a move privately favored by Hoffa, which would have set up a bi-coast teamster-longshore combination; but this did not materialize.

In October, 1956, the AFL made its last challenge to the ILA. But it was obvious that its chances were slim. Maritime union leader Joe Curran, mindful of the need for longshoremen co-operation on the docks, came out publicly in support of the ILA. When the votes were announced, the ILA had won by 11,827 to 7,428.

After all the strenuous efforts at clean-up, the old crowd was still in control. Some changes for the better had been made. The Waterfront Commission, by reducing the number of longshoremen eligible for work, had helped to regularize employment. The union itself had begun to set up orderly records and to organize welfare benefits. But the mob control was secure. Tough Tony Anastasia had extended his power over the Brooklyn docks. Ed Florio, after fourteen months in Atlanta prison, was again the power in Hoboken. The Bowers group that had organized the loading on the West Side were still entrenched. And the ILA itself had won a union shop which gave it even greater power over jobs on the watefront.

The Cycle Resumes

Looking back at the four decades, how could such a corrupt and fetid state of affairs have continued for so long? One simple answer is that most of the individuals concerned found it difficult to recognize the face of evil. Joe Ryan was not a vicious man. A morose and sentimental individual, he came to success through the "freight entrance" and knew the seamy side of life the way a well-worn *douanier* knows the little vices and hypocrisies of the great travelers. The waterfront is tough, and he accepted life that way. Like many self-made men, he scorned—and feared—"do-gooders" and reformers who have never known hard knocks.

In the union Ryan was a captive. Each little local around a pier or neighborhood was a molecular world of its own with its own traditions, prerogatives, cliques, and jealousies. Each warlord knew his particular work and felt at home there; the larger society, the complexities of the skyscraper world over the "shadow line," were beyond his ken. Joe Ryan was the emissary to this world. He was the "waxer" who, despite the rough manner, could talk and hold his own. That is why he reigned but did not rule.

The steamship companies also accepted the "tough world." It was easier to make a "deal." Besides, "the men are undisciplined, and need a strong hand." So, on loading and other lucrative concessions, the companies looked the other way—in exchange for the promise of the hiring boss that he would keep the men in line and get the ships in and out fast. Besides, many of the costs of doing business were met by government maritime subsidies—so what was the point of getting excited?

For the loaders, tough punks from the tough West Side world, the waterfront was a place where everybody was out to make a buck, so why not they? "The steamship companies couldn't complain; it cost them nothing to have loaders on the pier. The truckers? They objected to loading only because they wanted to do the job themselves so they could make the buck out of the customer rather than us. The consignee? Why should they object; they could pass the costs along to the customers easily. The public? What's that? Everybody is out to make a buck; some pay, some don't; that's life."

Underneath all three, bearing the load, were the longshoremen. Fifty years ago, the Irish were the dominant group. Many of the West Side Hudson piers are still manned by the Irish, but the majority of longshoremen today are Italians and "Austrians"—a vague waterfront term that covers all Slavs and East Europeans. Traditionally, most of the longshoremen have lived close to the docks, forming a homogeneous, self-contained community. Along with the house, there is the bar, the social club, and occasionally the parish house as the center of community life. St. Veronica's Parish on the West Side is typical longshore slum. The men live in a narrow band of tenements between Houston and the Federal Home of Detention. Slashed across the center is Pig Alley, a block-long cobblestoned, junk-strewn thoroughfare where in the daytime the boys play stickball and at night the souses lurch along until they slide down into the street to sleep off their drunk. In the summer, the street is the living-room. There are the usual number of brawls, and on Sunday the little girls walk self-consciously in their white organdies to communion. Most of the people live in the houses where they were born, and die there. There are the usual feuds and fights. But withal, it is a community, and no one is a "cop-hollerer." In recent years some longshoremen have sought to break away from the docks. They moved to Queens, the Bronx, and Washington Heights. The reason usually is "the kids." The world is a jungle, and they want to give their children a better start. On the docks, only the mobsters are successful, and they are a poor model for the devout.

As the Irish have moved out, the Italians have moved in, and the old patterns of exploitation in its many vicious forms appear once more. Many of the men are illegal aliens, smuggled into the country like cattle. Most of the aliens came from the hometowns of the ILA organizers. The dock is an anonymous place to work; subject to arrest and deportation, the men are unusually docile. Hence, it is easy to arrange "short gangs." Fifteen men do the work of the regular twenty-two whose "names" are entered on the books, and the difference is split between the hiring boss and the stevedore. The steamship companies don't mind; the men work fast and efficiently.

How can one break this vicious cycle? One answer is the "regularization" of work. The action of the Waterfront Commission is a step in that direction. But this is not enough. The matrix of the problem is the dilapidated physical condition of the port. The New York waterfront remains, aging, chipping, cracking, and congested by traffic. With everyone crowded by space, they became also crowded by "time" and sought to cut corners. And the fulcrum is still time. Ships still require a fast turn-around to equalize mounting dock costs. Trucks still wait long hours to load or discharge consignments. The pier facilities are still inadequate to speed the flow of cargo; the narrow, fringe-like piers still have little radial space to permit trucks to maneuver and unload. Forced into the narrow, gridiron-patterned streets built to accommodate the horse and wagon, the trucks force all traffic to back up behind them. And astride the ports stand the mobs; at this vantage point between trucker and steamship company, like medieval robber barons, they erected their sluice gates and exacted their tolls. The barriers may have been torn down. But the dilapidation remains.[48]

Chapter 10

The Capitalism of the Proletariat:

A Theory of American Trade-Unionism

TRADE-UNIONISM, said George Bernard Shaw, is the capitalism of the proletariat. Like all such epigrams, it is a half-truth, calculated to irritate the people who believe in the other half. American trade-unionism would seem to embody Shaw's description, but in fact it only half-embodies it—at most. True, the American labor leader will mock socialism and uphold capitalism; yet he has built the most aggressive trade-union movement in the world—and one, moreover, that has larger interests than mere economic gain. Abroad, the European Marxist hears the labor leader praise the free enterprise system as the most successful method yet devised for a worker to obtain a fair, and rising share, of the country's wealth; within the United States, the American businessman listens to the labor leader denouncing him in wild and often reckless rhetoric as a greedy profiteer, monopolist, and exploiter. How reconcile these contradictions? One U.S. labor leader sought to do so in these terms: *to* your wife, he said, you talk one way; *about* your wife, you talk another. Very clever; but, one might add, another half-truth—at most.

William James once said that whenever you meet a contradiction you must make a distinction, for people use the same words but mean two different things. One way out of this seeming contradiction, therefore, is to see American trade-unionism as existing in two contexts, as a *social movement* and as an economic force (*market-unionism*), and accordingly playing a different role in each. The social movement is an *ideological* conception, shaped by intellectuals, which sees labor as part of a historical trend that challenges the established order. Market-unionism, on the other hand, is an *economic* conception, a delimiting of role and function, imposed by the realities of the specific industrial environment in which the union operates.

Any labor movement finds itself subject to all the ideological pressures of the "left," whether social, communist, or syndicalist. After all, it is in the name of the workers that these social movements proclaim their slogans; and the labor movement itself is one of the chief vehicles of social change. But in the United States, the image of trade-unionism as a social movement took a unique course, as plotted in the theory—inspired largely by the "Wisconsin school" of John R. Commons and Selig Perlman—of "Laborism." The theory argues that the trade-union movement, although fashioned ideologically, has a different source of cohesion than the radical movement, i.e., the limited, day-to-day, expectation of social improvement. By its concentration on the specific issues at hand, it must necessarily reject the far-flung socialist and radical ideologies; unlike them, it is both in the world and *of* the world. In its operation, it can indeed become a force for social change, but only by "sharing" power rather than seeking the radical transformation of society. This sharing of power takes place both in the factory—through bargaining on wages and working conditions, and sometimes on production standards — and in the larger society, through seeking legislation for the increased welfare of the worker.

"Laborism" is the dominant ideology, to the extent that there is one, of the American labor movement. In the past it has been the conservative defense of the unions against the recriminations of the radicals; it was a rationalization of the purely economic role of the unions. Yet, despite its theorists, even it has come to have a political force of its own. Pale ideology though it is, it still conceives of unionism as a social movement, and it still conceives of itself as being opposed to the employer class as a whole. Contemporary American unionism could only have flourished with the aid of a favorable political—and social—climate, which was provided by the New Deal. More importantly, the Roosevelt Administration provided, through law, two extraordinary protections: first, the legal obligation of employer to bargain collectively with unions; and second, the granting of *exclusive* representation rights to a *single* union within a defined bargaining unit. This, plus the growth of various union security devices (e.g., maintenance-of-membership clauses, union shops, etc.) gave the unions a legal protection that few union movements enjoyed anywhere.[49] "Laborism" is associated usually with the New Deal and Fair Deal, and with the left wing of the Democartic party. It calls for improved social-welfare benefits, for a tax program which falls mostly on the wealthy, and it cries out incessantly against "monopolies."

But here lies an anomaly and the source of a contradiction; for *market-unionism,* collective-bargaining unionism, can only exist in monopoly situations, a monopoly created either by the employers or by the unions. In fact, the only industries in the United States where unionism is strong today are those where a monopoly situation, industry- or union-created, exists.

The reason is fairly simple. *The chief purpose of market-unionism is to eliminate wages as a factor in competition.* Where an industry is only partially unionized and wages therefore can be utilized as a competitive lever, a union must either impose a monopoly or go under; the erosion of the American textile unions is a case in point.

The pattern of monopoly follows that of the different markets. In oligopolistic markets, i.e., in industries dominated by a few giant firms, the unions eliminate wages as a competitive factor by "pattern bargaining," that is, by imposing wage agreement on all firms in the industry. While, theoretically, bargaining is still done with individual firms, in practice (as is seen in the case of steel) the agreement is industry-wide. In the highly competitive or small-unit-size fields, the unions have stepped in and provided a monopoly structure to the market, limiting the entry of firms into the industry, establishing price lines, etc. This has been true most notably in the coal industry, in the garment industry, and in the construction trades.

In coal, where the industry could not do it itself, the miners' union has enforced a basic price floor for the entire industry. This has been done in various ways: through legislative price-fixing, as in the Guffey Coal Act of the first years of the New Deal; outright production-restriction schemes, as in Pennsylvania, which limit the tonnage of anthracite that can be mined in the state; by keeping the mines open only three days a week; by staggered strikes in order to reduce coal surpluses, etc.

The garment unions have established a fixed series of price lines, or grades, for men's clothing and women's dresses, thus bringing order out of chaotic competition. By limiting the number of contractors who can sew and finish dresses for a single manufacturer, and by stopping firms from moving out of a fixed geographical area, the International Ladies' Garment Workers' Union has been able to restrict the number of firms in the industry and to police the market.

The most elaborate form of market stabilization exists in the construction trades. The power of the unions resides in the fact that they serve as a work contractor, i.e., as the

next decade, this group increased an additional 43 per cent, or two-and-a-half times as fast as the labor force as a whole. While the semi-skilled group remained almost constant over ten years (from 12.2 to 12.9 million workers), the technical and professional, the non-production worker, has increased over 50 per cent in the same period. If one excludes the service fields, the number of white-collar workers in the United States by 1956, for the first time in U.S. history, exceeded the number of blue-collar workers.[52]

These salaried groups do not speak the old language of labor. Nor can they be appealed to in the old class-conscious terms. Their rise poses a difficult problem for the leadership of the American labor movement.

4. *The loss of* élan *and the disfavor of the public.* The labor movement, in its present form, is less than twenty-five years old, and the men on top are the men who built it. But they are no longer young—the average age of the AFL-CIO executive council is in the middle sixties—and they have lost their *élan.* The organizing staffs, too, are old, and there is no longer the reservoir of young radicals to rely on for passing out leaflets at the plant sites.

But more than this, there is a crisis in union morality and public confidence. It is not simply a problem of racketeering.* Racketeering is shaped by the market. It has always had a hold in the small-unit construction trades, the longshoremen, and the teamsters, where the chief cost to an employer is "waiting time" and where one can therefore easily exact a toll from employers. And one finds no racketeering in the mass-production industries. Even in the fields where "shakedowns" are common, racketeering is on a considerably smaller scale today than twenty-five years ago, when the industrial gangster flourished in the U.S. The real sickness lies in the decline of unionism as a moral vocation, the fact that so many union leaders have become money-hungry, taking on the grossest features of business society, despoiling the union treasuries for private gain. And where there has not been outright spoliation—typical of the teamster, bakery, textile, and laundry unions—one finds among union leaders an appalling arrogance and high-handedness in their relation to the rank and file, which derives from the corruption of power. Such gross manifestations of power have alienated a

* Given my distinction between *market-unionism* and the *social movement,* one can say that racketeering is a pathology of market-unionism, while communism is the pathology of the social movement.

middle-class public which, for twenty years, was tolerant of, if not sympathetic to, unionism.

The future of any movement depends upon the character of its leaders, the strength of its traditions (the impelling force) and the sharpness of its goals (the compelling forces), and the challenges of the society of which it is a part.

Certainly the radical tradition of the labor movement has almost vanished, and of those individuals who came out of the Socialist or leftwing movement, such as Dubinsky, Potofsky, Rieve, Curran, Quill, and Reuther, only Reuther still has the drive and desire to widen labor's definition of its goals. The men at the top of labor unions today have little energy for intensive political action or a desire to take a leading political role. At the middle levels, which reflect themselves largely in the state and city rather than national scenes, many of the younger labor leaders are eager for means to enhance their status and power, and it is quite likely that these men will step into the political arena in order to gain recognition and will do so by becoming more active in the Democratic party.

On the national level, the men who hold the stage are George Meany, Jimmy Hoffa, and Walter Reuther. Meany, by taking command of a reunited labor movement, has already written his page in history. Hoffa is ambitious, but other than consolidating his power over a strong union and thus thumbing his nose at his detractors, there is little he can do politically. He is anti-intellectual, uneasy with ideas and those who articulate them because of his own inferiority in these realms, and lacking in any political or moral perspective. He can, on occasion, preach a primitive class war, more raw than anything Walter Reuther could or even would say, but this is a reflex of his temperament, which is to resolve all issues by action rather than ideas. He has extraordinary drive and ambition, but no direction. And the effort of various aides to provide him with one fell under Hoffa's own impatience. What ultimately will curb Hoffa is a craving for respectability, which is masked under the veneer of toughness. But it is there nonetheless; and this will tame him. Walter Reuther cares little for the respectability—the flattery of the press and the business community—which other labor leaders have sought, he has, still, a sense of mission (though the dogmatic edges have been dulled) and the respect of the liberal community which he gained twenty years ago. At age fifty (in 1958) Reuther still has a long future ahead of him. He is not popular with his labor peers. He makes them uncomfortable. He will not relax. His vices are few and his energies are great. Like the Jansenist confronting the "whiskey priests," his example calls them to account for their own moral failures. Yet, there is no one else in sight who can lead them. And Reuther temperamentally is an ideologist, though his skills are eminently practical; he can temper vision to reality, and his conception of the labor movement is a social one.

It is quite possible that the labor movement may sink, slowly, slothfully into the market role of being a junior partner to industry, as is now the case with the building trades. But it is more likely, in my opinion, that in the years ahead we will find U.S. labor seeking to redefine itself as a social movement.

Apart from the possible role of Reuther, one reason is that, with politics becoming so intertwined with bargaining, the need to extend labor's political power means that the unions will have to play a more direct role in the Democratic party and will have to build a liberal coalition in order to strengthen their own position in that party. If collective bargaining has reached a limit, then politics becomes an important arena.

A subtle change in the political process itself, molded by the spread of mass media and mass communication, reinforces this tendency. This is the emergence of what may be called "symbol" groups (or those bearing ideological tags), as against the "interest" groups (with their single focus on protecting the specific tangible interest of a specific, tangible group). For in a mass society, where public opinion is king, various groups are more than ever forced to assume some coherent identity and to clothe their aims in national or general-interest terms. This is particularly true where the poll concept of democracy takes hold, for polls can only formulate problems in symbolic terms, such as: what should *The Farmer do?* (without worrying about the complication that "The Farmer" is a whole spectrum of persons); or what should *Labor* do? (without enquiring further about the meaning of such a generic term as "Labor"). However, not only the nature of polls but also the new process of informal group representation in government becomes a shaping element in this fusion of coherent identities. Thus "Business" is asked to name its representatives to a government advisory board; and "Labor" is asked likewise. Political issues become national in scope, and "Labor," as a symbolic group, is asked to define "its" attitude toward such issues; and it has to learn to compose its internal differences in doing so. One of the pressures for unity between the AFL and CIO, for example, was the need to have a single set of spokesmen to speak for "labor" on various national issues.

A third element is the rise of "status anxieties" in the business community, a rising concern about the threat of "Big Labor" and its political influences at a time when the trade-union movement is ideologically exhausted and beset with hardening of its organizational arteries. The agitation over the "right-to-work" laws bore all the marks of an emotional crusade rather than a national *interest* attempt to deal with labor power. A study in 1958 by Frederic Meyers for the Fund for the Republic of the effects of the right-to-work law after five years in Texas showed that it had no effect at all. Unions were not hurt, industrial relations were no different than before, but employers had gained emotional satisfaction from the fact that a law which labor had fought was on the books. The right-to-work campaigns of California, Ohio, and other states in 1958 were sponsored predominantly by middle-sized concerns, while big business, with the exception of General Electric, stood aloof. For these employers, many of whom run multi-million-dollar industries, were clearly motivated by resentment of union power, even though that power had become stabilized and the pattern of industrial relations had become settled. It may well be that the business community thought that with the election and re-election of Dwight Eisenhower and the Republican party, the unions would roll over and surrender. But the unions didn't. The choleric reaction of many employers to the name of Walter Reuther—especially those who have never dealt with him and the UAW but to whom he is the symbol of perhaps new labor power—indicates that, on the national and political level, the labor-management tensions are no longer fired by interest-group conflict, though this exists, but in symbolic and emotional terms.

If American labor does develop more as a social movement in the next decade, what will be the political and ideological content of this new unionism? This is difficult to say. The "left" ideology has in recent years become utterly exhausted; and the idea of nationalization holds no appeal. Most likely we shall see the re-emergence of a rather more emphatic version of "Laborism," insisting more vigorously than ever before on such benefits as better housing, more schools, adequate medical care, the creation of a more "humanistic" work atmosphere in the factory, and the like. These are generally prosaic in nature, and it takes great skill on the part of an individual to dramatize them. The question is, who among the labor leaders could fire the imagination of the union leadership and rank-and-file? Walter Reuther thinks he can, but it is problematic whether he will be given the opportunity.[53] The opposition to him, among his labor peers, is so great that if he assumed the leadership of the labor movement, following the retirement of George Meany, a split might ensue. To avoid one, it seems likely that the AFL-CIO would choose a middle-of-the-road individual such as Albert J. Hayes, of the Machinists. And it is possible that Walter Reuther, like John L. Lewis, might become one more "lost leader" of labor. To the extent that personality and imagination count in social action—and I think their weight is great—this would be a loss indeed.

Chapter 11

Work and Its Discontents:

The Cult of Efficiency in America

> Before Jove's day no tillers subdued the land. Even to mark the field or divide it with bounds was unlawful. Men made gain for the common store, and Earth yielded all of herself more freely when none begged for her gifts. 'Twas he that . . . hid fire from view, and stopped the wine that ran everywhere in streams. . . . Then came iron's stiffness and the shrill sawblade—for early man cleft the splitting wood with wedges; then came divers arts. Toil conquered the world, unrelenting toil, and want that pinches when life is hard.
>
> —Virgil, *The Georgics*

THESE ARE "notes on work"—some reflections, some *aperçus*. Notes are an unfamiliar form for a reader. He demands to know one's thesis, or at least one's point of view. This essay has no thesis, in the ordinary sense of the word, and it has no answers to the conventional problems raised by the manager, the engineer, or the sociologist who writes about work. On point of view? "They go but faintly to work, as they say, with one buttock," wrote Montaigne. This is an ineluctable response in industrial society, for any moral standpoint must be ambiguous. It is as easy to condemn the "dehumanization" of the machine as to sing hosannas to the promises of technology. I seek not to be the ideologue or the moralist. What ties these notes together is a mood, and some questions. It is true that the way a question is asked limits and disposes an answer. But knowledge is gained, as Herbert Butterfield among others has pointed out, not by new observation and experiment, but by varying the questions, by new ways of looking at familiar facts, whether they be the problem of motion or the interpretation of dreams.

This essay, less ambitiously, concerns itself with the most familiar, yet unexamined, fact of modern industrial life—the concept of efficiency. We assume that in efficiency, as in geometry, the shortest distance between two points is a straight line. But what if something is in the way? Within the same week, once, the problem was posed in two different places. In New York, the new Thruway pushing down from New England came smack up against the old Huguenot cemetery at New Rochelle, the burial place of the French founders of the town; should the Thruway be diverted, or the cemetery moved? In England, a new fleet of square-topped, double-decker buses found themselves unable to proceed through the ancient Gothic arch of a historic town wall; should the vault be rebuilt, the double-deckers scrapped, or the buses rerouted some distance in miles? Which was the rational course in each case? In New York the cemetery was removed; in England the buses rerouted. Each choice reflected the contrasting values of the society.

The contrasting definitions of rationality, the costs of efficiency—as applied to work—are the themes of this essay.

The New Calculus of Time

For about twenty years of his busy life, Jeremy Bentham, the patriarch of modern reform, devoted much of his energies to the elaboration, in minutest detail, of plans for a perfectly efficient prison. This was the famous *panopticon,* a star-shaped building so intricately constructed "that every convict would pass his life in perpetual solitude, while remaining perpetually under the surveillance of a warder posted at the center."

Bentham, the leader of the philosophical radicals, had gotten the idea of the *panopticon* from his ingenious brother, Sir Samuel Bentham, a famous naval architect who, while employed by Catherine the Great to build ships for Russia, had designed a factory along just those lines. For many years, in fact, Jeremy Bentham sought money from Parliament to build a "five-storied" *panopticon,* one-half of which would be a prison, the other half a factory. The *panopticon,* he said, would be a cure for laziness, a "mill for grinding rogues honest and idle men industrious." (In 1813 he finally received £23,000 as compensation for money he had expended in his efforts to construct a model.)

This identification of factory and prison was, perhaps, quite natural for Bentham. Prison and factory were united in his philosophical mind by the utilitarian conceptions of tidiness and efficiency. The root of utilitarianism—this new mode of conduct which Bentham elaborated—is a passion for order, and the elaboration of a calculus of incentives which, if administered in exact measures, would stimulate the individual to the correct degree of rectitude and work. Utilitarianism provided a new definition of rationality: not the rule of reason, but the rule of measurement. With it, man himself could now be regulated. When the rule was applied by the engineer—the utilitarian par excellence—not only was work broken down in detail, but it was measured by detail, and paid for in time units defined in metric quantities.

With this new rationality came a unique and abrupt break from the rhythm of work in the past. With it came a new role of time. In the various ways it has been expressed, two modes of time have been dominant: time as a function of space, and time as *durée.* Time as a function of space follows the rhythm of the movement of the earth: a year is the curving ellipse around the sun; a day, the spin of the earth on its axis. The clock itself is round; and the hour, the sweep of a line in 360 degrees of space.[54] But time, as the philosophers and novelists —and ordinary people—know it, is also artless. There are the psychological modes which encompass the differing perceptions: the dull moments and the swift moments, the bleak moments and the moments of bliss, the agony of time prolonged and of time eclipsed, of time recalled and time anticipated—in short, time not as a chronological function of space, but time felt as a function of experience.

Utilitarian rationality knows little of time as *durée.* For it, and for modern industrial life, time and effort are hitched only to the clock-like, regular, "metric" beat. The modern factory is fundamentally a place of order in which stimulus and response, the rhythms of work, derive from a mechanically imposed sense of time and pace.* No wonder, then, that Aldous Huxley can assert: "Today every efficient office, every up-to-date factory is a panoptical prison in which the workers suffer . . . from the consciousness of being inside a machine."

The indictment, damning if true, lays its gravest charge against the United States. Contemporary America is, above

* "Order," said Freud, "is a kind of repetition compulsion by which it is ordained once for all when, where and how a thing shall be done so that on every similar occasion doubt and hesitation shall be avoided. The benefits of order are incontestable: it enables us to use space and time to the best advantage, while waiving expenditures of mental energy. One would be justified in expecting that it would have ingrained itself from the start and without opposition into all human activities; and one may well wonder that this has not happened, and that, on the contrary, human beings manifest an inborn tendency to negligence, irregularity and untrustworthiness in their work, and have to be laboriously trained to imitate the example of their celestial models." *Civilization and Its Discontents* (Hogarth Press, London, 1946), pp. 55-56.

all, the machine civilization. The image of tens of thousands of workers streaming from the sprawling factories indelibly marks the picture of industrial America, as much as the fringed buckskin and rifle marked the nineteenth-century frontier, or the peruke and lace that of Colonial Virginia. The majority of Americans may not work in factories, just as the majority of Americans never were on the frontier and never lived in Georgian houses; yet the distinctive ethos of each time lies in these archetypes.

What then is the nature of work in the life of present-day America?

The Watching Hand of God

The contemporary enterprise was set up to obey three peculiar technologics: the logic of size, the logic of "metric" time, and the logic of hierarchy. Each of the three, the product of engineering rationality, has imposed on the worker a set of constraints with which he is forced to wrestle every day. These condition the daily facts of his existence.

For the man whose working day is from eight in the morning to five in the afternoon, the morning begins long before the time he is to arrive at his place of work. After a hasty wash and a quick breakfast, he is off in his car or on the streetcar, bus, or subway; often he may have to spend an hour or more in getting to the plant. (There seems to be a law, as Bertrand Russell has noted, that improvements in transportation do not cut down traveling time but merely increase the area over which people have to travel.)

Although this is the most obvious fact about modern work, few writers have concerned themselves with it or with the underlying assumption: that large masses of human labor should be brought to a common place of work. The engineer believes that concentration is technologically efficient: under one roof there can be brought together the source of power, the raw materials, the parts, and the assembly lines. So we find such huge megaliths as Willow Run, now used by General Motors, a sprawling shed spanning an area two-thirds of a mile long and a quarter of a mile wide; or such roofed-over, mile-long pavements as the Boeing plant in Wichita, Kansas.

This belief in the efficacy of size was conditioned by the type of energy first used—the limited amount of power available through the use of steam. Since steam dissipates quickly, the engineer tended to crowd as many productive units as possible along the same shaft, or within the range of steam pressure that could be carried by pipes without losses due to excessive condensation. These considerations also led to the bunching of workers in the layout of work, since the machines had to be located along a straight-line shafting.

The introduction of electric power and electric motors opened the way to greater flexibility; and within the plant these opportunities were taken. Newer work-flow designs have avoided the antiquated straight-line shafts and aisles of the older factory. Yet the outward size of the factory remained unchallenged. Why? In part because the engineer conceives of efficiency in technological terms alone; and he is able to do so because a major cost—the travel time of the worker—can be discounted. But the question can be posed: should large masses of persons be brought to a common place of work? Which is cheaper to transport: working men twice daily or materials and mechanical parts, let us say, twice a week? As Percival and Paul Goodman so pertinently note in their book, *Communitias*: "The time of life of a piece of metal is not consumed while it waits for its truck; a piece of metal does not mind being compressed like a sardine." What the Goodmans propose is production in "bits and pieces" rather than integrated assembly. If the plants were located near workers' communities, the men would not have to travel; the processed materials would be brought to several places for manufacture, and the parts would then be collected for assembly. Yet the question is rarely considered, for few industries pay directly for their workers' travel time. Calculations in terms of market costs alone do not force the enterprise to take into account such factors as the time used in going to and from work, or the costs of roads and other transport to the factory site, which are paid for by the employee or by the community as a whole out of taxes.

In his travel to and from work the worker is chained by time. Time rules the work economy, its very rhythms and motions. (After consulting Gulliver on the functions of his watch, the Lilliputians came to the belief that it was his God.)

One of the prophets of modern work was Frederick W. Taylor, and his stop watch was his bible. If any such social upheaval can ever be attributed to one man, the logic of efficiency as a mode of life is due to him. With "scientific management," as enunciated by Taylor, we pass far beyond the old rough computations of the division of labor; we go into the division of time itself.

Frederick W. Taylor was born in 1856, the same year as Freud. As a boy and man, his biographer Roger Burlingame writes, Taylor split his world into its minutest parts. Playing croquet, he worried his fellows by plotting the angles of his strokes. When he walked, he counted his steps to learn the most efficient stride. Nervous, highstrung, although he neither smoked nor drank, not even coffee or tea, he was a victim all his life of insomnia and nightmares; and, fearing to lie on his back, he could sleep in peace only when bolstered upright in a bed or in a chair. He couldn't stand the sight of an idle lathe or an idle man. He never loafed, and he was going to make sure that nobody else did.

It was this compulsive character that Taylor stamped onto a civilization. In the shop where he first went to work, a machinist performed his operation by "rule of thumb." Machine speeds, choice of tools, methods of work, were decided by whim or hunch. Taylor set out to prove that these lazy rhythms, inherited from artisan days, should yield to the superior rationality of fractionated time.

The stop watch itself was not new. Before Taylor, work had been timed, but only for the entire job. What Taylor did was to split each job into its component operations and take the time of each. This, in essence, is the whole of scientific management: the systematic analysis and breakdown of work into the smallest mechanical component and the rearrangement of these elements into the most efficient combination. Taylor gave his first lectures to American engineers in 1895 (the year, one might note wryly, that Freud and Breuer published their *Studies in Hysteria,* the "breakthrough" of psychoanalysis). But it was in 1899 that Taylor achieved fame when he taught a Dutchman named Schmidt to shovel forty-seven tons instead of twelve and a half tons of pig iron a day. Every detail of the man's job was specified: the size of the shovel, the bite into the pile, the weight of the scoop, the distance to walk, the arc of the swing, and the rest periods that Schmidt should take. By systematically varying each factor, Taylor got the optimum amount of barrow load. By exact calculation, he got the correct response.

But Taylor also knew what such a mechanical regimen would do to a man or, rather, what sort of man could fit into this strait jacket. "One of the very first requirements for a man who is fit to handle pig iron as a regular occupation," he wrote, "is that he shall be so stupid and so phlegmatic that he more nearly resembles an ox than any other type."*

The logic of Taylorism was obvious: each man's work could be measured by itself: the time in which an operation could be performed could be established, "without bargaining," as an impersonal "standard time"; pay could then be computed on the basis of the amount of work done and the time taken to do it.† In the modern economy, shading of time is so important (as Benjamin Franklin, the prototype of Max Weber's ethical Protestant, remarked, "time is money") that a large company like General Motors contracts with its workers on a six-minute basis. (For purposes of payroll calculation, General Motors divides the hour into ten six-minute periods and, except for the guarantee of three hours' "call-in" pay, the worker is paid by the number of tenths of an hour he works.)

The significance of Taylorism lies in its attempt to enact a social physics. Once work was scientifically plotted, Taylor felt, there could be no disputes about how hard one should work or the pay one should receive for labor. "As reasonably might we insist on bargaining about the time and place of the rising and setting sun," he once said. For a managerial class which at the turn of the century had witnessed the erosion of its old justificatory *mystique* of "natural rights," the science of administration per se provided a new foundation for its moral authority.

While Taylor analyzed the relations of work to time, another engineer, Frank Gilbreth (1868-1924), carried the process one step further: he detached human movement from the person and made of it an abstract visualization. Not only could the pattern of machine work be broken down into elements, but human motion, too, could be "functionalized," and the natural movements of arms and legs could be ordered into a "one best way" of performance.

* Taylor was not the first to understand such consequences. One hundred and fifty years earlier, Adam Smith wrote: "The understandings of the greater part of men are necessarily formed by their ordinary employments. The man whose life is spent in performing a few simple operations . . . has no occasion to exert his understanding. . . . He generally becomes as stupid and ignorant as it is possible for a human creature to become." *The Wealth of Nations* (Modern Library, 1937), p. 734.

† Which is why the "protestant" industrial economy cannot adopt the system of "family wage," to be found in Italy and other countries where Catholic social doctrine applies, whereby a man with children receives more wages than the one who has none, though both do the same work.

Gilbreth (whose contemporary fame rests, ironically, on the movie story of the frenetically organized domesticity of his large family (*Cheaper by the Dozen*), isolated eighteen basic patterns of kinetic units or motions, e.g., reach, move, grasp, which he modestly called "therbligs" (or Gilbreth spelled backwards). And from the analysis of therblig combinations, Gilbreth came to his principles of "motion economy." For example: two hands should not be idle at the same instant except during rest periods; motions of the arms should be in opposite and symmetrical directions, and so on. The penalty for violating these rules is waste.

There was one further step in the inexorable logic of rationalization. While Taylor systematized factory operations and Gilbreth sought to reduce waste motion, Charles Bedeaux sought to combine these into a unit measurement of human power, not unsurprisingly called a "B," which would correspond to the "dyn," or the unit in physics of mechanical power. So defined, "a B is a fraction of a minute of work plus a fraction of a minute of rest always aggregating unity but varying in proportion according to the nature of the strain." Using this detailed calculus, Bedeaux formulated a complicated but mathematically neat system of wage payments which took into account not only the work done but the varying fractions of non-work or rest required in different operations, and increased or decreased payments correspondingly.[55]

The fragmentation of work, although atomizing the worker, also created a dependency and a hierarchy in work, for inherent in the division of labor is what Marx called "the iron law of proportionality." Thus, in the manufacturing process, the ratios between different numbers of workers required in different work processes are ordered by technological complexities. Marx cited an example in type manufacture: One founder could cast 2,000 type an hour, the breaker could break up 4,000, and the polisher could finish 8,000 in the same time; thus to keep one polisher busy the enterprise needed two breakers and four founders, and units were hired or discharged, therefore, in multiples of seven. In many other operations, notably an assembly line, similar inflexible ratios are established, and the hiring and firing of numbers of workers is dictated by the multiples of those ratios. But such dependency presupposes co-ordination and, with co-ordination, the multiplication of hierarchies.

The logic of hierarchy, the third of the logics created by

modern industry, is thus not merely the sociological fact of increased supervision which every complex enterprise demands, but a peculiarly technological imperative. In simple division of labor, for example, the worker had a large measure of control over his own working conditions, i.e., the set-up and make-ready, the cleaning and repairing of machines, obtaining his own materials, and so on. Under a complex division of labor these tasks pass out of his control, and he must rely on management to see that they are properly done. This dependence extends along the entire process of production. As a result, modern industry has had to devise an entirely new managerial superstructure which organizes and directs production. This superstructure draws all possible brainwork away from the shop; everything is centered in the planning and schedule and design departments. And in this new hierarchy there stands a figure known neither to the handicrafts nor to industry in its infancy—the technical employee. With him, the separation of functions becomes complete. The worker at the bottom, attending only to a detail, is divorced from any decision or modification about the product he is working on.

These three logics of size, time, and hierarchy converge in that great achievement of industrial technology, the assembly line: the long parallel lines require huge shed space; the detailed breakdown of work imposes a set of mechanically paced and specified motions; the degree of co-ordination creates new technical, as well as social, hierarchies.*

The Pit and the Pendulum

In the forty years since the death of Taylor, the search for the magical harmony of a kingdom of Micomicon has intensified. The old Puritan morality of a Captain John Smith, according to which he who will not work will not eat, becomes translated into the engineering morality according to which he who will not work a "fair day" should not receive "fair pay." Throughout U.S. industry today the lives of millions of

* It is remarkable how recent is the assembly line, both as a mode of operation and as a linguistic term. Oliver Evans developed a continuous production line for milling grain in 1800, and the packinghouse industry in the 1870's had adopted the use of overhead conveyors for the processing of slaughtered animals. But the assembly line as a modern achievement owes its success largely to Henry Ford and the establishment of an auto line at Highland Park, Michigan, in 1914. And only in 1933 did the Oxford English Dictionary legitimize the term when its supplement in that year added the contemporary meaning of the word. See Siegfried Giedion, *Mechanization Takes Command.*

persons are ordered by production standards which most engineers and managers feel are as little open to argument as the "time and place of the rising and setting sun."

How are the logics translated into practicalities? What does the establishment of a 'fair day's work" mean concretely? What is required of a worker? The basic wage contract between the U.S. Steel Corporation and the CIO Steel Workers can be taken as an example. The contract, first negotiated on May 8, 1946, defines a "fair day's work" as "that amount of work that can be produced by a qualified employee when working at a normal pace a normal pace is equivalent to a man walking, without load, on smooth, level ground at a rate of three miles per hour."

This viscerotonic definition then becomes a "benchmark" or gauge to define the degree of exertion in various jobs. For example·

Shoveling sand

> Material: River sand, moisture 5.5% approx., weight per cu. ft. 100-110 pounds.
> Equipment: Materials handling bos (steel) effective height above floor—32" shovel—No. 2 furnace.
> Working conditions: Under roof: smooth concrete floor, all other conditions normal.
> Production rate: For shoveling sand from pile to box—average weight sand on shovel—15 lbs; 12.5 shovelfuls per minute.

Packaging staples

> Material: 3/4 x 14 gauge staples; 1 pound per cardboard box.
> Equipment: 3 pound capacity metal scoop, platform scale; assembled cardboard boxes with one end open for filling; metal covered working surface.
> Working conditions: Inside, seated.
> Production rate: Filling scoop from pile of staples in tray, pouring one pound into tray on scale, picking up tray and pouring into cardboard box, closing flaps on box, placing aside approximately 24"—5.9 boxes a minute.

In the wage-rationalization program of the U.S. Steel Corporation, completed only in 1947, descriptions of 1,150 benchmark jobs within 152 representative classifications were worked out with similar exactitude. In all, 75,000 workers are covered by such specifications, and the company's incentive program is based on these minimal standards.

Throughout American industry one can find a dozen performance rating systems (some of them worked out pictorially in films), volumes of "standard data" on specific jobs, and other efforts to create objective, comprehensive, yet simple measuring rods of work. In the system of time-and-motion studies of clerical workers devised by Paul Mulligan, the partner of former Air Force Secretary Harold Talbott, all operations are pictured on a "flow chart," a schematic representation of office procedures. This quickly reveals any duplications, back-tracking, or unnecessary steps. From his thick reference guide, *The Manual of Standard Time Data for the Office,* Mulligan fills in the standard times for various manual and machine operations performed in the department under study. With slow-motion films, the efficiency expert can gauge whether a billing clerk, for example, is working at an expected speed. Each motion she goes through in performing her duty is filmed and then analyzed and timed against the "wink-counter," an electric clock constantly within camera view; each movement is expressed in decimal fractions of an hour.

Perhaps the ultima Thule in rationalization is the mathematical formula to determine the fine shadings of skill between jobs recently worked out by the Aluminum Corporation of America in order to set wage differentials scientifically. The program, which covered 56,000 jobs, took three and a half years to complete, at a cost of $500,000. The final equation, three pages long, juggles fifty-nine separate variables; it took thirty-five hours of Univac time, at a cost of $10,000, to compute.*

As Alcoa said diffidently, the formula is simply a "mathematical tool for resolving day-to-day wage problems rationally and without dispute."

Almost compulsively, like the theologian reaching for the perfect metaphysical system with which to encompass all thought, the engineer, going beyond the mere breakdown of work into its simplest detail, now reaches out for a simple, comprehensive system to encompass all time and motion—from the correct strokes of the janitor sweeping the floor to

* If a precise definition of one company's wage structure alone calls for so many variables, consider the problem for social science generally, which seeks to break down such complex variables as decision-making in international affairs, or policy formulation in economic matters

the movement of the typist drumming rhythmically on the keyboard of her electric typewriter. In each instance, the striving is toward the irreducible atom, the nuclear unit which, in alchemic fashion, can be recombined into almost infinite variations, yet be encompassed within the two dimensions of a single card. If such fundamental units could be isolated, then time studies of specific jobs would be rendered obsolete, and all that one would need would be the "periodic table" of elements in order to read how any compound operations would be gauged. That this is no literary metaphor can be seen from the most ambitious attempt to create such a table, the system called "Methods-Time-Measurement" (M-T-M). Elaborated by former Westinghouse engineers Maynard, Schwab, and Stegmerton, M-T-M is a concise catalogue of defined work motions (e.g., reach, move, turn, grasp, position, disengage), with a scale of predetermined time values for each motion, all pinpointed neatly on one handy card. With it, say the authors, a standard performance time may be established for every job in industry.

For the engineer, the unwillingness of the worker to accept such a definition of a "fair day's work" only shows how deeply rooted is his irrational temper. The puzzled manager does not understand, either, why workers persistently restrict output and so limit their income. Yet the revolt against work is widespread and takes many forms. Occasionally one still finds literary protests, either from novelists who have ventured into the factory or from factory workers who have described their experiences.

"This gadget was timed to turn out eight hundred welded shoes per hour," recalls a union organizer named Clayton Fountain. "To make his production, a skillful operator had to keep it going almost constantly. This required a degree of dexterity which a beginner believed impossible to attain—except for the cold fact that the old operator could do it. To master it, you had, in effect, to perform the old stunt of rubbing your belly and patting your head at the same time; that is, you had to learn to do one thing with one hand while doing something else with the other. The way the machine was timed, you just could not keep one hand idle while the other worked. When the dies were old and worn, the shoes stuck to them after they were welded and that added to the complication. It was then necessary to make another motion, banging one shoe with another to loosen it."

"You'd think that it would all become so automatic that

you could do a lot of serious thinking on the job," observes a Chicago worker, Casmir Pantowski. "But you've got to be careful in placing the steel under the press. So even 'daydreaming' is dangerous. Six guys on my shift have missing fingers."

Nor are the respites sufficient to provide relief. "After a few months . . . the regularity of the break and your dependence on it as a means for destroying the day, utterly rob it of its purpose," a young writer, Edward Wahl, notes. "Your first break on Wednesday . . . means that you have six hours left for that day and twenty-two for the rest of the week. Not half the required forty hours is yet past, and only one-fourth of Wednesday's."

But most workers, by and large, are not so articulate about their work. Their behavior itself is a judgment. It appears in the constant evasion of thought about work, the obsessive reveries while on the job and the substitution of the glamor of leisure for the drudgery of work. Yet the harsher aspects are present as well. These take the form of crazy racings against the clock to vary the deadly monotony, of slowdowns —the silent war against production standards—and most spectacularly in the violent eruptions of wildcat strikes against "speed-ups," i.e., changes in the time required to complete a job.

If "conspicuous consumption" was the badge of a rising middle class, "conspicuous loafing" is the hostile gesture of a tired working class. In many machine plants, as sociologist Donald Roy describes it, workers play the "make-out" game, i.e., working at a breakneck pace to fulfil one's piecework quota so that one can be free for the rest of the day. Piecework is often preferred to "day work" or to a flat payment of an hourly rate. On day work, an operator has only the pause at lunch time to break up the meaningless flow of time, like sand in an hourglass. On piecework, by racing the clock, one can mark time in intervals; a worker then has an hour-by-hour series of completions to mark his position in terms of the larger frame of the day's work. By "making out" early, one achieves a victory over the despised time-study man; and the greater the ease, the more vaunted the victory. By "making out" early, one flaunts one's freedom, too, in the face of the foreman: "Since worker inactivity, even after the completion of a fair day's work, seemed to violate a traditional supervisory precept of keeping the appearances of being busy even if there is nothing to do," writes sociologist Roy, "mak-

data" procedures developed by engineers. In standard data, it will be recalled, a work cycle on a job is broken down into its basic elements, each is timed, and standards are then developed for a whole host of comparable operations. Abruzzi sought to discover whether each of the elements was indeed statistically independent—that is, whether the time assignment for each operation could be assessed atomistically or whether each element was dependent on those preceding or following. He concluded that statistical independence could not be established; nor was there any constancy in the relations among operations. Variations in the timing of elements from worker to worker were so great as to cast doubt on the objectivity of the standard data.

Questioning of standard data led to the questioning, too, of the "one best way" of doing work, established by Gilbreth (now included in every textbook on the subject). As Abruzzi pointed out, one cannot add "bits of motion" and claim that the mechanical total of the bits add up to the most efficient motion; in any unified motion, as in any *Gestalt,* the whole is greater than the sum of the parts.

This point is underscored in a recent volume by James Gillespie, one of the foremost British industrial engineers. "Motion study," he writes, "has become micromotionism and with its motion cameras, therbligs, micromotion clocks . . . and its useless time charts, it has become a complex, unwieldy technique. Worse still, with its . . . publication of principles such as that of minimum movement, it has divorced itself from practical, humanitarian knowledge." And that "practical, humanitarian knowledge" is the finding that a man's characteristic or "natural" rhythms in the use of his hands may in the end be more efficient than the mechanistic concept of "the" one best way.

Form without Function

A philosophical radical had defined a new rationality, but the engineer had realized it in a radical way. One would expect the artist, a man who lives time as *durée,* to challenge it. But he too has been assimilated by the machine. Until the last decade and a half, "the machine" had been an object of lively interest and heated controversy. Some social thinkers like Veblen discerned a rationality in "the machine process"; others, like Karl Jaspers, took an opposite view and condemned its mechanistic character. Today the artist and the intelligentsia have become indifferent to the debate and to the challenge of progress which inspired it.

It was not so a century ago. The nineteenth century was an age of a new plasticity and new materials in which Da Vinci's airy draftsmanship was finding concrete application in engineering molds. Every thinker breathed the sense of progress. "The ultimate development of the ideal man is logically certain," wrote Herbert Spencer, "as certain as any conclusion in which we place the most implicit faith." For Walt Whitman's seventieth birthday, Mark Twain wrote a greeting which, as Lewis Mumford reminds us, exulted in the giant strides of mechanical progress—the steamship, the railroad, the telegraph, the electric light, and so on. In a burst of triumph, Twain concluded: "Wait thirty years, and then look out over the earth! You shall see marvels upon marvels added to those whose nativity you have witnessed; and conspicuous about them you shall see their formidable result—man at almost full stature at last!—and still growing, visibly growing while you look . . ."

It was an optimism breathed, too, by Winwood Reade, who, at the climax of his widely read Victorian tract *The Martyrdom of Man,* predicted three inventions—a fuel substitute for coal, aerial locomotion, and the synthetic composition of food. Only the extinction of disease and mortality would be left as man's final tasks on earth, before jumping out to conquer space.

The designers and architects were moved by these visions. In 1901 Frank Lloyd Wright wrote a panegyric on the "age of steel and steam." In the "machine age . . . locomotive engines and engines of industry . . . take the place of works of Art in previous history," he declared. Wright challenged the twentieth-century artist to integrate the machine into his style.

Out of this challenge emerged the "modern style." It was first elaborated in the famous Bauhaus, at Weimar and Dessau, where, in the work of Gropius, Klee, Kandisky, and Moholy-Nagy, a revolution in design began. "The Bauhaus believes the machine to be our modern medium of design and seeks to come to terms with it," wrote Gropius. Against the Art Nouveau, the frivolous ornament, the useless decoration, the sentimental object, the Bauhaus raised the banner of functionalism. In the creation of buildings, the arched baroque and the involuted rococo were replaced by stark geometrical planes and the unadorned curtain wall. Within a generation, the "modern style" had conquered, even though it had been repudiated by some forebears like Wright.

But, while the Bauhaus accepted the rationality of the machine, the revolution it wrought was in design, in materials, and in product—but not in the organization of work. The new aesthetic decree that "form followed function" rarely challenged the function. It took it for granted. More than that, like the technical division of labor, it too detached itself from the human scale and became fragmented. Just as Gilbreth's chrono-cyclographs—a worker's movements traced on a photographic plate—caught the abstract curves of motion divorced from the human mover, so Kandinsky's volatile color bursts or Klee's caressing arcs detached themselves from recognizable objects and became pure abstract visualization.[57] Marcel Duchamp's "Nude Descending the Staircase," the painting that symbolized the revolt against academicism, captured in its spastic oscillations the sense of movement, but lost the human form.

If in art there has been the loss of the human scale, and if in architecture the epigones of Mies and Gropius create an aseptic and sterile form without function, the literary protest, too, has become exhausted. The fascination with the machine, so fashionable in the twenties and thirties, is dulled. Such biting satire as Chaplin's *Modern Times* or René Clair's *A Nous la Liberté,* with their common motifs of factory and prison, is gone. Hart Crane in *The Bridge* sought to come to terms with the machine in order to express its rhythms in verse. But the poets have fled. The factory is now the province of the sociologist and the psychologist. But their interest is not in work either.

Drops in the Social River

By and large the sociologist, like the engineer, has written off any effort to readjust the work process; the worker, like the mythical figure of Ixion, is chained forever to the endlessly revolving wheel. But the spectacle has its unnerving aspect, and the sense of dehumanization is oppressive. Industry has been told, therefore, that production may suffer when only the mechanical aspects of production are considered. Hence the vogue in recent years of "human relations." Its rationale is stated by Cornell sociologist William F. Whyte. The "satisfactions of craftsmanship are gone, and we can never call them back," he writes. "If these were the only satisfactions men could get out of their immediate work, their work would certainly be a barren experience. There are other important satisfactions today: the satisfactions of human association and the satisfactions of solving technical and human problems of work."

The statement summarizes the dominant school of thought which has grown out of the work of the late Elton Mayo of the Harvard Business School and his followers. For Mayo, following the French sociologist Emile Durkheim, the characteristic fact about the modern scene is the presence of constant, disruptive change. The family, the primal group of social cohesion, breaks up as a work and educational unit; neighborhood roots are torn up, and social solidarity, the key to human satisfactions, gives way to *anomie*. If solidarity is to be re-established, it will have to be done within the corporation and factory.

Born in Australia in 1880, Elton Mayo came to the United States in 1923 as a research associate at the University of Pennsylvania. He conducted his first investigations in a textile mill in Philadelphia in 1925.[58] His problem was to determine why labor turnover among the workers in a particular operation—"mule-spinning"—was fifty times higher than in other parts of the plant. Efficiency engineers had been consulted, and several wage-incentive plans introduced, yet the turnover rate continued high. In other parts of the plant, conditions seemed fine. Morale was high; the factory head was a former army colonel under whom many of the workers had served in the war, and ties of personal loyalty were strong.

Mayo noticed that the machines in the mule-spinning room were so arranged that the men who tended them rarely came into contact with each other. The men were subject to spells of obsessive revery and day-dreaming and displayed melancholic traits. A nurse was called in as one of the investigating team, and the workers were encouraged to bring their problems to her. To the efficiency engineers, the men's complaints had seemed so improbable that their stories had been dismissed. Now finding a sympathetic ear, the workers began to pour out their troubles. In addition, Mayo prescribed two rest periods during the day. The results were startling. Turnover diminished, and for the first time, the men in the mule-spinning room were able to meet the production standards set by the time-study men.

At that time Mayo did not fully understand what had produced this change. The role of the nurse and the effect of the rest period were only the first clues, and these were followed up and utilized in the famous Hawthorne experiments (one zealot has exclaimed that the Hawthorne experiments are to social science what Galileo's demonstration of falling weights was to the physical sciences).

The Hawthorne Works in Chicago is one of the manufacturing plants of the Western Electric Company. Western Electric engineers had tried to determine the effect of different lighting conditions on output. They had naturally expected that better illumination would bring better work, and poorer illumination poorer work, but the experiment permitted no such conclusion. Every canon of scientific procedure was followed; there was an experimental group and a matched control group; changes were introduced in one group and not in the other. With improved lighting in the experimental room, production went up—but output rose in the control room, too, where lighting had not been improved. When lighting in the experimental room was reduced again, production continued to rise. And in the control room. where lighting was still held constant, production still continued to rise!

Mayo and the Harvard Department of Industrial Research were then brought in and initiated a series of experiments that was to last more than nine years.[59] The basic experiments, which took five years, were conducted in the "relay test-room," where five girls worked at assembling pieces of telephone equipment. The tests were designed to verify the fundamental hypothesis that output varies with the fatigue of workers, as measured by certain physiological tests. The following factors were isolated to see if they affected efficiency (as measured by output): (1) illumination; (2) amount of rest the previous night; amount of rest the two previous nights; (3) menstrual cycles; (4) humidity and temperature; (5) changes in the type of work; (6) holidays; (7) rest periods within a day's work, of different durations, and in different arrangements; (8) fatigue accumulation during the day, measured by blood pressure tests and vascular skin tests; (9) intelligence; (10) dexterity; (11) wage incentives of different kinds.

For a period of thirteen weeks at a time, one factor was changed or studied and all others were kept constant. "A skilled statistician," Roethlisberger reports, "spent several years trying to relate variations in the physical circumstances of these five operators. For example, he correlated the hours that each girl spent in bed the night before with variations in output the following day. Inasmuch as some people said the effect of being out late one night was not felt the following day but the day after that, he correlated variations in output with the amount of rest the operators had had two nights before. . . . The attempt to relate changes in physical circumstances to variations in output resulted in not a single correlation of enough statistical significance to be recognized by any competent statistician as having any meaning."

Then came the great *éclaircissement*. In period XII of the experiment, the girls were returned to a bread-and-water diet, so to speak—a 48-hour week without rest breaks, without lunches, and with the same illumination as when the experiment began. Yet output kept rising. It then became clear that the workers were responding, not to any of the physiological or physical variables, but to the interest and attention centered on them. The experiment itself, not any outside factor, was the missing link, the unknown determinant.

This led to the second phase of the Hawthorne experiment: the introduction of ambulatory confessors, or walking counselors, ready at any moment to stop and listen to a harassed worker air his woes. Counseling for Mayo was meant to be "a new method of human control." But of this, as of all such objectives, one can ask: Control of whom for what purposes? The answer has been given by Roethlisberger: In counseling, one seeks to shift "the frame of reference," so that the worker sees his grievance in a new light. As one Hawthorne counselor described this process: "In the case of the down-graded employee . . . her focus of attention shifts from alleged inequities, transfer and down-grading grievances, etc. . . . to her unhappy home life; then, when she returns to her original grievance, things do not look so bad." [60]

As a result of the Hawthorne studies and later studies along the same lines, the Mayo group discarded the older hypotheses of industrial psychology that output varies largely with fatigue and was able to elaborate certain "theoretical frames" to guide future research:

1. A factory has to be conceived as a social system, with the relations of its parts defined not only by the formal logical structure but also by the informal structure and by the ceremonials, rituals, and non-logical sentiments that motivate behavior. The worker cannot be abstracted from his social situation.

2. The function of the executive is not only to make policy but to ensure its acceptance "down the line" by subordinates. Since human beings usually resist change, accept-

ance of change involves translating orders into terms that circumvent this resistance. Programs have to be "sold" to the personnel, as a product is "sold" to the public.

3. A factory system, like any stable social system, must be conceived as tending toward an equilibrium in which its different parts are functionally adjusted to each other. When change upsets equilibrium, the function of the executive is to observe which parts need adjustment in order to redress the balance. (The concept of equilibrium came from the Italian sociologist Vilfredo Pareto and from L. J. Henderson, the physiologist who had greatly influenced the Mayo group.)

The great prestige of the Hawthorne studies lay in its claim to scientific objectivity. Certainly few investigations in the social sciences had ever before been conducted on such an enormous scale. But though the methods were neat and precise, and though all the canons of experimental method were duly observed in varying the conditions, some reflection will show that the Hawthorne study and a host of studies it inspired have deep biases which vitiate the claim to completely objective results. These researches rested on the unstated assumption that mechanical efficiency and high output are the sole tests of achievement—of "good" results. And the concepts used were not, thus, objective operational concepts but flowed from the unstated value assumptions. Take the key concept of "restriction of output" which guided the Mayo group in the follow-up experiment at Western Electric, in the study of the bank-wiring room. In the bank-wiring room the Mayo team discovered the existence of an "informal group" which imposed a "bogey" or output restriction mark which was not to be exceeded by any group member, lest the performance of any single man be found wanting. The meaning of this behavior was conceptualized around the term "restriction." But the term "restriction of output," simply represents a contrasting definition of rationality. What may be "resriction" to management may be "a fair day's" work to a worker.

Being "scientists" the researchers were concerned with "what is" and were not inclined to involve themselves in questions of moral values and larger social issues. They operated as technicians, approaching the problem as it is given to them and keeping within the framework that is set. Many sociologists have conceived of themselves as "human engineers"—counterparts to the industrial engineers: where the industrial engineer plans a flow of work in order to assure mechanical efficiency, the "human engineer" tries to "adjust" the worker to the job so that the human equation will match the industrial equation. Some sociologists deny that workers in a plant tend to be unhappy, and point to survey data—much of it collected by management—to show that workers are fairly well satisfied with the job. The argument, however, misses two essential points: there are of course many other aspects of the work environment, *other than the job,* which provide satisfactions (such as the clique group, the joking, loafing, etc.), but this cannot be used to disprove the debilitating aspect of the organization of work and *its* failure to provide satisfactions; secondly, no question about satisfaction is meaningful unless the worker is *aware* of *alternative* possibilities of work. (This is, I suppose, the meaning of the old saw, How can you keep them down on the farm once they've seen Paree? A farmer never having seen or known of Paree may be satisfied with his lot; but is he still satisfied once he has known wider horizons?)

The idea that a scientist simply studies "what is," as John Dewey has argued, is a parochial conception of science.* Few industrial sociologists seem to be aware of the fact that one of the functions of social science is also to explore alternative (and better—that is, more human) combinations of work and not merely to make more effective those that already exist. Without such exploration, one has no notion of the hu-

* "I welcome the quotation marks around 'what is,'" wrote John Dewey, "for it is the supreme business of scientific inquiry to ask about and find out about *what is* . . . the trouble with the [industrial sociology] inquiries is that they fail to be genuinely scientific precisely because, instead of taking *what is,* the facts of the case in human relationships as the subjects of their investigations, they start with a prejudgment as to what is: one that automatically limits the inquiries carved on . . . When this unscientific limitation is removed, "larger social issues" (and moral values as involved in these issues) are necessarily and inevitably an integral part of the subject matter of inquiry" ("Liberating the Social Scientist," *Commentary,* October, 1947).

Professor Dewey was responding to an article by this writer, "Adjusting Men to Machines" (*Commentary,* January, 1947) which analyzed a dozen or more studies in industrial sociology that were made in terms of the above framework. That article, along with one by Nathan Glazer, "Government by Manipulation" (*Commentary,* July, 1946), questioned the method of sociological researches which simply accepted a social problem as "given." In discussing the articles by Glazer and myself, Professor Dewey argued that the attitude which restricted social inquiry to "existing" social arrangements grew out of a historical division, created by the religious culture, which sought to limit the range of social science. As Dewey said forcefully on another occasion: "Anything that obscures the fundamentally moral nature of the social problem is harmful, no matter whether it proceeds from the side of physical or psychological theory. Any doctrine that eliminates or even obscures the function of choice of values and [the] enlistment of desire and emotions in behalf of those chosen weakens personal responsibility for judgment and for action."

man potential and of the real range of social behavior. But as Burleigh Gardner, one of the researchers at Hawthorne, who in recent years has become one of the leading management consultants in the country, succinctly phrased the objectives of these sociological researches: "The more satisfied [the worker] is, the greater will be his self esteem, the more content he will be, and therefore more efficient in what he is doing." A fitting description not of human, but of "cow" sociology.[61]

In this, as in many instances, social engineering imitates art. Twenty years ago the first "solidarity hymn" was penned by Aldous Huxley in his *Brave New World,* and the refrain voiced by the Alphas and Betas could be the school song for industrial sociology:

> Ford, we are twelve; oh make us one
> Like drops within the social river.
> O make us now together run
> As swiftly as thy shining flivver.

While "human relations," as a result of the tremendous publicity given to the Hawthorne findings and of Mayo's further work, became a great vogue, personnel counseling in the broader sense did not spread widely for a while, even within the Bell Telephone System where it originated. The reason, in large measure, was that management itself did not fully understand its function. There seemed to be no tangible "payoff" in diminished cost or increased production that management could point to; moreover, it seemed to some to represent too much "coddling."

Since World War II, however, and largely because of the continuing influx of women into the work force, counseling has become more and more an adjunct of a company's medical service to its employees. Some large companies, like Du Pont and Eastman Kodak, maintain staff psychiatrists. Many, like Hughes Aircraft and Raytheon, have full-time social workers who advise employees on a multitude of problems, financial and marital. But, ironically, it was the psychologist in this instance who taxed the manager for not appreciating the benefits of what Huxley called "advanced emotional engineering." And it was the growing prestige of the management consultant that led management to accept these psychological gimmicks.

While counseling lagged, "communication and participation" quickly became great management fads. In theory, "communication" is supposed to open a two-way street whereby those down the line can talk back to those above and thus "participate" in the enterprise. In few instances have such systems become operative. In most cases communication consists simply of employee newsletters or "chain-of-command" conferences in which vice-presidents meet with managers, managers with supervisors, supervisors with foremen, and so on down the line. In some cases, the system operates with a characteristic advertising-agency twist. At Westinghouse, for example, statements of company policy were recorded on tape, and by dialing on the interplant telephone system one could listen to the messages given to the hundreds of top supervisors. The dial number ostensibly was a secret, confined to 1,200 supervisory employees. In practice, it was a secret in name only, since supervisors were instructed to "leak" the number "confidentially" to various employees, and these men, gleeful at knowing a secret, quickly spread the information to others. The result was that thousands of workers eagerly rushed to listen to hortatory talks which at other times might have been received with utter indifference.

There are two points to be noted about the vogue of "human relations." One is that, in the evident concern with understanding, communication, and participation, we find a change in the outlook of management, parallel to that which is occurring in the culture as a whole, from authority to manipulation as a means of exercising dominion. The ends of the enterprise remain, but the methods have shifted, and the older modes of overt coercion are now replaced by psychological persuasion. The tough brutal foreman, raucously giving orders, gives way to the mellowed voice of the "human-relations oriented" supervisor. The worker doubtless regards this change as an improvement, and his sense of constraint is correspondingly assuaged. In industrial relations, as in large areas of American society, accommodation of a sort has replaced conflict. The second point is that these human-relations approaches become a substitute for thinking about the work process itself. All satisfactions are to be obtained in extracurricular areas: in the group, in leisure pursuits. Thus the problems of work are projected outward and swathed in psychological batting.

This tyranny of psychology has led management into a curious discounting of the "economic man." We are told that what the worker really wants is security, recognition, reward-

Ure wrote a century ago, became tamed, and diligence was regularized. Even the American worker—a man, according to the national stereotype, of boisterousness, individualism, and independence—submitted to the tyranny of the clock.

But in our day, surely, it is not physical hunger which is the driving force; there is a new hunger. The candied carrot, the desire for goods, has replaced the stick; the standard of living has become a built-in automatic drive. Aided and abetted by advertising and the installment plan, the two most fearsome inventions of man since the discovery of gunpowder, selling has become the most striking activity of contemporary America.[62] Against frugality, selling emphasizes prodigality; against asceticism, the lavishness of display. No creature in history is more uxorious than the American consumer, and this submissiveness drives him to buy. The "golden chain" is the deferred-payment plan. By mortgaging his future, the worker can buy a house, a car, appliances, and other comforts. By possession of these products he enters the provinces hitherto tenanted only by the *haut monde*. The aural nerve of *homo Americanus* has been tightened to the most excruciating pitch. The American citizen, as *Fortune* once noted, lives in a state of siege from dawn until bedtime. "Nearly everything he sees, hears, touches, tastes, and smells is an attempt to sell him something. . . . To break through his protective shell the advertisers must continuously shock, tease, tickle or irritate him, or wear him down by the drip-drip-drip or Chinese water torture method of endless repetition. Advertising is the handwriting on the wall, the sign in the sky, the bush that burns regularly every night."

If the American worker has been "tamed," it has not been through the discipline of the machine but by the "consumption society," by the possibility of a better living which his wage, the second income of his working wife, and easy credit all allow. Nowhere was this more evident than in Detroit. In American radical folklore, the auto worker was considered the seedling of the indigenous class-conscious radical—if there was ever to be one in America. Uninhibited, rootless (many were recruited from the Ozark hills), with his almost nihilistic temper he was the raw stuff for revolutionary sentiment—once he realized (or so the Marxists thought) that he was trapped by his job. Few auto workers today have a future beyond their job. Few have a chance of social advancement. But they are not radical. What has happened is that old goals have been displaced, and the American Dream has been given a new gloss. Success at one's job becomes less important than success in one's style of life. A worker sees himself "getting ahead," as Eli Chinoy points out in a recent study, not by promotion in the plant—he knows that *that* ladder has vanished, even though Henry Ford and Walter P. Chrysler began from the mechanics' bench[63]—but because he is working toward a "nice little modern house." These changes in values are reflected most sharply among younger workers. The desire for immediate gratifications — a car, spending money, a girl—burn strong. Rather than spend hard years at study, a man goes immediately into a plant at its attractive starting wage. Once in the plant, he may realize, sickeningly, that he has made a devil's bargain. His advancement depends upon educational training; but this he has foregone. He becomes restless. But dissatisfactions on the job lead not to militancy, despite occasional sporadic outbursts, but to escapist fantasies—of having a mechanic's shop, a turkey farm, a gas station, of "owning a small business of one's own." An idle dream!

Bootstraps

This essay has concerned itself largely with "the" factory worker and the constraints imposed upon him. Certainly any large-scale generalizations become fuzzy if matched against complex and protean reality. And factory work, after all, comprises only a fraction of the kinds of work done in the United States. Other occupational groups have their own work psychology and problems. A skilled worker may find his job monotonous, and a chambermaid in a bustling metropolitan hotel may not. Nothing may be more deadly, perhaps, than the isolated, hermetic life of the bank teller in his cage or of the elevator operator in his sealed jack-in-the-box. Longshoremen swear by their occupation, gaining satisfactions in the free use of muscle and the varieties of excitement on a big city pier, while scorning those who are tied down to the bench or lathe. Musicians, typographers, miners, seamen, loggers, construction workers, all have their special cast of work. Yet the factory is archetypical because its rhythms, in subtle fashion, affect the general character of work the way a dye suffuses a cloth; and, equally, because the rhythms of mechanization spill over into once individualized modes of work. Coal mining, once spoken of as "underground farming," now, with mechanization of the cutting and conveying, takes on much of the aspects of factory work. In offices the installation of rapid high-speed calculators, tabulators, and billing machines turns the white-collar workers into mechanically paced drones. The spread of mechanization into "materials handling" (i.e., warehouses and supermarkets) has introduced mechanical rhythms into the distributive sector of the economy.

These changes accentuate, too, the tendencies to evade work which are so characteristic of the American factory worker and which today obsess all workers. The big lure of escape remains the hope of "being one's own boss." The creed of "the 'individual enterprise' has become by and large a working-class preoccupation," sociologists Reinhard Bendix and S. M. Lipset report. "Though it may have animated both working class and middle class in the past, it is no longer a middle-class ideal today. Instead, people in the middle class aspire to become professionals and, as a second choice, upper-white-collar workers." Fewer people, of course, actually try to go into business than those who think of it as a goal, "but here again the manual workers report more such efforts than the white-collar group."

How realistic are these aspirations? We know that the labor force of the economy is being transformed. Colin Clark, in his *Conditions of Economic Progress,* long ago pointed out that, as incomes rose and the quantity and quality of goods produced increased, large sections of the economy would shift to service and other "tertiary" occupations. Since 1910, the proportion of farmers, farm owners, and unskilled workers in the labor force has decreased sharply as an aggregate; skilled workers have held their own; service workers have increased slightly; professional persons have moved up from 4.4 to 7.5 per cent, and proprietors and managers from 6.5 to 8.8 per cent, of the work force in that period. The largest increases have come in the categories of semiskilled labor and in clerks and sales personnel. Between 1910 and 1950 the semiskilled group increased from 14.7 to 22.4 per cent, the white-collar worker from 10.2 to 20.2 per cent.

Followers of Clark, seeking to refine the conceptual scheme, have talked of "quarternary" occupations (communications, finance, transport, commerce) and "quinary" occupations (medical care, education, research, recreation). Certainly the expansion of the American economy has made many new careers possible, and these new occupations are located, on the whole, outside the factory. But the fascination with these *rates* of growth should not mislead us into failing to consider the limited number of such positions available or the fact that social mobility in the United States occurs *between* generations—it is the children who may get ahead, not the father; the father reaches a point and stays there. The study of occupational mobility by Bendix and Lipset showed that individuals held an average of 4.8 jobs over a twenty-five-year work history. But while workers do change jobs, "between those who work with their hands and those who do not, there is . . . relatively little shifting." All those who work with their hands have spent 80 per cent of their working lives in manual occupations; all who do not work with their hands have spent 75 per cent of their working lives in non-manual occupations.

The sense of having a fixed place is grinding. And even, as in the large corporations, if one still thinks of moving up, the escalator-like process is slow. In compensation, there is a considerable—and sometimes pathetic—effort, if not to lift oneself, to lift one's occupation by its bootstraps. A man will do an infinite amount of physically dirty work, says sociologist Everett Hughes, if the status and prestige arrangements are right; the physically unpleasant jobs of the doctor, for example, are legion. The effort to "professionalize" work has become the major means of giving one's job a badge of honorific quality which the nature of the work itself denies. We have schools of hotel management, as well as of social work. The garage becomes the "lubritorium"; individuals do not say "I sell pots and pans" but "I am in selling"; the janitor becomes the "superintendent"; the hospital superintendent turns into the "administrator"; the secretary becomes the "executive assistant"; and the minister, if he is unable to rise to bishop, measures his success in terms of the social class of his parishioners.

Prophets of Play

The most significant form taken by the flight from work is the desperate drive for "leisure." Work is irksome, but if it cannot be evaded, it can be reduced. In modern times, the ideal is to minimize the unpleasant aspects of work as much as possible by pleasant distractions (music, wall colors, rest periods) and to hasten away as quickly as possible, uncontaminated by work and unimpaired by its arduousness. A gleaming two-page advertisement in *Life* magazine shows a beautiful Lincoln car in the patio-living room of an elegantly simple house, and the ad proclaims: "Your home has walls of glass. Your kitchen is an engineering miracle. Your clothes and your furniture are beautifully functional. *You work easily; play hard.*"

The theme of play, of recreation, of amusement are the dominant ones in our culture today. They are the subject of the "hard sell." Sports clothes, travel, the outdoor barbecue, the portable TV set, all become the hallmarks of the time. In his passivity, there are already the seeds of decay. Yet some serious social critics see in the development of leisure time the potentialities of achieving a spontaneity of spirit, free of the restraints of work and of the older moral injunctions which frowned uopn undisciplined expression. David Riesman mocks those who would seek to introduce "joy and meaning" into modern industrialism. "In a fallacy of misplaced participation," he says, they would like to "personalize, emotionalize and moralize the factory and white collar worlds." But "it makes more sense," he argues, "to work with rather than against the grain of impersonality in modern industry: to increase automatization in work—but for the sake of pleasure and consumption and not for the sake of work itself."

What Reisman wants is "freedom in play." "Far from having to be the residue sphere left over from work-time and work-feeling, [play] can increasingly become the sphere for the development of skill and competence in the art of living. Play may prove to be the sphere in which there is still room left for the would-be autonomous man to reclaim his individual character from the pervasive demands of his social character."

Few can quarrel with the idea, perhaps because it is so amorphous. ("Admittedly we know very little about play," writes Reisman; "research has been concerned mainly with the 'social character' of the producer.") But can "play" be divorced from work? Play, it should be pointed out, is not leisure—at least not in the classical image as it has come down from Plato to T. S. Eliot. A leisure civilization is one with the fixed task of exploring and extending a specific cultural heritage. Leisure is not, as Josef Pieper points out, a dalliance or wanton play, but a full-time cultivation of the gentle arts, a "working at" pursuits which make up the calling of the gentleman. Nor is relaxation play. Relaxation, whether it be puttering or daydreaming, is an interstice between efforts, a trough between peaks. It is not "free time," as any man who takes a "break" from work knows, but lapsed time, an integral part of the rhythms of work.

Play (not leisure or relaxation) is a release from the tension of work, an alternate use of muscle and mind. But a tension that is enervating or debilitating can only produce wildly aggressive play or passive, unresponsive viewing. To have "free time" one needs the zest of a challenging day, not the exhaustion of a blank one. If work is a daily turn round Ixion's wheel, can the intervening play be anything more than a restless moment before the next turn of the wheel?

Edward Bellamy in his *Looking Backward* foresaw a state wherein an individual spent twenty to twenty-five years of his life in drudging routine for a few hours a day and then was free to pursue his own desires. Here, in the United States in mid-twentieth century, in a curious fashion, Bellamy's vision is being realized. The average work week has been reduced from 70.6 hours (in 1850) to 40.8 (in 1950). The two-day weekend is now standard in American life, and the seven-hour workday is at the threshold. But what workers have been denied in work, they now seek to recapture in manifold ways. Over the past decade there has been a fantastic mushrooming of arts-and-crafts hobbies, of photography, home woodwork shops with power-driven tools, ceramics, high fidelity, electronics, radio "hams." America has seen the multiplication of the "amateur" on a scale unknown in previous history. And while this is intrinsically commendable, it has been achieved at a high cost indeed—the loss of satisfaction in work.

The Exhaustion of the Left

If work has lost its rationale in the capitalist industrial order, it has failed to find any new meaning under the socialist regimes. Perhaps one of the most significant sociological facts of recent years is the exhaustion of socialist thought on the European continent and in England. Socialists are not wholly at fault. The European national economies, so insular or landlocked, are peculiarly dependent upon world-trade balances, and the area of maneuverability is limited; in fact, in a silently emerging "managerial revolution," technical decision-making by the economic expert now shapes the politician's pronouncements.

But socialist doctrine is not quite free of responsibility for its present miseries. Socialism was primarily a distributive philosophy. The *Manifesto* of Marx, the *Finanzkapital* of Hilferding, the Fabian essays of the Webbs, all blithely assumed that the problems of production were solved by capi-

whereby incoming orders are simultaneously translated, through tapes, into production, scheduling, traffic, and shipping orders for the relevant plant; into volume and income information for the company's operating and financial records; and into billing, invoicing, and price notices to the customers. The Bank of America has a 25-ton "bank clerk," an electronic machine made up of 17,000 radio tubes and a million feet of electric wire, coyly named "Erma," which is capable of handling the bookkeeping details on 50,000 checking accounts a day. It accepts "stop" payments and "hold" orders, catches overdrawn accounts, and prints monthly statements at a speed of 600 lines a minute.

(3) Self-correcting control devices which "instruct" machines through punched tapes, very much like the ones in old player-pianos. An automatic lathe developed by the Arma Corporation, through punched-tape instructions, machined a workpiece in four minutes to tolerances of 0.0003 of an inch, which normally was machined in thirty minutes by a skilled machinist working with drawings. A concrete-mixing plant, in use by the Cleveland Builders Supply Company, loads onto ready-mix trucks any one of 1,500 different mixing formulas. A punched card, coded for the formula, is inserted into an electronic control panel, and the desired mixture is delivered by conveyors onto the waiting truck; the control mechanisms even measure and compensate for any deficiency or excess of water in the sand, coarse rock, and slag that go into the mixture.

(4) Automatic assembly. Admiral Corporation and several other major electrical manufacturing companies have machines that can "spit out" completely assembled radios. A machine called Autofab, produced by General Mills, will put together in one minute the number of electronic units that previously took a worker a full day to assemble.

While some of these plants resemble the image of the "robot factory" which science-fiction writers have conjured up for decades, they are still one step away from "true" automation. Today, fully automatic assembly is possible only when a large output of a single product is called for, but such inflexible, single-purpose machinery is too costly for medium or short production runs, and consequently the adoption of such machines tends to "freeze" the design and the technological stage of the product. True automation, as envisaged by Eric Leaver and John J. Brown, would design products in terms of a multi-purpose machine, rather than a machine for each product. If such machines ever were produced, they would create a revolution not only in technology but in aesthetics as well. The concept of what a radio or a stove should look like, for example, might have to change drastically. In the first industrial revolution, fixed aesthetic habit dominated the design of a machine. When, in the famous Crystal Palace Exhibit of 1851, iron was introduced for the first time into construction other than machinery, the first structures and artifacts, true to the predominant imagination, were ornamental and baroque rather than utilitarian. Only gradually did the "modern" emphasis that the form should express, rather than hide, the function gain the upper hand. Yet, although the designer is no longer conservative, the engineer still is. It is easier for him to create single-purpose automatic machinery that can produce quick, spectacular results. But the adoption of these expensive machines will only delay the coming of the flexible automatic machines, capable of turning out a wide variety of products, and producing a true machine revolution.

Americans, with their tendency to exaggerate innovations, have conjured up wild fears about changes that automation may bring. Norbert Wiener, whose book on "cybernetics" was responsible in part for the vogue of "communication theory," has pictured a dismal world of unattended factories turning out mountains of goods which a jobless population will be unable to buy. Such projections are silly. Even if automatic controls were suddenly introduced, regardless of cost considerations, into all the factories that could use them, only about eight per cent of the labor force would be directly affected.

It is evident that automation will produce disruptions; and many workers, particularly older ones, may find it difficult to ever find suitable jobs again. It is also likely that small geographical pockets of the United States may find themselves becoming "depressed areas" as old industries fade or are moved away. But it is unlikely that the economic effects of automation will be any greater, say, than the social disruptions which follow shifts in taste, or substitution of products, or changes in mores. The rise of a functional style in architecture, for example, has meant a decrease in the ranks of brick masons, plasterers, painters, and molders. The substitution of oil for coal has cut in half the required number of miners. The fact that young people now marry at an earlier age has produced a sharp slump in the textile and clothing industries, for marrying earlier means that one dresses up less, dresses more casually, and spends more of the family budget for house and furniture.

Whether the nation can absorb all such disruptions depends on the general level of economic activity, and this itself is a function of the productive growth of the economy. Over the last decade and a half Americans have learned, through a flexible tax and fiscal policy, how to regulate the economy and to stimulate its growth. The government, as gyroscope, can offset overproduction and underconsumption. The question is largely one of politics rather than economics, of the willingness of the government to act when necessary.

Automation, however, will have enormous social effects. Just as factory work impressed its rhythms on society, so the rhythms of automation will give a new character to work, living, and leisure.

Automation will change the basic composition of the labor force, creating a new *salariat* instead of a *proletariat,* as automatic processes reduce the number of industrial workers required in production. In the chemical industry, for example, output rose, from 1947 to 1954, over 50 per cent, while the number of "blue-collar" workers increased only 1.3 per cent. At the same time, the number of non-production workers, that is, professional, supervisory, clerical, and sales personnel, increased by 50 per cent. In 1947, the ratio of production workers to non-production workers was 3:1. In 1954, in a seven-year period, the ratio had dropped to 2:1.

In its most important consequence, the advent of automation means that a corporation no longer has to worry about a large labor supply. This means that new plants can be located away from major cities and closer to markets or to sources of raw materials and fuels. Sylvania, for example, which has forty-three plants, has built its most recent ones in such out-of-the-way places as Nelsonville, Ohio; Burlington, Iowa; and Shawnee, Oklahoma. The company has also insisted that its plants be smaller, and it placed a limit of 700 persons to be employed in a plant. In this way, the corporation can exercise new social controls. The works manager can know all the men personally, and the social divisions of the small town will recapitulate the social gradations in the plant. Under these conditions a new manorial society may be in the making.

The decentralization of industry may equally revolutionize the social topography of the United States as a whole. As new plants are built on the outskirts of towns and as more and more workers live along the radial fringes of the spreading city, the distinction of the urban and the suburban becomes increasingly obliterated. In its place may appear one scenery, standard for town, suburb, countryside, and wild. An environment, as William James has noted, is an extension of ego. In the new topography, we may arrive at what the editors of the British *Architectural Review* have called "subtopia."

But more than topographical changes are involved. The very matutinal patterns will change as well. The major economic fact is that, under automation, depreciation rather than labor becomes the major cost. And when labor is relatively cheap, it becomes uneconomical to keep an enormously expensive machine idle. To write off the high capital investment, more and more of the automated plants may expand shift operations in order to keep the plant running twenty-four hours a day. And so more and more workers may find themselves working "out of hours." In such work communities, the rhythms of sleeping, eating, social, and sexual life become skewed. A man on the regular eight-to-four shift follows a cycle of *work, recreation, and sleep,* while during the same day the fellow on the four-to-twelve shift is on a cycle of *recreation, work, and sleep,* while the night man goes through his twenty-four hours in *sleep, recreation, and work.* Where this occurs, friendship patterns may change abruptly. When the wife and children follow a "normal" routine while the man sleeps through the day, home and sex life become disjointed.

This breakup of the workday—and why should men work while the sun is shining? the practice is a relic of rustic days —is accentuated by a different aspect of the changing economic pattern of the country. As incomes rise and hours are reduced, more and more families begin to spend increasing amounts of money on recreation and travel. This rising demand for entertainment and services, for hotels, motels, vacation resorts, garages, theaters, restaurants, television, requires more individuals to work "out-of-hours" — evenings and weekends—in catering to these desires. In the next decade, perhaps a fourth or more of the labor force will be working special hours. The multiplication of such special work groups, with their own internal life and modes of recreation, is one of the features of a consumer-oriented culture.

For the individual worker, automation may bring a new concept of self. For in automation men finally lose the "feel" of work. Whatever the derogating effects, the men who use power-driven tools sense these instruments, almost as in driving an automobile, as an extension and enlargement of their own bodies, their machines responding, almost organically, to their commands and adding new dexterity and power to their own muscle skills. As a machine tender, a man now stands outside work, and whatever control once existed by "setting a bogey" (i.e., restricting output) is finally shattered. As one steelworker said, "You can't slow down the continuous annealer in order to get some respite." With the new dial-sets, too, muscular fatigue is replaced by mental tension, by the interminable watching, the endless concentration. (In the Puritan morality, the devil could always find work for "idle hands," and the factory kept a man's hands busy. But that morality ignored the existence of the fantasy life and its effects. Now, with machine-watching, there will be idle hands but no "idle minds." An advance in morality?)

Yet there is a gain for the worker in these new processes. Automation requires workers who can think of the plant as a whole. If there is less craft, less specialization, there is the need to know more than one job, to link boiler and turbine, to know the press and the borer and to relate their jobs to each other.

Most important, perhaps, there may be an end, too, to the measurement of work. Modern industry began not with the factory but with the measurement of work. When the worth of the product was defined in production units, the worth of the worker was similarly gauged. Under the unit concept, the time-study engineers calculated that a worker would produce more units for more money. This was the assumption of the wage-incentive schemes (which actually are output-incentive schemes) and of the engineering morality of a "fair day's pay for a fair day's work."

But under automation, with continuous flow, a worker's worth can no longer be evaluated in production units.[68] Hence output-incentive plans, with their involved measurement techniques, may vanish. In their place, as Adam Abruzzi foretells, may arise a new work morality. Worth will be defined not in terms of a "one best way," not by the slide rule and stop watch, not in terms of fractioned time or units of production, but on the basis of planning and organizing and the continuously smooth functioning of the operation. Here the team, not the individual worker, will assume a new importance; and the social engineer will come into his own. And work itself?

Ananke and Thanatos

In Western civilization, work, whether seen as curse or as blessing, has always stood at the center of moral consciousness. "In the sweat of thy brow," says Genesis, "shalt thou eat bread." The early Church fathers were intrigued about what Adam did before the Fall; in the variety of speculations, none assumed he was idle. He devoted himself to gardening, "the agreeable occupation of agriculture," said St. Augustine.

In the Protestant conception, all work was endowed with virtue. "A housemaid who does her work is no farther away from God than the priest in the pulpit," said Luther. Every man is "called," not just a few, and every place, not just a church, is invested with godliness. With Zwingli, even with dour Calvin, work was connected with the joy of creating and with exploring even the wonders of creation.

In the nineteenth century, beginning with Carlyle, man was conceived as *homo faber,* and human intelligence was defined as the capacity for inventing and using tools. If man in the Marxist sense was "alienated" from himself, the self was understood as a man's potential for "making" things, rather than alienation as man being broken into a thing itself. (Man will be free when "nature is his work and his reality" and he "recognizes himself in a world he has himself made," said Marx in his early philosophical-economic manuscripts, adopting an image that A. E. Housman later turned into a lament.) In the same vein, John Dewey argued that a man "learned by doing," but the phrase, now a progressive-school charade, meant simply that men would grow not by accepting prefigured experiences but by seeking problems that called for new solutions. ("Unlike the handling of a tool," said Dewey, "the regulation of a machine does not challenge man or teach him anything; therefore he cannot grow through it.")

All these are normative conceptions. In Western history, however, work has had a deeper "moral unconscious." It was a way, along with religion, of confronting the absurdity of existence and the beyond. Religion, the most pervasive of human institutions, played a singular symbolic role in society because it faced for the individual the problem of death. Where death was but a prelude to eternal life, hell and heaven could be themes of serious discourse, and domination on earth had a reduced importance. But with the decline in religious belief went a decline in the power of belief in eternal life. In its place arose the stark prospect that death meant the total annihilation of the self. (Hamlet, as Max Horkheimer points out, "is the embodiment of the idea of individuality for the very reason that he fears the finality of death, the terror of the abyss.")

Many of these fears were staved off by work. Although religion declined, the significance of work was that it could still mobilize emotional energies into creative challenges. (For Tolstoy, as later for the Zionists in the Israeli *kibbutzim,* work was a religion; A. D. Gordon, the theoretician of the co-operative communities, preached redemption through physical labor.) One could eliminate death from consciousness by minimizing it through work. As *homo faber,* man could seek to master nature and to discipline himself. Work, said Freud, was the chief means of binding an individual to reality. What will happen, then, when not only the worker but work itself is displaced by the machine?

PART III

The Exhaustion of Utopia

Chapter 12

The Failure of American Socialism:

The Tension of Ethics and Politics

> The Rabbi of Zans used to tell this story about himself: "In my youth when I was fired with the love of God, I thought I would convert the whole world to God. But soon I discovered that it would be quite enough to convert the people who lived in my town, and I tried for a long time, but did not succeed. Then I realized that my program was too ambitious, and I concentrated on the persons in my own household. But I could not convert them either. Finally it dawned upon me: I must work upon myself, so that I may give true service to God. But I did not accomplish even this."
>
> —Hasidic Tale

> He who seeks the salvation of souls, his own as well as others, should not seek it along the avenue of politics.
>
> —Max Weber

SOCIALISM WAS AN unbounded dream. Fourier promised that under socialism people would be at least "ten feet tall." Karl Kautsky, the embodiment of didacticism, proclaimed that the average citizen of the socialist society would be a superman. The flamboyant Antonio Labriola told his Italian followers that their socialist-bred children would each be Galileos and Giordano Brunos. And the high-flown, grandiloquent Trotsky described the socialist millennium as one in which "man would become immeasurably stronger, wiser, freer, his body more harmoniously proportioned, his movement more rhythmic, his voice more musical, and the forms of his existence permeated with dramatic dynamism."

America, too, was an unbounded dream. When the American colonies broke away from England, they inscribed upon the back of the great seal authorized by Congress *Novus Ordo Seclorum*—we are "the new order of the ages," the beginning of the American era. The American continent, with its vast lands and mighty riches, was destined to be a great social laboratory. Here the unfolding design of "God, Master Workman," would be manifest. Such a disguised deism, emphasizing the aspect of God as a craftsman rather than as a fixed revelation, was congenial to the growth of a pragmatic temper. It was a society which, if it did not welcome, would at least abide without scorn the efforts of small bands to explore the design of the millennium. And if in places the response was hostile, there was the Icarian wilderness, stretching from Texas to Iowa, in which utopian colonies might find refuge, safe from prying eyes, to continue their chiliastic search. Small wonder then that such colonies arose in prodigal number.

Here, too, it seemed as if socialism would have its finest hour. Inspired, perhaps, by the expanse of the virgin wilderness, Marx and Engels felt a boundless optimism. In 1879 Marx wrote, "the United States have at present overtaken England in the rapidity of economical progress, though they lag still behind in the extent of acquired wealth; but at the same time, the masses are quicker and have greater political means in their hands to resent the form of a progress accomplished at this expense."[69] Engels, who wrote a score of letters on the American scene in the late 1880's and early nineties, repeated this prediction time and again. In his introduction to the American edition of *The Conditions of the Working Class in England,* written at the height of enthusiasm over the events of 1886—notably the spectacular rise of the Knights of Labor and the Henry George campaign in New York—he exulted: "On the more favored soil of America, where no medieval ruins bar the way, where history begins with the elements of modern bourgeois society, as evolved in the seventeenth century, the working class passed through these two stages of its development [a national trade union movement and an independent labor party] within ten months." And five years later, his optimism undiminished by the sorry turn of events, Engels wrote to Schleuter: ". . . continually renewed waves of advance followed by equally certain set-backs are inevitable. Only the advancing waves are becoming more powerful, the set-backs less paralyzing. . . . Once the Americans get started it will be with an energy and violence compared with which we in Europe shall be mere children."[70]

But there still hovers the melancholy question posed by Werner Sombart at the turn of the century in the title of a book, *"Why Is There No Socialism in the United States?"* To this Sombart supplied one set of answers. He pointed to the open frontiers, the many opportunities for social ascent through indivdual effort and the rising standard of living. Other writers have expanded these considerations. Selig Perlman, in his *Theory of the Labor Movement,* advanced three reasons for the lack of class consciousness in the United States: the absence of a "settled" wage-earner class; the "free gift" of the ballot (workers in other countries who were denied such rights—for example, the Chartists in England—developed political rather than economic motivation); and third, the impact of successive waves of immigration. It was immigration, said Perlman, which gave rise to the ethnic, linguistic, religious, and cultural heterogeneity of American labor and to the heightened ambitions of immigrants' sons to escape their inferior status. Count Keyserling, a traveler here in the twenties, observed that Americanism, with its creed of egalitarianism, was a surrogate for socialism; and the "conversions" of many German socialists who came here in the late nineteenth century attests to the acuity of this remark. Some writers have stressed the agrarian basis of American life, with the farmer seesawing to radicalism and conservatism in tune to the business cycle. Others have pointed to the basically sectional rather than functional organization of the two-party system, with its emphasis on patronage, its opportunism, and its vacuity of rhetoric as the mode of political discourse; hence compromise, rather than rigid principle, becomes the trading concern of the interest-oriented political bloc. In the end, all such explanations have fallen back on the natural resources and material vastness of America. In awe of the fact that the Yankee worker consumed almost three times as much bread and meat, and four times as much sugar, as his German counterpart, Sombart exclaimed: "On the reefs of roast beef and apple pie socialistic Utopias of every sort are sent to their doom."[71]

Implicit in many of these analyses was the notion, however, that such conditions were but temporary. Capitalism as an evolving social system would of necessity "mature," crisis would follow crisis, and a large, self-conscious wage-earner class and a socialist movement on the European pattern would emerge. The great depression was such a crisis—an emotional jolt which shook the self-confidence of the entire society. It left scar tissue on the minds of American workers. It spurred the organization of a giant trade-union movement which, in ten years, grew from less than three million to over fifteen million workers, or almost 30 per cent of the wage and salaried force of the country. It brought in its train smoking-hot organizing drives and sit-downs in the Ohio industrial valley which gave the country a strong whiff of class warfare. It spawned strong anticapitalistic and antiplutocratic populist movements (e.g., Huey Long's share-the-wealth, Father Coughlin's social justice, Dr. Townsend's old-age pension scheme). Here, seemingly, was the fertile soil which socialist theorists had long awaited.

Yet no socialist movement emerged, nor did a coherent socialist ideology take seed either in the labor movement or in government. It would seem that the general reasons adduced earlier simply held—and that the New Deal, like the earlier ideology of Americanism, had become a somewhat different surrogate for socialism. But all such explanations are "external," so to speak, to the radical movement, and, even if true, are simply one side of the coin. The other is: How did the socialist see the world, and, because of that vision, why did the movement fail to adapt to the American scene? Why was it incapable of rational choice?

A general answer why the socialist movement did not face up to the real situation—and these judgments are always after the fact—involves *the interplay of social character* (i.e., the social composition of the movement and the kind of allegiance it demanded of its members), *the degree of "access" to other institutions,* and *the nature of its ideology.*[72] A full explanation of the failure—or success—of a social movement would have to describe how these three elements affect each other. Thus, a movement completely alienated from the society, for ethnic or emotional reasons, would find it harder to make compromises with an existing order; in such cases, the social character of the movement might be the decisive explanation for its failure to adapt to changing reality. A social movement with a high proportion of union members, one with a high proportion of professional persons, might have an easier "bridge" to other political groups; hence, "degree of access" might be the important factor. In other instances, the nature of the ideology might be the agent that creates the dilemma of action. For some movements, ideology is a pose, easily dropped; for others it is a bind.

This chapter concerns itself with the ideology of socialism. It is my argument that the failure of the socialist movement in the United States was rooted in its inability to resolve a basic dilemma of ethics and politics: the socialist movement, by the way in which it stated its goal, and by the way in which it rejected the capitalist order as a whole, could not relate itself to the specific problems of social action in the here-and-now, give-and-take political world. In sum: it was trapped by the unhappy problem of living *in* but not *of* the world; it could only act, and then inadequately, as the moral, but not political, man in immoral society. It could never resolve, but only straddle, the basic issue of either accepting capitalist society and seeking to transform it from within, as the labor movement did, or of becoming the sworn enemy of that society, like the Communists. A religious movement can split its allegiances and (like Lutheranism) live *in* but not *of* the world (after all, it is not concerned with this life but the after-life); a political movement cannot.

The Two Ethics

In the largest sense, society is an organized system for the distribution of rewards and privileges, the imposition of obligations and duties. Within that frame, ethics deals with the *ought* of distribution, implying a theory of justice. Politics is the concrete *mode* of distribution, involving a power struggle between organized groups to determine the allocation of privilege. In social action there is an ineluctable tension between ethics and politics. Lord Acton posed the problem in a note: "Are politics an attempt to realize ideals, or an endeavour to get advantages, within the limits of ethics?" More succinctly, "are ethics a purpose or a limit?"[73]

In some periods of history, generally in closed societies, ethics and politics have gone hand in hand. There, in theory, the moral law and the just price rule, and each stratum receives its privileges according to fixed status. But a distinguishing feature of modern society is the separation of ethics and politics—since no group can, through the civil arm, impose its moral conceptions on the whole society; and ideology—the façade of general interest and universal values which masks specific self-interest—replaces ethics. The redivision of the rewards and privileges of society can only be accomplished in the political arena. But in that fateful entry into politics, an ethic stated as purpose (or end), rather than as a limit (or simply the rules of the game), becomes a far-reaching goal which demands a radical commitment that necessarily transforms politics into an all-or-none battle.

Acton's dilemma was most clearly reformulated by Max Weber in his dicussion of politics as a way of life. One can see the political game, he said, as an "ethic of responsibility" (or the acceptance of limits), or as an "ethic of conscience" (or the dedication to absolute ends). The former is the pragmatic view which seeks reconciliation as its goal. The latter creates "true believers" who burn with pure, unquenchable flame and can accept no compromise with faith.

Weber, arguing that only the ethic of responsibility is possible in politics if civil peace is to be maintained, writes: "The matter does not appear to me so desperate if one does not ask exclusively who is morally right and who is morally wrong, but if one rather asks: Given the existing conflict how can I solve it with the least internal and external danger for all concerned?"[74]

Such a view of politics, rather than the dedication to some absolute (whether it be Bolshevism as an active, disruptive force of society or religious pacifism as a passive withdrawal from society), is possible, however, only when there is a basic consensus among contending groups to respect each other's rights to continue in the society. The foundation of a pluralist society rests, therefore, on this separation of ethics and politics and on the limiting of ethics to the formal rules of the game. In practice, the socialists accepted this fact; in theory, because of its root rejection of the society, the socialist movement could never wholeheartedly accept this basic approach, and on crucial doctrinal issues it found itself stymied.

The question of which ethic one accepts becomes crucial, for the distinctive character of "modern" politics is the involvement of *all* strata of society in movements of social change, rather than, as in feudal or peasant or backward societies, the fatalistic acceptance of events as they are. The starting point was, as Karl Mannheim elegantly put it, the "orgiastic chiliasm" of the Anabaptists, the ecstatic effort to realize the Millennium at once. Martin Luther had torn down the monastery walls which separated the sacred from the profane life. Each man now stood alone, in the "equality of believers," forced to make his affirmation and to realize the Christian life himself, directly, rather than through the vicarious atonement of the saints. But if all men were equal, how could there be master and servant? If all men stood naked before God in the matter of salvation, should they not be equal in sharing the material goods of the worldly life? These were the disturbing questions asked by Thomas Munzer and the radical Anabaptists. Suddenly, other-worldly religious quietism became transformed into a revolutionary activism to realize the Millennium in the *here and now*. Thus the religious frenzy of the chiliasts which burst the bonds of the old religious order threatened to buckle the social order as well;

for unlike previous revolutions, which aimed at single oppressors, chiliasm sought to overthrow the entire, existing social order.*

The characteristic psychological fact about the chiliast is that for him "there is no inner articulation of time"; there is only "absolute presentness." "Orgiastic energies and ecstatic outbursts began to operate in a wordly setting and tensions previously transcending day to day life became explosive agents within it."[75] The chiliast is neither in the world nor of it. He stands outside of it and against it because salvation, the Millennium, is immediately at hand.

Where such a hope is possible, where such a social movement can transform society in a cataclysmic flash, the "leap" is made, and in the pillar of fire the fusion of ethics and politics is possible. But where societies are stable and social change can only come piecemeal, the pure chiliast, in despair, turns nihilist, rather than make the bitter-tasting compromises with the established hierarchical order. "When this spirit ebbs and deserts these movements," writes Mannheim, "there remains behind in the world a naked mass-frenzy and despiritualized fury." In a later and secularized form, this attitude found its expression in Russian anarchism. So Bakunin could write: "The desire for destruction is at the same time a creative desire."

Yet not only the anarchist, but every socialist, every convert to political messianism, is in the beginning something of a chiliast. In the newly found enthusiasms, in the identification with an oppressed group, there is the unsuppressed urgency and hope that the "final conflict" might soon be in sight. ("Socialism in our time," was the banner which Norman Thomas raised for the new recruits to the Socialist party in the 1930's.) But the "revolution" is not always nigh, and the question of how to discipline this chiliastic zeal and hold it in readiness has always been the basic problem of radical strategy.

The anarchist had the vision of *die Tat,* "the deed." Like Paul Munnumit, in Henry James's *Princess Casamassima,* he

* Munzer's millennarian dreams kindled the literary utopias, more than a century later, of Robert Burton's idyllic land, in his preface to the *Anatomy of Melancholy,* and the technological paradise of Bacon's New Atlantis, and found political expression in the egalitarian demands of the Levellers and Diggers during the Cromwell rebellion. A century and a half later, the same impulses flickered strongly, during the French Revolution, in Gracchus Babeuf's "conspiracy of the equals," and passed into the common currency of the revolutionary movements of the nineteenth century.

could live a drab, humdrum life because of his secret, omnipotent conviction that "a shot" could transform the world in a flash and that he could command the moment when the shot would come. Powerful as the image was, its believers could only live, like sleepwalkers, in a fantasy world. Yet only through fantasy could the anarchists keep the believer from becoming tired or dispirited. The most radical approach was that of Georges Sorel, with his concept of the revolutionary myth (*images de batailles*), a myth which, for the anarcho-syndicalists, functioned as a bastardized version of the doctrine of salvation. These unifying images, Sorel wrote, can neither be proved nor disproved; thus they are "capable of evoking an undivided whole" from the mass of diverse sentiments which exist in society. "The syndicalists solve this problem perfectly by concentrating the whole of socialism in the drama of the general strike; thus there is no longer any place for the reconciliation of contraries in the equivocations of the professors; everything is clearly mapped out so that only one interpretation of Socialism is possible." In this "catastrophic conception" of socialism, as Sorel called it, *"it is the myth in its entirety which is alone important.*[76]

But how long can a myth sustain, when the reality constantly belies it?

The Veils of the Proletariat

What of the proletariat itself? What is its role in the socialist drama of history? How does the proletariat see through the veils of obscurity and come to self-awareness? Marx could say with Jesus, "I have come to end all mysteries, not to perpetuate them." His role, in his own self-image, was to lay bare the fetishes which enslave modern man and thus to confute Hegel's claim that freedom and rationality had already been achieved. But like his old master he could only deal with "immanent" forces of history, not the mechanics of social action.[77]

All political movements, Marx wrote, have been slaves to the symbols of the past. ("Thus Luther donned the mask of the Apostle Paul, the Revolution of 1789 to 1814 draped itself alternately as the Roman Republic and the Roman Empire," he wrote in *The Eighteenth Brumaire*.) But history is the process of progressive disenchantment; men are no longer bound to the river gods and anthropomorphic deities of the agricultural societies; nor need they be bound to the abstract impersonal deity of bourgeois Protestantism. Man was potential. But how to realize his potentiality? The intellectual was, in part, capable of self-emancipation because he possessed the imagination to transcend his origins. But the proletariat, as a class, could develop only to the extent that the social relations of society itself revealed to the slave the thongs that bound him. Man is not freer, said Marx in *Das Kapital,* because he can sell his labor power to whom he wishes. Exploitation is implicit in the very structure of capitalist society, which, in order to live, must constantly expand by extracting surplus value and accumulating new capital. In the process, the proletarian would be reduced to the barest minimum of human existence (the law of increasing misery) and thus be robbed of any mark of distinction. In the agony of alienation he would realize a sense of identity which would unite him with others and create a cohesive social movement of revolution. In action he would no longer be manipulated but would "make" himself.[78]

Thus the scene is set for the grand drama. Out of the immanent, convulsive contradictions of capitalism, conflict would spread. The proletariat, neither in nor of the world, would inherit the world.

But History (to use these personifications) confounded Marx's prophecy, at least in the West. The law of increasing misery was refuted by the tremendous advances of technology. The trade union began bettering the workers' lot, and, in the political struggles that followed, it found that it could sustain itself not by becoming a revolutionary instrument against society but by accepting a place within society.

A Place in the Sun

In the America of the nineteenth century, almost every social movement had involved an effort by the worker to escape his lot as a worker. At times the solution was free land, cheap money, producer's co-operatives, or some other chimera from the gaudy bag of utopian dreams. The rise of the American Federation of Labor signaled the end of this search for the land of Prester John. "The working people," said Gompers, "are in too great need for immediate improvement[s] in their condition to allow them to forego them in their endeavour to devote their entire energies to an end however beautiful to contemplate. . . . The way out of the wage system is through higher wages."[79]

It was the obstinate manner in which the sectarians ignored the bread-and-butter aspect of the situation that soured him completely on the political socialists. In the 1880's, the cigarmakers union, headed by Gompers, sought legislation outlawing the manufacture of cigars in tenement homes. He marked for reprisal those legislators who voted against the measure and called for support of those who voted for the bill. But the political socialists were dead-set against voting for old-party candidates, even the pro-labor ones, charging that such a move might provide temporary gains for the cigarmakers but would "corrupt" the labor movement. Even when the first tenement-house bill was enacted, the socialists refused to support for re-election Gompers' man, Edward Grosse, who had been instrumental in pushing through the measure. It was a lesson that Gompers never forgot.

But there was another side to the seeking for a place in the world to which Gompers was no less sensitive, though he was more masked in his statement of the case. Gompers, the son of Dutch-Jewish parents, came to the United States at the age of thirteen and, for most of his life, was acutely aware of his foreign birth. Most of the leaders of American labor have been immigrants or close to immigrant stock, and the desire to be accepted, as Marcus Lee Hansen has noted, was part of the intense status drive of most immigrants. In effect, the immigrant has not been a radical force in American life; on the contrary, the immigrant generation has tended to be conservative. When in the early 1900's the AFL took the much debated step of entering the National Civic Foundation, an organization headed by Republican political boss and president-maker Mark Hanna, Gompers explained the move in the following terms: "It helped to establish the practice," he wrote, "of accepting labor unions as an integral social element and logically of including their representatives in groups to discuss policies."[80] This was labor's single ambition: to win acceptance as a "legitimate" social group, equal with business and the church as an established institution of American life. For Gompers, the immigrant boy, it was a personal crusade as well. He sought to win recognition for labor in all civic aspects of American life: an entry and a hearing at the White House, an official voice in government, and acceptance in the community at large. To become respectable—this was Gompers' and labor's aim. And, by the mid-century, labor had indeed become the new parvenu force of American life.

Wating for Socialism

Neither nineteenth-century American radicals nor the American socialists faced up to this problem of social compromise. The utopias that were spun so profusely in the nineteenth century assumed that in the course of evolution "reason" would find its way and the perfect society would emerge. But so mechanical were the manikin visions of human delights in such utopias that a modern reading of Bellamy, for example, with its plan for conscript armies of labor ("a horrible cockney dream," William Morris called *Looking Backward*), only produces revulsion.

The "scientific socialist" movement that emerged at the turn of the century mocked these utopian unrealities. Only the organization of the proletariat could bring a better world. But this apparent relatedness to the world was itself a delusion. The socialist dilemma was still how to face the problem of "in the world and of it," and in practice the early socialist movement "rejected" the world; it simply waited for the new. Although the American Socialist party sought to function politically by making "immediate demands" and pressing for needed social reforms, it rarely took a stand on the actual problems that emerged from the everyday functioning of society. "What but meaningless phrases are 'imperialism,' 'expansion,' 'free silver,' 'gold standard,' etc., to the wage worker?" asked Eugene V. Debs in 1900. "The large capitalists represented by Mr. McKinley and the small capitalists represented by Mr. Bryan are interested in these 'issues' but they do not concern the working class."

These "issues" were beside the point, said Debs, because the worker stood outside society. Thus Debs and the socialist movement as a whole would have no traffic with the capitalist parties. Even on local municipal issues the party would not compromise. The socialist movement could "afford" this purity because of its supreme confidence about the future. "The socialist program is not a theory imposed upon society for its acceptance or rejection. It is but the interpretation of what is, sooner or later, inevitable. Capitalism is already struggling to its destruction." So proclaimed the Socialist national platform of 1904, the first issued by the Socialist party.

And the Socialist party and its leader, Gene Debs, waited. To the extent that any one person can embody the fantastic contradictions inherent in the history of the socialist movement—its deep emotional visions, its quixotic, self-numbing political behavior, its sulky, pettish outbursts—it is Eugene Debs. Debs had what the theologians call charism, the inner light of grace, or, as put by a laconic southerner, "kindlin' power." "He was a tall shamblefooted man, had a sort of gusty rhetoric that set on fire the railroad workers in their pine-boarded halls . . . made them want the world he wanted, a world brothers might own where everybody would split even," wrote Dos Passos.

Yet while Debs fully *realized* the messianic role of the prophet, he lacked the hard-headedness of the politician, the ability to take the moral absolutes and break them down to the particulars with the fewest necessary compromises. He lacked, too, the awareness that a socialist leader must play both of these roles and that in this tension there arise two risks—the corruption of the prophet and the ineffectuality of the politician. But Debs never even had the strength to *act* to the hilt the role of the prophet. A shallow dogmatism gave him the illusion of an inflexible morality. "If his mind failed to grasp a direct connection between a proposed reform and socialism," writes a sympathetic biographer, "he refused to waste time with reform. Then argument became futile; he could not be swayed."[81]

This dogmatism had its roots not in an iron revolutionary will, as with Lenin, but in an almost compulsive desire to be "left" of orthodox labor opinion. Nor did this thick streak of perpetual dissidence flow from the spirit of a dispossessed rebel, like Haywood. Its wellspring was a sentimental nineteenth-century romanticism. He had been named for Eugene Sue and Victor Hugo, and their concern for the underdog, as well as the naive optimism of a Rousseau, soared in him. Yet in his personal life, manner, and habits (except for a later private addiction to drink), Debs was respectable and almost bourgeois; his wife Kate was even more so. His literary tastes were prosaic: his favorite poet was Elbert Hubbard. But in his politics Debs wore romanticism like a cloak—and this was his strength as well as his weakness. It allowed him to be rhetorical and emotional, touching people at the ragged edge of their desire for a purpose outside themselves. But it also caused him to shun the practical and to shirk the obligations of day-to-day political decision. His fiercest shafts were reserved for the bureaucrat and party boss; his warmth and affection for those who led turbulent and dissident careers like his own. But, at bottom, it was the easiest path.

Withal, the lonely figure of Debs, his sagging, pleading gauntness, pierced all who beheld him. It was perhaps because, in a final sense, he was the true protestant. Debs stood at the end of the long road of the Reformation. He had an almost mystical—at times omniscient—faith in the dictates of his inner self. Like the Anabaptists of old, all issues were resolved by private conscience. From the priesthood of all believers he had become the solitary individual, carrying on his shoulders the burdens of humanity. That sense of loneliness—and grandeur—touched others who were equally afflicted with the terrible sense of isolation. By his standing alone, he emphasized the individual and his rights, and at best, such an attitude of "autonomy" provides a unique defense of the dignity of the person. But in its extreme antinomianism, in its romantic defiance of rational and traditional norms, it shirks the more difficult problem of living in the world, of seeking, as one must in politics, relative standards of social virtue and political justice instead of abstract absolutes. It is but one pole—a necessary one—in creating standards of action. But as the isolated protestant refuses to join the community of "sinners," so the isolated prophet evades the responsibility of political life. The prophet, once said Max Scheler, stands on the mountain as a signpost; he points the way but cannot go, for if he did, there would no longer be a sign. The politician, one might add, carries the sign into the valley with him.

Straddling for Socialism

Unlike the other-wordly movements toward salvation, which can always postpone the date of the resurrection, the Socialist party, living in the here and now, had to show results. It was a movement based on a belief in "history"; but it found itself outside of "time." World War I finally broke through the façade. For the first time, the party had to face a stand on a realistic issue of the day. And on that issue almost the entire intellectual leadership of the party deserted; and, as a result, the back of American socialism was broken.

The socialist movement of the 1930's, the socialism of Norman Thomas, could not afford the luxury of the earlier belief in the inevitable course of history. It was forced to take stands on the particular issues of the day. But it too rejected completely the premises of the society which shaped these issues. In effect, the Socialist party acknowledged the fact that it lived "in" the world, but refused the responsibility of becoming a part "of" it.

But such a straddle is impossible for a *political* movement. It was as if it consented to a duel, with no choice regarding weapons, place, amount of preparation, etc. Politically, the consequences were disastrous. Each issue could only be met by an ambiguous political formula which would satisfy neither the purist nor the activist, who lived with the daily problem of choice. When the Loyalists in Spain demanded arms, for example, the Socialist party could only respond with a feeble policy of "workers aid," not (capitalist) government aid; but to the Spaniard, arms, not theoretical niceties, were the need of the moment. When the young trade-unionists, whom the socialists seeded into the labor movement, faced the necessity of going along politically with Roosevelt and the New Deal in order to safeguard progressive legislative gains, the socialists proposed a "labor party," rather than work with the Democrats, and so the Socialist party lost almost its entire trade-union base. The threat of fascism and World War II finally proved to be the clashing rocks through which the socialist argonauts could not row safely. How to defeat Hitler without supporting capitalist society? Some socialists raised the slogan of a "third force." The Socialist party, however, realized the futility of that effort; in characteristic form, it chose abnegation. The best way to stem fascism, it stated, "is to make democracy work at home." But could the issue be resolved other than militarily? The main concern of the anti-fascist movement had to be with the political center of fascist power, Hitler's Berlin, and any other concern was peripheral.

In still another way the religious, chiliastic origin of modern socialism revealed itself: in the multiplication of splits, in the constant formation of sectarian splinter groups, each hotly disputing the other regarding the true road to power. Socialism is an eschatological movement; it is sure of its destiny, because "history" leads it to its goal. But though sure of its final ends, there is never a standard for testing the immediate means. The result is a constant fractiousness in socialist life. Each position taken is always open to challenge by those who feel that it would only swerve the movement from its final goal and lead it up some blind alley. And because it is an ideological movement, embracing all the realm of the human polity, the Socialist party is always challenged to take a stand on every problem from Vietnam to Finland, from prohibition to pacifism. And, since for every two socialists there are always three political opinions, the consequence has been that in its inner life the Socialist party has never, even for a single year, been without some issue which threatened to split the party and which forced it to spend much of its time on the problem of reconciliation or rupture. In this fact lies one of the chief clues to the ecklessness of American socialism as a *political movement* in the last thirty years.* But if in politics it proved to be impotent, it remained a moral force, and in Norman Thomas it had a new signpost.

If Debs was, at bottom, the sentimentalist of American socialism, Norman Thomas has been its moral figure. A communist critic once sneered at Norman Thomas for entitling his study of poverty in the United States *Human Exploitation* rather than *Capitalist Exploitation.* The critic, unwittingly, had a point, for what arouses Thomas is not the analytical and sociological but the ethical and emotional. Intellectually, Thomas would know that "the system" is to blame; but such abstractions have rarely held meaning for him. His interest has always been the personal *fact* of injustice, committed by individuals; and while socialism might analyze the impersonal "basic" causes, he was always happiest when he could *act* where the issue was immediate and personal. In speaking out against shorecropper terror in Birdsong, Arkansas; in defying martial law in Terre Haute, Indiana; in exposing the Klan in Tampa; in uncovering the municipal corruption of Jimmy Walkers' New York; in combating the anti-free-speech ordinances of Jersey's Boss Hague—in all these instances, Thomas's voice has rung out with the eloquent wrath of an Elijah Lovejoy or of a William Lloyd Garrison.

These impulses came naturally to Norman Mattoon Thomas. Religion, orthodox Presbyterianism, was the center of his boyhood home. His father was a minister, as was his Welsh-born grandfather. He was raised in a strict sabbatarian code, but the harshness of his ancestral Calvinism was modified by the kindness of his parents. "My father who

* Beyond the reaches of this essay is the problem of the psychological types who are attracted by a sectarian existence. Yet one might say that the illusion of settling the fate of history, the mimetic combat on the plains of destiny, and the vicarious sense of power in demolishing opponents all provide a sure sense of gratification which makes the continuance of sectarian life desirable. The many leadership complexes, the intense aggressiveness through gossip, the strong clique group formations, all attest to a particular set of psychological needs and satisfactions which are filled in these opaque, molecular worlds.

believed theoretically in eternal damnation," wrote Thomas, "would never say of any one that he was damned."[82]

Thomas, born in Marion, Ohio, in 1884, was a sickly little boy who grew too fast, became an awkward, skinny kid, shy with his peers and talkative with his elders, and who found his main satisfaction in reading. Norman was the eldest of six children, and the family was always busy with household chores and other activities of small-town middle-class life. Of the parents, Emma Mattoon was the more outstanding personality, and "father was content to have it so." In thinking back on his boyhood in the small Ohio town, Thomas remarked: "What a set-up for the modern psychologically-minded biographer or novelist. A study in revolt of reaction from Presbyterian orthodoxy and the Victorian brand of Puritanism in a midwest setting. The only trouble is that this isn't what happened."

With the financial help of an uncle, Thomas satisfied a boyhood dream and entered Princeton, graduating in 1905 as class valedictorian. Entering the ministry was a more or less destined fact. But in the age of genteel faith in progress, acceptance of the old orthodoxies seemed out of place. As with many social-minded ministers of the day, the modernist and liberal gospel of Walter Rauschenbusch had its appeal. But it was the filth and poverty of the cold-water flats of the Spring Street slums on New York's west side that turned Thomas actively to social reform. And it was World War I and the influence of the Fellowship of Reconciliation, a religious pacifist organization, that made him a socialist. "God, I felt, was certainly not the 'God and Father of Our Lord Jesus Christ' if his servants could only serve him and the cause of righteousness by the diabolic means of war." Thomas' stand took him from the ministry into politics and journalism. (Rather than endanger the financial support his church received, he resigned the pastorate.) A tall handsome man with strongly-etched patrician features, rich resonant voice, and fine American credentials, he quickly became an outstanding leader in a party depleted of public figures. In 1924 he was nominated for governor of New York; four years later—because the two veteran party leaders, Morris Hillquit and Victor Berger, were European-born and because Dan Hoan was busy being mayor of Milwaukee—Thomas was nominated for the presidency.

As a party leader, Thomas had two serious flaws. For one, he strikingly distrusted his own generation and surrounded himself with considerably younger men who stood in an admiring and uncritical relation to him. The other was a profound fear of being manipulated, so that every political attack was taken personally. Unlike Debs, Thomas was intent on being party leader. Often a situation would develop—particularly in the late thirties—when, if party policy tended in a direction other than his, Thomas would threaten to resign (otherwise how could he speak on an issue with pure conscience?). Yet many of Thomas' decisions were made not with an eye to the political results but to the moral consequences as he saw them. Moreover, by background and temperament, Thomas was concerned largely with issues rather than ideas. In a party whose main preoccupation has been the refinement of "theory" at the cost, even, of interminable factional divisions, Thomas' interest in specific issues often meant shifting alliances with different factions while maintaining aloofness from the jesuitical debates that gave rise to these groups. Thus in the late thirties Thomas was with the right wing on the labor-party issue and shifted to the pacifist and left wing on the war problem. Thomas was probably most unhappy during the early and middle thirties, when as a professed non-Marxist, he was involved in the conflicts of fifty-seven varieties of claims to revolutionary orthodoxy.

As a man whose instincts are primarily ethical, Thomas has been the genuine moral man in the immoral society. But as a political man he has been caught inextricably in the dilemmas of expediency, the relevant alternatives, and the lesser evil. As a sophisticated modern man, Thomas has been acutely aware of his ambiguous role and feels he has made the political choice. "One is obliged," he wrote in 1947, "to weigh one's actions in terms of relative social consequences . . . and the tragedy is that no choice can be positively good. . . . Positively [the pacifists] had nothing to offer in the problem of stopping Nazism before its triumph could not only enslave but corrupt the world. Nothing, that is, except for a religious faith in the power of God, a faith stronger if it could include a belief in immortality. It was something but not enough to affirm that the method of war was self-defeating for good ends. It was not enough to say 'if all Americans would act like Gandhi' we should more surely defeat avowed fascism. Possibly, but since almost no Americans would thus act the question remained of the lesser evil." Thomas did learn the lesson of the lesser evil: instead of being an absolute pacifist, however, he became an indecisive one. When the

Franco rebellion broke out, Thomas gave up his religious pacifism, but was led to an ambiguous distinction whereby he supported the right of individuals to volunteer and fight but not "American official intervention by war which would involve conscription." After Pearl Harbor, Thomas came out in "critical support" of the United States government, a position which consisted in the first years largely of ignoring foreign policy and of speaking out against injustices on the home front. Fearful of another split, the Socialist party adopted a formula sufficiently elastic and ambiguous to permit pacifists, anti-war socialists, and pro-war socialists to continue together inside the party.[83] But to little avail. No one was satisfied with the compromise, and since factions were robbed of the incentive to split, the members simply resigned. From that point on, the Socialist party simply wasted away.

The Alien Outsider

For the twentieth-century Communist, there are none of these agonizing problems of ethics and politics. He is the perpetual alien living in the hostile enemy land. Any gestures of support, any pressure for social reforms, are simply tactics, a set of Potemkin villages, the façades to be torn down after the necessary moment for deception has passed. His is the ethic of "ultimate ends"; only the goal counts, the means are inconsequential.[84] Bolshevism thus is neither in the world nor of it, but stands outside. It takes no responsibility for the consequences of any act within the society nor does it suffer the tension of acquiescence or rejection. But the Socialist, unlike the Communist, lacks that fanatical vision, and so faces the daily anguish of participating in and sharing responsibility for the day-to-day problems of the society.

It is this commitment to the "absolute" that gives Bolshevism its religious strength. It is the commitment which sustains one of the great political myths of the century, the myth of the iron-willed Bolshevik. Selfless, devoted, resourceful, a man with a cause, he is the modern Hero. He alone, a man of action, a soldier for the future, continues the tradition of courage which is the aristocratic heritage bestowed on Western culture and which has been devitalized by the narrow, monetary calculus of the bourgeoisie. (Can the businessman be the Hero?) Such is the peculiar myth which has taken deep hold among many intellectuals. It is a myth which is also responsible for the deep emotional hatred and almost pathologic resentment felt most keenly by the ex-communist intellectual, the "defrocked priest," toward the party. For the "Bolshevik," through the myth of absolute selflessness, claims to be the "extreme man," the man of no compromise, the man of purity. The intellectual, driven to be moral, fears the comparison and resents the claim. Thus he bears either a sense of guilt or a psychological wound.

In addition to the myth of the Bolshevik as iron-willed Hero, twentieth-century communism has made several other distinctive contributions to the theory and practice of modern politics. Like so many other social doctrines, these were never put down systematically in a fully self-conscious fashion; yet over the years they have emerged as a coherent philosophy. Of these contributions some five can be linked schematically. These are central for understanding the history of the Communist party in this country.

One of the major innovations of the Bolsheviks is their theory of power. Against the nineteenth-century liberal view which saw social decisions as a reconciliation of diverse interests through compromise and consensus—this was a theory which social democracy gradually began to accept after World War I, when it was called upon to take responsibility for governments—power was defined as a monopoly of the means of coercion. Power was thought of almost in terms of physics, its equation being almost literally "mass times force equals power." The individual, central to the liberal theory of a market society, was for the Bolshevik a helpless entity. Only the organized group counted, and only a mass base could exert social leverage in society.

But a mass requires leadership. The great unresolved dilemma of Marxian sociology was the question of how the proletariat achieves the consciousness of its role. To await the immanent development of history was to rely on the fallacy of misplaced abstraction. "Spontaneity" was not for Lenin a reality in mass politics; nor was the trade-union an effective instrument. His answer, the most significant addition to revolutionary theory, was the vanguard role of the party.

Against the "economism" which glorified the role of the trade-union, Lenin argued that the mere organization of society on a trade-union basis could only lead to wage consciousness, not revolutionary consciousness; against the spontaneity theories of Rosa Luxemburg he argued that the masses, by nature, were backward. Only the vanguard party, aware of the precarious balance of social forces, could assess the play and correctly tip the scales in the revolutionary direction. This was the classic formulation of revolutionary avant-gardism which Lenin outlined in his *What Is to Be Done?*

In it he wrote that without the "dozen" tried and talented leaders—and talented men are not born by the hundred—professionally trained, schooled by long experience, and working in perfect harmony, no class in modern society is capable of conducting a determined struggle. "I assert," said Lenin, "(1) that no movement can be durable without a stable organization of leaders to maintain continuity; (2) that the more widely the masses are spontaneously drawn into the struggle and form the basis of the movement, the more necessary it is to have such an organization and the more stable must it be (for it is much easier for demagogues to sidetrack the more backward sections of the masses); (3) that the organization must consist chiefly of persons engaged in revolution as a profession."[85]

If the party were to become a vanguard, it needed discipline in action, and thus there arose the principle of party hierarchy and "centralism." A line was laid down by the leadership which was binding on all. Lenin's promulgation of these doctrines in 1903 split Russian socialism and brought about the emergence of the Bolshevik and Menshevik factions. In the beginning Trotsky opposed Lenin's ideas, but later he capitulated. As he wrote in his autobiography: ". . . there is no doubt that at that time I did not fully realize what an intense and imperious centralism the revolutionary party would need to lead millions of people in a war against the old order. . . . Revolutionary centralism is a harsh, imperative and exacting principle. It often takes the guise of absolute ruthlessness in its relation to individual members, to whole groups of former associates. It is not without significance that the words 'irreconcilable' and 'relentless' are among Lenin's favorites."[86]

From the principle of power and the theory of party organization rose two other key tenets of Bolshevism. One was the polarization of classes. Because it looked only toward the "final conflict," Bolshevism split society into two classes, the proletariat and the bourgeoisie. But the proletariat could only be emancipated by the vanguard party; hence anyone resisting the party must belong to the enemy. For Lenin, the maxim of the absolute ethic meant that "those who are not for me are against me." Hence, too, a formulation of the theory of "social fascism," which in the early 1930's branded the Social Democrats rather than Hitler as the chief enemy and led the Communists to unite, in several instances, with the Nazis in order to overthrow the German Republic.

The second tenet, deriving from the backward nature of the masses, was the key psychological tactic of formulating all policy into forceful slogans. Slogans dramatize events, make issues simple, and wipe out the qualifications, nuances, and subtleties which accompany democratic political action. In his chapter on slogans[87] Lenin wrote one of the first manuals on modern mass psychology. During the Revolution, the Bolsheviks achieved a flexibility of tactic by using such slogans as "All Power to the Soviets," "Land, Peace, and Bread," etc. The basic political tactic of all Communist parties everywhere is to formulate policy primarily through the use of key slogans which are transmitted first to the party rank and file and then to the masses.

The consequence of the theory of the vanguard party and its relation to the masses is a system of "two truths," the *consilia evangelica,* or special ethics endowed for those whose lives are dedicated to the revolutionary ends, and another truth for the masses. Out of this belief grew Lenin's famous admonition: one can lie, steal, or cheat, for the cause itself has a higher truth.

Except for the period from 1935 to 1945, the decade of fascism and war, the Communist party did not achieve any sizeable following in the United States. In the misnamed "Red Decade," the Communist party, though never a national political force, did achieve important influence in the CIO (controlling at one time unions with about 20 per cent of the membership of the Congress, but, more important, holding almost all the major staff positions in the national CIO and running the large state and city CIO councils in New York, Illinois, California, and other key states) and did attain a position of respectability in the liberal and cultural community of the country.

The greatest triumph of Communist propaganda—the fifth innovation — was the creation of the papier-mâché front organizations. These fronts, sought to "hook" famous names and exploit them for Communist causes by means of manifestoes, open letters, petitions, declarations, statements, pronouncements, protests, and other illusions of opinion groundswells in the land. The viciousness of the front technique was that it encouraged a herd spirit whereby only "collective opinion" carried weight; and if a critic dared challenge a tenet of Soviet faith, he was drowned out by the mass chorus of several score voices. As Eugene Lyons put it: "Did rumor-mongers charge that a horrifying famine had been enforced by the Kremlin to 'punish' forty million Soviet citizens in an area as large as the United States? Half a hundred experts on nutrition and agronomy, all the way from Beverly Hills to Park Avenue penthouses, thereupon condemned the capitalists and Trotskyites responsible for the libel, and the famine was liquidated."

The corruption of the front technique was that many poor dupes, imagining that they were the leaders of the great causes, found themselves enslaved by the opium of publicity and became pliable tools of the Communist manipulators behind the scenes. In other instances upper-class matrons and aspiring actresses found in the Communist "causes" a cozy non-conformism to replace their passé conventions. The ultimate betrayal was of the masses of front members who gained a sense of participation which they sadly discovered to be spurious when the party lines changed and they found that they themselves were victims of party manipulations.

But such influence was only possible because the Communist party was, at the time, moving in parallel direction with the liberal community whose emotions had been aroused by Hitler and Franco. Because of its superior organization, the Communist party was able to assume the leadership of many "causes." And yet, curiously enough, its very success was almost a corrupting influence. In the late 1930's, in the days of the Popular Front, the Communists suddenly found themselves accepted in areas (labor movement, Hollywood, urban politics) where they had been ostracized or scorned. But the Popular Front was a tactic. It had been dictated by Moscow as part of its policy of seeking national alliances. The Communists had not given up their belief in revolution or power; the liberals were a force to be manipulated. In 1943, however, in the so-called Teheran phase of national unity, there was a new phase. Browder took the decisive step of dissolving the Communist party as a political party and reconstituting it as a political association. But more than tactics was involved. The previous success in the Popular Front had given the party a new perspective. Browder himself was pleased by the new recognition and respectability of the party. In place of the Socialist party, it was becoming the acknowledged "left," occupying a "legitimate" place in American life. How far this revisionism would have gone is a moot point, for in 1945, abruptly and savagely, Browder was dumped, and the party was ordered into a new, sectarian phase, in accordance with the new, anti-Western agressive line of Moscow. The Wallace campaign of 1948 was a desperate effort to salvage the old liberal support for the new extreme line. But the effort only resulted in isolating the Communists from the labor and liberal movements and leading to their exclusion.

In sum, the main appeal of the Communist party was to the dispossessed intelligentsia of the depression generation and to the "engineers of the future" who were attracted by the elitist appeal described above. It stirred many Americans to action against injustices and left them with burnt fingers when, for reasons of expediency, the party line changed and the cause was dropped. It provided an unmatched political sophistication to a generation that went through its ranks, and it gave an easy-going, tolerant, sprawling America a lesson in organizational manipulation and hard-bitten ideological devotion which this country, because of its tradition and temperament, found hard to understand. But most of all, through the seeds of distrust and anxiety it sowed, communism helped spawn a reaction, a hysteria and bitterness that democratic America may find hard to live down in the years ahead.

From the sixteenth-century chiliast, burning with impatient zeal for immediate salvation, to the twenty-century American labor leader, sunning himself on the sands of Miami Beach, is a long, almost surrealist jump of history. Yet these are antipodal figures of a curving ribbon which binds all movements that have sought to change the hierarchical social order in society.

The chiliast and the anarchist live in crisis, at the edge of History, expecting the world to be changed in a flash. The Bolshevik identifies himself with History and confidently expects that the turn of the wheel will put him forward, replacing the old. For these, then, the questions of social compromise, of the tension of ethics and politics, have had no meaning. But for others, particularly the socialists, the dilemma has been insoluble.

Living in the world, one cannot refuse the responsibility

of sharing in the decisions of the society. In the here and now, people do not live at the extreme (in the "entirety" which was Sorel's myth), but they live "in parts," parceling out their lives amidst work, home, neighborhood, fraternal club, etc. Nor does History, as Acton put it, "work with bottled essences." Compromise is the "soul if not the whole of politics . . . and progress is along diagonals." For the socialist movement, living in but not of the world, it was a wisdom which it could not accept. Doctrine remained; but the movement failed.

Chapter 13

The Mood of Three Generations:

A. The Once-Born, the Twice-Born, and the After-Born

> **We get the belief in the old age of mankind, the belief at all times harmful, that we are late survivals, mere Epigoni.**
>
> **—Nietzsche**

IT IS DIFFICULT for me to know if I am, or am not, of the "young generation." I came to political awareness in the Depression and joined the Young People's Socialist League in 1932, at the precocious age of thirteen. At the age of fifteen I was writing resolutions on the "road to power." At C.C.N.Y., in the late thirties, I was already a veteran of many factional wars. Since graduating, in 1938, I have worked for twenty years, half my life, as a writer or teacher — a respectable period, yet whenever biographical details are printed, I am, almost inescapably, referred to as a *young* American sociologist, or a *young* American writer. And so are others of my generation of the same age or slightly older. To take some random examples: Harvey Swados, now thirty-nine, is still called a promising "young" writer although he has published three novels; Richard Hofstadter, who, at the age of forty-two, has published four first-rate historical interpretations, is called a young American scholar; James Wechsler, over forty, a young editor; Saul Bellow, over forty, a young American novelist; Leslie Fiedler, aged forty-three, a young American critic; Alfred Kazin, aged forty-four, a young American critic, etc., etc.

Two generations ago, a man of forty would not have been considered young. The Founding Fathers of the American Republic were largely in their thirties when the country was formed; so, too, were the leaders of the Russian Revolution. But this is an older man's world, and in the lengthening of the "shadow line" a damper is put on the younger generations.

But, beyond the general change in the tone of the culture, there is a more specific reason why the college generation of "the thirties" has been, until now, at bay. This is because those who dominated "the thirties" were young themselves when they became established, and, until recently, have held major sway in the culture. *Partisan Review,* for example, is twenty-three years old, yet its editors, William Phillips and Philip Rahv, are not "old" men (say, fifty, give or take a year). Our intellectual nestors—Lionel Trilling, Sidney Hook, Edmund Wilson, Reinhold Niebuhr, John Dos Passos, Newton Arvin, F. W. Dupee, James T. Farrell, Richard Wright, Max Lerner, Elliott Cohen—were in their late twenties and early thirties when they made their mark as a new generation. The reason why there has been no revolt against them, as they, in asserting a radical politics, had ousted their elders, is that they led their own "counter-revolt." They had both iliad and odyssey, were iconistic and iconoclastic. They were intense, horatory, naive, simplistic, and passionate, but, after the Moscow Trials and the Soviet-Nazi pact, disenchanted and reflective; and from them and their experiences we have inherited the key terms which dominate discourse today: irony, paradox, ambiguity, and complexity.

Curiously, though they—and we—are sadder and perhaps wiser than the first political generations of the century, we are not better or greater. There are few figures today, or of the last twenty years, and few books, that can match the stature and work of Dewey, Beard, Holmes, Veblen, Brandeis. But to read these men today is to be struck by their essential optimism (even Veblen: read his *Engineers and the Price System,* and its technocratic vision of the future), which was based upon an ultimate faith in the rationality or common sense of men. Ours, a "twice-born" generation, finds its wisdom in pessimism, evil, tragedy, and despair. So we are both old and young "before our time."

The remarkable fact about the recent post-college generation, as one of its spokesmen, Norman Podhoretz, has pointed out, is its sober, matter-of-fact, "mature" acceptance of the complexities of politics and existence; but also, as he concludes, an underlying restlessness, a feeling of being cheated out of adventure, and a search for passion. There is a hankering for the misspent life that was never misspent. (But, I suspect, there has been, along with the strong emphasis on estheticism, homosexuality, and the like, a greater *sub-rosa* exploration of the decadent than Mr. Podhoretz admits.) And, among the more serious-minded, a longing for "a cause to believe in," although the self-conscious awareness of the desire for "a cause" itself is self-defeating.

Yet no generation can be denied an experience, even a

negative one. Previously sane periods have seen such efflorescences as the "Yellow Book estheticism" of England in the nineties, or the mysticism and debauchery of Russian intellectuals (cf. Artzybesheff's *Sanine*) in the 1910's. In England today, in Kingsley Amis's *Lucky Jim* or John Osborne's *Look Back in Anger,* we have the flowering of what Christopher Sykes has called "redbrickism, provincialism, and all this belly-aching"—meaning a revolt against the cultural inbreeding of Oxford and Cambridge, and the grayness of the Welfare State. What will happen in the United States is difficult to foresee, for all expressions of revolt, whether it be Zen, or abstract expressionism, or Jungianism, or progressive jazz, quickly become modish and flat.* In the Christian trials of conversion (i.e., a genuine experience that transformed one's life) one had to be lost to be saved. Today, experiences are transposed from the moral to the psychological level, and to become "ecstatic" (literally, "ex-stasis," or outside one's self) one has to "let go" completely. But consciousness of self has become so inbred that even an impulse to "let go" becomes self-conscious; and so there is, almost, an infinite regress.

But the problem for the generation is less, as Mr. Podhoretz says, the "fear of experience" than an inability to define an "enemy." One can have causes and passions only when one knows against whom to fight. The writers of the twenties—Dadaist, Menckenian, and nihilist—scorned bourgeois mores. The radicals of the thirties fought "capitalism," and later, fascism, and for some, Stalinism. Today, intellectually, emotionally, who is the enemy that one can fight?

The paradox is that the generation wants to live a "heroic" life but finds the image truly "quixotic." This is, as for Cervantes' Don, the end of an age. For the younger generation, as for all intellectuals, there is this impasse. It is part of the time which has seen the end of ideology.

The ideologist — Communist, existentialist, religionist — wants to live at some extreme, and criticizes the ordinary man for failing to live at the level of grandeur. One can try to do so if there is the genuine possibility that the next moment

* This was written before the Beatnik fad unfolded, and dealt with the complaint of Mr. Podhoretz that his generation had found it difficult to adopt a radical political stance. Jack Kerouac, the "spokesman" of the Beat Generation, is, it should be pointed out, thirty-seven years old—a curious reversal of role, since the effort of the Beats is, like Peter Pan, the denial of growing up. It is, of course, an apolitical movement. See the essay by Norman Podhoretz, "The Know-Nothing Bohemians," *Partisan Review,* Spring, 1958.

could be actually, a "transforming moment" when salvation or revolution or genuine passion could be achieved. But such chiliastic moments are illusions. And what is left is the unheroic, day-to-day routine of living.

Max Weber, more than forty years ago, in a poignant essay entitled "Politics as a Vocation," posed the problem as one of accepting the "ethics of responsibility" or the "ethics of ultimate ends." For the latter—the "true believer"—all sacrifices, all means, are acceptable for the achievement of one's belief. But for those who take on responsibility, who forgo the sin of pride, of assuming they know how life should be ordered or how the blueprint of the new society should read, one's role can be only to reject all absolutes and accept pragmatic compromise. As Edmund Wilson once described Theodore Roosevelt's attitude, politics, in a society where there is a shared consensus, becomes a "matter of adapting oneself to all sorts of people and situations, a game in which one may score but only by accepting the rules and recognizing one's opponents, rather than a moral crusade in which one's stainless standard must mow the enemy down."

In this sense, the generation of the thirties, whose representative men are Lionel Trilling and Reinhold Niebuhr, were prodigal sons who, in terms of American culture, had returned home. But one can't tread the same road twice. And a generation that knows it has to be "moral" and "responsible" is a generation that is destined to stay home.

B. The Loss of Innocence in the Thirties

For a small group, the thirties have a special meaning. These are the individuals who went through the radical movement and who bear, as on invisible frontlets, the stamp of those years on their foreheads. The number is small. Of the four million college and high-school youths, less than twenty thousand, or one-half of one per cent, took part in radical activity. But, like the drop of dye that suffuses the cloth, this number gave the decade its coloration.

A radical is a prodigal son. For him, the world is a strange place whose contours have to be explored according to one's destiny. He may eventually return to the house of his elders, but the return is by choice, and not, as of those who stayed behind, of unblinking filial obedience. A resilient society, like a wise parent, understands this ritual, and, in meeting the challenge to tradition, grows.

But in the thirties, the fissures were too deep. Seemingly,

there was no home to return to. One could only march forward. Everybody seemed to be tramping, tramping, tramping. *Marching, Marching* was the title of a prize-winning proletarian novel. There were parades, picketing, protests, farm holidays, and even a general strike in San Francisco. There was also a new man, the Communist. Not just the radical—always alien, always testing, yet open in his aims — but a hidden soldier in a war against society.

In a few short years, the excitement evaporated. The labor movement grew fat and bureaucratized. The political intellectuals became absorbed into the New Deal. The papier-mâché proletarian novelists went on to become Hollywood hacks. And yet it is only by understanding the fate of the prodigal sons and the Communists that one can understand the loss of innocence that is America's distinctive experience of the thirties.

Murray Kempton, in his book *Part of Our Time,* has looked at the small band who dreamed, and who—because of having a dream "possessed no more of doubting"—sought to impress that dream into action. But in action, one defies one's character. In some, the iron became brittle, in some it became hard; others cast the iron away, and still others were crushed. In the end, almost all had lost the dream and the world was only doubt.

The story opens, naturally enough, with Alger Hiss and Whittaker Chambers. Kempton retells the familiar story, but with a special nuance. What united the strange pair was their symbiotic relation to Baltimore, a mildewed city which was Kempton's home and whose musty character he captures so well. Hiss, from a shabby, genteel Baltimore family, fled its faded elegance to meet Chambers, the tortured man from the underground, who settled gratefully into its Victorian dust. Each found, in the secret craving of the other, the lives they were rejecting, until, locked in defeat, they both sank beneath the waters.

The story spreads out and touches on the writers attracted by the myth of the revolutionary collective, the "rebel girls," the militant labor leaders, the youth movement, and others who were riding the crest of history's waves. It is not a formal history of the left, but a series of novellas. What gives it its special cast and enormous appeal is the elegiac mood, the touch of adolescent ache in the writing.

A descendant of an old Southern family, James Murray Mason Ambler Kempton carries many bloodlines in his full name. In the thirties, he was, briefly, a college Communist, went to sea, became a Socialist, and, fleeing the deracinated talk of New York intellectuals, enlisted and found a community, for a while, in the fighting platoons of New Guinea. Like all utopian moments, this communion had vitality only in memory, rather than enduring reality, and Kempton returned to New York, where, for the past six years, as a widely read columnist of the New York *Post,* he has been another Brann the iconoclast.

There are no villains in the book—none so wholly black that some degree of pity does not remain—only the pathos of those who, by living a lie, became consumed by it: John Howard Lawson, whose nervous *Processional* promised a new style in the American theater, but who, as a Hollywood commissar, played at revolution by smuggling lines of "progressive dialogue" into banal movies; Lee Pressman, the taut, brilliant labor lawyer, who chose Henry Wallace and the Progressives over Phil Murray and the C.I.O., and found, too late, that he had made the wrong choice; Ann Moos Remington, the prototype of the "rebel girl," who would only marry ardent William Remington if he would join the Young Communist League, but later, as his ex-wife, testified against him in a perjury trial.

There are heroes, for, unlike many disenchanted, Kempton has some—that radical breed, who, though patronized by the later "realists' who equated revolution with tough-mindedness, retained their kindness and idealism: James T. Farrell, an unpolished novelist, perhaps, but one whose bullheaded grasp of truth sent him rampaging against the Communist writer fronts; Gardener (Pat) Jackson, who organized the Sacco-Vanzetti defense but ran afoul of the Communist amoralists; Mary Heaton Vorse, who wrote of labor not as an abstract collective but as individuals; Edmund Wilson, whose canon of criticism kept him on an inviolate path of honesty.

There are many others: the incredible J. B. Matthews, a political Reverend Davidson, who, having slept with the red Sadie Thompsons, got lascivious contrition in exposing them; John Dos Passos, who found the Communist manipulations too frightening for his anarchist impulses and turned Republican; Joe Curran, who in going from park bench to labor leader became trapped by the dilemmas of responsibility and was forced to sweep aside his old rebel cohorts; the Reuther boys, uncomplicated by bohemian trappings, who soberly have sought to install a sense of social discipline in America. And many others—the middle-class Vassar girls, the boy who died in Spain, the Negroes who rebuffed the Communists and obtained a new dignity. Like Malcolm Cowley's *Exile's Return* or Vincent Sheean's *Personal History,* Kempton's book is the story of a generation, and if it sometimes lacks the personal element of those accounts of the twenties, it has a sweep and power fired by the ache for the lost Arcadia.

In the end, the generation failed. Not because the idealistic impulses became exhausted; this is the inevitable trajectory, perhaps, of any radical generation. Not because events had belied the predictions, this is a healthier America. But because this may well have been the *last* radical generation for a time—the last because it was the first that tasted power and became corrupt. (Yet it is not only that power corrupts, for, as Alex Comfort once said, corrupt men seek power.) But the seed of the corruption was the *hubris* of the "possessed." Generous of impulse, it sought the end of injustice, but in the single vision the dogmatism grew hard and the moral sense cynical, so that, when reality proved the vision false, all that was left was the hardness, or the despair.

C. Politics in the Forties

DWIGHT MACDONALD MADE his political debut in 1937 by writing a five-page letter to the *New Republic* protesting Malcolm Cowley's pusillanimous review of the official transcripts of the Moscow trials; after considerable haggling, the *New Republic* printed one-third of the letter. Earlier, he had formed an exclusive club at Phillips Exeter Academy under the revolutionary motto of *Pour Epater les Bourgeois.* Following uneventful, non-revolutionary years at Yale, he worked briefly, during the opening of the Depression, at Macy's, as a member of its Executive Training Squad (in reaction to which, I suppose, he acquired the habit of wearing the loud pink-and-black striped shirts he now sports), and subsequently, like Jacob for Laban, he worked seven years on *Fortune.* For two years, Macdonald was a Trotskyite, making his exit from organized politics in 1940, when the Schachtmanites printed only 4,000 words of a 30-000-word study characterizing Nazi society as a new social form, that of bureaucratic collectivism. Writing an 8,000-word letter to the Political Committee, Macdonald made as a "minimum demand" for his continued collaboration the publication of an additional 4,000 words of his article. When the committee collectively and bureaucratically refused, he resigned. Reflecting on the incident, he declared that the party was not seriously "engaged in politics, but in metapolitics." (More seriously, it would seem to have been micropolitics.) Macdonald now concentrated his attention on *Partisan Review,* but resigned in 1943, when his pacifism led to growing disagreement with his co-editors. In 1944, Macdonald founded his monthly, later quarterly, periodical, *Politics,* an extraordinary achievement in personal journalism. In 1949, exhausted by these efforts, Macdonald surrendered *Politics* and politics, and turned to the more genteel pastures of the *New Yorker.*

This, then, is the career which unfolds in the lead essay of *The Memoirs of a Revolutionist.* These "memoirs," subtitled "Essays in Political Criticism," are not, apart from the introductory essay, autobiographical or reflective. They are, fifty selections in all, *aperçus,* editorials, reviews, the majority of them from *Politics,* the shorter and often insubstantial chips from the writer's block. The book does not contain Macdonald's most celebrated essay, on Popular Culture, or his most ambitious, "The Root Is Man," or (except for the profile of the latter-day Franciscan, Dorothy Day) any of the longer pieces from the *New Yorker,* e.g., the demolition of Mortimer Adler's *Syntopicon,* the do-it-yourself craze, etc.

And yet, these *cosettes* reveal Macdonald at his best—lively, witty, versatile—and at his worst—sardonic, superior, irritating. Macdonald is what may be called "an inconstant dogmatist." At any particular moment, he is completely cocksure of his position and unmerciful to an opponent. (When he is doing a literary demolition job, of which he is a master, woe to the writer who uses clumsy metaphors or commits stylistic gaucheries.) But then, like Heisenberg's particle, he is off in the next historical moment on a new, erratic tack, and often as dogmatic in the new stance as in the old.

There are several—saving—reasons why one is not annoyed at these inconstancies (apart from the grace of Macdonald's own good humor and his willingness to laugh at his own faults). Macdonald is a journalist-*cum*-intellectual, not a social scientist or a philosopher. The intellectual takes as a starting point his *self* and relates the world to his own sensibilities; the scientist accepts an existing field of knowledge and seeks to map out the unexplored terrain. The impulse of the journalist is to be novel, yet to relate his curiosities to the urgencies of the moment; the philosopher seeks what he conceives to be true, regardless of the moment. The changing nature of experience, thus, always seduces the intellectual. That is why Macdonald, temperamentally, is not really interested in ideas but in moral posture, and his is a constant search for inconstant verities.

These impulses, plus a remarkable devotion to his craft, did lead him for a moment to a unique place in American intellectual history. For when we come to look more closely at the forties, as our curiosities are now turned to the earlier decades, we may see that *Politics* was the only magazine that was aware of and insistently kept calling attention to, changes that were taking place in moral temper, the depths of which we still incompletely realize.

The singular theme of *Politics* was the event of depersonalization: the denigration of the individual through the impersonality of killing; the role of terror and extreme situations; how things happen to people and people became "things," the turning of society into a mechanism. The theme of depersonalization has now been made abstract and objectified, almost a literary commodity, by existentialism, Tillich's theology, and the popular sociology of the mass society. But in *Politics* it was there, palpable, in concrete detail, and illustrated in the ways in which individuals lost their humanness.

The best essays in the book, unfortunately only a fifth of the total, are those written during the war, when Macdonald, with his remarkable eye for significant detail, illuminated the psychology of killing, the pathetic attempts to expiate guilt, the mock bravado of war. Perhaps the most extraordinary article that *Politics* ever published was the abridgement of Bruno Bettelheim's account, from the *Journal of Abnormal and Social Psychology*, of "Behavior in Extreme Situations." The sense of fear that it evoked arose not from the descriptions of sadism in the concentration camps, but from the horrifying awareness that a victim, out of the deep, infantile, regressive aspects in one's own nature, would willingly take on the hideous mask, stance, and code of the brutes. Whatever we have heard subsequently about confessions, brainwashing, and the like, hardly matched the awesome revelation of those first disclosures.

Macdonald was more sensitive to these concerns because, as a pacifist, he was more alive to and horrified by these changes than those who justified the war; he was also influenced by Nicola Chiaramonte and other refugees who had had first-hand contact with these sickening events.

Yet, more fundamentally, this awareness derived from a singular innocence about politics. One of the accusations that

Ortega y Gasset brought against liberalism, as Mrs. Judith Shklar reminds us in her interesting book *After Utopia,* is that it forgot the violence inherent in politics. Ortega's indictment derived from the liberal's inability to understand the "fierce nature of the State," which, owing to the Hobbesian need to maintain order, must rule by threat against all. (And it followed for Ortega that all political activity was degrading, especially for the intellectual, whose vocation—the desire for truth—brought him into opposition to the politician, with his need for expediency, compromise, and myths.) Macdonald's fall from innocence came in the horrifying realization that violence—and the drive for domination—was a craving in man, and, following Hannah Arendt, that modern society had become a bureaucratized apparatus for periodically, and necessarily, evoking and suppressing such violence. And since the indictment of innocence could be leveled against radicalism as well, politics—and *Politics*—had to come to an end.

There remains the difficult question—far beyond the scope of this essay—of how true such a theory is. These political images are conceptions that derive from "heroic" and ultimately romantic images of life and man's place in it. To see politics on the more mundane, and civil, level of reconciling diverse interests may be naive. But this has been the British experience and, McCarthy apart, that of America, too. We do not live "at extremes" (and when we do, as in popular culture, this represents vicarious violence, not real experience, and is perhaps a useful displacement). That is why, perhaps, we have avoided some of the extreme ideological conflicts that wrecked Europe.

Apart from the apathy of the fat fifties, one reason, perhaps, why *Politics* could not last is that it drew from alien experiences. Is the fabric of American life strong enough to resist such rents as occurred in Europe? Did the war really leave us unmarked? It is the merit of Dwight Macdonald's *Memoirs* that he forces us once again to confront such desperate questions.

D. Dissent in the Fifties

Dissent is one of the few cultural periodicals in the United States avowedly socialist in politics and radical in its criticism of contemporary culture. It is, like *Universities and Left Review* in England and *Arguments* in France, at odds with the doctrinaire interpretation of orthodox Marxism, and at one with the search for a new socialist humanism. But in important respects the differences are greater than the similarities. *Universities and Left Review* arose out of the ferment in the Communist world following the Khrushchev admissions that the Stalin regime had criminally murdered thousands of innocent Communists. *Arguments* came into being after the 1956 events in Poland and Hungary, and, in its intense philosophical absorption, reflects the revisionist discussions that have taken place in Eastern Europe. *Dissent,* five years older than the other two, was founded largely by individuals who had left the Trotskyite movement a few years before (the "class of 1950"), and who were long schooled in the doctrinal debates of Marxist exegetics.

The difference in origin accounts for the differences in tone and content. The first two are products of the fifties, cut off from the past by the war and the tales of their tired elders; the latter is an echo of the thirties, repeating, in mournful anger, the concerns and debates of the past. *Universities and Left Review* and *Arguments* represent a new generation with all the earnestness and questing freshness of the young; *Dissent* is a magazine of the epigone, the after-born, jejune, and weary. *Universities and Left Review* and *Arguments* are intense, frenetic, naive, bursting out with a new sense of autodidact wonder about theoretical issues that had been wrangled over by the Left twenty years before; *Dissent* is querulous, scornful, magisterial, sectarian, yet infinitely more sophisticated.

These differences in style caricature, as extreme statements are wont to do, the gulf between European and American radicalism. It is not only that America has become an affluent society, offering place (in the universities and in the publishing houses) and prestige (if not in the society as a whole, certainly in the universities and the publishing houses) to the onetime radicals—and it is interesting to note that the two chief editors of *Dissent,* Irving Howe and Lewis Coser, are university professors—but American radicalism had, intellectually, long ago disposed of the very questions that rack the serious European Left today. It is that fact—as well as the one that American society, through the modifications introduced by Roosevelt and Truman, belied Marxist predictions of "fascism and collapse"—which explains much of the difference in intellectual atmosphere between the two continents.

This is a seeming paradox. Europe, in legend, has always been the home of subtle philosophical discussion; America was the land of grubby pragmatism. Questions laid to rest in

Europe found their reincarnation (an old quip had it) twenty years later in the United States. Whatever the truth of the remark once, the reverse is true today. Take any of the questions that in the last five years have preoccupied Sartre and Camus in France, Wolfgang Harich in East Germany, Kolakowski in Poland—the questions of ends and means, of class truth, the meaningfulness of dialectic materialism as a scientific construct, the definition of a workers' State, party democracy, the nature of bureaucracy, the relationship of literature to propaganda, the mixed economy—and you will find that these were thrashed out more than twenty years ago by Sidney Hook, Ernest Nagel, Lewis Corey, Edmund Wilson, Philip Rahv, John Dewey, and dozens of others in the pages of *Partisan Review,* the *New International,* and the *New Leader.* It is not that these men had greater theoretical acumen than Marxists in Europe, many of whom, individually (most notably Ignazio Silone, in *Bread and Wine*), had explored these same problems. But while in Europe only a small number of intellectuals left the Communist orbit before the war, in the United States almost the entire group of serious intellectuals who had been attracted to Marxism had broken with the Communist party by 1940. Thus, as an intellectual problem, Bolshevism disappeared from the American scene almost twenty years ago.

The sociological reasons for these differences in behavior are varied. Being 3,000 miles from Europe, the American radicals were not caught up in the immediate political struggles of fascism—and the possibility of having to become refugees—so there was less reason to suppress the political doubts which had been fired by the Moscow Trials and the Nazi-Soviet Pact. In the United States, moreover, the Communist party never had a large following in the labor movement, so there was no emotional force the party could use to hold the intellectuals. And, being free-floating intellectuals, rather than functionaries or officials who had to swing a large political movement with them, the discussions were more "irresponsible," yet by the same token freer and more intense.

As a result of such free-spiritedness, the basic political drift of the former Left intelligentsia in the United States in the forties and fifties has been anti-ideological—that is to say, skeptical of the rationalistic claim that socialism, by eliminating the economic basis of exploitation, would solve all social questions; and to a great extent this anti-rationalism is the source of the intellectual vogue of Freudianism and neo-orthodox theology (i.e., Reinhold Niebuhr and Paul Tillich), with their anti-rational stoicism. Moreover, the American intellectuals found new virtues in the United States because of its pluralism, the acceptance of the Welfare State, the spread of education, and the expanding opportunities for intellectual employment. And, in the growing Cold War, they accepted the fact that Soviet Russia was the principal threat to freedom in the world today. These political attitudes were reflected largely in the pages of *Partisan Review, Commentary,* and the *New Leader,* the three magazines, and the writers grouped around them, that originally made up the core of the American Committee for Cultural Freedom. On the academic level, these re-evaluations called into question the populist basis of American radicalism and argued that the political conflicts of the fifties, such as McCarthyism, were more fruitfully explained by sociological concepts such as "status anxiety" than by the more conventional notions of class or interest group conflicts. The changes in intellectual temper can be seen in Lionel Trilling's *The Liberal Imagination,* Richard Hofstadter's *The Age of Reform,* Edward Shils' *The Torment of Secrecy,* and the various essays on "McCarthyism" in *The New American Right,* edited by this writer.

It was in this context of the breakup of the old Left, and in reaction to these re-evaluations, that *Dissent* arose. Its targets were those who were calling the old radical clichés into question, and the internal debate was carried on, as it has usually been in the United States, in that large, exotic cauldron that is the New York intellectual world. While *Dissent* talked of the conformism of American society, and the need for "new ideas," there was little path-breaking thought on radicalism. "What Shall We Do?" asks one of the editors, Lewis Coser, in a programmatic essay. "Above all, it would seem to me," says editor Coser, the radical "must be concerned with maintaining, encouraging, fostering the growth of the species 'radical.' If it becomes extinct, our culture will inevitably ossify from want of challenge." But challenge to what? Radical about what? *Dissent* attacked *Partisan Review* and *Commentary* for not being radical. But, other than attacking these magazines, there was little in *Dissent* itself that was new; it never exemplified what it meant by radicalism; and it has not been able, especially in politics, to propose anything new.

For actually *Dissent* has been hoist, as has been the Left

as a whole, on the meaninglessness of the term. In the past, radicalism had vitality because it was a form of *apocalyptic* thought—it wanted to wash away an entire society in one tidal wave. ("I went to Cuba," writes Livio Stecchini in a recent issue of *Dissent,* in an article which expresses in extraordinary fashion the romantic pathos of the magazine, "because over the years I have become disappointed with revolutionary ideas and experience. Selfishly I wanted to share the exhilaration that comes from living by hope and desire *before the dawn of reality.*") But where the problems are, as Karl Popper put it, of "piecemeal technology," of the prosaic, yet necessary questions, of school costs, municipal services, the urban sprawl, and the like, bravura radicalism simply becomes a hollow shell.

If *Dissent* has had a single unifying idea—and this is what gives any radical magazine its character—it is its conceptualization of America as a *mass society,* and its attack on the grotesque elements of such a society. And here *Dissent* begins to merge in identity with *Universities and Left Review,* and other new voices of the Left which attack modern society. The concept of the *mass society,* however, has a peculiar amorphousness. Those who used the older vocabulary of radicalism could attack "the capitalists" or even "the bourgeoisie," but in the *mass society* one simply flails out against "the culture," and it is hard to discover who, or what, is the enemy. This is not true of the older group of writers who first employed the idea of the mass society, principally Ortega y Gasset, Joseph Pieper, Karl Jaspers, and T. S. Eliot. They have had an aristocratic, or Catholic, or elite conception of culture, and for them the standards of taste and excellence, once set by the educated and the cultivated, have been torn down by the mass. They stood against equalitarianism and industrial society. In effect, they did not want to give the masses "cultural voting rights." But it is difficult for the "young radical" to adopt this stance. Nor can they easily absorb, intellectually, though many have done so without seeing the contradiction, the pastoral-romantic image (which derives from German sociology)—that the roots of the old *Gemeinschaft* have been torn up by the impersonal, mechanized society. This protest has always been the cry of the rural society against the rootlessness, anonymity—yet privacy and freedom—of the city. (But the young radicals are not rural idiots.) I believe the image of the mass society, as used by *Dissent* and *Universities and Left Review,* to be misleading. The bringing of the "mass" *into* a society from which they have been excluded is, as Edward Shils has been arguing, a long and difficult process. Yet against the "traditional society," in which people led the same dull, rote, often brutalized lives (Saul Padover, in a study of France, has pointed out that a large number of Frenchmen have never traveled, belonged to a voluntary association, or even seen the inside of a museum), modern society, with its possibilities for mobility, occupational choice, theater, books, and museums, is more differentiated, variegated, and life-enhancing.

The pages of *Dissent* and *Universities and Left Review* are full of attacks against advertising, the debaucheries of mass culture, and the like. And, often, phrasing these criticisms in the language of the early Marx, particularly in terms of alienation, gives these attacks a seeming political content. But the point is that these problems are essentially cultural and not political, and the problem of radical thought today is to reconsider the relationship of culture to society. Certainly few persons will assume the relationships of culture to politics to be as direct as Marxist critics assumed them to be twenty-five years ago. And when, with the lesson of totalitarianism and bureaucracy in mind, one comes to accept—in the mixed economy and political pluralism—moderation in social politics, specifying the content of "cultural radicalism" becomes even more difficult. The paradox is that whatever is deemed radical in culture is quickly accepted, and whatever calls itself avant-garde, be it abstract expressionism or Beatnik poetry, is quickly acclaimed. When the products of high culture, from Schönberg to Matisse to *l'école de New York,* become best-selling cultural items, the problem of locating the source of the "corruption" of standards becomes a difficult one. The acceptance of the avant-garde has become so vexing that Hilton Kramer (an editor of *Arts*), writing in *Dissent,* was moved to say, "The fact of the matter is that since 1945 bourgeois society has tightened its grip on all the arts by allowing them a freer rein." (And, one might say, a freer reign.)

In part, some of this is due to the desire for novelty and sensation in American life. But on a more serious level, these changes are also a feature of the absorption of radicalism into the society. Just as managerial authority is shared, in part, by the unions, and political power is shared, in part, with the ethnic and labor groups, so the culture, too, in part, has been transformed. Many of the new cultural arbiters (Clement

Greenberg and Harold Rosenberg in painting, Lionel Trilling and Alfred Kazin in literature) were part of the *ancien* Left, and their tastes have affected not only the serious painters and novelists but the standards of the larger public as well. One other important consideration must be noted. The cultural elite—to the extent that there is one, and I believe there is—is primarily a university culture, that of Harvard, Columbia, Berkeley, and other large centers; and, in contrast to fifty years ago, it is a "liberal culture," receptive to ideas, critical in its outlook, and encouraging of (and sometimes nostalgic for) dissent. To that extent, and this is the final paradox, even *Dissent* is an accredited member of that culture, and a welcome one.

Chapter 14

Ten Theories in Search of Reality:

The Prediction of Soviet Behavior

SURELY, MORE HAS BEEN written about the Russian Revolution and the ensuing forty years of Soviet rule than about any comparable episode in human history! The bibliography of items on the French Revolution occupies, it is said, one wall of the Bibliothèque Nationale. A complete bibliography on the Soviet Union—which is yet to be compiled and may never be because of the geometric rate at which it multiplies—would probably make that earlier cenotaph to scholarship shrink the way in which the earlier tombs diminished before the great complex at Karnak.

And yet, how little of this awesome output has stood the test of so short a span of time! If hell, as Thomas Hobbes once said, is truth seen too late, the road to hell must now be paved twice over with the thousands of books claiming to discover the "truth" about Russia—while the tortures of the damned are reserved for those, diplomats especially, who committed the fates of millions in the confident belief that they could predict correctly the way in which the Soviet rulers would respond.[88]

In the last ten years there has been, presumably, a new sophistication, and an extraordinary amount of research and writing on Soviet society, particularly in the United States. Some of this research has come from Russian defectors; most of it has been done in special institutes set up by universities under government or foundation research grants in an effort to obtain reliable knowledge about Soviet behavior. We have seen, too, the entry of new disciplines—anthropology, sociology, and psychiatry—into the study of political phenomena. In some instances these newer approaches have claimed to provide a total understanding of Soviet behavior; in others, to supplement existing explanation. So thick and heavy is this research that an outside observer, seeking to push his way through the marshes, often finds himself mired (as that wonderful Russian onomatopoeic evocation has it) in *splosh*. And one is bogged down further by the fact that much of this newer research is couched in a special jargon which owes allegiance to other modes of discourse than the common tongue. (As R. P. Blackmur has said of the literary "New Criticism," the terminology rigidifies in the course of time and the "normal pathology of a skill becomes a method, and the method a methodology.")

In this chapter, the writer has attempted a description and, in representative cases, a detailed assessment of these methodologies. This is not a "national estimate" of Russian capabilities and weaknesses, social, military, or economic, such as is made by the government's National Security Council. Nor is it a "survey" of empirical research. The writer has sought to distinguish ten approaches in social theory, each of which, despite some shading or overlap, represents a coherent judgment of Soviet behavior. It is hoped that by "reading" each against the other, some sense of the crucial differences, analytical or methodological, may emerge. Beyond that, such a reading may aid in the formulation of the two judgments which are essential in any stock-taking—namely: (1) Which theories or approaches have "stood up" in explaining events, and which have not? (2) If one were a policymaker, which research would one underwrite in the future, and why?

I. Enter Pirandello

Hegel once said that what was reasonable was real. Each of the theories to be discussed seems reasonable, yet not wholly real. Something may be wrong with Hegel, the theories, or both. The reader will have to be the judge.

CHARACTEROLOGICAL THEORIES

(1) *Anthropological.* Beginning with the work of Ruth Benedict, and taken up by Linton and Kardiner, Margaret Mead, and Clyde Kluckhohn, contemporary anthropologists have developed the concept of "culture and personality." The argument is that members of a given culture share certain common, sufficiently distinct ways of handling emotional drives and regulating social conduct which form a unique life style that differs, often markedly, from the life style of other cultural groups. The "norms" of the group specify how an individual must manage the key tensions generated in social living (i.e., attitudes to authority, frustration of impulses, aggression, etc.) and how the social controls against violation of those norms (i.e., mechanisms of guilt and shame, disposal of repressed hate, etc.) operate.

Margaret Mead,[89] Geoffrey Gorer and John Rickman,[90] and Henry V. Dicks[91] have sought to apply these "culture and personality" concepts to Russian behavior. Gorer, particularly, has gained a certain notoriety for what skeptics have dubbed "diaperology." Together with the late John Rickman, a respected British psychiatrist who lived in Russia during World War I, Gorer argued that the maternal practice of tightly swaddling the Russian infant produces a privation-gratification cycle. This predisposes the "Great Russian" national character to pendulum swings of submissiveness and violent eruption, of apathy and diffuse persecutory anxiety, or "oral" greed and abstinence.* This accounts, too, for the willingness of the Russian adult to submit to brutal authority.

Dicks's work is more specific. A British psychiatrist at the Tavistock Institute (which set up the War Office Selection Boards), Dicks's generalizations are based, principally, on long interviews with Russian defectors.[92] The outstanding trait of Russian personality, says Dicks, is its ambivalence. On one side is the omnivorousness, the tendency to rush at things and to "swallow them whole," the need for quick and full gratification, the spells of manic omnipotence, the anarchic demand for abolition of all bounds and limitations; on the other, the melancholy closeness and suspicion, the anxious and sullen submissiveness, the "moral masochism and grudging idealization of a strong and arbitrary authority which is thought of as the only safeguard against the excesses of Russian nature." Authority, thus, if it is to be *authority,* must be hard, deprivational, arbitrary, and capricious; if the *vlast* were weak, nobody would obey it.

Against the traditional untidiness, lack of system, and formlessness of the Russian masses is the contrasting behavior of the elite. It has to be puritanical, in full control of all sentimentality and self-indulgence, and strong enough to renounce the gratifications which "traditional" Russian character seeks. At important points there are congruities. The people expect and the elite satisfies the image of authority as severe, arbitrary, and fickle. The system, further, permits the most au-

* A dichotomy, like an atom once split, can seemingly be multiplied indefinitely. Thus Dinko Tomasic, in his study of *The Impact of Russian Culture on Soviet Communism* (Glencoe, Ill., 1953), finds the Russian national character is a bisect of two contrasting influences, that of the "power-seeking and self-oriented nomadic horsemen of the Eurasian steppes" and of the "anarchic and group-oriented [Slavic] tillers of the land." One can also point to antinomies, such as Gordon Wasson's discovery that Russians are mycophiles and Anglo-Saxons are mycophobes.

thoritarian fraction of the population "to act out their introjected bad-object relations"—i.e., to step into the shoes of a hated, yet, deep down, secretly identified-with father figure (Tsar, landlord, etc.). "By this hypothesis," says Dicks, "I would explain the rise in Soviet Russia of a rigid, gold-braided, intensely status-conscious and anxious bureaucracy, which is winning in the struggle against the very tendency originally successfully attacked by the new system and its founders during the Revolution.[93]

But this very transformation of goals, on a conscious or an unconscious level, provides the "salient" divergence between the Soviet system and the traditional Russian culture-pattern. For the elite, faced with the need of quickly producing a new type of technological and managerial personality, "is using the impetus of its own imperfectly assimilated and conflict-laden goal-drives to force and mould the people into a new cultural norm." Since the greater the pressure, the more intensive the inner conflicts, the elite "projects its own compulsive and sadistic authoritarian dominance needs on to foreign outgroups." Thus it creates a psychological situation of "encirclement" and attributes all failures to the work of the external enemy. "It is difficult to estimate," says Dicks, "how much of this paranoid behavior is the result of conscious design and how much is the effect of an inner compulsion due to cultural-psychological forces into which the top leaders have little insight. In this respect, I can only refer to the amazing discovery of the psychiatric pictures presented by a comparable power clique whom we were able to study: Hitler's entourage. We had assumed a cynical and cold-blooded exploitation of this paranoid dynamic by people like Goebbels and Himmler—and we found they were its victims." [94]

The acceleration of industrialization, says Dicks, will increase the tensions between the elite and the people. The coercions are "resented and stored up against the regime"; the deprivations in the name of some ultimate and impersonal good are interpreted as "withdrawal of love and nurturance." But such unconscious rage also leads to a sense of guilt for having defied authority, and this becomes projected onto the elite (i.e., it creates a feeling, at all levels, that the elite is angry at the masses and wants to punish them), leading to an increase in the atmosphere of "persecutory anxiety and diffuse fear (*strakh*)." The guilt thus also reduces a tendency to strike out at, or oppose, the regime.

(2) *Psychoanalytic.* An attempt to analyze not Russian

but Bolshevik character structure, particularly as exemplified in the Politburo, has been made by Nathan Leites in his RAND study, underwritten by the U.S. Air Force.[95] But Leites' work goes beyond the mere codification of behavior in operational terms. In guarded, almost esoteric fashion, Leites undertakes a psychoanalytic explanation which is fairly breathtaking in its attempt. Bolshevik elite behavior is seen in contrast to that of the nineteenth-century intelligentsia. The latter were moody, nervous, soul-searching, brooding, introspective. "The Bolshevik" is rigid, suspicious, unyielding, ever-aggressive. This character is stamped in the primal image of Lenin, and is derived, psychoanalytically speaking, as a "reaction-formation" to fears of death and latent homosexual impulses. (Since Leites' massive work—639 pages—is the most ambitious attempt yet to read an "operational code" of Bolshevik behavior, particularly in international strategy, a more detailed exposition of the theory is undertaken in Section II below.)

SOCIOLOGICAL THEORIES

(3) *The Social System.* This socio-psychological theory, developed at Harvard in the Russian Research Center, and expressed most concisely in the recent book by Raymond Bauer, Alex Inkeles, and Clyde Kluckhohn,[96] seeks to identify the functionally relevant "operating characteristics" of the Soviet system—e.g., the overcommitment of resources to particular objectives; "storming"; the refusal to allow independent concentration of power—and the effect of these behavior patterns on the various social groups. In this fashion, the authors seek to locate the points of strain in the Soviet system. (Because it is the summary volume of the largest single research project on Soviet behavior, it is discussed in greater detail in Section III below.)

(4) *Ideal Types.* This approach, exemplified largely in the writings of Barrington Moore, Jr., at Harvard[97] (though it has influenced the thinking of W. W. Rostow at M.I.T. and Henry Dicks at Tavistock), sets up a number of models for the organization of power in a society and seeks to establish how far any society, and the Russian in particular, can go in its commitment to one or another of these forms.

According to Moore, power and position in a society are held in one of a combination of three ways: (*a*) *traditional*: power and position are transmitted through the family or kinship system, from father to son; (*b*) *rational-technical:* power and position are attained by an individual on the basis of skill and technical ability, regardless of the status of one's parent; (*c*) *political:* power and position are awarded on the basis of loyalty to a political leader, party or clique.

The use of any one criterion limits the range of workable alternatives for the solution of other problems. Rationality (*b*) emphasizes that technical competence should be the criterion for employment. But the nature of power struggles (*c*) demands that jobs should go to the faithful, to the commissar rather than to the manager, while purges, the most drastic expression of politics, remind individuals that obedience is the first law of the Soviet system. Meanwhile, traditionalism (*a*) is still the "natural" mode of the peasantry, and *sub rosa,* within large sections of Soviet industry, and informal ties have become a necessary means of protection against arbitrary orders.

The political criterion of power in Russia (e.g., the commissars in the army, the control functions of the party in relation to industry) has been employed too ruthlessly, says Moore, at the expense, even, of sacrificing large classes of technicians and experienced army officers (e.g., the *Yezhovschina,* the dreaded 1937-38 purges which bear the name of Yezhov, the head of the secret police at the time). The power of the dictator to intervene arbitrarily at any point in the administrative hierarchy creates a level of insecurity which an ongoing system may find difficult to maintain. The choice now, Moore feels, lies between "creeping rationality" or traditionalism, or some combination of both.

Since the Soviet Union is intent on industrialization, the rationalizing elements are likely to become more deeply embedded in the society: this would mean that technical criteria would replace political decisions, jobs would be allocated according to skill, career expectations would have a higher degree of stability, family privileges could be passed on to the children. In turn, the power and prestige of the industrial manager, the engineer, and the technician would rise, and the share in power and prestige held by the "control" apparatus —the party and the secret police—would decline.

An alternative evolution in a traditionalist direction, which Moore finds politically "somewhat more plausible," would mean that the party and military elements would retain control, but abritrary intervention would diminish as personal cliques and machines within the bureaucracy become the focal point of such loyalties. Such a development would also imply a rise in local autonomy and a resistance to innovation and change.

Plausible as these alternatives seem, if there is any sense to Khrushchev's vast "decentralization" scheme, it would seem to mean the reassertion of a political criterion, rather than economic rationality, in the handling of economic affairs. Genuine economic decentralization, as Richard Lowenthal points out,[98] would leave the party as a parasitic appendix to the economy. Despite the absorption of managers into the party, the division of function between managers and party whips has been a source of conflict; and this was utilized by Malenkov, speaking for the managerial group. What Krushchev, whose strength has been in the party secretariats, has now done is to create a union of function, whereby the party secretaries, at the Republic and regional levels, will be responsible for the economic performance of the plan. As Lowenthal concludes: "It is the 'irrational' Khrushchev with his party bosses, and not the 'rational' Malenkov with his managers and economic administration, who has won the latest round; and the reason is to be found precisely in the logic of self-preservation of the party regime." [99]

If Moore is correct, such logic may yet lead to economic crises; but that remains to be seen. What Moore has done is to focus attention on Soviet development primarily as a function of "forced industrialization," rather than of Marxist or even Bolshevik ideology, and to see Stalinist repression as much the necessary outcome of the speed of industrialization as of internal power struggles or the desire of Stalin to consolidate his rule. This is a theme which has commanded increasing attention from writers with such diverse views as Raymond Aron and Isaac Deutscher, and forms the core of E. H. Carr's interpretative analysis of Soviet history.[100] It has the merit, which few of the writings on Russia have had, of speculating on the possibly different "profiles" of Soviet society once industrialization has been achieved.

POLITICAL THEORIES

(5) *Marxist.* Expressed most directly by Isaac Deutscher, this approach sketches a theory of Soviet development based on the proposition that the level of productive power always acts as a constraint on the possibility of action. It argues that the Stalinist dictatorship was a historically "necessary" stage, therefore, in overcoming the resistance of the masses to industrialization, but that once this social stage has been

achieved the dictatorial apparatus will "come into social conflict" with the requirements of the new, higher stages of economic development.[101]

As developed by Deutscher—agreement can be found in the writings of E. H. Carr—the year 1920 represented the crossroads of the revolution:[102] the working class was exhausted, demoralized, shrunken to half its size, anxious for relaxation; in a free election, the Bolsheviks would have been ousted; only the iron will of the Bolshevik leadership saved the revolution, at the expense of putting down democracy in the party (i.e., suppressing the workers' opposition faction, the "levelers or Utopian dreamers"). The result was an anomaly, a workers' revolution without working-class support. The rationale for this paradox was "historical necessity": nationalized property represented a higher stage of social development and therefore had to be defended, even against the workers.

The theory, *sans* Stalinist apologetics, had its origin in Trotsky's *The New Course* (1923) and later *The Revolution Betrayed* (1937). There Trotsky argued that in the growth of bureaucracy Russia faced a crisis: either the release of productive forces from the heavy hand of bureaucracy, or a "Thermidor," a return to some capitalist form, state or otherwise. Deutscher, at this point, feels otherwise. The backwardness of the peasant masses and their reluctance to make the sacrifice for industrialization, he says, required the harsh measures and iron discipline of Stalinism. But with the progress that was achieved in the 1930's, says Deutscher, the Stalinist terrorism and "primitive magic" had outlived their usefulness and were coming into conflict with the "new needs of Soviet society." Industrialization, he believes, "tends to awaken the democratic aspirations of the masses," while the "phenomenal growth of Soviet wealth . . . tends to soften class privileges, and the orthodoxy, the iron curtain and the elaborate mythology of Stalinism tend to become socially useless. . . . Stalinism is untenable in this expanding society at its present level of productive forces."[103]

This theme, with a greater emphasis on the working class as a "political power of a magnitude hitherto unknown in Russian history," has been expanded by Deutscher in a recent publication.[104] The post-Stalin reforms, he notes, are reforms from "above," intended largely to provide some security for the bureaucracy. But the working class, particularly the skilled elements in engineering (which employs about one-third of Russia's industrial manpower), is now displaying long-suppressed egalitarian aspirations. This is evident in the revision of the old "progressive" piece-rate system, the narrowing of wage differentials, the introduction of a new pension scheme, and the abolition of all tuition fees in education.

This egalitarian drive—which is reinforced by the formal ideology that the workers are the ruling power in the country—says Deutscher, must come into conflict with the bureaucracy, which will seek to maintain its privileges and to preserve the status quo. And such an impending conflict must create a problem for a regime. With the power of the secret police diminished, there is only the army as the guardian of the order. But the army, rather than keeping order for the benefit of the party, sooner or later will do so on its own account. "In other words," concludes Deutscher, "the strains and stresses caused by a stormy revival of mass movements lacking leadership and clear political purpose, may lead to the establishment of a dictatorship of the Bonapartist type. All the more so as the military could hardly view with indifference a situation in which they must see a threat to Russia's positions of power and to all the strategic gains she won in the last war." [105]

It is highly debatable whether industrialization leads to a striving for *freedom* (even though it may lead to a demand by workers for a greater distributive share of wealth), or whether the expansion of wealth tends to diminish class privileges. Relative scarcities in the Soviet Union are bound to exist for a long period, however "phenomenal" the growth of Russian productivity. And the congealing of class privileges may become the real brake on any relaxation of the dictatorship, although key social groups at the top may win a measure of security. Certainly, in the downfall of Zhukov, the military has, for the time being at least, once again come under the control of the party. Deutscher clearly underestimated the role of the party, and in *Russia: What Next?* (published in 1953) failed even once to mention Khrushchev—so remote was he from the inner-elite struggles. What is relevant, however, for this presentation is that in Deutscher's scheme of analysis there is a clearly determinable sense (whether substantively right or wrong) of a mainspring of change; and thus it focuses attention on the question which all social theory must confront: the sources of change in social systems.

(6) *Neo-Marxist.* Leading out of Trotsky's discussion of the nature of Soviet policy, a group of theorists argued that Russia, despite nationalized property, was no longer a work-

ers' state but a new social form, namely, "bureaucratic collectivism."[106] The distinction has been important for the *political* orientations of the Marxist parties and sects. The orthodox Trotskyites, for example, claimed that Russia, although a "degenerated" workers' state, was, because of nationalized property, "historically progressive" and therefore worth defending in the event of a conflict with capitalist powers. The dissident Trotskyites, claiming that a new exploitative class society had been established, took a "neither-nor," "third-camp" position. Analytically—i.e., in terms of its predictive utility—the view that Russian society is bureaucratic collectivist leads its proponents either to adopt a scheme similar to that of Moore, or to analyze the regime in political terms not very different than those who see the USSR as a totalitarian society.

(7) *Totalitarian.* Expressed most forcefully in the categories of political philosophy by Hannah Arendt,[107] this theory argues that a radically new social form, different from tyranny, dictatorship, or authoritarianism, was created in Germany and exists now in Russia. The essentially new fact of totalitarianism is that all intermediate or secondary institutions between the leader and the "masses" have been eliminated, and that the ruler, unrestrained by legal or political checks, rules by terror. The theory, as applied to the Soviet Union by Bertram D. Wolfe, holds that no essential change in the nature of the regime is possible and that totalitarianism, through an inner "ideo-logic" of its own, can never relinquish its combative posture vis-à-vis democratic societies. As a "working tool" to explain specific political situations, the theory of totalitarianism, which Mr. Wolfe draws also from Karl Wittfogel's *Oriental Despotism,* is too sweeping. From such heights the terrain of politics, its ridges and gullies, becomes flattened, and the weary foot-traveler finds few guides to concrete problems. Even on a simpler, intuitive basis, one can question the basic assumption of the theory—namely, that society becomes completely atomized and rule is anomic and direct. In a *crisis* situation, a state can fragment all social life, and through terror, perhaps, mold a people to its will. But can a society live in permanent crisis? Can it hold such a rigid posture without either exploding into war or relaxing? The basis of all social life requires not only a minimum of personal security but the reasonable expectation by parents that their children will be educated, develop careers, and so

forth. To that extent, a tendency toward "normalization" is at work in any crisis state.

(8) *Kremlinological.* These speculations, identified principally with the writings of the late Franz Borkenau and of Boris Nicolaevsky, focus primarily on the power struggle within the core elite and seek to identify the shifting coalitions ("who is doing-in whom") within the Kremlin, as a basis for predicting political events. While open to easy satire, it is the supercilious who mock it at their peril, as the New York *Post* once learned when it scoffed at the speculations arising from the fact that all the Bolshevik leaders *but* Beria had appeared en masse at the Bolshoi Ballet. "Perhaps Beria doesn't like ballet," said the *Post* archly. Perhaps he didn't, but we never had the opportunity to find out, for two days later came the announcement that Beria had been arrested as a traitor.

In one form or another, Kremlinology is practiced today by every foreign office and by most journalists. Its emphasis is largely on personality and power groups, and less on the social systems and the way such systems can or cannot constrain these leaders. (See Section IV for an enlargement of this discussion.)

HISTORICAL THEORIES

(9) *Slavic Institutions.* Represented in an earlier generation by Nicholas Berdyaev, Sir Bernard Pares, and Sir John Maynard, and today to some degree by Edward Crankshaw, Ernest Simmons, and Werner Philipp (of the Free University of Berlin), this school states that much of contemporary Russian behavior can be accounted for by traditional Slavic character and institutions. "Too often we forget," said Professor Ernest Barker, in introducing Maynard's *The Russian Peasant: And Other Studies* (London, 1942), "that Russia, with all her changes, still largely remains the same." The theme is elaborated in Sir John's book: "All Russian regimes have been sudden and arbitrary. . . . Old Russia was always rough, with its Siberian exile. . . . Planning . . . a characteristic feature of the new regime, is not as new at first glimpse as it looks to be. . . . Even the 'Party'—that misnomer of the vocation of leadership—is not really new: but rather a new application of an ancient institution: the priesthood . . . ," etc., etc.

One finds a similar argument in the November, 1951, lecture by Professor Werner Philipp on the "Historical Presuppositions of Political Thought in Russia," inaugurating the

Osteuropa Institute of Berlin.[108] As a reviewer summarizes Professor Philipp's argument: "Conditions and traditions have produced a definite political mentality in Russia which goes back for several centuries. . . . The Russian distrust of the West, the cult and consciousness of the precedence of the community over the individual, the recognition of the unlimited power of governmental authority over society, and the discrepancy between political reality and the professed ideal aim, all these phenomena of Soviet thought and life have their roots in conditions which developed in Russia between the beginning of the thirteenth and the end of the sixteenth century." [109] The theme of an "eternal Russia" is propounded, too, by Crankshaw in his *Cracks in the Kremlin Wall* (New York, 1951).

To argue that the roots of Soviet life go down deep in the Russian past is not, of course, to justify those practices (although the argument lends itself sometimes to apologetics, and in the 1930's and 1940's apologists like Bernard Pares or Maurice Hindus did justify Russian behavior in such terms). But like the characterological theories ("parallel travelers," one might call them), the Slavophile theory argues in effect that since Soviet institutions were shaped by historical social forms, and since they are deeply rooted in the traditions of the people, they will change only slowly.

(10) *Geo-political.* This school, which had some vogue during World War II (e.g., Nicholas Spykman at Yale, and William T. R. Fox's *The Super-Powers,* New York, 1944) and still has some supporters, holds that Russian foreign policy is dictated primarily by long-range strategic interests deriving from its position as a great land-mass power, and that its contemporary political aspirations (e.g., in the Middle East) reflect the historic drives of Great Russian policy. The school generally tends to minimize ideology (viz., Walter Bedell Smith's introduction to the Marquis de Custine *Diaries,* New York, 1951) and to see Russian policy primarily as a function of strategic power position. To some extent the early policy views of George Kennan (see his Princeton University lectures, *Realities of American Foreign Policy,* Princeton, N. J., 1954) and those of Henry Kissinger are shaped by these considerations.

II. Kto-Kovo—the Id and Ego of Bolshevism

During the truce negotiations in Korea, a slim book, *The Operational Code of the Politburo,* by Nathan Leites, was used by the American negotiators as a tactical manual. Leites's research, embodied in the larger *Study of Bolshevism,* was sponsored by the U. S. Air Force's Project RAND. The fact that RAND has given strong support to the pioneering method of Leites (which is now being applied to the study of French politics) makes a more detailed examination of his work worthwhile.

Leites begins by attempting to define "Bolshevik character" as a type distinct in social history. The attempt to define historic character is not new. (We have the image, somewhat overworked these days, of the "inner-directed Protestant.") What makes Leites' work unique are the novel categories he chooses and, above all, his method. There is no observation of behavior. Like Max Weber, who drew his "Protestant ethic" from the writings of Luther, Calvin, Baxter, and others, Leites scans the writings of Lenin and Stalin to infer similar norms which guide the Bolshevik party. He reads the Bolshevik character as a "reaction" to the Oblomovs, who slept away their lives; to the Rudins, the high-flown talkers but never-doers; to the indecisive, soul-sick, moody students. The Bolshevik, as Boris Pilnyak put it, is "against the old peasant roots of our old Russian history, against its aimlessness, its non-teleological character . . . against the philosophy of Tolstoy's Karataev." The moral training of the Russian intelligentsia stressed the prohibition against egotism and the prohibition against "dirtying oneself." Chekhov once said, "If all Socialists are going to exploit the cholera for their own ends, I shall despise them." But, for the Bolshevik, refusal to use bad means is merely an expression of sentimentality and stupidity; in Bolshevik doctrine, the worst egotist is precisely he who refuses to soil his hands. The party strives for humanity, and "purity" lies not in a personal refusal to act immorally but in dedication to the party. In such dedication the individual finds his defense against both egotism and personal impurity.

In contrast to the Russian intelligentsia, who spoke of ultimate things and sacred values, the Bolsheviks maintain silence about the sacred. Against the vice of outpouring emotion, the Bolsheviks uphold the virtue of reserve. Against the old Russian tendency to depressed passivity, introspection, nervous impressionability, and excited babbling, against the protracted searching for metaphysical truths and the posing of unanswerable questions—against all these, there is the determinism of history, the certainty of purpose, the commitment to action,

is to minimize death by work, and, more important, to express a kind of personal omnipotence through the dissolution of the self into the all-embracing, undying party. Thus, Leites writes, "The earlier Russian feeling that life is empty because of death has been replaced by the Bolshevik feeling that death is empty and small and unable to interfere with life."[111]

The code of work becomes all-important. It is a basic defense against threatening feelings. Krupskaya, Lenin's wife, tells of the time in exile when Lenin was absorbed for hours in playing chess. "On his return to Russia Vladimir Ilyich abandoned chess-playing. 'Chess gets hold of you too much, and hinders work . . .'," he said. "From his early youth," she continues, "Vladimir Ilyich was capable of giving up whatever activity hindered his main work." In exile, many political refugees went often to the cinema, while others, scorning this mode of enjoyment, preferred to take physical exercise in walking. The group divided, said Krupskaya, into cinemists and anti-cinemists, who were jokingly called "anti-Semites." "Volodya," wrote Krupskaya to Lenin's mother, "is a decided anti-cinemist and a fierce walker."[112]

The theme of latent homosexuality, lying deep in the arcanum of psychoanalysis, is seen as a pervasive yet repressed element of Russian intellectual desire. In Dostoevsky, the utmost demonstration of emotion by the usually overwrought and emotionally charged characters is to embrace and clasp one another. To Bolshevism, the fantasy of men embracing each other is repulsive and frightening. When Lenin described those once close to him who had now made common cause with his enemies, he would say that they "kissed" and "embraced" one another. ("The Scheidemannites kiss and embrace Kautsky"; "The followers of Bernstein are impudently blowing kisses to [Plekhanov].")

To Leites, a further significant clue lies in the number of Lenin's intimate friendships which ended in violent ruptures. These included Struve, a close collaborator in the 1890's; Potresev, an early *Iskra* associate; Plekhanov, Lenin's "ambivalently loved master" who "capitulated" to the Mensheviks; Alekinsky, perhaps Lenin's most intimate associate in the years after 1905, who later denounced him as a German agent; and Malinovsky, the Bolshevik whip in the Duma, of whom Lenin said, "He will not be another Alekinsky," and who turned out to be a police agent.

"One might speculate—" says Leites, "the data discussed here allow no more than that—whether the Bolshevik insistence on, in effect, killing enemies and being killed by them is not in part an effort to ward off fear-laden and guilty wishes to embrace men and be embraced by them. This hypothesis is consistent with the existence of certain pervasive Bolshevik trends described in this study; the fear of being passive, the fear of being controlled and used, the fear of wanting to submit to an attack. Once one denies one's wish to kiss by affirming one's wish to kill, this is apt to reinforce one's belief in the enemy's wish to kill by virtue of the mechanism of projection, probably heavily used by the Bolsheviks."[113]

On the basis of what documentation can one make such sweeping inferences? Even if we fully accept the psychoanalytic theories, how does one validate these judgments without putting the Bolshevik leaders on the couch, so to speak? Leites' method is to examine the imagery fantasy, the characteristic literary metaphors employed by Bolshevik leaders, and the fictional models in Russian literature with which the Bolsheviks identify, or those they assail. Russian literature and the Russians' attitude toward it seem to make this possible. In few cultures have fictional characters become such sharply defined national types: Dostoevsky's gallery — the Karamazovs, Raskolnikov, Myshkin, Verkhovensky; Turgeniev's Rudin, Gogol's Chichikov, Goncharov's Oblomov, Chekhov's multifarious characters.* These are all models which are accepted or rejected by Russians as psychological masks. The Bolsheviks, as Leites points out, cite these types in their own speech and homiletics with great frequency and emphasis (e.g., "Oblomovism" as a disease of slothfulness which the party must avoid).

Taking off from these literary sources, Leites draws on Freudian theory to highlight the latent meanings of specific imagery. For example, fear of impotence, fear of being beaten (in Stalin's famous speech to the managers of Soviet industry in 1931, the image of beating or being beaten occurs eleven times in a single paragraph), jokes about "cleaning out" the party, fear of being used as a "tail," etc. As chief evidence for his theories Leites relies on the marshaling of images, in a vast profusion. The result is a strange and fascinating medley of quotations—roughly three thousand cited for various points.

This method of analysis immediately provokes a charge of

* Less easily and much less intensely and completely, we accept or reject Hemmingway's character, Fitzgerald's youths, Horatio Alger's theories, Huck Finn, the cowboy and the gangster as American types, embodying aspects of our national character.

"reductionism," namely, that all ideas are seen as being *au fond* something more primitive. Thus, Lenin's fierce attack on solipsism is seen as expressing panic about annihilation, while his attack on the "spontaneity of the masses" is seen as a defense against desires for impulsive, orgiastic gratification. In what sense, one may ask, is the primitive impulse behind an idea more "real" than the idea itself? This is a difficulty one often encounters in connection with psychoanalytic thinking. It is obvious that the psychological impulse *behind* an idea is no test of its truth; the test of truth comes *after* the idea has originated. Yet we have learned not to scoff at these hidden mainsprings, *for we are dealing less with the ideas than with the way in which they are held and used.* What Leites is arguing is that any view held with stubbornness, exaggeration, and intensity—as all Communist views are held—and which violently rejects all rational tests, raises the presumption that it may constitute a defense agains strong unconscious wishes or fears which stand in contradiction to the idea. To follow a pronouncedly masculine profession like soldiering does not label a man as a "latent homosexual," but if we find him compulsively, violently, and beyond reason insisting on his military posture, "common sense" permits us to suspect that he may be afraid of being less a man that he would like to appear.

Granting even the validity of the psychoanalytic method in the study of personality, we must still ask whether it can legitimately be extended to the analysis of politics.

Erich Fromm has argued in *Escape from Freedom* (New York, 1941), that the sado-masochistic character, typical of the German middle class, found an outlet in the Nazi party. T. W. Adorno and his associate authors of *The Authoritarian Personality* (New York, 1950) have pointed to the rigid, compulsive individuals who seek authoritarian values. Harold Lasswell, in the early *Psychopathology and Politics* (Chicago, 1930), sought to show how the political arena acts as a displacement of personal needs. (For example, adolescents, feeling guilty about sex strivings, find sublimation in the generalized "love" appeal of political movements that emphasize brotherhood.) In these studies, characteristic of modern social science, the social structure is taken as fundamental and the personality components are seen as the responses.[114]

Leites' view, however, goes beyond this. He says, in effect, that *character determines politics.* Since the mainspring of

Bolshevism is action, the movement, by impressing its character on others, transforms all politics and, in the end, the social structure itself. (Compare the purposeful Bolshevik-type organization with interest-group parties, or tepid ideological parties, to see the difference.) Bolshevism, in this sense, can be considered as one of the few successful movements of pure will in history; its only competitors in this respect are certain religious orders. Because, in modern life, ideas (abstract, philosophical conceptions of truth) have become transformed into ideologies (active strivings to implement a creed as truth), Leites' type of analysis is possible, reflecting as it does a social reality. For ideologies are, in effect, attempts to unite ideas, behavior, and character; they demand a hardening of commitment. The Communist (or the Fascist, or the kibbutznik, or the 100 per cent American) is not only supposed to believe certain things; he is supposed to act, to *be* something, and, in acting, to fix his character. If one is "serious," one "lives" one's ideology. Thus ideology may be said to presuppose character.

But again, what basically determines character? The liberal and utopian answer, as given, say, by Robert Owen in his *New View of Society* or by Edward Bellamy in *Looking Backward,* was that environment bred character: e.g., the rapacious nature of capitalism shaped the competitive character ("Withdraw these cirmustances in order to create crime in the human character and crime will not be created," said Owen in a classic phrasing of the liberal belief; in the utopian society where abundance prevailed, a different character would emerge).

What determined Bolshevik character? Leites stops short of an answer to this question, possibly because the purpose of his book lies elsewhere: he is interested in describing the pattern of Bolshevik action in order to develop a practical way of counteracting communism. Whether or not his picture of this operational code is a true one is, he argues, independent of the origins of Bolshevik impulses. Formally he is correct, for the code's validity depends upon its internal consistency, upon its confirmation by other analysts using the same data, and finally upon its usefulness in making predictions. Yet, intellectually, the sources of that code are important, for only by tracing them can we have a complete model of social analysis.

The conventional answer regarding Bolshevik character is

that the conspiratorial nature of the conditions of underground work in the days before the Revolution—the environment—shaped the peculiar structure of the Bolshevik elite and its unique code and discipline. But there were other parties, Marxist and Social Revolutionary, which operated in the same environment. And the ideological debates between Lenin and Martov in 1903 on the nature of the party membership antedated the development of "party work": Martov argued that a Social Democrat was one who sympathized generally with the party's program, while Lenin argued that only a professional revolutionary, only a conspirator, could be a party member. Thus the pattern was prefigured in the thinking of Lenin.

Leites, it seems to me, would be forced to argue that the Bolshevik pattern was a product of pure will shaped by the intense unconscious drives. Further, if he is to be consistent with the psychoanalytic approach, he would have to argue that *it was the character of Lenin, the "primal father," which shaped the party* (his followers did call themselves Leninists) *rather than the party organization and the environment which shaped Lenin* and the other Bolsheviks. And it was the will of Lenin alone which altered the party's politics, as in the crucial decisions in April and July, 1917. The Bolshevik party, more than any other party in history, has demonstrated the nature of will. It was, and is, one of the most highly self-conscious movements in history. Its patristic writings are not only canonical; they are also "training documents" in the tempering of a "hard core" party membership. Individuals may join from a variety of motives, but all must be stamped in the mold or driven out. "The Narodniks," Lenin jibed, "are more united . . . and with them the abundance of grouplets is not accompanied by sharp splits . . . [yet] the Narodniks are politically impotent . . . incapable of carrying through any political mass action . . . [while] the dogmatic 'Marxists' who have an endless number of splits . . . are successfully active."

The splits and expulsions (becoming blood purges after power is achieved) which characterize Communist parties may thus be seen in a different, sociological light, as a process of personnel, and personality, selection: the true Bolshevik is the man who has thus been tempered, and remains.

If we can sum up the argument schematically: Bolshevik character is a reaction, consciously and unconsciously, to elements in the character structure of the old Russian intelligentsia.* This is seen most characteristically in the person of Lenin and his emotional and intellectual temper. In Lenin's mold the party became stamped.

With the Leites study we come full circle in the theories of history and politics. It was the fashion a hundred years ago to ascribe historical change to "great men" and the force of their personalities. Subsequently we interpreted history in terms of abstract "social forces"—population pressure, search for markets, etc.—which somehow, but never fully understandably, translated themselves through individual actors into tangible events. The glaring inadequacies of these deterministic theories have led to the reintroduction of psychological and, through Freudian influence, of characterological explanations. Even ex-Marxists have not been immune. Is not the current fashionable theory of the "primacy of politics" over economic forces simply a smuggled-in psychological theory of "power"? Most attempts to explain the situation in Russia today find expression in the "power" formula. But actually the formula of "power" explains little. It tells nothing about different tactics, different social groups, the different purposes for which power will be used. If a psychological theory of politics is to be employed, then the Leites view — with its emphasis on character as blending a power drive with ideology—is, in spite of all its limitations and uncertainties, far more subtle and imaginative than the contraband psychology of the political scientist.

However, two questions remain to be asked of the method: How are continuities of character established, and how, and with what difficulties, does an elite group impress its character upon a country?

In the Leites model, as we have seen, there is the implication that the initial change in the character of the intelligentsia —the emergence of Bolshevism—was a reaction-formation, and that the character of the "primal father" determined its political course. If that was true of Lenin, how does it apply to Stalin and to his heirs? In his study of *Hamlet,* Ernest Jones remarks that there are two kinds of sons: those who reject their fathers, and those who take over and internalize

* Leites has elaborated his view in a subsequent volume, *Ritual of Liquidation* (Glencoe, Ill., 1954), to explain the Moscow Trials of the late thirties. His view, briefly, is that the old Bolsheviks were caught, psychologically, in the wheel of their own logic and, having lost, fatalistically submitted and confessed.

the essential characteristics of the father, often caricaturing his features in the process.[115] From this point of view, Stalin was the son who took over the lineaments of the father. The touches, however, were grosser. Where in Lenin's time it was the party that had the monopoly on foresight, under Stalin it became a group within the party, and eventually the Leader alone, in whom all wisdom resided. Devices once reserved for the enemy, particularly deception and terror, were exercised on the masses which the party claimed to represent, and later against rivals within the party itself. Lenin had opposed personal touchiness and insisted on the irrelevance of personal prestige; Stalinism reacted intensely to minor slights, but only after giving them a political interpretation. Lenin opposed bragging; the Stalinist regime went in for the greatest self-glorification in history. Lenin opposed the creation of "scandals" in the party; Stalin liquidated the party cadres under the most fantastic charges.

These changes in Bolshevik behavior *do not necessarily reflect changes in the unconscious wishes and fears* which Leites posits as the ultimate sources of the Bolshevik character. Psychological *defense* patterns may change; indeed, they often *must* change as older defenses become inadequate. But when such changes take place on a broad political scale, they become extremely important, and we are bound to ask why the changes in defense mechanisms have occurred, why *these* particular changes, and what further changes are likely to occur. Here Leites offers little assistance. His theory deals with the dynamics of Bolshevism in the process of its formation, but once Bolshevism has come to birth, the model, as he presents it, is static. Take, for example, the initial turning on Stalin by Khrushchev and company. One could say that this, in turn, represents a reaction to the overbearing, almost paranoid Stalin; or there may be more "rational" explanations: the need to win mass support, etc. Further, how are we to explain the seeming "openness" and marked vulgarity of Khrushchev's character? We have no guide in the model itself to the possibility or the nature of the change.

The static quality of the model comes in part from its methodology. The basic outlines of Bolshevik character are drawn not from the empirical world of action, but from the abstract canons of Bolshevik doctrine. In itself this is not too great a fault, since the doctrine itself is evident. The greater fault of the theory—and, paradoxically, its strength—lies in the fact that, starting from static doctrine, it posits a static force called "character" and then gathers all human action into that one hedgehog force.* But how often in social action does character or will actually impose itself on events? People live largely in social systems, and they are "chained" to one another in complex ways. All of us, no doubt, would like to impose our "character" on the world, but in practice we find ourselves forced to modify our demands to conform with *possibilities.* Leites may thus be claimed to have given his concept of "character" a false autonomy, and in applying this concept to politics, which is par excellence a phenomenon of change within possibilities, to have falsified the nature of the subject.

III. How the Harvard System Works

Turning now to the sociological approach, the study by three Harvard social scientists, Raymond A. Bauer, Alex Inkeles, and Clyde Kluckhohn, *How the Soviet System Works,* is the best that contemporary sociology offers, and on this score alone merits attention. Their book is a revised presentation of a report, *Strategic Psychological Strengths and Vulnerabilities of the Soviet Social System,* that was prepared for the U. S. Air Force, the agency which commissioned and paid for the five years' research that went into the study. In one respect, the study illustrates the hazards of such sponsored research, since the authors found themselves under pressure to produce a "popular" book which the Air Force sponsors could show to their own controllers. The result is not a happy combination: "theses" are condensed and presented with only partial documentation; the book is written in an attempted vernacular style which just does not come off. The project, based on systematic interviewing of defectors, drew data from 329 extended life-history interviews, including detailed personality tests; 435 supplementary interviews; almost 10,000 questionnaires on special topics; 2,700 general questionnaires, and 100 interviews and psychological tests, administered for control purposes, to a matched group of Americans. In all, 33,000 pages of data were accumulated. These, together with the list of over fifty specialized unpublished studies and thirty-five published articles on which the

* As George Ivask has said, if all men may be divided into foxes and hedgehogs, they may also be divided, following the satire of Saltykov-Schedrin, into boys with pants and boys without pants. If Lenin wore pants, is Khruschev without them?

authors drew in preparing the book, indicate how rich their source materials were.

Economic and political matters were not considered to be within the scope of the project. The key concept was that of the "social system," and this is the heart of the Harvard contribution. A "social system" is simply the characteristic ways in which societies, or sub-groups, organize their activities to achieve specific goals. Since the resultant institutions or behavior patterns are linked, presumably in meaningful fashion, variations in one area should be accompanied by regular—and determinate—variations in others. (Thus a change in the rate of capital accumulation, one of the fundamental determinants of an economic system, must precipitate changes in the rate of consumption, etc.) In the social system, reorganization of the structure of authority in the factory would presumably entail corresponding changes in the organization of the school system, the family, etc. For example, when Stalin introduced one-man rule and tight labor discipline in the factories in 1931, one could imagine a manager, confronted with a disrespectful student from a "progressive" school, asking, "What kind of a hooligan is this?" and insisting that school methods be changed so that students would learn obedience. The educational commissars, however, confronted with "wild" children from broken homes, would be forced to demand that the family be strengthened and divorce be made more difficult. And so, in linked fashion, we find the reintroduction of older, traditional forms of authority.[116] Yet such social change may become self-defeating, for as repression in the factory becomes pervasive, individuals need to find protection and do so in close family ties. And thus, after a while, the regime begins to complain about undue familialism. This example oversimplifies a social process, but it is not unjust.

The Harvard group has concentrated, however, not on locating change in the conventional institutions of society—family, political system, education, industry—but on the typical adaptive patterns of behavior which regulate the life of the ruled. These "central patterns" are: the need to conform to an explicit ideology; the refusal to allow independent sources of power; the centralization of all planning and control; the overcommitment of resources to particular objectives; the use of terror and forced labor; "storming" as a method of reaching objectives; the tolerance of evasions which fulfil the plan (e.g., *blat,* the network of informal deals), etc. On the basis of these "operating characteristics," the Harvard group seeks to identify the general strengths and weaknesses of the *system.* To wit: Weaknesses: there are no orderly processes of succession in office; economic growth in heavy industry is disproportionate to that in consumer industries; there are constant purges and insecurities. Strengths: the atomization of resistance; the Russians' ignorance of the realities of the outside world; the deep loyalties to the system on the part of the managerial groups.

One trouble with this approach is that one does not know, actually, which of these "operating characteristics" are central and which are not, for the Harvard group seems to lack an organizing principle which determines the selections. Is "forced labor," for example, an "inherent" aspect of the system, or a fortuitous element which got out of hand and may be discarded? And, if the latter, how is the judgment made?—on the basis of the fact that the terror has become self-defeating or that it is uneconomic, or because of moral disapprobation from the outside, or what? Moreover, if one seeks to forecast the "likely responses . . . of various segments of the Soviet leadership" in order to gauge the degree of loyalty and disaffection among the major social groups, the "central patterns" may be of less importance than an accurate definition of the different interests of such segments and of their power vis-à-vis other interest groups. The question is, What do we look for in a mode of analysis?

A mode of analysis is a function of the particular categories one uses to group together related characteristics. In political theory, one can classify regimes, as Aristotle did, as monarchies, oligarchies, or democracies; or, as Max Weber did, as traditional, rational, and charismatic. One's purpose dictates one's perspectives. The danger is that one tends to think of categories as realities rather than as theoretical constructs. This error has been appallingly true of Marxist thought, which in rudimentary fashion first employed the concept of a social system. Since in a simple Marxist model of capitalism, classes are formed in relation to the means of production, to the simple-minded Communist there could be no exploitation in Russia since the "people" owned the factories and there were, therefore, no exploiting classes. Hence, too, the fierce doctrinal debates as to whether Russia was a "workers' state," a "degenerated workers' state," or what.

But, given all these pitfalls, the gain in trying to define the *essential* nature of a system is that one can locate the causal factors (in modern jargon, the independent variables), the

in the Gosplan? If the "managers" include all three categories, is there an identity of interests among them? (Surely one would expect considerable friction between a factory seeking greater control over its own activities and a ministry in Moscow.) And, if not, which of the three are the real "managers"?

A second difficulty arises from mechanically countering bloc with bloc. While it is true that there are often interest conflicts between functional groups, the very nature of a political power struggle carried on by small cliques and coteries requires the power figure to have his allies within *all* groups. Thus the fight may not be simply "managers" vs. "party," or "army" vs. "party," but may cut across these groupings. Is the army, for example, a unitary interest group (united on what interests?), or does Zhukov line up with X and Koniev with Y and Vasilievsky with Z? From what we know of armies elsewhere, certainly such internal conflicts and differing outside alliances take place—e.g., in the U.S. Army the Marshall-Eisenhower group vs. MacArthur. The problem, then, is to locate those issues on which the army would stand united and those on which its top officers would divide. And, in so doing, one faces the problem of determining what it is that ties cliques and coteries together: school affiliation, loyalties to one who has made promotion possible, differences in generation, common wartime or service experiences, etc., etc.

Nor can one say that ideology determines alignments, for on key policy issues — consumer goods vs. heavy industry, tough or soft line toward the West, tough or soft line toward the satellites—there may be no unitary ideology which dictates a consistent attitude toward such issues. Malenkov may have wanted relaxation at home so as to be more tough with the West. Moreover, a top figure will often switch ideological sides opportunistically in a bid for support. Certainly Stalin's history is instructive in this regard. (The question is often put: does Khrushchev represent the "Stalinist" faction or does Malenkov? The difficulty with these formulations is that what we are observing is the breakup of a faction and, in such a highly personal situation, few of the formal sociological criteria for charting allegiances seem to hold.)

Even greater difficulties are faced in the task of locating the links of support down the line. Every foreign office and propaganda organization maintains extensive biographical dossiers on members of the Soviet elite in an effort to keep track of the shifting personnel as a means of measuring the relative strength of the contenders at the top. And often, as the example cited below shows, the method is highly tenuous.[118] How far one can go with this detailed, yet mechanical, scoring is open to question. One observer, in reviewing Boris Meissner's *Das Ende des Stalin-Mythos,* complains: ". . . he believes that he can say of any party functionary, from the top on down through lower ranks, whether he is a Khrushchev or a Malenkov man, a supporter of this or that tactical nuance of party policy. Very often these assertions are based on extraneous biographical information. Whoever served under Malenkov at some time in the past must, in Meissner's opinion, be considered a Malenkov adherent in all present-day situations. Whoever worked with Khrushchev twenty years ago in the Ukraine still must be his confidant today."[119]

And sometimes the same event—in this instance, the appointment of Frol R. Kozlov to the key post of candidate member of the party Presidium—is interpreted in diameterically opposite fashion. Harrison Salisbury, in the New York *Times* of February 16, 1957, reported that Kozlov was a member of a group to which Mr. Pervukhin belonged, and was "probably an adherent of Mr. Malenkov." Kozlov, said Salisbury, was one of the authors of the key propaganda documents of the "doctor's plot" of 1953; and one can surmise, therefore, in line with the logic of Kremlinology, that Malenkov was one of the directors of the plot. But Richard Lowenthal commented a day later in the London *Observer:* "Mr. Khrushchev's inner-party position has been reinforced not only by Mr. Shepilov's return to the party Secretariat, but by the promotion of Frol Romanovich Kozlov, the first secretary of the Leningrad region, to candidate membership of the party Presidium. . . . Having returned to obscurity during the early Malenkov era, he was at the end of 1953 promoted by Khrushchev's personal intervention to take the place of Malenkov's protege, Andrianov, as head of the Leningrad party organization." And, by equal logic, since Kozlov had signaled the campaign of vigilance at the start of the "doctors' plot," Khrushchev was thus tied to the execution of the plot.

This is not to say that the method is wrong, but that someone's information is inadequate. (For the record, Mr. Lowenthal was right about Kozlov, and Salisbury wrong.) How excruciatingly difficult the problems of Kremlinology can be is seen from a report in the New York *Times* of

And with one more step we come full circle. Whatever the importance of power at the top, no group of power figures, however absolute their rule, can wield infinite power. The problem with the Kremlinological approach is the same as with that of Leites. Every attempt to impose one's will has to take into account the finite limits of natural resources and the recalcitrance of human institutions[121]—but how?

V. The One Road and the Many—Exit Pirandello

Now that we have investigated many roads, are there some which can lead us to reality better than others? (Says a passage in the Talmud: "If you don't know where you are going, any road will take you there.") Perhaps a few distinctions—and questions—are in order.

THE DIFFERENT MOMENTS

There should be a clear distinction between the types of change which take place: between changes in Soviet society (the social system) and in Soviet politics, although in crucial moments one is dependent on the other. The difference is one of distinguishing between a process and an event; or, to revive an old distinction of the crusty sociologist William Graham Sumner, between *crescive* and *enacted* change.

Crescive changes are those which surge, swell, go on willy-nilly, and develop with some measure of autonomy. They variously derive from organic growth of tradition, or from changes in values (e.g., the decision of people to have fewer children or more), or from technical imperatives, once a key decision has been taken (e.g., the need for training more engineers, once a country industrializes).

Enacted changes are the conscious decisions or intents of legislators or rulers (e.g., the declaration of war, the collectivization of agriculture, the location of new industry, etc.). Those who enact change have to take into account the mores of the people and the resources at their disposal, but these serve only as limiting, not determining, factors.

Sociological analysis is most sure when it deals with crescive changes. These can be identified, their drift charted, and, like iceberg floes, their course and even their breakup specified more readily than others. But sociological analysis often fails in predicting political decisions. There are in history what Hegel called the "unique moments," and, in calling the turn, not pure reason but practical judgment (that unstable compound of information, intuition, and empathy) has to take hold. Bolshevism has been par excellence a movement minutely conscious of the past and supremely aware of the tactical and strategic nuances of events. It has been this constant awareness of "unique moments" (the "revolutionary situation," as Lenin first conceived it) and its ability to adapt its timing to the changing situation that have given Bolshevism its unique political advantage in the past.

THE PROBLEM OF PREDICTION

The nature of the changes which one describes conditions the kind of prediction one can make. One can define, and predict, the limits of broad crescive changes (e.g., if one knows the resource pattern of the Soviet Union—amount of arable land, minerals, manpower—one can make a guess about the slowdown in the rate of economic growth), but in predicting the short-run policy turns one comes up against the variabilities of accident, folly, and simple human cantankerousness. The situation is reminiscent of two radicals in the 1920's debating the future course of Soviet politics. "The objective situation," said one, "requires that Trotsky do so and so and so and so." "Look," replied the other, "you know what Trotsky has to do, and I know what Trotsky has to do, but does Trotsky know?"

One of the key problems in the analysis of power is the mode of succession. In the Soviet system, as opposed to a constitutional regime, there seems to be no formal definition of legitimacy, and no system of investiture of power. In seeking to duplicate Stalin's rise, Khrushchev used the party secretariat as a power lever. But in doing so he was taking a big gamble. In the war years and after, Stalin had emphasized his governmental and military titles rather than his party position. At the time of his death in 1953, Stalin was only one of nine party secretaries, but was, uniquely, the Chairman of the Council of Ministers of the USSR. Malenkov relinquished his post as party secretary, when forced to make a choice, and sought to legitimize his authority through the post of Premier and the Council of Ministers. It is the measure of Khrushchev's shrewdness that he assumed correctly that, despite the rise of the technical and military classes, the mechanics of political power had not changed essentially since the 1930's. Yet can we assume that these "laws of mechanics" will hold in the naming of Khrushchev's successor? How do we define the balances of forces and predict the direction in which they will tip?

(Given all these problems and pitfalls, it would be a forward step in the social sciences if a group of Soviet experts were, at regular intervals, to make predictions, at different levels, of probable Soviet developments and state the reasons for their inference. Bauer, Inkeles, and Kluckhohn, for example, stated that the collegial system of power in Russia *could stabilize itself;* Myron Rush said that it would not, and predicted Khrushchev's bid for power.[122] By systematic review of the predictions, the successes and failures, one could probably obtain a more viable operational model of Soviet behavior.)

THE ROLE OF THE IRRATIONAL

In social theory, the weight of analysis has always been thrown on the side of the rational explanation. The presumption (cf. Moore, Rostow, Deutscher, Aron, etc.) is that a society ultimately makes its choices on the basis of the rational alternatives which confront it. But how much meaning can one make of the role of pique (e.g., Tito's anger, as reported in the Dedijer biography,[123] at the fact that "we were treated like Komsomols," or Khrushchev's resentment at being forced by Stalin to dance the *Gopak*) in explaining the precipitateness or intensity of political acts? And, taking into account the researches of Leites, what weight can be given to the role of emotional components, conscious or unconscious, as a clue to political stance? Is it simply that rationality dictates the political course, and emotions the choler, or what?

MYTH AND MONOLITH

One difficulty with analysis in social science is that it deals with categories, not people. In recent analyses of the Communist movement, particularly in the United States, the movement has been seen as a monolith, with each adherent a disciplined soldier or a "true believer" ready always to follow orders of "the party."

To some extent, the West itself has been seduced by the very image of "The Bolshevik" with which the Communist rulers have sought to mold the "new" Soviet man. For, like any human group, the Communists have not been immune to personal rivalries and, more important, they have not been immune to the inherent factionalism which besets all radical movements. In fact, one might argue that factionalism, if only the need at times to chop off a "left" wing or a "right" wing, has been necessary in order for the party to maintain a myth of inviolate correctness. Certainly, however, the strains and factions of earlier years (the defections of Levi, Ruth Fischer, Brandler, Thalheimer, Souvarine, Rappaport, Rosmer, Bordiga, Silone, Cannon, Lovestone, Wolfe) have had their counterparts—although the struggles were more hidden and suppressed—in the defections and expulsions and murders of Marty, Tillon, Lecoeur, Hervé, Cucchi, Magnani, Reale, Tito, Petkov, Gomulka, Rajk, Nagy, and thousands of others. In fact, not monolithism but factionalism has been a basic law of the Communist movement. And we have failed to see this and exploit it. For from general political experience—whether it be in the trade-union movement or political parties—we know that ruling groups rarely collapse, but fall through the defection of key power figures who control substantial followings. This was the experience of the CIO with the "Communist problem" in the United States, and the meaning of Tito, Nagy, and (perhaps) Gomulka in the international Communist movement.

But more than a tactical inability to exploit the fissures and cracks is involved. In the character approach, and in Kremlinology, too, there has often been a "false concreteness." One saw all Communists as "the enemy," as "The Bolshevik," and any unrest, particularly in the satellites, purely as power conflicts between rival leaders. But there was more than this. There was also the simple recalcitrance and the simple decency of the human being which lay underneath. Who becomes the *apparatchik*, seduced by sadism and power, and who does not? Who the bureaucrat and who the lurking idealist? Who the Rakosi and who the Gyulya Hay? These questions are not, as we saw in Poland and Hungary in 1956, a closed book.

We can now see, in retrospect, the real meaning of the first Nagy regime in 1954-1955, how the momentum gathered when people were able to communicate with each other, exchange experiences, and realize that some hope of change was possible.* But why did almost all the specialists in Soviet

* We realize, too, the profound wisdom of de Tocqueville: ". . . it is not always when things are going from bad to worse that revolutions break out. On the contrary, it oftener happens that when a people which has just put up with an oppressive rule over a long period of time without protest suddenly finds the government relaxing its pressure, it takes up arms against it. . . . Patiently endured so long as it seemed beyond redress, a grievance comes to appear intolerable once the possibility of removing it crosses men's minds. For the mere fact that certain abuses have been remedied draws attention to the others and they now appear more galling. . . ." Alexis de Tocqueville, *The Old Regime and the French Revolution* (Anchor ed.; New York, 1955), pp. 176-77.

affairs fail to catch the significance of those clues in 1954-55? Was it because they were so mesmerized by the thought of "power" alone as the singular clue to the meaning of social conflict as to forget its impact on people?

Having said this, we must also recognize that political events do not return in the same trajectory. Having failed to catch the "unique moment," we are apt to forget that the moment may not return. The lesson of the last few years, from East Berlin to Budapest, is that a "thaw" breaks up glaciers and log jams, creates rifts and fissures, and sends massive floes down the sea of history. But have not the Russians—who are more sensitive than most to the lessons of history—seen this as well and, learning from these events, may they not have decided that, if they can help it, to control any new "thaws."

THE WORD AND THE DEED

Every society, every social organization, lives for certain goals which in considerable measure are dictated by its ideology. We know—to use an example from modern trade-union experience—that many individuals act quite pragmatically when their doctrinaire ideological goals conflict with the ongoing reality, and they compromise accordingly. Yet, when called upon to take a stand on issues far removed from their immediate experience, the only vocabulary, the only rhetoric, the only categories of analysis or even simple formulae available to them, are the old ideological banners. They use them and become trapped; for ideology is a hardening of commitment, a freezing of opinion.

Since the Bolshevik ideology is the only formal canon of Soviet intentions that we have, an answer to this question is of prime importance: To what extent are the Soviet leaders committed to the formal Bolshevik ideology (e.g., the incompatibility of compromise, the attribution to capitalism of inherent imperialist aims, etc.), and to what extent are they prepared to modify it on the basis of experience and reality?

The answers are contradictory: (1) If one accepts the "characterological evidence" (e.g., Dicks, Leites), compromise is precluded. The rigid psychological postures and even paranoid suspicions of the Soviet rulers make it difficult for them to appraise realistically the changes in the Western world. (2) An extreme Kremlinologist might say that the Soviet rulers are cynical and regard the ideology simply as a necessary myth for the masses. (3) A geopolitical theorist, taking a completely rationalist view, would argue that strategic interests rather than ideology determine the behavior of Soviet rulers. (4) The weight of some evidence (see pp. 29-35 of the Bauer, Inkeles, and Kluckhohn book) is that ideology, even though cynically used by the Soviet rulers, is a real factor in the way they think and in the formulation of their goals.

But all this was before Khrushchev. While in the fields of literature and the arts the party has moved to reassert *partinost* (ideological control), in other fields practical considerations rather than ideology seem to determine policy. Soviet economists, for example, in conformity with the Marxist theory of value, could not admit of the productivity of capital or utilize the interest rate to measure the rational allocation of capital. But even under socialism, capital scarcities exist, and if cost economies were to be achieved, some disguised techniques had to be created in order to carry out the functions of the interest rate. After the war, these evasions of dogma were attacked by the ideologists. "In the hot debate which followed," writes Robert Campbell, "the conflict between the very real problem of the planners and the demand of purity in doctrine was made quite clear. The Soviet leaders faced an impasse; one of the central assumptions of Marxist economic theory had been proved wrong by their own experience, and they were faced with a painful choice between ideology and rational expediency. . . . So long as Stalin was alive, no official line emerged to break the deadlock. About a year after his death, however, the Gordian knot was cut, and cut in such a way as to constitute a surrender of orthodoxy to reality." [124]

In the field of agriculture, Khrushchev has taken the dramatic, drastic step of abolishing the machine and tractor stations, which, in the Stalinist scheme, represented a giant step forward in the elimination of the peasantry, and is turning their equipment over to the *kolkhozes*. And, we can surmise, in the fields of nuclear physics, the pressure to squeeze all theories into the ritualistic formulae of dialectical materialism has diminished. Certainly no one today talks, as they did twenty-five years ago, of the "bourgeois" physics of Einstein.

And yet, at some point—but where?—some essential aspects of the regnant ideology—but which?—must be maintained, for without a central belief system with some continuity, disintegrative opinions begin to spread (e.g., Poland). Nothing demonstrates better the incalculable effects of such opinions, and of the role of single events in politics, than the

Chapter 15

Two Roads from Marx: *The Themes of Alienation and Exploitation and Workers' Control in Socialist Thought*

Historical Hindsight: A Parable as Introduction

IN 1899 A LITTLE-KNOWN, NOW long-forgotten, Polish revolutionist named Waclaw Machajski published a small book, *The Evolution of Social Democracy,* which provoked consternation in the nascent Marxist movement in Russia. Its thesis was that the new messianism of socialism masked an ideology of discontented intellectuals, and that the new socialist society would simply replace one ruling class with another, so that the workers would still remain exploited, albeit this time by a new class of professional leaders.*

The book was avidly discussed by the young revolutionists who had been deported to Siberia, including the future rulers of Russia. "For several months," wrote Trotsky in his auto-

* The fear of the role of the intelligentsia was not a new one; it was, in fact, the root issue that divided the Russian revolutionary movement at the start. In the early 1870's, the *Zemlya i Volya* (Land and Freedom) movement set out to consolidate the various strands of revolutionary populism. Its prophet, Peter Tkachev, declared at the time that revolutions did not arise spontaneously but were made by people with creative energy, and that the intlligentsia—rather than the masses, who were passive or apathetic—were the only force capable of making a revolution. He demanded the formation of a conspiratorial organization based on the principle of "centralization of power and decentralization of function," since only a "conscious minority" was able to act.

Tkachev was answered by Paul Akselrod, one of the founders of Russian Marxism, who declared that the development of the revolutionary consciousness of the masses, to allow them to act for themselves, was the main task for socialists. And the subsequent debate, in fact, brought Russian Marxism into being. For in answering the claim of the Populists that only the intelligentsia could make the revolution, George Plekhanov, the intellectual father of Russian Marxism, argued that any movement that disregarded the "objective laws of social development" or the "inexorable laws of history" was doomed to failure. Plekhanov, using a metaphor that was to become a favorite of Russian Bolsheviks, warned that one could not "force birth" of a new system, although one could ease the labor pains. Thus the task, at the moment, was to wait for "objective" social conditions to develop. In contrast to the Populist intelligentsia, who openly declared the necessity of leading the masses, the Marxists identified themselves with the proletariat (although Lenin, shortly after, in terms completely reminiscent of Tkachev, spoke of the necessity for tutelage of the proletariat). Hence the charge by Machajski that the Marxists wanted to dominate the proletariat seemed to be aimed at the wrong party and could be easily dismissed.[126]

biography, "the work of Machajski held the first place in the interests of the Lena exiles." And in his first encounter with Lenin, in 1902 in London, Trotsky, who was then only twenty-one years old, told the 32-year-old Lenin that the two works which had held the attention of the men in exile were Machajski's tract and Lenin's *The Development of Capitalism in Russia*. Of the two, it was Lenin's book which was remembered. Machajski's gloomy theory made little mark, quite inevitably perhaps, on the enthusiasm of the burgeoning revolutionists in exile. "A theory very sweeping in its verbal negations, it gave me a powerful inoculation against anarchism," recalled Trotsky thirty-two years later.[127] But that was all.

In 1904, in Geneva, Machajski published his major study, *The Intellectual Worker,* which restated and enlarged his thesis. The theory of socialism, he repeated, had not been worked out in the interests of the proletariat but of a new force, "the growing army of intellectual workers and the new middle class." A revolution undertaken in the name of socialism would end, he said, as an exploitative form of state capitalism in which the technicians, organizers, administrators, educators, and journalists (i.e., the intellectuals) would constitute the "great joint stock company known as the State, and become, collectively, a new privileged stratum over the manual workers." Thus, said Machajski, there could not be any such thing as a "workers' government"—the conquest of power would simply mean the installation of a new ruling class in place of the old. History was a permanent class struggle in which the workers would be forced to continue their revolutionary struggle, even after the revolution. Their aim would be not to abolish the state—for the state as an instrument of class domination would exist so long as there was a separate class of managers—but to force the state to raise the wages of the manual workers until their standard of living was equal to that of their "educated masters." Only equality of income, concluded Machajski, would create educational opportunities for the offspring of intellectual and worker alike.[128]

The doctrine of *Machayevstchina*—antagonism between the manual workers and the intellectuals—had a slight vogue in Russia in the wake of some disillusionment after the abortive revolution of 1905. Machajski formed a small organization, the *Rabochi Zagovor* (Workers' Conspiracy), which influenced the anarcho-syndicalists and the "left" Communists during the October Revolution. After the Bolshevik seizure of power, Machajski issued a single number of a magazine called *Rabocha Revolutsia* (Workers' Revolution), in July, 1918, in which he repeated his warnings of eighteen years before. "The workers will not have their workers' government even after the capitalists have disappeared," he said. "As long as the working class is condemned to ignorance, the intelligentsia will rule through the workers' deputies."

It was his last word, and in the dawn of October the warning went unheeded. Few prophets with a single theme, repeated almost tiresomely as Machajski did his, can command an audience for long. Few prophets die with honor. Unknown and ignored, Machajski lived in obscurity in Russia after the Revolution, working as an economist for the Gosplan. He died in 1926, one year before Trotsky lost his fight for power with Stalin on the issue which Machajski had warned about and Trotsky had dismissed twenty-seven years before—the issue of bureaucracy.

Alienation Transformed

To the arguments of Machajski, as to later critics, Marxist theory had provided a simple and "logical" answer to the question whether a new, exploiting class might not arise in the socialist society: exploitation was an economic phenomenon that arose out of the system of private property which allowed the capitalist to "extract" surplus value from the worker through the exchange process; once private property was socialized, the "surplus" would belong to the people, and the material basis for exploitation, a product of a specific stage of history, would disappear.* Thus, as in all such crucial

* Even as sophisticated a socialist as Sidney Hook, in his first major exposition of Marx, felt that the problem of bureaucracy under socialism was relatively simple. Seeking to refute the contention of Robert Michels, who held that, as a result of the "iron law of oligarchy," "socialists may be successful but socialism (true democracy) never," Hook wrote, in 1933: ". . . what Michels overlooks is the social and economic presuppositions of the oligarchical tendencies of leadership in the past. Political leadership in past societies meant economic power. Education and tradition fostered the tendencies to predatory self-assertion in some classes and at the same time sought to deaden the interest in politics on the part of the masses. In a socialist society in which political leadership is an administrative function, and, therefore, carries with it no economic power, in which the processes of education strive to direct the psychic tendencies to self-assertion into 'moral and social equivalents' of oligarchical ambition, in which the monopoly of education for one class has been abolished, and the division of labor between manual and mental worker is progressively eliminated—the danger that Michels' 'law of oligarchy' will express itself in traditional form, becomes quite remote." (Sidney Hook, *Towards the Understanding of Karl Marx* [New York, 1933] p. 312.)

problems of responsibility and choice, the Marxist theory found its comfort in "history."

And yet, the curious fact is that in the complex route of Marx becoming a "Marxist," this argument—which led to the rationalization of Russia as a worker's state—was only one road out of a great debate which had divided the radical followers of Hegel, the debate over the nature of alienation. And it is in this debate that we find the source of the most seminal, yet untapped ideas of Marxist sociology, and the transformation of this idea into a narrow economic conception which mesmerized several political generations of intellectuals.

The goal of man for Hegel was freedom, a condition where man would be self-willed and in which his "essence" would become his own possession—in which he would regain his "self." But man was "separated" from his essence and bound by two conditions which seemed inherent in the world: necessity and alienation. Necessity meant a dependence on nature and the acceptance of the limitations which nature imposed on men, both in the sense of the limitations of natural resources and the limitations of physical strength. Alienation, in its original connotation, was the radical dissociation of the "self" into both actor and thing, into a *subject* that strives to control its own fate, and an *object* which is manipulated by others.

In the development of science, man could, perhaps, overcome necessity and master nature. But how was one to overcome the Orphic separateness of subject and object? Alienation was an ontological fact, in the structure of grammar as well as of life, for the self, the individual, was not just an "I," seeking to shape the world according to its intentions, but also a "me," an object whose identity is built up by the pictures that *others* have of "me." Thus the condition of complete freedom, in which the self seeks only to be an "I," a shaper of events in accordance with its own will, rather than being shaped by others, is a seeming impossibility. In the face of this irreducible dualism of subject-object, of "I" and "me," how does one achieve the goal of being "self-willed"?

Bruno Bauer, one of the first teachers and friends of Marx, felt that the solution lay in developing a "critical" philosophy which exposed the "mystery" of human relationships (i.e., the *real* motives behind social acts). Most human beings born into the world, said Bauer, simply accept it and are oblivious to the sources of their morals and beliefs, of their rationality or irrationality; they are "determined" by the world. By subjecting all beliefs to criticism, however, men would become self-conscious, reason would be restored to them, and therewith their self-possession. The overcoming of the dualism, therefore, was to be through the achievement of self-consciousness.

Feuerbach, to whom Marx, at first, gave the credit for making the real breach in the system of Hegelian abstractions, sought to locate the sources of all alienation in religious superstition and fetishism. Man was bound, he said, because he took the best of himself, his sensibility, and projected it onto some external object or spirit which he called divine. The way to overcome alienation was to bring the divine back into man, for man to reintegrate himself through a religion of humanity, not of God, through a religion of self-love. The function of criticism—using the radical tool of alienation or self-estrangement—was to replace theology by anthropology, to dethrone God and enthrone Man. Men's relation to each other, said Feuerbach, in his first employing terms that, ironically, were adopted later by Martin Buber for religious purposes, had to be on an I-Thou basis. Philosophy was to be directed to life; man was to be liberated from the "spectre of abstractions" and extricated from the thongs of the supernatural.

This uncompromising attack on religion was equally a sharp attack on all established institutions. But beyond that, the concept of alienation in the minds of the left-Hegelians had more radical consequences: it ushered in the period of modernity, and initiated a direct break in the history of philosophy. In classical philosophy, the ideal man was the *contemplative* one. Neither the Middle Ages nor the transitional period to contemporary times (the seventeenth to the nineteenth century) was ever wholly able to detach itself from the ideal of the Stoa. Even Goethe, who gave us in *Faust* the first modern man, the man of ambition unchained, in his ethical image of the human ideal reverted to the Greek. In discussing freedom, however, Hegel introduced a new principle, the principle of *action*. For man, in order to realize his "self," had to strive actively to overcome the subject-object dualism that bound him. In action, a man finds himself; by his choices he defines his character. For Hegel, the principle of action had remained abstract. In Feuerbach, while the principle of alienation is sharply defined and the source is located in religion, an abstraction remains because Feuerbach was talking of Man in general, of generic Man. In Marx, action was given a specificity in a radical new emphasis on *work*. Man becomes man, becomes alive, through work, for through work man loses his isolation and learns to become a social or co-operative being and thus learns of himself; and through work, he is able to transform nature as well.

In locating man's alienation in work, Marx had taken the revolutionary step of grounding philosophy in concrete human activity. The steps by which he "freed" himself from the tyranny of abstraction was a long and difficult one.[129] As a Hegelian, Marx first thought of the alienation of work in terms of idealistic dualities. Man, in working, reifies himself in objective things (i.e., in products which embody his work). This is *labor* (*arbeit*) and is part of the "alien and hostile world standing over against him." Labor is driven (*nicht freiwillig*). In labor, man is "under the domination, compulsion and yoke of another man." Against this is the state of freedom where man would transform nature, and himself, by free, conscious, spontaneous, creative work. But what stood in the way of achieving this freedom? The fact that in the alienation of work man lost control of the process of work, and, of the product of his labor. For Marx, therefore, the answer to Hegel was clear: the source of alienation lay, ultimately, in the property system. (Religion was an opiate to disguise this fact; hence Feuerbach's analysis was secondary.) In the organization of work—in labor becoming a commodity—man became an object used by others, and unable, therefore, to obtain satisfaction in his own activity. And by becoming a commodity, he lost his sense of identity; he lost the sense of "himself."*

The extraordinary thing was that Marx had taken a concept which German philosophy had seen as an ontological fact, and had given it a social content.† As ontology, as an ultimate, man could only accept alienation. As a social fact, rooted in a specific system of historical relations, alienation could be overcome by changing the social system. But in narrowing the concept, Marx ran two risks: of falsely identify-

* Some of the confusion about the term alienation, as Morris Watnick has pointed out to me, is that Marx used it in a double sense, or rather in a way that permits of two readings: in our contemporary psychological meaning of feeling estranged from the world, and, in a philosophical, Aristotelian sense, of a departure from what men would ideally be in the historical future.

† At the other extreme, Kierkegaard, also drawing from Hegel, had taken the concept of alienation and given it a religious content. Since man, by any rational act, could not overcome the subject-object dualism, the world was forever completely *absurd*. Thus, in the world, man was forever bound; only by a leap of faith, in the acknowledgment of some religious meaning beyond himself, could man find some integration with an absolute.

ing the source of alienation only in the private-property system; and of introducing a note of utopianism in the idea that once the private-property system was abolished, man would immediately be free.[130] Unfortunately, both risks proved hazardous, and Marx's followers drew the "vulgar" implications from these conclusions. The steps are worth tracing in detail.

The question why men were propertyless turned Marx to economics. For a man whose name is so linked with the "dismal science," Marx was never really interested in economics. His correspondence with Engels, in later years, is studded with contemputous references to the subject (which he at one time referred to as the "economic filth"), and he resented the fact that his detailed explorations in the economic mechanisms of society prevented him from carrying on other studies. But he continued because, for him, economics was the practical side of philosophy—it would unveil the mystery of alienation—and because he had found in the categories of political economy the material expression of that alienation: the process of *exploitation.*

This development is seen most clearly in the studies written in 1844, when Marx was twenty-six years old, called the *Economic-Philosophical Manuscripts.* The *Manuscripts* was an "anthropology," a discussion of the nature of man. It is, in the history of Marxist thought, however, a key document, for it is the bridge from the left-Hegelianism of the early Marx to the Marxism we have come to know. In it one finds the first conceptualization of alienation as rooted in work (rather than in abstract spirit, or religion), and the beginnings of the analysis of property. And in the analysis of property, one finds the direct transmutation, which is so crucial in the development of Marx's thought, of philosophical into economic categories.

All along, Marx had been searching for the way in which the human being was being robbed of his potential. For Feuerbach, religion was the means whereby man was alienated from himself; for in religion man externalized his real "self." For Marx, however, the idea of the "self" was too abstract. He had found a key in the nature of work, but in looking at the economic system he saw that individuals, in the capitalist economy, were formally free, that in the contract between worker and employer a basic bargain was made. What, then, was the mechanism whereby a man, unbeknownst even to himself, was alienated and enslaved? Marx found the answer in *money*. Money is the most impersonal form of value. It is seemingly neutral. A man who has a direct obligation to another, as a serf does to a master, knows directly the source of power over him. But one who sells his labor power for money may feel himself to be free. The product of the laborer can thus be easily "abstracted" into money and, through the exchange system, be "abstracted" from him.

Money, thus, is the concrete embodiment of a philosophical abstraction which Hegel had airily described as "spirit," and the commodity process a means whereby the laborer, by exchanging his labor power for money, is robbed of his freedom, unaware that "surplus value" is being extracted from him. This, then, was the concrete answer Marx had found to the initial conundrum posed by Hegel as to the source of alienation; this was the means of bringing Hegel down to earth. Thus, political economy became for Marx what religion was for Feuerbach, a means whereby human values are "projected" outside of man and achieve an existence independent of him, and over him.* And so, *alienation,* initially conceived by Marx to be a process whereby an idividual lost his capacity to express himself in work, now became seen as *exploitation,* or the appropriation of a laborer's surplus product by the capitalist. Thus, a philosophical expression, which embodied, actually, a socio-psychological condition, became transformed into an economic category.

Having found the answer to the "mysteries" of Hegel in political economy, Marx promptly forgot all about philosophy. ("The philosophers have only *interpreted* the world differently; the point, however, is to change it," he had scrawled in his *Theses on Feuerbach.*) In 1846, Marx and Engels had completed a long criticism of post-Hegelian philosophy in two large octavo volumes, and (except for some gnomic references in the *Critique of the Gotha Programme* in 1875) neither of them returned to the subject until forty years later when Engels, after the death of Marx, was asked by the *Neue Zeit,* the German socialist theoretical magazine, to review a book on Feuerbach by C. N. Starcke, a then well-known anthropologist. Engels reluctantly consented and wrote a long

* It is this conception of money as the hidden mechanism whereby people became exploited that lay behind Marx's withering analysis of the Jew in economic society; and this fetish, too, taken in doctrinaire terms, which was the basis of the effort of the Bolsheviks, in the first days of the Revolution, to abolish money altogether.

review which, slightly expanded, was published two years later, in 1888, as a small brochure entitled *Ludwig Feuerbach and the Outcome of Classical German Philosophy*. In writing the review Engels went back to some mouldering manuscripts of Marx and found among his papers the hastily scribbled "eleven theses on Feuerbach," totaling in all a few pages, which he appended to the brochure. In the Foreword, Engels alluded to the large manuscript (without even mentioning its title, *The German Ideology*), and says, merely, that because of the reluctance of the publishers it was not printed. "We abandoned the manuscript to the gnawings of the mice all the more willingly," said Engels, "as we had achieved our main purpose—to clear our own minds." [131] (The gnawing was literal, since many pages, in fact, had been completely chewed up!)

But it is also clear that while, as young philosophy students, the debates with the other young Hegelians were necessary for the purposes of "self-clarification," the absorption of both into concrete economic study and political activity had made the earlier philosophical problems increasingly unreal to them. In a letter to Florence Kelley Wischnewetsky, his American translator, in February, 1886, Engels writes, apropos of his 1845 work, "the semi-Hegelian language of a good many passages of my old book is not only untranslatable but has lost the greater part of its meaning even in German."[132] And in 1893, a Russian visitor to Engels, Alexei Voden, found Engels incredulous when the question of publishing the early philosophical manuscripts was raised. In a memoir, Voden recalled: "Our next conversation was on the early works of Marx and Engels. At first Engels was embarrassed when I expressed interest in these works. He mentioned that Marx had also written poetry in his student years but it could hardly interest anybody. . . . Was not the fragment on Feuerbach which Engels considered the most meaty of the 'old works' sufficient?" Which was more important, asked Engels, "for him to spend the rest of his life publishing old manuscripts from publicistic works of the 1840's or to set to work, when Book III of *Capital* came out, on the publication of Marx's manuscripts on the history of the theories of surplus value?" And for Engels the answer was obvious. Besides, said Engels, "in order to penetrate into that 'old story' one needed to have an interest in Hegel himself, which was not the case with anybody then, or to be exact, 'neither with Kautsky nor with Bernstein.' "[133]

In fact, except for *The Holy Family,* a crazy-quilt grab bag of essays deriding Bruno Bauer and his two brothers, who with their friends constitute the "holy family,"* none of the early philosophical writings of Marx were published either in his lifetime or that of Engels. Nor is it clear whether the major exegetes, Kautsky, Plekhanov, and Lenin, were ever aware of their content. None of the questions on alienation ever appear in their writings. The chief concern of the post-Marxist writers, when they dealt with philosophy, was simply to defend a materialist viewpoint against idealism.

The contemporary "rediscovery" of the idea of alienation in Marxist thought is due to Georg Lukacs, the Hungarian philosopher, who did have an interest in Hegel. The idea of alienation, because of its natural affinity to romanticism, had already played an important role in German sociology, particularly in the thought of Georg Simmel, who had been a teacher of Lukacs. Simmel, writing about the "anonymity" of modern man, first located the source of alienation in industrial society, which destroyed man's self-identity by "dispersing" him into a cluster of separate roles. Later, Simmel widened the concept to see alienation as an ineluctable outcome of the clash between man's creativity and the pressure of social institutions, much as Freud, in his *Civilization and Its Discontents,* in 1927, saw man's unhappiness as the inescapable outcome of the tensions between instinctual needs and the repressions of civilization.

Lukacs, coming onto Marx after World War I, was able, without knowing of the early *Manuscripts,* to "read back," from Marx unto Hegel, the alienation of labor as the derivative of the self-alienation of man from the Absolute Idea. The Kautsky-Lenin generation had construed Marxism as a scientific, non-moral analysis of society. But in Lukacs's interpreta-

* The first part of *The Holy Family,* subtitled the "Critique of Critical Critique," is devoted to an alleged misreading by Edgar Bauer of Proudhon's work on property. The book then jumps to a detailed analysis of Eugene Sue's *The Mysteries of Paris* and to the alleged misreading of this volume—which is about the sick and wretched of Paris—by a supporter of Bauer who had used the volume to demonstrate the "critical method." The last sections deal with the French Revolution and the rise of French materialism. In his heavy-handed irony, Marx was fond of pinning religious tags on his opponents. Not only are the Bauers called the "holy family," but in *The German Ideology* Max Stirner is called "Saint Max." Although Marx drew most of his ideas from his peers—self-consciousness from Bauer, alienation from Feuerbach, communism from Moses Hess, the stages of property from Proudhon—he was not content, simply, to synthesize these ideas, but had to attack, and usually viciously, all these individuals in the determined effort to appear wholly original.

tion, Marx's economic analysis of society was turned inside out and became the work, as Morris Watnick put it, "of a moral philosopher articulating the future of man's existence in the accents of a secular eschatology." Lukacs's interpretation, which was included in a collection of essays entitled *Geschichte und Klassenbewusstein* ("History and Class Consciousness"), published in 1923, to the orthodox Marxists smacked of idealism, and Lukacs quickly came under fire in Moscow. The book was proscribed, although the work continued to enjoy a *sub rosa* reputation among the Communist intelligentsia, less for its discussion of alienation, however, than for another essay which, in covert form, rationalized the elite position of, and the need for outward submission of, the Communist intellectual in his relation to the Communist movement. When Lukacs fled Germany in the early thirties and took refuge in the Soviet Union, he was forced, eleven years after the publication of the essays, to again repudiate his book, and this time in an act of abject self-degradation.[134]

When the early philosophical works of Marx were unearthed and finally published,[135] Lukacs had the satisfaction of seeing how accurately he had been able to reconstruct the thought of the young Marx. But this did not spare him from attack. What is remarkable, in fact, is that in the last few years in Europe, a whole school of neo-Marxists, taking inspiration from Lukacs, have gone back to the early doctrines of alienation in order to find the basis for a new, humanistic interpretation of Marx. To the extent that this is an effort to find a new, radical critique of society, the effort is an encouraging one. But to the extent—and this seems as much to be the case—that it is a form of new myth-making, in order to cling to the symbol of Marx, it is wrong. For while it is the early Marx, it is not the *historical* Marx. The historical Marx had, in effect, repudiated the idea of alienation. The term, because of its Hegelian overtones, was, for him, too abstract. And, because it carried psychological echoes of ideas such as "man's condition," it was too "idealistic." Estrangement, for Marx, had to be rooted in concrete social activity; and Marx felt that he had found the answer in the idea of exploitation, the economic precipitate, so to speak, of alienation.

The irony, however, is that in moving from "philosophy" to "reality," from phenomenology to political economy, Marx himself had moved from one kind of abstraction to another. For in his system, self-alienation becomes transformed: man as "generic man" (i.e., Man writ large) becomes divided into *classes of men.* The only social reality is not Man, not the individual, but economic *classes.* Individuals, and their motives, count for nought. The only form of consciousness which can be translated into action—and which can explain history, past, present and future—is class-consciousness.

In *The German Ideology,* written in 1846, the idea of "self" has disappeared from Marx's writings. Marx now mocks the left-Hegelians for talking of "human nature, of Man in general, who belongs to no class, has no reality and subsists only in the realm of philosophical fantasy." The attack is made even more explicit, and cruelly sardonic, in *The Communist Manifesto.* The German *literati,* said Marx, "wrote their philosophical nonsense beneath the French original. For instance, beneath the French criticism of the economic functions of money, they wrote 'alienation of humanity'." And, mocking his erstwhile philosophical comrades, Marx speaks scornfully of "this transcendental robe in which the German Socialists wrapped their sorry 'eternal truths' . . . the robe of speculative cobwebs, embroidered with the flowers of rhetoric, steeped in the dew of sickly sentiment."

But in saying that there is no human nature "inherent in each separate individual" (as Marx does in his sixth thesis on Feuerbach) but only in *classes,* one introduces a new *persona,* a new abstraction. Marx himself points out explicitly, in his preface to *Capital,* written in 1867, that "to prevent possible misunderstanding . . . I paint the capitalist and the landlord in no sense in *couleur de rose.* Here individuals are dealt with only insofar as they are the personifications of economic categories, embodiments of particular class-relations and class-interests. My standpoint, from which the evolution of the economic formation of society is viewed as a process of natural history, can, *less than any other,* make the individual responsible for relations whose creature he socially remains, however much he may subjectively raise himself above them." [136]

Thus individual responsibility is turned into class morality, and the meaningfulness of individual action transformed into impersonal mechanism.*

The argument can now be quickly summarized. In his early

* Some Marxist-minded sociologists, such as Lewis Coser, insist that such a statement is an anticipation of role theory, which deals with the compulsions on individuals to act in particular ways in order to fulfill their roles as capitalist or workers, but this claim reads too much into the statement.

philosophical writings Marx had seen, against Hegel, that alienation, or the loss of a sense of self, was rooted primarily in work rather than in the abstract development of consciousness. In the organization of work men become "means" for the aggrandizement of others rather than "ends" in themselves. As alienated labor, there was a twofold loss: men lost control over the *conditions* of work, and lost the *product* of their labor. This dual conception is present somewhat in the later Marx: the loss of control of work was seen as *dehumanization,* occasioned by the division of labor and intensified by technology; the loss of product, as *exploitation,* because a portion of man's labor (surplus value) was appropriated by the employer. But other than as literary references in *Capital,* to the dehumanization of labor and the fragmentation of work, this first aspect of the problem was glossed over by Marx. In common with later sociologists, Marx felt that the solution to dehumanized work lay in the reduction of the hours of work, the automization of labor, and the development of leisure. What became central to *Capital* was the concrete social relationship created by private property, that of employer-employee, rather than processes generated by technology. Dehumanization was a creature of technology, exploitation of capitalism. In the key chapter of *Capital,* the section on the "fetishism of commodities," Marx sought to expose the process of exploitation: i.e., that while labor was formally free, in the complicated exchange process, surplus value was taken from the worker. The solution, therefore, was simple: abolish private property, and the system of exploitation would disappear. When critics asserted that socialism itself might become an exploitative society, the Marxist had a ready answer: the source of power was economic, and political office was only an administrative extension of economic power; once economic power was socialized, there could be no basis for man to exploit man. Q.E.D. Thus the goal and rationalizations of socialism were fashioned.

The Socialist Society: The View from the Distance

One of the most extraordinary facts in the history of social thought is that the leaders of socialism, from Marx down, sought to win millions of people for the idea of a new society without the slightest thought about the shape of that future society and its problems. In part, these men could do so, confidently, unthinkingly, because of the apocalyptic belief that "the day after the revolution," rationality would make its

Revolution." It is, however, a dull schoolboy tale, told by a pedant. The picture of how power would be taken can only be described as naive. The road to Socialism would be taken, said Kautsky, simply by removing from the capitalists "the whip of hunger." The chief power of the capitalist, he argued, lay in the threat of unemployment. Once the proletariat obtained political power it would take measures to maintain all the unemployed; then—and here Kautsky sketched a picture which would confirm any hidebound Tory's fear of full employment—the worker would "no longer need capitalists, while the latter [could] not continue his business without him. Once things have gone thus far, the employer would be beaten in every conflict with his employees and be quickly compelled to give in to them. The capitalists could then perhaps continue to be the directors of the factories, but they would cease to be the masters and exploiters. Once the capitalists recognized however that they had the right to bear only the risks and burden of capitalist business, these men would be the very first ones to renounce the further extensions of capitalist production and to demand that their undertakings be purchased because they could no longer carry them on with any advantage." [142]

Thus, capitalism, like the dead scales of the snake, would fall, withered and unused, by the roadside of history. Afterwards the major industries would be nationalized, while other, local, industries such as electric power and transit would be run by municipalities or co-operatives. What would be the incentive of the worker to work? "The discipline of the proletariat" as represented by the trade-union. "The maintenance of social discipline," wrote Kautsky, "could only be secured by the introduction of union discipline into the processes of production. This would however not be carried out in the same manner, for each industry has its own peculiarities according to which organization of the laborers must conform. There are, for example, industries which cannot be operated without a bureaucratic organization as, for example, railroads. The democratic organization can be so formed that the laborers choose delegates, who will constitute a sort of parliament, which will fix the conditions of labor and control the government of the bureaucratic machinery. Other industries can be given over to the direction of the unions, and others again can be operated cooperatively." [143]

This is all, in an essay of 86 pages, on the questions of

management, democratic control, etc., in industry under socialism.*

Except for this essay of Kautsky, there is little more in continental socialist thought on this subject until the Bolsheviks. The classic Bolshevik statement, of course, of the organizations of the economy in the socialist society is to be found in Lenin's *State and Revolution,* which was completed in August, 1917, barely two months before the Bolsheviks seized power. The pamphlet is well known, but some recapitulation of its picture of administration is instructive.

A German Social-Democrat of the 1870's, said Lenin, had wittily called the post office an example of the socialist system. (Why "wittily" is hard to understand.) "To organize the *whole* national economy like the postal system, in such a way that the technicians, managers, bookkeepers, as well as

* It should be pointed out that the Fabians, who were not mesmerized by the doctrine that one could not envisage the "laws" of a new "historical phase," were much more specific in their inquiries on the question of administration in a socialist society. In her essay on "Industry Under Socialism," in the Fabian Essays, Annie Besant, who later became a misty-eyed theosophist, wrote a hard-headed statement on the problem of management. Writing in 1889, she said: "The best form of management during the transition period, and possibly for a long time to come, will be through the Communal Council, which will appoint committees to superintend the various branches of industry. These committees will engage the necessary manager and foremen for each shop, factory, etc., and will hold the power of dismissal as of appointment. I do not believe that the direct election of the manager and the foreman by the employees would be found to work well in practice or to be consistent with the discipline necessary in carrying out any large business undertaking. It seems to me better that the Commune should elect its Council—thus keeping under its own control the general authority—but should empower the Council to select the officials, so that the power of selection and dismissal within the various sub-divisions should lie with the nominees of the whole Commune instead of with the particular group immediately concerned." (*Fabian Essays in Socialism,* London, 1948 edition, p. 147.)

Daniel De Leon, the American Marxist, has an undeserved reputation for theoretical acumen. Although he talked of replacing the geographical or local district election system of parliaments by a functional or syndicalist organization, he never actually dealt with the problems of production and exchange in a socialist society, other than, like Kautsky, to emphasize the greater simplicity of the task under socialism than under capitalism. Speaking of the socialist industrial parliament, he said: "Their legislative work will not be the complicated ones which a society of conflicting interests, such as capitalism, requires, but the easy one which can be summed up in the statistics of wealth needed, the wealth producible and the work required" (cited in Arnold Peterson, *Proletarian Democracy vs. Dictatorship and Despotism* [4th ed.; New York, 1937], p. 29).

Actually De Leon drew most of his ideas from the French Syndicalists, after he embraced industrial unionism in 1905. For the best account of De Leon, see "The Intellectual and Historical Influences Shaping the Political Theories of Daniel De Leon," by Donald McKee, unpublished Ph.D. thesis, Columbia University, 1955.

all officials, should receive no higher wages than 'workingmen's wages' all under the control and leadership of the armed proletariat—this is our immediate aim." [144] "Capitalist culture," wrote Lenin, "has created large-scale production, factories, railways, the postal services, telephone, etc., and *on this basis* the great majority of functions of the 'old state power' have become so simplified and can be reduced to such simple operations of registration, filing, and checking that they will be quite within the reach of every literate person, and it will be possible to perform them for 'workingmen's wages,' which circumstance can (and must) strip these functions of every shadow of privilege, of every appearance of 'official grandeur.' "

It was all, said Lenin, easily at hand. "Overthrow the capitalists . . . break the bureautic machinery of the modern state —*and you have before you a mechanism of the highest technical equipment, freed of 'parasites,' capable of being set into motion by the united workers* who hire their own technicians, managers, bookkeepers and pay them *all,* as indeed every state official, with the usual workers' wage." All officials, said Lenin, without exception, would be elected and subject to recall at any time. Here was a "concrete, practicable, immediately realizable" program, *based upon the experience of the Commune.* "Such a beginning," concluded Lenin, "on the basis of large-scale production, of itself leads to the gradual 'withering away' of all bureaucracy, to the gradual creation of a new order, an order without question marks, an order which has nothing to do with wage slavery, an order in which the more and more simplified functions of control and accounting will be performed by each in turn, will then become a habit, and will finally die out as *special* functions of a special stratum of the population."

Reading this, it is strange to see that a man who was so self-conscious about the crucial nature of organization, whose chief contribution to the history of political practice was the conception of the *party* as a special form of organization within the amorphous mass, could be so purblind to the problems of managerial control, interest conflicts, and bureaucracy. If *State and Revolution* as read against Lenin's hardheaded statements about power, before 1917, is considered in the light of his realistic judgments about the inchoate nature of the Russian regime six months after power,* and against

* At the meeting of the All-Russian Central Executive Committee in April, 1918, Lenin opened a polemic against the "left communists" who saw in the

his evident and increasing concern in the last years of his life with the growth and threat of a monstrous state bureaucracy, it is evident that *State and Revolution,* much as it became a canonical document for the ideological faithful, was an aberration.

But why? In part, I think, because of the assumption of rationality as an automatic consequence of the elimination of the capitalists. It is also quite evident, as Michael Polanyi has pointed out, that neither Lenin or any of the Bolsheviks had any notion of the meaning of economic rationality—of the meaning of a market, of pricing, of resource allocation, and the like. And any attempt to picture the economic workings of a socialist society would inevitably be callow. But *State and Revolution* is not only an economic, but a political, document. And only as a political document does it gain meaning. It was, curiously, an act of desperation.

Like most Marxists, Lenin had believed that the socialist revolution would come first, because of intensified economic crises, within the fully matured capitalist economics. The revolution which all foresaw in Russia would, of necessity, be a "bourgeois revolution." How could it be otherwise, without a large *working class?*† But once the thought—and possibility—arose, after April, of seizing power, the question of tactics, of assessing the mood of the workers, and of the immediate measures to be taken in power came to the fore. And Lenin turned to the only historical experience available, the Paris Commune.‡

---

actions to restore managerial authority the "road to state capitalism." Actually, said Lenin, "state capitalism would be a step forward for us. If we were capable of attaining state capitalism in Russia within a short time this would be a victory . . . then the transition to full socialism would be easy and certain. For state capitalism is a system of centralization, integration, control, and socialization. And this is precisely what we lack." (V. I. Lenin, *Socheniia,* XXII, 482, cited in Herbert Barcuse, *Soviet Marxism* [New York, 1958], p. 44.)

† When the new German Socialist Workers party, of 1875, adopted the Gotha Program and called for the organization of producer co-operatives under the democratic control of the "toiling people," Marx chided them, saying "the majority of the 'toiling' people in Germany consists of peasants and not proletarians" (*Critique of the Gotha Programme,* p. 25).

‡ In the essay, "Will Bolsheviks Retain State Power?" written October 7-14, 1917, Lenin wrote: "Marx taught us from the experience of the Paris Commune, that the proletariat *cannot* simply lay hold of the ready-made state machinery and set it in motion for its own purpose, that the proletariat must *destroy* this machinery and replace it by a new one. (This I treat in detail in a pamphlet, *The State and Revolution—The Teachings of Marxism about the State,* and *The Tasks of the Proletariat in the Revolution.*) This new state apparatus was created by the Paris Commune and of the same type of 'state apparatus' are the Russian Soviets of Workers', Soldiers', and Peasants' Deputies." (V. I. Lenin, *Collected Works,* XXI, 25.)

Now the major impulse of the Commune, as of all spontaneous manifestations of workers, was a primitive egalitarianism, an egalitarianism which was expressed, later, most forcefully by the anarchists and syndicalists. And the "left" mood of the workers in Russia, with its primitive demands, was clearly anarcho-syndicalist. Lenin, fearing isolation, moved in step with this mood. The demand for workers' control, which Lenin took over at this time, was therefore an opportunistic *political* effort to ride the gathering waves. But in being opportunistic, Lenin was forced to come to grips with the problem of just how the socialist society would operate.

Lenin later asserted that he had never believed such utopian dreams, stating that the war communism decrees of late 1917 and early 1918 were only propagandistic, designed to be an inspiration to the proletariat in other countries, since the Revolution might fail, and some historical cenotaph was necessary to mark its place in history.[145] This, itself, if true, is an interesting reflection on Lenin's assessment of the fundamental impulses of workers. Yet it is quite likely that, embarrassed later by the naive 1917 formulations, Lenin too easily dismissed these writings as merely tactical. It is quite true that Lenin was faced with a practical problem. But in meeting a problem, one takes the tools one is accustomed to; and for Lenin, the only "language" of analysis, the only conceptual framework that he understood, was Marx; and in this he was also the prisoner of the "naive" conceptions of rationality and administration. If one follows Lenin's thinking in detail during this period, one can see how these conceptions were employed.

In January-February, 1917, Lenin kept a notebook entitled "Marxism on the State," which is extraordinary for its extracts and marginal annotations on the *Critique of the Gotha Programme*. Having never thought about the concrete problems of the nature of social organization during and after a seizure of power, Lenin desperately grasped whatever fragments were at hand. And these were Marx's reflections on the Commune and on the nature of the State as embodied in the *Critique*. And from it he obtained the crucial notion for *State and Revolution* of the stages of communist society, the transition society with payment according to work, and the "higher" phase of pure communism "from each according to his ability, to each according to his needs."[146]

What emerges from all this is that Lenin simply did not

have *any* notion of the meaning or specific content of socialism when he was forced to confront the issue in 1917. Not only is this evident on the theoretical level but in the extraordinary terminological confusions before and just after the October Revolution. At the crucial April, 1917, Bolshevik party caucus of the All-Russian Conference of Soviets, Lenin, just returned from abroad, had presented some fundamental theses on strategy, including one on changing the name of the party (still Social-Democrat) to the Communist party. The key thesis, number eight, stated: "Not the 'introduction' of socialism as an immediate task, but the immediate placing of the Soviet of Workers' Deputies in control of social production and distribution of goods," is the task of the Party. But six months later, Lenin defended the seizure of power, since a "socialist state" was possible through quick nationalization (since "technically . . . the work has been accomplished for us by capitalism") and through the operation of workers' control.[147]

The magic phrase "workers' control" promised to solve all administrative difficulties in operating the State. In this, Lenin was hoist by his opportunism and by his naive rationality. It seems clear that at some moment, Lenin believed that workers' control could run a complex society. The extent of his "naiveté" can best be seen by quoting at length from an extraordinary essay, written *just before* the Revolution, to illustrate his "magical" concept of administration. It was in answer to an article in Maxim Gorky's *Novy Zhin.*

"We are told," wrote Lenin, "that Russia will not be able to be governed by the 240,000 members of the Bolshevik Party . . . [but] we have a 'magic' means for increasing *tenfold* our state apparatus with one stroke, a means which never has been and never could be at the disposal of a capitalist state. This magic thing is the drawing of the workers, the poor people, into the everyday work of managing the state.

"To explain how simple is the application of this magic means, how faultless is its action, we shall take a most simple and obvious example.

"The state has forcibly to evict a family from a house and to install another in it. This is done time and again by the capitalist state, and it will have to be done by ours, by the proletarian or Socialist state.

"The capitalist state evicts a workers' family which has lost its bread-winner and does not pay rent. There comes upon the scene a bailiff, policeman or militiaman, with a whole platoon of men. In a working-class district a whole detachment of Cossacks is necessary for the eviction. Why? Because the bailiff and policeman refuse to go without military protection of considerable strength. They know that the sight of an eviction brings forth such mad fury among the neighbouring population, among thousands and thousands driven well nigh to despair, such hatred against the capitalist and the capitalist state, that the bailiff and the squad of police might at any moment be torn to pieces. Large military forces are necessary; several regiments of soldiers must be brought into the town from a province, necessarily distant, so that the soldiers may know nothing of the life of the town poor, so that the soldiers may not be 'infected' with Socialism.

"The proletarian state has forcibly to move a very needy family into the dwelling of a rich man. Our detachment of workers' militia consists, let us say, of 15 people—two sailors, two soldiers, two class-conscious workers (of which only one needs to be a member of our Party or sympathizing with it), one intellectual, and eight poor labourers, of whom there would be at least five women, servants, unskilled workmen, and so on. The detachment comes to the rich man's house, investigates, and finds five rooms for two men and two women. 'For this winter, citizens, you must confine yourselves to two rooms and prepare two rooms for two families that are now living in cellars. For the time, until with the help of engineers (you are an engineer, I think?) we build good houses for all, you will have to put yourselves out a bit. Your telephone will serve ten families. This will save about a hundred hours' work in running to the stores, and so on. Then in your family there are two unoccupied semi-workers capable of doing light work—a woman of 55 and a boy of 14. They will be on duty for three hours daily, superintending the distribution of products for the ten families, and they will keep the necessary accounts. The student in our detachment will write out two copies of the text of this state order and you will kindly give us a signed declaration of your undertaking to carry out the duties accurately.'

"Thus, in my view, could be demonstrated in very clear examples the difference betweeen the old bourgeois and the new Socialist state apparatus and state administration."

Thus Lenin, writing in the week of October 7-14, to answer those who belittled the ability of the Bolsheviks to run the state.[148] With this bare notion, the Bolsheviks held and transformed power, and began to build a new order.

Workers' Councils: The Crossroads

But what could "workers' control" actually mean? In his famous formulation in *What Is To Be Done,* Lenin had stated that the workers, if left to themselves, would achieve only *economic* consciousness through the trade-unions; only under the active leadership of the vanguard party and its cadres of professional revolutionaries would the workers achieve *socialist* consciousness. But even before World War I, Lenin's ideas had been opposed, not only by the Mensheviks (and Trotsky) within Russia, but by a small group of theoretical Marxists, notably Rosa Luxemburg in Germany and Poland, and Hermann Gorter in Holland. Luxemburg and Gorter argued that Lenin's conception was shaped by the backward conditions of Russia. The development of modern industrial society, they said, would lead to the creation of a self-conscious, educated proletariat who would no longer be dependent for tutelage on party leaders but would be able to act on their own initiative. Under conditions of crises, they said, the workers would act spontaneously, and through "mass action."*

The extraordinary fact was that the proletarian stirrings of 1917-19 were not of the sort envisaged by Lenin, and, just as the Paris Commune was not Marxist, so the Workers' Councils which arose and spread with amazing rapidity at the close of World War I were not Leninist. If anything, they confirmed the Luxemburg-Gorter conception of the "spontaneity of the masses." The pattern had been first set in 1905 in

* The question of consciousness and spontaneity is probably the most crucial question in the history of radical politics, for it involves on the one hand the nature of party organization, and its relation to the masses, and on the other the role of the intellectual. Further, if the masses, by themselves, are unable to achieve socialist consciousness, what does this mean for the entire theory of Marxist materialism, that existence determines consciousness? And further, if such ideas derive from the intellectuals, and as Kautsky, from whom Lenin drew many of his ideas in *What Is To Be Done,* puts it, that science is the source of radical consciousness, what does this mean for a Marxist theory of ideas? Such a discussion, however, goes too far beyond the context of this essay. For a treatment of these questions in detail, see the chapter on Leninism in my forthcoming study of Communism and the American labor movement.

A careful discussion of the history of the Russian debate over party organization is contained in Leopold Haimson's study of the Russian Marxists, *op. cit.,* Parts II and III. Unfortunately Mr. Haimson does not trace these debates in other socialist parties, and the impression may be left that the question of consciousness and spontaneity was peculiarly a product of Russian conditions. For an earlier, now neglected, but still one of the most thoughtful accounts of the background of Leninism and of these questions, see Arthur Rosenberg's *A History of Bolshevism* (New York, 1934), esp. pp. 57-63. For a detailed discussion of Gorter's ideas, see H. Gorter, "Mass Action: The Answer," *International Socialist Review,* Chicago, September, 1916. For a discussion of Rosa Luxemburg's ideas, see Haimson, *op. cit.,* pp. 194-96.

Russia. The Councils of Workers' Deputies were, initially, spontaneous strike committees in local factories, formed by metal workers and textile workers, which then merged into a general-strike organization. This syndicalist pattern was repeated in Russia in 1917 and in Central Europe. Most of the Workers' and Soldiers' Councils that arose sprang up spontaneously in the defeated countries as a consequence of the crumbling of central administration and authority. But these were quickly taken over by the political parties for *political purposes.* In only few places were real attempts made to take over control of economic life. In Bremen, a Workers' and Sailors' Council held power from January 10 to February 3, 1919, and in Bavaria, a Soviet Republic set up on April 13, 1919, introduced workers' control in the factories and nationalized the banks, before being overthrown little more than a fortnight later by the German government. In Austria, workers' councils checked production and sought to control prices until they submitted to the authority of Karl Renner, the socialist head of the new republic. In Hungary, the Soviet Republic set up by Bela Kun was established through top-level political maneuvers rather than through workers' councils. But it was not only in the defeated countries that such spontaneous action was seen. In England, on a lesser scale, the shop-steward movement showed the restlessness of the rank and file against bureaucratic union control, as well as the ready response of the masses of workers to create their own institutions, responsive to their needs, when the unions had become agencies to control the workers.

It is quite likely that the experience of these spontaneous movements was a factor in convincing Lenin, at least in the first year or two after the Russian Revolution, that the "self-conscious discipline" of the proletariat would allow for the easy administration of the economy of socialist societies; and that these experiences accounted for the syndicalist imagery in his writings during 1917-19.

But the political failures of the left socialists in Europe, especially Germany, were to create a profound change of mind in Lenin. These experiences, plus the emerging centralizing role of the Bolshevik party in Russia, brought once again to Lenin's mind the emphasis on centralized organization and the necessity of the leading role of the party. This reversal, warned Rosa Luxemburg, would lead to disaster. In a remarkable prescient warning, written while still in jail in 1919, she stated that the attempt to install party control over the proletariat would lead to the dictatorship of the party, and eventually, within the party, of the dictatorship of a few.[149] But the warning went unheeded.

At the Second Congress of the Communist International (July-August, 1920), the experience of the workers' council was debated and the idea rejected. A set of theses, drafted by Zinoviev, was adopted, which stated, in conclusion: "the only certain way to ensure the victory of the principle for which the workers' councils are fighting—and therefore of putting them in power, is to insure that they are led by workers' political party. . . ." These theses[150] were designed to counteract the syndicalist and direct-action tendencies which still prevailed in France and Spain and which were present, in somewhat different form, in the German KAPD, the American IWW, and the British shop-steward movement. Jack Tanner, speaking for the British shop stewards, told the Russians that they had much to learn from the West. But the Russians were now in complete control, and would not listen. Their experiences, and theirs alone, were to serve as the model for all other parties. Citing the failure of the Paris Commune, Zinoviev said: "If the working-class had had a disciplined Communist Party. . . ." The lesson was obvious. The adoption of the theses made it clear that from that time on the Communist parties and the movements they controlled would be run on a basic pattern of centralized organization and iron military discipline. All "spontaneous" action would be canalized or crushed. This was the proclamation of the Comintern, and the way was already being shown in Russia.

The Fate of Workers' Control in Russia: The Road Down

For a brief instant, Russia in 1917-18 was truly a workers' society. Those were heady days in the feeling that the new society would come with the quick proclamation of revolution. Immediately following the October revolution, and without waiting for decrees, the workers began taking over the factories and driving out the capitalists. National workshops were to be created. Much like the exchange bank schemes of 1848, short-term tickets entitling one to commodities were circulated. Since money, in the simple-minded Marxist view, was a tool of capitalist exploitation, it was to be abolished. (Even as late as 1921, Soviet economists were busily engaged in drawing up a plan to eliminate money entirely and replace it by a labor unit of accounting to be called the "treb.") As with all chiliasts, there was the sense of an "absolute presentness of time."

The first Russian trade-union Congress of 1918 took seriously the idea of workers' control of production. The unions were charged to "participate most energetically in all administrative departments of production; to organize labor boards of control, the registration and distribution of labor, and the exchange of labor between village and the city."

This view was endorsed by the Communist party, which at the Eighth Congress in March, 1919, adopted a new program replacing the old one of 1903. "The organizing apparatus of national industry must be based primarily on the trade unions." Industry was to be centralized into a "single economic unit," and the trade-unions were to persuade the toiling masses to participate immediately in the administration of economics."[151]

But given the chaos of the time, worker's control was inevitably a mockery. In January, 1918, for example, the management of the railways was entrusted to a committee of workers, and in a few months the roads were in a state of collapse. The shop committees were powerless to discipline a recalcitrant worker. If a committee did so, it was voted out and another replaced it. In three months, control of the railroads was taken out of the hands of the workers and centralized under the Commissar of Communications, who was given complete dictatorial powers. Decrees extending nationalization were passed to take other enterprises *out* of the hands of workers, and the enterprises were brought under state control.

The breakdown of workers' control was followed by new industrial discipline, one-man management, and the employment of non-communist specialists. More importantly, the experience opened a major debate in the Bolshevik party which ended, finally, in the destruction of the independent role of the trade-unions, and of any democracy within the party itself.

The year 1920 represented the crisis of the Revolution. The working class was exhausted, demoralized, shrunken to half its size. In a free election, as E. H. Carr and Isaac Deutscher have admitted, it is likely that the Bolsheviks would have been ousted from power. It was at this point that the iron will of Lenin and Trotsky saved the Bolsheviks—at the expense of workers' democracy.

The issue was opened by Trotsky, who in a brochure, "About the Role of the Trade Unions," attacked the clause in the basic program of the Communist party Eighth Congress which spoke of the goal of transferring the management of the economy to the trade-unions. Since the Soviet state is proletarian, he said in a magnificent tautology, it is meaningless to talk about protecting the proletariat from the state. Trotsky proposed, as a long-run goal, to merge the unions with government administrative departments. More immediately, he proposed the militarization of the entire civilian life, with strict centralization of both political and practical work by the council of the appropriate labor army. The army, said Trotsky, was a model for industrial efficiency. He proposed to convert military formations into worker battalions. His supporter, Goltsman, a trade-union leader himself, proposed the creation in industry of an "officer class," a workers' aristocracy composed of managers trained from the ranks, who would run the factories.[152]

These proposals were too extreme for Lenin, and Zinoviev, who had become a factional rival of Trotsky, attacked him in Lenin's name. But the sharpest attacks came from the unions and from the "Workers' Opposition" group. The shoe was on the wrong foot, they said. Not the unions, but the party itself should be reorganized. The party was corrupted by peasant and middle-class elements. And, in the spirit of Machajski, they said: "The great majority of administrative positions must be occupied by workers who have not abandoned physical labor."

The opposition proposed that "every member of the Communist Party shall be obliged to perform annually at least three months of physical labor in the factories, mills, or mines, or coal pits. No member of the Party could hold a post for more than a year without such labor and living under the same conditions as the workers did." Bukharin, who later was to swing in the opposite direction, said: "since the entire housekeeping must be under the administration of the unions, it follows that the candidates for the Supreme Soviet of the National Economy should be chosen by the unions—and accepted by the Government."

Lenin turned abruptly on this "syndicalist twaddle." The entire "syndicalist absurdity," he said, "must be thrown into the waste basket."[153] "If we should say," he replied to Bukharin, "that not the Party nominates the candidates and governs, but the trade unions alone, it will sound very democratic, but it destroys the dictatorship of the proletariat."[154]

In a tortuous casuistry, Lenin sought to prove that the

sentence in the party program that he had written on trade-union control of the national economy did not mean what it patently said. The sentence, "the trade unions must concentrate in their own hands the complete administration of the *entire* national economy," meant, he said, the top direction of the economy, but *not* the specific branches of industry, which should be run by managers. And at the second All-Russian Congress of Miners, in December, 1920, he turned full circle from his famous theoretical pronouncement of three years before. "Does every worker know how to rule the country?" he exclaimed. "Practical people know that these are fairy tales."

But who had spun these tales?

The issue between the workers' opposition and the party leadership came to a head in 1921. Ostensibly the issue was one-man management in the factories. Actually the larger issue was the independence of the trade-unions from party control.

In 1918-19, the system of workers' committees in control of factories had been replaced by a cumbersome form of "co-determination," or a board system of collegial rule, in which a non-party specialist shared control with the union. But this was ended when the party's Ninth Congress, in March, 1920, voted to establish the principle of one-man management. In such a setup, the unions could challenge the authority of management and bargain, but little more. But the unions feared that even these rights would be lost, and these fears were soon justified when, in the crucial area of transport, all union rights were suspended. Thus the issue of union independence came sharply to the fore. It centered on an institution known popularly as the *Tsektran.*

In August, 1920, a Joint Central Transport Committee, called, for short, *Tsektran,* was created, with Trotsky, as Commissar for Transport, in charge. The *Tsektran* cut across the authority of the unions. It substituted a centralized government control over powers that previously the unions had exercised. Moreover, union officials were now appointed from above, not elected from below.

Trotsky, in his vision of military discipline, made no secret of his intention to smash union opposition and even to imprison the leaders if necessary. To justify his position, Trotsky made the theoretical argument that "In the workers' state . . . the parallel existence of economic organs and of trade union organizations can only be tolerated as a temporary phenomenon." Lenin opposed the position as too doctrinaire. The unions, he said, should have some leeway; the question of fusing the two organs was a matter of tempo.

Feeling that the *Tsektran* would become the reality of the future, a group of trade-unionists led by Shlyapnikov, of the Metal Workers, formally raised the issue of workers' control before the Tenth Congress in 1921. Citing the official declaration of the party that the trade-unions should achieve the management of the national economy, the workers' opposition proposed a syndicalist reorganization of Soviet society which bears striking resemblance to the plans proposed by the American Marxist Daniel De Leon thirty years before. It called for organization of industrial unions and the control of industry by a central body elected from the constituent unions. Within individual factories, control would be vested in an elected workers' council, subordinate only to the trade-union organization next in the hierarchy. The key demand, however, was the principle of *election* of all officers. Its aim was to break the power of the Central Committee of the party and of the local party over the unions. For if the Central Committee lost the power of appointing union officials and members of committees, the central apparatus would not be able to put its policies into practice.

In 1921, three positions had crystallized within the Bolshevik party. One position, represented by Trotsky, wanted, in effect, to eliminate unions, to centralize power, and to exercise stringent controls, but to allow for freer access, to the top by young, talented workers in place of the aging bureaucrats. The majority position, whose spokesman was Zinoviev, wanted a looser structure, less rigid controls, and the freezing of the power of existing bureaucrats. Lenin backed Zinoviev's position. He felt that the unions should not be antagonized, since their roots were in the working class, although they should not exercise direction of the economy of the party. In a remarkable statement at the time, Lenin said: "Ours is a workers' government with a bureaucratic twist. Our present Government is such that the proletariat, organized to the last man, must protect itself against it. And we must use workers' organization for the protection of the workers against their Government."[155] The third group was that of the syndicalists, the workers' opposition.

The chief spokesman for the workers' opposition, paradoxically, was not a worker but Alexandra Kollontay,[156] the daughter of a Czarist general who had become a Bolshevik

generations weighs like a nightmare on the brain of the living," wrote Marx.) Feuerbach, the most radical of all the left Hegelians, called himself Luther II. Man would be free, he said, if we could demythologize religion. The history of all thought was a history of progressive disenchantment, and if finally, in Christianity, God had been transformed from a parochial deity to a universal abstraction, the function of criticism—using the radical tool of alienation, or self-estrangement—was to replace theology by anthropology, to substitute Man for God. Philosophy was to be directed at life, man was to be liberated from the "specter of abstractions" and extricated from the bind of the supernatural. Religion was capable only of creating "false consciousness." Philosophy would reveal "true consciousness." And by placing Man, rather than God, at the center of consciousness, Feuerbach sought to bring the "infinite into the finite."[165]

If Feuerbach "descended into the world," Marx sought to transform it. And where Feuerbach proclaimed anthropology, Marx, reclaiming a root insight of Hegel, emphasized History and historical contexts. The world was not generic Man, but men; and of men, classes of men. Men differed because of their class position. And truths were class truths. All truths, thus, were masks, or partial truths, but the real truth was the revolutionary truth. And this real truth was rational.

Thus a dynamic was introduced into the analysis of ideology, and into the creation of a new ideology. By demythologizing religion, one recovered (from God and sin) the potential in man. By the unfolding of history, rationality was revealed. In the struggle of classes, true consciousness, rather than false consciousness, could be achieved. But if truth lay in action, one must act. The left Hegelians, said Marx, were only *littérateurs.* (For them a magazine was "practice.") For Marx, the only real action was in politics. But action, revolutionary action as Marx conceived it, was not mere social change. It was, in its way, the resumption of all the old millenarian, chiliastic ideas of the Anabaptists. It was, in its new vision, a new ideology.

The analysis of ideology belongs properly in the discussion of the intelligentsia. One can say that what the priest is to religion, the intellectual is to ideology. This in itself gives us a clue to the dimensions of the word and the reason for its multivariate functions. The word *ideology* was coined by the French philosopher Destutt de Tracy, at the end of the 18th century. Together with other Enlightenment philosophers, notably such materialists as Helvetius and Holbach, de Tracy was trying to define a way of discovering "truth" other than through faith and authority, the traditional methods encouraged by Church and State. And, equally, under the influence of Francis Bacon, these men were seeking some way to eliminate the accidents of bias, the distortions of prejudice, the idiosyncracies of upbringing, the interventions of self-interest or the simple will to believe, all of which, like shadows in Plato's cave, created illusions of truth.* Their aim was to "purify" ideas in order to achieve "objective" truth and "correct" thought. Some of them, Helvetius, for example, believed that one had to go bock to the origin and development of ideas in order to see how distortions entered. De Tracy believed that one "purified" ideas by reducing them to sense perceptions—a belated French variant of British empiricism with a barely concealed anti-religious bias—and this new science of ideas he called "ideology."

The negative connotations of the term arose with Napoleon. Having consolidated his power, he forbade the teaching of moral and political science at the Institut National and denonuced the "ideologues" as irresponsible speculators who were subverting morality and patriotism. As a republican, Napoleon had been sympathetic to the ideas of the philosophers; as Emperor, he recognized the importance of religious orthodoxy for the maintenance of the State.

But it was with Marx that the word "ideology" went through some curiously different transmutations. For Marx, as in his work *The German Ideology,* ideology was linked to philosophical idealism, or the conception that ideas are autonomous, and that ideas, independently, have the power to reveal truth and consciousness. For Marx, as a materialist, this was false since "existence determined consciousness" rather than vice versa; any attempt to draw a picture of reality from ideas alone could produce only "false consciousness."

* Francis Bacon in the *Novum Organum* sought to release Reason from the "imperfections of the mind" by positing different kinds of distortion. These he called *The Idols of the Tribe; The Idols of the Cave* ("everyone . . . has a cave or den of his own, which refracts and discolors the light of nature; owing . . . to his education and conversation with others; or to the reading of books, and the authority of those he esteems and admires . . ."); *The Idols of the Market-Place; and The Idols of the Theatre* ("because in my judgment all the received systems [of philosophy] are but so many stage-plays representing worlds of their own creation after an unreal and scenic fastion"). For a discussion of the history of the idea of bias in the social sciences in relation to ideology, see Reinhard Bendix's *Social Science and the Distrust of Reason* (University of California Press, 1951).

Thus, for example, in following Feuerbach—from whom Marx drew most of his analysis of ideology and alienation—he considered religion to be a false consciousness: Gods are the creation of men's minds and they only appear to exist independently and determine man's fate; religion therefore is an ideology.

But Marx went one step further. Ideologies, he said, are not only false ideas, but they mask particular interests. Ideologies claim to be truth, but reflect the needs of specific groups. In his early essays on *The Jewish Question,* one of the few places where he dealt specifically with the philosophical problems of State and Society, Marx sharply attacked the concept of "natural rights" as it appeared in the French Revolution's Declaration of the Rights of Man, and as these rights were specified in the State constitutions of Pennsylvania and New Hampshire. The presumption of "natural rights"—the freedom to worship or the freedom to own property—was that they were "absolute" or "transcendant" rights; for Marx, they were only "bourgeois rights," historically achieved, which made false claim to universal validity. The function of the State, Marx pointed out, was to create some basis for the "general will." In the "civil society" which the bourgeoisie had created, the State presumably was to be negative or neutral. Each man would pursue his own self-interest, and a social harmony would prevail. But in fact, he argued, the State was used to enforce the rights of particular groups. Thus the claim of "natural rights" simply masked the demand of the bourgeoisie to be able to use property to their own advantage. Marx believed that the individualism of "natural rights" was a false individualism, since man could only "realize" himself in community, and that true freedom was not freedom *of* property or freedom *of* religion, but freedom *from* property and freedom *from* religion—in short, from ideology. The attempt, therefore, to claim universal validity for what was in fact a class interest, was ideology.

Marx differed from Bentham, and other utilitarians, in recognizing that individuals were not always motivated by direct self-interest. (This was "vulgar hedonism.") Ideology, he said, was a meaningful force. "One must not form the narrow-minded idea," he wrote in *The Eighteenth Brumaire,* "that the petty-bourgeoisie wants on principle to enforce an egoistic class interest. It believes, rather, that the *special* conditions of its emancipation are the *general* conditions through which alone modern society can be saved and the class struggle avoided." The "unmasking" of ideology, thus, is to reveal the "objective" interest behind the idea, and to see what function the ideology serves.*

The implications of all this are quite direct. For one, a rationalistic analysis of politics alone is inadequate. What people say they believe cannot always be taken at face value, and one must search for the structure of interests beneath the ideas; one looks not at the *content* of ideas, but their *function.* A second, more radical conclusion is that if ideas mask material interests, then the "test of truth" of a doctrine is to see what class interests it serves. In short, truth is "class truth." Thus, there is no objective philosophy, but only "bourgeois philosophy" and "proletarian philosophy"; no objective sociology but only "bourgeois sociology" and "proletarian sociology." But Marxism is not, simply, a relativistic doctrine: there is an "objective" ordering of the social universe, which is revealed through "history." History, for Marx as for Hegel, is a progressive unfolding reason, in which society, through man's conquest of nature and the destruction of all mythologies and superstitions, moves on to "higher stages." The "truth" of doctrine, therefore, is to be determined by its "closeness of fit" to the development of history; and in practice, it has meant that "truth" was determined by whether or not it contributed to he advancement of revolution.

There are many difficulties to the theory of the "social determination of ideas." One is the role of science. Marx did not speak of the natural sciences as ideologies. Yet a number of Marxists, particularly in the Soviet Union in the 1930's, did claim that there was a "bourgeois science" and a "bourgeois physics" and a "proletarian science" and a "proletarian physics." Thus, the relativity theories of Albert Einstein were attacked as "idealistic." And while today in the Soviet Union, there is hardly any talk of "bourgeois physics," the theories of Sigmund Freud are officially condemned as "idealistic." Yet if science is not class-bound, is this equally true of the social sciences? The question of the autonomy of science is one that has never been satisfactorily resolved in Marxian thought.

A second difficulty is the deterministic presumption that there is a *one-to-one* correspondence between a set of ideas and some "class" purpose. Yet this is rarely the case. Empiri-

* To this extent, the "unmasking of ideology" is somewhat akin to the theory of "rationalization" in the Freudian system. A rationalization hides an underlying motive. This does not mean it is necessarily false. In fact to function effectively, a rationalization has to have some "close fit" with reality. Yet an ulterior or underlying motive exists as well, and analysis seeks to point this out.

cism is usually associated with liberal inquiry. Yet David Hume, the most "radical" empiricist, was a Tory, and Edmund Burke, who had argued the most vigorously against rationalist efforts to blueprint a new society, was conservative. Hobbes, one of the most profound of materialists, was a royalist, and T. H. Green, one of the leaders of the idealist revival in Great Britain, a liberal.

And the third diffculty is the definition of class. For Marx (though class was never rigorously defined in his work) the key social divisions in society arose out of the distribution of property. Yet in a politico-technological world, property has increasingly lost its force as a determinant of power, and sometimes, even, of wealth. In almost all modern societies, technical skill becomes more important than inheritance as a determinant of occupation, and political power takes precedence over economic. What then is the meaning of class?

And yet, one cannot wholly discount the force of the proposition that "styles of thought" are related to historic class groups and their interests, or that ideas emerge as a consequence of the different world-views, or perspectives, of different groups in the society. The problem is how to specify the relationships between the existential base and the "mental production." Max Weber, the sociologist, argued, for example, that there is an "elective affinity" between ideas and interests. The social origin of an idea, or of a theorist, or a revolutionist, is less relevant than the fact that certain ideas become "selected out," so to speak, by social groups that find them congenial and thus espouse them. This was the basis for the theory of the "Protestant Ethic," in which he argued that certain features of Calvinistic thought, and the kind of personality that such a doctrine sanctioned, became necessary, and causal, in the development of capitalism, despite the other-worldly foundation of these ideas. Karl Mannheim, another sociologist, sought to divide social thought into two fundamental styles, which he called "ideological" and "utopian." He accepted the proposition, derived from Marx, that ideas are "time-bound," but insisted that Marx's ideas, as those of all socialists, came within the same stricture. Since all ideas serve interests, those which defended the existing order he called "ideological" and those which sought to change the social order he called "utopian." But was all effort, then, at objective truth hopeless? Was Bacon's quest therefore a mirage? Mannheim felt that one social group could be relatively objective—the intellectuals. Since the intelligentsia were a "floating stratum" in society, and therefore were less bound than other class groups, they could achieve multi-perspectives that transcended the parochial limits of the other social groups.

In the development of the social sciences, the problem raised by Bacon, de Tracy, Marx and others—the clarification of the role of ideas in social change—has become part of a technical field known as the "sociology of knowledge." (For a clear discussion of these issues, see the chapter by Robert K. Merton in his *Social Theory and Social Structure.*) But in popular usage the word *ideology* remains as a vague term where it seems to denote a world-view or belief-system or creeds held by a social group about the social arrangements in society, which is morally justified as being right. People then talk of the "ideology of the small businessman," or of liberalism, or fascism, as an "ideology." Or some writer will talk of "the dream-world of ideology (in which) Americans see their country as a place where every child is born to 'equality of opportunity,' where every man is essentially as good as every other man if not better." In this sense, ideology connotes a "myth" rather than just a set of values.

Clearly, such usages, by mixing together many things, create only confusion. Some distinctions, therefore, are in order.

We can, perhaps, borrow a distinction from Mannheim, and distinguish between what he called "the *particular* conception of ideology," and "the *total* conception of ideology." In the first sense, we can say that individuals who profess certain values do have interests as well, and we can better understand the meaning of these values or beliefs, or the reasons why they come forth where they have, by linking them up with the interests they have—though the interests may not always be economic; they may be status interests (such as an ethnic group that wants higher standing or social approval in a society), political interests, such as representation, and the like. It is in this sense that we can talk of the *ideology* of business, or of labor, or the like. (When Charles E. Wilson, the Secretary of Defense in the Eisenhower Administration and one-time president of General Motors, said, "What is good for the United States is good for General Motors, and vice-versa," he was expressing ideology—i.e., the view that economic policy should be geared to the needs of the business community, since the welfare of the country depended on the health of business.) A *total* ideology is an

The differences between the intellectual and the scholar, without being invidious, are important to understand. The scholar has a bounded field of knowledge, a tradition, and seeks to find his place in it, adding to the accumulated, tested knowledge of the past as to a mosaic. The scholar, qua scholar, is less involved with his "self." The intellectual begins with *his* experience, *his* individual perceptions of the world, *his* privileges and deprivations, and judges the world by these sensibilities. Since his own status is of high value, his judgments of the society reflect the treatment accorded him. In a business civilization, the intellectual felt that the wrong values were being honored, and rejected the society. Thus there was a "built-in" compulsion for the free-floating intellectual to become political. The ideologies, therefore, which emerged from the nineteenth century had the force of the intellectuals behind them. They embarked upon what William James called "the faith ladder," which in its vision of the future cannot distinguish possibilities from probabilities, and converts the latter into certainties.

Today, these ideologies are exhausted. The events behind this important sociological change are complex and varied. Such calamities as the Moscow Trials, the Nazi-Soviet pact, the concentration camps, the suppression of the Hungarian workers, form one chain; such social changes as the modification of capitalism, the rise of the Welfare State, another. In philosophy, one can trace the decline of simplistic, rationalistic beliefs and the emergence of new stoic-theological images of man, e.g. Freud, Tillich, Jaspers, etc. This is not to say that such ideologies as communism in France and Italy do not have a political weight, or a driving momentum from other sources. But out of all this history, one simple fact emerges: for the radical intelligentsia, the old ideologies have lost their "truth" and their power to persuade.

Few serious minds believe any longer that one can set down "blueprints" and through "social engineering" bring about a new utopia of social harmony. At the same time, the older "counter-beliefs" have lost their intellectual force as well. Few "classic" liberals insist that the State should play no role in the economy, and few serious conservatives, at least in England and on the Continent, believe that the Welfare State is "the road to serfdom." In the Western world, therefore, there is today a rough consensus among intellectuals on political issues: the acceptance of a Welfare State; the desirability of decentralized power; a system of mixed economy and of political pluralism. In that sense, too, the ideological age has ended.

And yet, the extraordinary fact is that while the old nineteenth-century ideologies and intellectual debates have become exhausted, the rising states of Asia and Africa are fashioning new ideologies with a different appeal for their own people. These are the ideologies of industrialization, modernization, Pan-Arabism, color, and nationalism. In the distinctive difference between the two kinds of ideologies lies the great political and social problems of the second half of the twentieth century. The ideologies of the nineteenth century were universalistic, humanistic, and fashioned by intellectuals. The mass ideologies of Asia and Africa are parochial, instrumental, and created by political leaders. The driving forces of the old ideologies were social equality and, in the largest sense, freedom. The impulsions of the new ideologies are economic development and national power.

And in this appeal, Russia and China have become models. The fascination these countries exert is no longer the old idea of the free society, but the new one of economic growth. And if this involves the wholesale coercion of the population and the rise of new elites to drive the people, the new repressions are justified on the ground that without such coercions economic advance cannot take place rapidly enough. And even for some of the liberals of the West, "economic development" has become a new ideology that washes away the memory of old disillusionments.

It is hard to quarrel with an appeal for rapid economic growth and modernization, and few can dispute the goal, as few could ever dispute an appeal for equality and freedom. But in this powerful surge—and its swiftness is amazing—any movement that instates such goals risks the sacrifice of the present generation for a future that may see only a new exploitation by a new elite. For the newly-risen countries, the debate is not over the merits of Communism—the content of that doctrine has long been forgotten by friends and foes alike. The question is an older one: whether new societies can grow by building democratic institutions and allowing people to make choices—and sacrifices—voluntarily, or whether the new elites, heady with power, will impose totalitarian means to transform their countries. Certainly in these traditional and old colonial societies where the masses are apathetic and easily manipulated, the answer lies with the intellectual classes and their conceptions of the future.

Thus one finds, at the end of the fifties, a disconcerting caesura. In the West, among the intellectuals, the old passions are spent. The new generation, with no meaningful memory of these old debates, and no secure tradition to build upon, finds itself seeking new purposes within a framework of political society that has rejected, intellectually speaking, the old apocalyptic and chiliastic visions. In the search for a "cause," there is a deep, desperate, almost pathetic anger. The theme runs through a remarkable book, *Convictions*, by a dozen of the sharpest young Left Wing intellectuals in Britain. They cannot define the content of the "cause" they seek, but the yearning is clear. In the U.S. too there is a restless search for a new intellectual radicalism. Richard Chase, in his thoughtful assessment of American society, *The Democratic Vista*, insists that the greatness of nineteenth-century America for the rest of the world consisted in its radical vision of man (such a vision as Whitman's), and calls for a new radical criticism today. But the problem is that the old politico-economic radicalism (pre-occupied with such matters as the socialization of industry) has lost its meaning, while the stultifying aspects of contemporary culture (e.g., television) cannot be redressed in political terms. At the same time, American culture has almost completely accepted the avant-garde, particularly in art, and the older academic styles have been driven out completely. The irony, further, for those who seek "causes" is that the workers, whose grievances were once the driving energy for social change, are more satisfied with the society than the intellectuals. The workers have not achieved utopia, but their expectations were less than those of the intellectuals, and the gains correspondingly larger.

The young intellectual is unhappy because the "middle way" is for the middle-aged, not for him; it is without passion and is deadening.[168] Ideology, which by its nature is an all-or-none affair, and temperamentally the thing he wants, is intellectually devitalized, and few issues can be formulated any more, intellectually, in ideological terms. The emotional energies—and needs—exist, and the question of how one mobilizes these energies is a difficult one. Politics offers little excitement. Some of the younger intellectuals have found an outlet in science or university pursuits, but often at the expense of narrowing their talent into mere technique; others have sought self-expression in the arts, but in the wasteland the lack of content has meant, too, the lack of the necessary tension that creates new forms and styles.

Whether the intellectuals in the West can find passions outside of politics is moot. Unfortunately, social reform does not have any unifying appeal, nor does it give a younger generation the outlet for "self-expression" and "self-definition" that it wants. The trajectory of enthusiasm has curved East, where, in the new ecstasies for economic utopia, the "future" is all that counts.

The end of ideology is not—should not be—the end of utopia as well. If anything, one can begin anew the discussion of utopia only by being aware of the trap of ideology. The point is that ideologists are "terrible simplifiers." Ideology makes it unnecessary for people to confront individual issues on their individual merits. One simply turns to the ideological vending machine, and out comes the prepared formulae. And when these beliefs are suffused by apocalyptic fervor, ideas become weapons, and with dreadful results.

There is now, more than ever, some need for utopia, in the sense that men need—as they have always needed—some vision of their potential, some manner of fusing passion with intelligence. Yet the ladder to the City of Heaven can no longer be a "faith ladder," but an empirical one: a utopia has to specify *where* one wants to go, *how* to get there, the costs of the enterprise, and some realization of, and justification for the determination of *who* is to pay.

The end of ideology closes the book, intellectually speaking, on an era, the one of easy "left" formulae for social change. But to close the book is not to turn one's back upon it. This is all the more important now when a "new Left," with few memories of the past, is emerging. This "new Left" has passion and energy, but little definition of the future. Its outriders exult that it is "on the move." But where it is going, what it means by Socialism, how to guard against bureaucratization, what one means by democratic planning or workers' control—any of the questions that require hard thought, are only answered by bravura phrases.

It is in attitudes towards Cuba and the new States in Africa that the meaning of intellectual maturity, and of the end of ideology, will be tested. For among the "new Left," there is an alarming readiness to create a *tabula rasa,* to accept the word "Revolution" as an absolution for outrages, to justify the suppression of civil rights and opposition—in short, to erase the lessons of the last forty years with an emotional alacrity that is astounding. The fact that many of these emerging social movements are justified in their demands for freedom, for the right to control their own political and economic destinies, does not mean they have a right to a blank check for everything they choose to do in the name of their emancipation. Nor does the fact that such movements take power in the name of freedom guarantee that they will not turn out to be as imperialist, as grandeur-concerned (in the name of Pan-Africanism or some other ideology), as demanding their turn on the stage of History, as the States they have displaced.

If the end of ideology has any meaning, it is to ask for the end of rhetoric, and rhetoricians, of "revolution" of the day when the young French anarchist Vaillant tossed a bomb into the Chamber of Deputies, and the literary critic Laurent Tailhade declared in his defense: "What do a few human lives matter; it was a *beau geste.*" (A *beau geste* that ended, one might say, in a mirthless jest: two years later, Tailhade lost an eye when a bomb was thrown into a restaurant.) Today, in Cuba, as George Sherman, reporting for the *London Observer* summed it up: "The Revolution is law today although nobody has said clearly what that law is. You are expected to be simply for or against it and judge and be judged accordingly. Hatred and intolerance are wiping out whatever middle ground may have existed."

The problems which confront us at home and in the world are resistant to the old terms of ideological debate between "left" and "right," and if "ideology" by now, and with good reason, is an irretrievably fallen word, it is not necessary that "utopia" suffer the same fate. But it will if those who now call loudest for new utopias begin to justify degrading *means* in the name of some Utopian or revolutionary *end,* and forget the simple lessons that if the old debates are meaningless, some old verities are not—the verities of free speech, free press, the right of opposition and of free inquiry.

And if the intellectual history of the past hundred years has any meaning—and lesson—it is to reassert Jefferson's wisdom (aimed at removing the dead hand of the past, but which can serve as a warning against the heavy hand of the future as well), that "the present belongs to the living." This is the wisdom that revolutionists, old and new, who are sensitive to the fate of their fellow men, rediscover in every generation. "I will never believe," says a protagonist in a poignant dialogue written by the gallant Polish philosopher Leszek Kolakowski, "that the moral and intellectual life of mankind follows the law of economics, that is by saying today we can have more tomorrow; that we should use lives now so that truth will triumph or that we should profit by crime to pave the way for nobility."

And these words, written during the Polish "thaw," when the intellectuals had asserted, from their experience with the "future," the claims of humanism, echo the protest of the Russian writer Alexander Herzen, who, in a dialogue a hundred years ago, reproached an earlier revolutionist who would sacrifice the present mankind for a promised tomorrow: "Do you truly wish to condemn all human beings alive today to the sad role of caryatids . . . supporting a floor for others some day to dance on? . . . This alone should serve as a warning to people: an end that is infinitely remote is not an end, but, if you like, a trap; an end must be nearer—it ought to be, at the very least, the labourer's wage or pleasure in the work done. Each age, each generation, each life has its own fullness. . . ."[169]

Afterword, 1988

The End of Ideology Revisited

—In memory of Raymond Aron

THERE ARE SOME BOOKS that are better known for their titles than their contents. Mine is one of them. Various critics, usually from the Left, pointed to the upsurge of radicalism in the mid-sixties as disproof of the book's thesis. Others saw the work as an "ideological" defense of "technocratic" thinking or of the "status quo." A few, even more ludicrously, believed that the book attacked the role of ideals in politics. It was none of these.[1]

The frame of the book was set by its subtitle, "On the Exhaustion of Political Ideas in the Fifties." Yet the last section looked ahead. After observing young left-wing intellectuals express repeated yearnings for ideology, I said that new inspirations, new ideologies, and new identifications would come from the Third World. I wrote:

> the extraordinary fact is that while the old nineteenth-century ideologies and intellectual debates have become exhausted, the rising states of Asia and Africa are fashioning new ideologies with a different appeal for their own people. These are the ideologies of industrialization, modernization, Pan-Arabism, color and nationalism. In the distinctive difference between the two kinds of ideologies lie the great political and social problems of the second half of the twentieth century. The ideologies of the nineteenth century were universalistic, humanistic, and fashioned by intellectuals. The mass ideologies of Asia and Africa are parochial, instrumental and created by political leaders. The driving forces of the old ideologies were social equality and, in the largest sense, freedom. The impulsions of the new ideologies are economic development and national power. (p. 403)

1. The charade continues. Quentin Skinner, in his introduction to a 1985 volume on "Grand Theory," writes of the "notorious title of Daniel Bell's" the claim that " 'the end of ideology' had been reached," which Skinner equates with the belief that political philosophy is finished and that one should "get on . . . with the purportedly value-neutral task of constructing . . . 'empirical' theories of social behaviour." Quentin Skinner, ed., *The Return of Grand Theory in the Human Sciences* (Cambridge: University Press, 1985), pp. 3-4.

And, as is evident in these pages, I said that, given the culture of the West, there would always be the hunger for a cause, for those impulses lie deep in the utopian and chiliastic roots of Christian thought.

The End of Ideology, as a work, did not stand alone. As a cautionary tale it was part of the war of ideas that was taking place among intellectuals, especially in Europe, about the future of the Soviet Union and Stalinism. On the one side were Jean-Paul Sartre and Maurice Merleau-Ponty in France; those who had returned "East," such as Bertolt Brecht and Ernst Bloch in Germany; and Georg Lukács, the *éminence grise* who had reemerged from the shadows. On the other side were men such as Albert Camus, Raymond Aron, Arthur Koestler, Ignazio Silone, George Orwell, and Czeslaw Milosz. One might have thought that the Moscow Trials, with their gruesome execution of almost the entire cadre of old Bolshevik leaders, such as Zinoviev, Kamenev, Bukharin, as well as hundreds of others; the revelations about the Yezhovshchina—the sweeping purge of hundreds of thousands of old party activists during the tenure of N. I. Yezhov as head of the secret police—and the imprisonment of millions in the labor camps (which Solzhenitsyn later dramatized as the Gulag Archipelago); and the Nazi-Soviet pact (when the swastika was hoisted over Moscow airport in honor of Ribbentrop's arrival and the Red Army band broke into the *Horst Wessel Lied*)—that all this would have ended the infatuation of intellectuals with the Soviet Union. But the great resistance and sacrifices by the Soviet people during the war, and the hopes for a new relaxation by the regime, fed the longings of many for the resumption of the *marche générale* of History to the promised land of socialist society. Merleau-Ponty, the French phenomenologist philosopher, and an editor (with Sartre) of *Les temps modernes,* wrote a book, *Humanisme et terreur,* justifying the repressions as the logic of the dialectical spiral of progress. Bloch published his ponderous *Der Prinzip Hoffnung,* a philosophy of history embodying the unfolding of a utopian principle of men's aspirations (which he had written in New York, during the war, before returning to East Germany). Sartre, the philosopher of existential decision, stated that the historical choice as heir to the future was either the Soviet Union or the United States; and that the Soviet Union as the incarnation of the working class, the universal class, was preferable to the United States, the embodiment of the vulgar bourgeois world. The claims of "the future" had resumed their march under the banner of ideology. And, as always the case with intellectuals, culture became the battleground in the combat for hegemony.

In the postwar debate, the first person to use the phrase "the end of ideology" was Albert Camus who in 1946 wrote that if the French socialists renounced Marxism as an absolute philosophy, limiting themselves to its critical aspect, "they will exemplify the way our period marks the end of ideologies, that is, of absolute Utopias which destroy themselves, in History, by the price they ultimately exact." The context of the phrase was a debate within the French Socialist Party in which one faction sought to reaffirm Marxism as the unyielding logic of History, the other to restate socialism as an ethical force. Camus wrote: "The chief task of the last party congress was to reconcile the desire for a new morality superior to murder with the determination to remain faithful to Marxism. But one cannot reconcile what is irreconcilable."[2] Ideology, for Camus, was a form of deception.

The theme of ideology as a form of self-deception was developed subsequently in a number of powerful arguments, personal and intellectual. *The God That Failed* (1949), edited by R. H. Crossman, carried the testimony of Koestler, Silone, André Gide, Richard Wright, Louis Fischer, and Stephen Spender about the illusions of Bolshevism. Czeslaw Milosz, in *The Captive Mind* (1953), used the Muslim term *ketman* to show the way intellectuals deceive themselves by embracing the *diamat* (dialectical materialism) as a new theology; *ketman* was an emblem of the contortions of ideology. George Orwell's *1984*, with its portrayal of the intoxication of power when ideology and politics are fused in a totalitarian system ("If you want a picture of the future, imagine a boot stamping on a human face—forever"), was unmistakably aimed at Stalin and the Soviet Union. And Raymond Aron's *The Opium of the Intellectuals* (1955) was a withering demolition of the arguments for "historical necessity" as the justification of terror.

Khrushchev's 1956 revelations of the malign crimes of Stalin; the subsequent Polish October, led by young intellectuals,

2. Albert Camus, "Ni victimes, ni bourreaux," in *Actuelles: Chroniques 1944-1948* (Paris, 1950). The essay first appeared in the newspaper *Combat* in November 1946 and was reprinted in *Politics*, July-August 1947, translated by Dwight Macdonald, under the title "Neither Victims, Nor Executioners." The essay was republished as a brochure by Continuum Books (New York, 1980), with an introduction by Robert Pickus; the quotations here are from pp. 39 and 36 of that edition.

which forced out the old Moscow-imposed regime; and the Hungarian Revolution in 1956–57 (led by the Communist prime minister Imre Nagy, who was executed by the Russians) closed the book for another generation of believers, just as the events of the late 1930s had marked the close for an earlier generation.

Aron had concluded his 1955 volume with a chapter entitled "The End of the Ideological Age?," and that question became the theme of an international conference in Milan in 1955, sponsored by the Congress for Cultural Freedom. It was in the papers for that conference that the ideas of Aron, Michael Polanyi, Edward Shils, C.A.R. Crosland, Seymour Martin Lipset, and myself found common ground. In the next several years, though emphases and themes differed somewhat, the central thought was elaborated in various seminars and books. Though the theme of my book drew its inspiration from that particular ground, there were several other sources and intentions as well. This book is not a unified study but a collection of essays held together by some common threads:

- A sociological examination of the role of intellectuals engaged in the combat of ideas.
- A view of ideology, in its historical context, as contrasted with the earlier role of religion in mobilizing passions and beliefs; in short, as a faith system.
- Some sociological studies of American society to show why many of the analytical categories derived from Marxism, particularly the concept of "class," were inadequate to deal with the distinctive complexities of American society.[3]
- And a "sermon" for the next generation of intellectuals.

The themes of utopian hopes and political limits, embodied in the reflections on my contemporaries, were explored in the

3. One long essay, "Interest and Ideology: On the Role of Public Opinion in Industrial Disputes," in the first edition (1960, chap. 10), was omitted in the paperback editions because of its narrow topicality, the Taft-Hartley law. Yet a general point about the relation between *interest* and *ideology* remains relevant. In that essay I sought to distinguish, using Bentham and utilitarian theory, between a "social decision" and the "sum total of individual decisions," between a symbolic or ideological attitude and market behavior. The context of the essay was the kind of public opinion that is created in modern society. When ideology and interests collide, I wrote: "A public opinion which claims to reflect a public interest is inherently, therefore, an unstable compound of ideological and market decisions. The question whether such opinions can lead to action, and of what kind, depends upon the degree of tension between the two types of motive and upon the degree of identification with one or the other" (p. 192). The essay here on "The Capitalism of the Proletariat: A Theory of American Trade-Unionism" generalizes this question by dealing with the two kinds of union behavior, that of a social movement, actuated often by ideological purposes, and a market organization, forced to consider first the interests of its own members and trade, even at the expense of other unions.

essays on "The Mood of Three Generations." And the final pages of my expanded epilogue (written in 1961) noted, in melancholy fashion, a new phase:

> The end of ideology closes the book, intellectually speaking, on an era, the one of easy 'left' formulas for social change. But to close the book is not to turn one's back upon it. This is all the more important now when a 'new Left' with few memories of the past is emerging . . .
>
> It is in attitudes towards Cuba and the new States in Africa that the meaning of intellectual maturity, and the end of ideology, will be tested. For among the 'new Left,' there is an alarming readiness to create a *tabula rasa,* to accept the word 'Revolution' as an absolution for outrage . . . in short, to erase the lessons of the last forty years with an emotional alacrity that is astounding.[4]

Though this is a "political" book, in the sense that I have been a participant in these intellectual wars, intertwined with the politics is also a sociological concern, the effort to break free of the strictures of conventional sociological categories; and in this context Marxism is also conventional in its holistic or totalistic view of society. Against the holistic modes, my thinking about society has proceeded on the assumption of a disjunction between culture and social structure. A Functionalist or a Marxist view sees these two either as integrated, with the

4. What I had in mind was the nascent Students for a Democratic Society. Tom Hayden, who was to be one of its founders, came to see me at Columbia University shortly after his graduation in 1961 from the University of Michigan, where he had been the editor of the college newspaper and a leader of a chapter then affiliated with the League for Industrial Democracy. It was those early conversations with Hayden that led to my disquiet, conversations that demonstrated in him a strange mixture of romantic posturing with a manipulative cynicism about organizational maneuvering. It is perhaps just that, many years later, one of his former comrades called him the Richard Nixon of the Left (see "Radical Soap Opera" by Richard Parker, *New Republic,* November 17, 1979).

For a recent, somewhat more positive view (because somewhat nostalgic and still romantic) of the founding of the SDS and its hopes for participatory democracy, see James Miller, *"Democracy Is in the Streets, From Port Huron to the Siege of Chicago* (New York: Simon and Schuster, 1987). The phrase "participatory democracy" has been the lodestar of the New Left. It declares that people should have control over the decisions that affect their lives—a good populist belief. Yet it assumes, naively, that the "people" are progressive and somehow barred from such control by "elites," or "them," or some other malevolent force. Yet the radicals rarely confronted the moral dilemma that the people might be reactionary or bigoted. Did the people of the South (or of South Boston) have the right to keep out blacks from their schools because they wanted to control their own lives and maintain their community as they saw it? And is there not also, as Tocqueville once put it, the "tyranny of the majority," which may override liberty? Typically, rhetoric here substituted for thought.

value system regulating behavior, or as a totality, in which the substructure of the material world "determines" the political, legal, and cultural orders. I have argued that such views confuse the different rhythms of change in the different levels of the history of societies. Changes in economy or technology, since they are instrumental, proceed in "linear" fashion, for there is then a clear principle of substitution: if something new is more efficient or more productive then, subject to cost, it will be used (though Marxists would argue that in practice the "social relations" of property inhibit the expanding "forces" of production). In culture, however, there is no such principle of substitution: the portals of culture either are guarded by tradition or they swing wildly through syncretism. But aesthetic innovations do not "outmode" previous forms; they widen the cultural repertoire of mankind. Historically, the several realms may sometimes be joined loosely (as in the coupling of the bourgeois character, culture, and economy in the eighteenth century), but more often, as today, they are in tension with one another. But there is no necessary unity.[5]

This division of focus is reflected in the organization of this book. The first two sections deal with structural changes in American society as a way of testing the adequacy of dominant sociological categories. These are the emerging role of the state as an economic arbiter; the breakup of family capitalism (a mode that Marx never discussed) and the sundering of an owning class from a ruling group; the change from a frugal society, fearing personal debt, to a hedonistic consumption society; the rise of status groups as a force in politics; and the basic changes in occupational patterns (the shrinking of the industrial working class, the plateau of trade-union membership, and the changes in the class structure of the society). Structural changes, if accurately identified, take a long time to unfold, and I find it satisfying to note that more than twenty-five years later these

5. This mode of analysis underlies my two books of the 1970s, *The Coming of Post-Industrial Society* and *The Cultural Contradictions of Capitalism*. And it is most strongly exemplified in the discussion of secularization in my Hobhouse lecture, "The Return of the Sacred." There I argued that the term "secularization," which most sociological commentators use to describe the modern Western world, confuses changes in two different realms: in the *institutional* realm, where there is a shrinking role of ecclesiastical authority, and changes on the level of *beliefs*. But the rise and fall of belief systems in religion do not derive from change in institutions. Thus I divide my analysis, using the terms sacred and secular to deal with institutions, and holy and profane for the character of beliefs. The lecture is reprinted in my book of essays, *The Winding Passage* (New York: Basic Books, 1980).

analyses and conclusions, especially on occupation and class, still hold true.

The third section of the book deals with beliefs, and the crystallization of one kind of faith system, ideology, as a kind of secular religion. Clearly, however, more than a dispassionate interest is evident here, for the analysis, the tone, and the intensity fuse the experiences of my generation with a judgment about human nature and history. I had, like many others, joined the Young Socialist movement at an early age (in 1932, at thirteen). Living through the thirties and forties was a hearbreak house limned with dread. There had been the Nazi death camps, barbarism beyond all civilized imagining; and the Soviet concentration camps, which had cast a pall on all utopian visions. How was one to explain them? A naturalist view, such as that advanced by Sidney Hook, argued that they were shaped by the cultural patterns of those societies and were therefore distinctive historical phenomena. Against this was the neo-Augustinian view of Reinhold Niebuhr, who saw in such ghastly actions the recurrent duplicity of human nature, of man as *homo duplex,* who in modern times seeks for self-infinitude and ends in idolatry when he transgresses the bounds of finitude. For myself and my friends, Niebuhr's was the more persuasive explanation. As I wrote here, "ours is a generation that finds its wisdom in pessimism, evil, tragedy, and despair."

Out of this came the fear of mass action, of emotion in politics, and of the politics of passions and hatreds; and this has framed my views throughout my life. In early form, it was shaped by a study of populist movements in the United States and the discovery not only of their conspiratorial view of the world but of their anti-semitism and their identification of Jews with money, a set of notions that strikingly anticipated Nazi ideology. Yet this was largely ignored if not suppressed by "progressive" historians in the United States, who saw in populism only a virtuous form of agrarian radicalism.[6]

6. These ideas were first expressed in an essay in 1944 and noticed by Richard Hofstadter, who later wrote: "It is characteristic of the indulgence which Populism has received on this count that Carey McWilliams in his *A Mask for Privilege: Anti-Semitism in America* (Boston, 1948) deals with early American anti-Semitism simply as an upper-class phenomenon. In his historical account of the rise of anti-Semitism he does not mention the Greenback-Populist tradition. Daniel Bell: 'The Grass Roots of American Jew Hatred,' *Jewish Frontier,* Vol. XI (June 1944), pp. 15–20, is one of the few writers who has perceived that there is any relation between latter-day anti-Semites and the earlier Populist tradition." Richard Hofstadter, *The Age of Reform* (New York: Knopf, 1955), pp. 80–81, n. 3.

And this fear was expressed in my monograph, *Marxian Socialism in the United States* (1952), which explored the tensions of ethics and politics, what Niebuhr had called "moral man in immoral society." The controlling metaphor I used was the dilemma of a political movement (not just an individual person) as living "in but not of the world." The Bolshevik movement, I argued, was neither in nor of the world and was therefore unencumbered by questions of "usual" (for them "bourgeois") morality, so that any and all means—including terror and murder—were ethically acceptable by the justification of their ends. The trade-union movement, living in the here-and-now of a continuing reality, had to make its accommodations to the society. But the socialist movement, rejecting capitalist society, found itself hoist by the dilemma of taking responsible actions which might strengthen that society and yet contradicted its political theology; and so it often found itself paralyzed.[7]

For me, this tension between ethics and politics was stated most forcefully by Max Weber, in the conclusion of his poignant essay "Politics as a Vocation" where he posed the polarities of the "ethics of responsibility" and the "ethics of ultimate ends" as the modes of action that any political activist has to confront. As I explained in these pages (and later), my choice has invariably been the ethics of responsibility.[8]

And yet, in the postwar West, there was some political hope. (Optimism of the will, pessimism of the heart, has been the unresolved tension of my temperament.) In Great Britain the Labour government of Clement Attlee had introduced in seven short years the foundations for a just welfare state, with the Beveridge social security and the National Health systems. At-

7. The main such issue, before World War II, was the question of entering "bourgeois" governments. In 1938, the Socialist International debated the so-called Bauer–Dan–Zyromski thesis (initiated by the revered leader of Austrian Marxism, Otto Bauer, and seconded by the Russian Menshevik Theodor Dan and the French leftist Jean Zyromski), which condemned any socialist participation in "bourgeois cabinet coalitions" as a betrayal of socialism. Yet after World War II one could not find a single West European country where, at some time or another, a socialist party leader did not serve as prime minister in a coalition—the most successful of which was Austria, where a joint Socialist-Catholic coalition ruled for more than thirty years.

8. The last pages of Weber's essay had always seemed to me to be a hidden dialogue with a younger man who was taking the political step of "ultimate ends" that Weber disapproved of. In my essay "First Love and Early Sorrow" (*Partisan Review*, 4, 1981), I tell of the unraveling of this "moral detective story" and the uncovering of that hidden face, Georg Lukács.

tlee's successor as the leader of the Labour Party, Hugh Gaitskell, had launched a campaign to drop the stilted Clause Four from the Labour Party constitution (written by Sydney Webb), which had focused on the nationalization of industry as the principal goal of the Party. And Gaitskell's protégé, Anthony Crosland, with whom I had many conversations at the time, was engaged in a rethinking of socialist philosophy that placed equality, opportunity, and merit at the center of Labour's hopes, a set of themes he developed in his influential *Future of Socialism* (1964). In Germany the Social Democratic Party, at Bad Godesberg (1959), had adopted a new party program that scrapped the orthodox Marxism to which it had been bound since the Erfurt program of 1891, written by Karl Kautsky under the supervision of Friedrich Engels. The German SDP proclaimed that it would no longer be a "class party," that democracy was central to any socialist political order, and that it sought reform rather than revolution.[9]

These political developments were buttressed by theoretical explorations. Ralf Dahrendorf, the German sociologist, argued in his book *Class and Class Conflict in Industrial Society* (American edition, 1959) that class could no longer be the division that polarized society along a single axis, as was true before World War II. The theme of the "shrinking of the ideologically oriented nineteenth-century party" was emphasized (in 1957) by Otto Kircheimer, a sometime member of the Frankfurt School, who succeeded Franz Neumann in political philosophy at Columbia. Most striking, perhaps, were the intellectual reversals by two men who in the 1930s had been immensely influential in persuading the intellectual public of the inevitable collapse of capitalism and the necessity of socialism. One was John Strachey, the English writer, whose book *The Coming Struggle for Power* became a bestseller in the Depression, and Lewis Corey, whose *Decline of American Capitalism* (1932) argued that an irreversible crisis had set in because of the falling rate of profit. Twenty years later, both

9. The view of German Social Democracy as reformist has always been distorted by the prism of Lenin who, having taken that party as a future model in such early writings as *What Is To Be Done?*, scorned the party for its support of the Kaiser at the outbreak of the war and its refusal to support the Bolshevik revolution in October 1917. A reformist program had been proposed by Eduard Bernstein, but was defeated within the party with Kautsky as the orthodox spokesman. Throughout Europe, and particularly among the socialist parties, the Bad Godesberg declaration was thus recognized as a major historical turn in the repudiation of classical Marxism.

men had become proponents of the mixed economy and of economic planning but, as Corey put it, "without statism."[10]

Perhaps the strongest formulation of the theme of the decline of ideology was that of the noted Swedish political commentator, Herbert Tingsten, who, reflecting on the Scandinavian experience, wrote in 1955: "The great [ideological] controversies . . . have been liquidated in all instances . . . Liberalism in the old sense is dead, both among the Conservatives and in the Liberal Party; Social Democrat thinking has lost nearly all its traits of doctrinaire Marxism . . . The actual words 'socialism' or 'liberalism' are tending to be mere honorifics." This was also one of the themes at the 1955 meeting of the Congress for Cultural Freedom in Milan.[11]

10. Under his original name, Louis C. Fraina, Corey was one of the founders and first leaders of the American Communist Party. He had been sent by Lenin to Mexico in the early 1920s to reorganize the party there but dropped out of political activity, returning quietly to the United States. He began writing prolifically in the 1930s as an independent radical and subsequently became professor of economics at Antioch College. I was associated with Corey in the activities of the Union for Democratic Action (forerunner of the Americans for Democratic Action) in the 1940s, and in an abortive political movement called the National Educational Committee for a New Party, from 1945 to 1947. The documents for that effort, written largely by Corey and myself, foreshadow many of the themes in *The End of Ideology*.

The theoretical basis for the mixed economy was given its most elaborate formulation by A. P. Lerner, in his *Economics of Control* (1944). A onetime Trotskyist, Lerner had come into prominence in the 1930s when, together with Oskar Lange, he had written some notable articles on the economic theory of socialism, which responded to the challenge of Ludwig von Mises and Frederick Hayek on the problems of setting rational prices in a planned economy. This argument for "market socialism" was repudiated or shuffled aside by Lange when he returned to Poland after the war and became one of the officials of the new Soviet-controlled regime. Lerner, who emigrated to the United States, was one of the first writers to apply Keynesian principles to the management of the economy, as allowing a greater protection for democracy. Lerner first popularized these views in a five-part series of articles in *The New Leader* (November-December 1944) when I was managing editor of the journal.

11. The individual most appalled by these developments was Frederick Hayek, author of *The Road to Serfdom* (1944). In a closing speech at the 1955 conference, Hayek deplored the consensus on this view. As Seymour Lipset has described Hayek's talk: "He alone was bothered by the general temper. What bothered him was the general agreement among the delegates, regardless of political belief, that the traditional issues separating the left and right had declined to comparative insignificance. In effect, all agreed that the increase in state control which had taken place in various countries would not result in a decline in democratic freedom. The socialists no longer advocated socialism; they were as concerned as the conservatives with the danger of an all-powerful state. The ideological issues dividing left and right had been reduced to a little more or less government ownership and economic planning . . . Hayek, honestly believing that state intervention is bad and inherently totalitarian, found himself in a small minority of those who still took the cleavages within the democratic camp seriously." See S. M. Lipset, "The End of Ideology," *Political Man*, rev. ed. (Baltimore: Johns Hopkins University Press, 1981), pp. 440–441.

The nineteenth-century ideological vision, with its roots in the French Revolution, had been framed in terms of the total transformation of society. The normative consensus emerging in the postwar years in the West held that civil politics could replace ideological politics; that the dream of organizing a society by complete blueprint was bound to fail; that no comprehensive social changes should be introduced, necessary as they might seem, without some effort to identify the human and social costs; and that no changes in the way of life (such as collectivization of land) should be undertaken if they could not be reversed. In short, it was—and is—a view that is mistakenly called pragmatism in politics (a word with less philosophical freight would be *prudence*), or what Dewey would have called, ambiguously, "intelligence"—the focus, *within a framework of liberal values,* on problem solving as a means of remedying social ills and inadequacies.

This, then, was the political and intellectual background of the theme, "the end of ideology." It was a theme that, not surprisingly, gained resonance, after the publication of my book, in the words and beliefs of John F. Kennedy. In a commencement address at Yale University in June 1962, President Kennedy said:

> the central *domestic* problems of our times are more subtle and less simple. They do not relate to basic clashes of philosophy and ideology, but to ways and means of *reaching common goals*—to research for sophisticated solutions to complex and obstinate issues . . . What is at stake in our economic decisions today is not some grand warfare of rival ideologies which will sweep the country with passion but the practical management of a modern economy . . . political labels and ideological approaches are irrelevant to the solutions.[12]

* * *

The publication of *The End of Ideology* struck a nerve. Though praised by Lionel Trilling (the book was a selection of the Mid-Century Book Club, which Trilling headed with

12. The Yale speech is in *Public Papers of the Presidents of the U.S.*, no. 234 (U.S. Government Printing Office, 1963), pp. 470–475. A month earlier, President Kennedy had given a less noticed speech before the Economic Conference in Washington, on myth and reality in economic affairs and the increasingly technical nature of economic issues. Both speeches were drafted by Arthur M. Schlesinger, Jr., who had attended the 1955 Milan conference of the Congress for Cultural Freedom, where the end-of-ideology theme was first raised.

structure; in part because of the "coexistence" of many overlapping social forms, such as property, and technical skill as the basis of power), and my aim has always been to avoid a single conceptual term (such as "capitalism") and to make analytical distinctions relevant to the complexities. These analytical distinctions run through almost every discussion of structural changes in this volume. Thus it has been easy for polemical critics to pick up one or another side of these distinctions in order to enter a critical objection.[16]

These are questions of intellectual misreading. But other, emotional, elements were involved. Given the underlying tone of disenchantment and the repudiation of romantic radicalism, many critics read their *own* presuppositions—and anger—into the volume and reacted accordingly. As Dennis Wrong put it in his dissent to my book: by accepting the "end of ideology," intellectuals "are failing to perform their roles as unattached critics and visionaries." To which one can only respond: Are intellectuals only to be critics, and not "constructive"? And don't they have to accept the responsibility of their visions?

The argument that *The End of Ideology* reinforces the status quo is a resounding vacuity. What is the "status quo"? As I have pointed out several times, no society is monolithic, nor can any single term, such as "capitalism," embrace its different dimensions: a democratic polity, with contending groups espousing different values and different claims to rights, a mixed economy, a welfare state, a pluralist diversity of social groups, a syncretistic culture, the rule of law. Nor is any of these directly dependent on the others. A democratic polity is not the product of a market economy but has independent roots in the legal systems and the tradition of rights and liberties of societies. Occupational structures change in consequence of technology, but not social relations. The expansions of civil rights—witness the inclusion of blacks in the political process

16. "At the root of Bell's ambiguity," writes Howard Brick, "there is an essential issue of method. 'Whenever you meet a contradiction,' Bell wrote as he paraphrased William James . . . 'you must make a distinction.' Indeed, *The End of Ideology* is full of 'analytical distinctions'—between the economic functions of labor unions and the political role of the labor movement, between cooperative politics rooted in rational economic 'interests' and disruptive politics rooted in irrational 'status' sentiments, between long term objective or 'crescive' change and the 'enacted' change that takes hold in 'unique moments' when 'political decision' and 'practical judgement' come to bear. All of these distinctions formalize the basic dualist structure of Bell's thought, the poles of skepticism and morality, interests and ideals, objective structures and subjective purpose" (p. 425).

in the past twenty-five years—was not dependent on economic class conflicts. The book did advocate "piecemeal" change in a social-democratic direction. If that is the "status quo," so be it.

Equally null is the argument that the book advocated technocratic guidance of society and, in the phrase of C. Wright Mills, made a "fetish of empiricism" out of sociology.[17] Both phrases are meaningless since a number of essays in the book (see particularly "Work and Its Discontents") deplore the rationalization of life, the thread of Max Weber's concerns, and more than half the essays (as Howard Brick again has noted) are devoted to detailed discussions of theories "not merely for the purpose of debunking them or revealing their misperceptions of empirical fact but also to show the necessary presuppositional role of theory in the observation of fact and in the formulation and resolution of 'problems' in social analysis."[18] And while I have always recognized the need for empirical grounds for social policy, there has always been as well the insistence on the primacy of principles and values—and the necessary play of politics—in the forumulation of policy.

The charge that the end of ideology means "an end to *moral* discourse and the beginning of consistent 'pragmatic discourse' in every sphere of political life," a charge leveled by the philosopher Henry D. Aiken, is particularly wide of the mark.[19] For example, he misconstrued my call for an "end of rhetoric" (see p. 406) to mean the end of eloquence, of moral judgment, of philosophical statements (such as "general welfare," "common good"), of political abstractions, of poetry (for "since

17. The further the distance in time, the greater the distortion and the more farfetched the generalization. A recent book by a young historian of science, Howard P. Segal, states (apropos of myself, Lipset, Shils, and Brzezinski): "They preferred that, wherever possible, decisions should not be made on the basis of political negotiation or popular voting but strictly on technical grounds. In effect, they wished to replace politics by *technology* [sic!]." *Technological Utopianism in American Culture* (Chicago: University of Chicago Press, 1985), p. 135.

18. In this book I wrote: "There is now more than ever some need for utopia, in the sense that men need—as they have always needed—some vision of their potential, some manner of fusing passion with intelligence . . . The ladder to the City of Heaven can no longer be a 'faith ladder,' but an empirical one; a utopia has to specify *where* one wants to go, *how* to get there, the costs of the enterprise, and some realization of, and justification for, the determination of *who* is to pay" (p. 405).

19. Aiken's "The Revolt Against Ideology" appeared in the April 1964 issue of *Commentary* and was followed by an exchange in October 1964. These are reprinted in the Waxman volume.

Plato, rationalists have been afraid of poetry''), of figurative language, and accused me of promoting a pessimistic *carpe diem* philosophy, ''which would render us helpless in the world struggle against the ideology of Communism.''

What is one to make of the bewildering pinwheel of accusations? I can only guess that Aiken identified the end of ideology with pragmatism, and pragmatism (in his own version) is opposed to political discourse and first principles. But all that this showed, as I pointed out in my reply, was a hopeless confusion between political *philosophy* and political *ideology*. It is a confusion that has not been restricted to Aiken alone.[20]

A very different turn was the sharp, bitter (and personal) attack by C. Wright Mills, who called *The End of Ideology* ''a celebration of apathy.'' In 1952, when *Partisan Review* ran a symposium under the rubric ''Our Country, Our Culture,'' Mills, with the habitually truculent posture of the outsider, wrote: ''Imagine 'the old PR' running the title 'Our Country' . . . You would have cringed.'' For Mills, this was not ''our'' country. In 1959 he went to Cuba, was charmed by Castro, and wrote the book *Listen Yankee*. In 1960 Mills went on the offensive, writing a famous ''Letter to the New Left'' (published in the English *New Left Review*) in which he declared that the ''end of ideology'' is ''historically outmoded,'' that the working class as an agency of change is ''historically outmoded,'' and that a new force, ''a possible immediate radical agency for change,'' was rising, the students and the intellectuals.

Since the battlefield of hegemony was the cold war of the intellectuals, Mills centered his attack on what he called ''the NATO intellectuals,'' Western counterparts of Soviet intellectuals, making a moral equivalence between the two, often to the discredit of the former. He ended his essay with a ringing

20. For two, I think disinterested, discussions of this issue, see Martin Seliger, *Ideology and Politics* (London: Allen and Unwin, 1976), pp. 87, 291–292; and Walter Carlnaes, *The Concept of Ideology and Political Analysis* (Westport: Greenwood Press, 1981), pp. 237–238. As the two point out, both Aiken and Joseph La Palombara, a writer who made a similar argument, equate ideology with political discourse and philosophy so that, on *semantic* grounds, there could not be an ''end of ideology.'' Yet both men ignored the empirical evidence for the decline of ideology presented in Rejai's volume, while Aiken simply evaded the questions I posed of specifying the costs of change (such as collectivization in the Soviet Union) made in the name of ideology.

cry, "Let the old women complain wisely about 'the end of ideology.' We are beginning to move again."[21]

It is difficult to derive a coherent argument from Mills's essay: it is written in a peculiar staccato style, punctuated by interior monologues, and contains repeated exhortations for "radical change"; but of *what* there is nary a word. In the classic ploy of sectarian rhetoric, one does not make an argument but "locates" the players (calling it the sociology of knowledge) and assumes that derision is sufficient. As intellectual substance it is worthless; as polemic it is highly effective. Mills had sensed a rising mood, and his essay became an ensign for the young New Left.[22]

The event that seemed to contradict the end-of-ideology thesis was the upsurge of radicalism in the mid-sixties and seventies. Its intensity, its anger, its rhetoric, its calls for radical change, all seemed to bespeak a new phase of ideology. Yet little or none of this radicalism spoke to economic issues or was even able (except when some later latched onto a heretical

21. This simplistic doctrine of "moral equivalence" is particularly meretricious, especially about the 1950s. In the Soviet Union, Stalin had renewed the crackdown on dissent and Andrei Zhdanov had reinstated the orthodoxy of "socialist realism," denouncing, for example, the great poet Anna Akhmatova, whose poems about Leningrad had helped to inspire the defense of the city, as "half nun–half whore." After the war, the Jewish artists Feffer and Michoels, who had organized the antifascist resistance, were executed, along with Bergelson, Markish, and other noted Jewish writers. And we know that Stalin was preparing a show trial of sixteen Jewish doctors from the Kremlin hospital, with plans for public executions, a new campaign of antisemitism, and mass deportation of Jews from major cities, a grisly plan aborted by Stalin's death in 1953.

Throughout Eastern Europe there were new purges and show trials. In Czechoslovakia, following the takeover of the country and the defenestration of Jan Masaryk in 1948, the Czech and Slovak party leaders, Rudolf Slansky and Vlada Clementis, along with a dozen others, "confessed" to being Zionist agents in league with R. H. Crossman and Koni Zilliacus, left-wing leaders of the British Labour Party, and were hanged. (The episodes are related in the book by Artur London, one of the survivors, and dramatized in the film of Costas Garvas, *L'aveu* [The Confession].) Similar trials were held in Hungary and Bulgaria, resulting in the execution of Laszlo Rajk and Nikola Petkov, the agrarian leader. The full history of those events still has not been told. This was an aspect of the cold war not discussed by Mills, nor by most of those in the New Left, even though many resigned from the communist parties after 1956.

22. Mills's "Letter" is reprinted in Waxman, pp. 126–140. I replied in *Encounter,* December 1960, under the title "From Vulgar Marxism to Vulgar Sociology"; reprinted in my book of essays, *The Winding Passage*. There is a critical account of Mills by Irving Louis Horowitz, *C. Wright Mills: An American Utopian* (Glencoe: The Free Press, 1983), who had been one of his literary executors. That book contains a discussion of my early friendship with Mills, whom I first published in *The New Leader* in 1942.

Marxism) to formulate a coherent political philosophy. It was moral and moralistic.

The radicalism of the sixties and seventies conjoined four diverse currents: the emergence of a youth culture flaunting a freer lifestyle, with sex and drugs; the dramatic rise of black-power movements, especially in the "five hot summers" that saw widespread burning and looting in a number of major cities in the United States; the spread of "liberation" movements and the rhetorical manifesto of a Third World that declared itself, self-consciously, in opposition to the West; and the Vietnam War, which, like the Algerian war against France, radicalized a large portion of the student population.

1. The inchoate youth culture in the fifties, symbolized by the Beats, who had dropped out of what they deplored as the dullness of American society. In principle, this was little different from recurrent and similiar bohemian and youth movements of the past hundred years—of Rimbaud's adolescent homosexual vagabondage with Verlaine and, at age twenty-two, seeking adventure in darkest Africa; or, a century or so later, Allen Ginsberg taking his troupe to Katmandu. The divergences, however, lay in two crucial facts: first, the extraordinary expansion in numbers of the youth cohort as a result of a postwar baby boom, a cohort conscious of its distinct identity; second, the extraordinary broadcast, through the mass media and the burgeoning music and record industry, of these tantalizing models and the avid embrace by so many more youths of this presumed liberation, the "democratization of Dionysus."

The flaunting of sex, at the center of the new rock-and-drug culture, was a conceit. It proclaimed itself in opposition to "bourgeois prudery," an attitude that had almost vanished fifty years before in the jazz age of their parents. What it was, in fact, was the acting out of the *liberal culture*, which had accepted these attitudes in literature and the imagination (and often behind closed doors) but could not condemn such views when they transgressed the boundaries of the imagination and became a defiant lifestyle. And it flourished, ironically, because the affluence of the society allowed these flower children to drop out and live off remittances sent by their parents.

2. The emergence of the black movement, too, was an instance not of repression but of the liberal polity. The Democratic administration of John F. Kennedy (after almost a decade of Republican rule) had promised reform but, as Tocqueville

had foretold more than a century before, once reform is underway, it invariably seems too slow to those who had long waited for change. The resentment could now be more openly expressed, for it was abetted by the guilt of white liberals for the years of injustice.

Much of this was exploited by the Black Panthers, a group of black nationalists in Oakland, California, who proclaimed a new ideology: that the oppressed were not the working class but the criminal, the junkie, the drifter—those whom Marx, in a classic passage in the *18th Brumaire,* had called "the lumpen proletariat" and who were now hailed as the historic agents of revolutionary change. Eldridge Cleaver, a prisoner convicted of rape, put forth these ideas in an eloquent book, *Soul on Ice* (largely ghost-written by his white female lawyer, a sometime lover), which became a bestseller. And the Black Panthers achieved national publicity in a dramatic photo of their leader, Huey Newton, sitting in a wicker chair holding a rifle in his hand, as an African chief may have once held a spear.[23]

The Black Panthers, given their revolutionary ideology, found themselves increasingly torn, as is true of any movement which has to live "in the world," between making every more extreme pronouncements and demands or of coming to terms with the system. In the end, the Panthers collapsed. Cleaver fled abroad, was feted in Cuba and Algeria, but returned home years later, claiming disillusionment and reemerging as a born-again Christian and a supporter of Ronald Reagan.

The more serious side of the black movement did begin the slow climb into the political system and reaped some political gains: a civil-rights law, affirmative action, and considerable electoral success, so that in the 1980s there were black mayors in Los Angeles, Chicago, Detroit, Philadelphia, Atlanta, Newark, and hundreds of other small towns and cities, though large pockets of poverty still remained. But in the sixties and seventies, the turbulence generated by the blacks fed into the wider tumult of the times.

3. If there was a striking new word in those two decades—a word that derived from the movements of the Third World—

23. The irony—again, for irony is the hallmark of this period—is that Newton and Cleaver were both employed on a U.S. government community agency project while fashioning their ideas and spreading their propaganda. Stalin had to rob banks to gain funds for the revolution, but he lived under a reactionary tsar; Newton and Cleaver were more fortunate in living under advanced capitalism. White liberals on Park Avenue rushed to throw fundraising parties for the Panthers, a phenomenon savaged in Tom Wolfe's memorable essay "Radical Chic."

it was "liberation." Liberation had two connotations, one psychological, the other political. The psychological aspect was most vividly dramatized in the work of a French-educated, black North African psychiatrist, Frantz Fanon, who in *The Wretched of the Earth* argued that blacks could gain emancipation from the heritage of colonial oppression only by a cleansing act of violence, even if this violence was directed against the innocent descendents of the old oppressors. What was unique in Fanon's thinking was not his justification of violence, though this received the most notice, but his subtle and original diagnosis of *humiliation* as the source of radicalism. Eighty years before, Nietzsche had stressed the idea of *ressentiment* as the source of lower-class motivation and morality, but *ressentiment* in Nietzsche's and (Scheler's) sense was based on envy and the desire to strike out against one's superiors. Fanon's work provided a much more acute sense of the impulses of affirmation that lay behind the anger of those who had been living under colonial rule. His book, introduced by Jean-Paul Sartre, had a profound influence on French intellectuals—especially as France found itself, after Indo-China, engaged in a "dirty war" in Algeria—and, or course, on black intellectuals everywhere.[24]

More dramatic was the electrifying triumph of Fidel Castro and Ché Guevara, men just thirty years old, who reignited the flame of revolution at the time when Marxists had decided that revolution was a foregone impossibility in Western industrialized societies. The idea—the word—*revolution* had been a magic talisman for intellectuals since 1789. The unanticipated victory of Lenin and Trotsky in October 1917, seizing power at the head of a small disciplined party, had fed the fantasies of café intellectuals before World War II, longing for similar theatrical roles. The spectacle of a small band of guerrillas, from a base in the Sierra Maestra mountains, toppling an army-based regime, thrilled young radicals, and as Ché then carried the torch of revolution first to Africa and then to Bolivia, thousands of youths in New York, London, and Paris placed his picture like an icon on their walls, sporting berets and beards

24. Irony, again. Fanon was struck by cancer, asked for American help, and was brought to the U.S. by CIA agents who had been courting him; he died in an American hospital.

as they strode the streets in defiance of the local bourgeosie to denounce United States imperialism.[25]

The emergence of the Third World, and the spread of national liberation movements—a set of events no one had predicted before World War II—provided a new set of actors on the stage of world history. Nkrumah, Sukarno, Nehru, and Zhou En Lai seemed to be the major figures in a new phase of world politics. And behind all this was the looming presence of Communist China, of the holy presence of Mao, and, in the Cultural Revolution, a new transformation of man in which purity, selflessness, and moral incentives all seemed to prove that Utopia could be a reality. If Marx was wrong in believing that socialism would arise as an historic necessity out of capitalist forms of production, History could take a leap of faith when propelled by those who remained pure in heart, and when there was sufficient *will* fused with ideas—which is, after all, the "authentic" definition of ideology. So the new appeal was fashioned.

4. The Vietnam War posed three problems: the moral ambiguity of its purposes; the argument that, in opposing an indigenous people's movement seeking to end colonialism, the United States was like Canute, trying to hold back the tides of History; and the ideological displacement of the cold war against the Soviet Union onto the selfless idealism of a Ho Chi Minh.

The crucial fact, again was that it was a liberals' war. The escalation of forces in Vietnam was initiated by John F. Kennedy (on the advice of General Maxwell Taylor and the national security adviser, McGeorge Bundy) and inflated by Lyndon Johnson at the very time, ironically, that he was expanding the Great Society programs in education, health, social security, and affirmative action. The Kennedy administration had stepped in after the French colonial forces had left and the reactionary emperor Bao Dai had been replaced by Ngo Dinh Diem, an ascetic Catholic from the north. But the idea of democratic forces opposing communism could never be made convincing against the "people's" myth of the Vietcong, while the bomb-

25. The prosaic facts were otherwise. The United States, at the close of World War II, had opposed colonialism, and Roosevelt, at Yalta and after, had pressured the English, the French, and the Dutch (who had ruled Indonesia) to dismember their empires. Even in Cuba it was not the strength of Castro but actions of the United States that had led directly to the fall of Batista (by denying arms he sought), a set of circumstances swept under the historical rug by both Castro and the United States, as embarrassing to both.

ing and use of napalm, seen nightly on television, made the war increasingly abhorrent to the public.

The leaders of the protest were the students, especially when conscription made them liable for military service, though in fact the deferment of those still in school meant that working-class and black youth made up the bulk of the troops under fire.[26] Student radicalism exploded in the *événements* of 1968: at Berkeley, at Columbia, and, in the contagion of defiance, at the Sorbonne and other European universities. If one looks for some interrelated structural elements underlying these student explosions, one can perhaps identify three factors. One was the "bunching" of the cohort. From 1940 to 1950, the youth cohort, as a proportion of the population, had been stable; from 1950 to 1960, it was stable; from 1960 to 1968, as a result of the postwar baby boom, it increased 54 percent in eight years.[27] The second element was the sense of an "organizational harness" that seemed to loom as the future of this generation. The size of the cohort increased the competition (and frustration) to get into good colleges, increased the pressures to get into graduate school and professional schools (in the Ivy League colleges at that time, more than 90 percent of each graduating class planned to continue in school, a career purpose reinforced by the fear of conscription), and heightened the competition and pressure to push through the narrow funnels of school admissions. And third, if one seeks an idealistic cause, there was a rejection of "white-skin privileges" and an identification with the Third World and the idea of liberation.

26. The administration, in order to reduce opposition, initiated a system of rotation so that no individual served longer than eighteen months in Vietnam. The effect, however, was to widen the pool of eligible persons who could be called up and to diminish the motivations of those in Vietnam as they neared the end of their tour of duty. Not only did the soldiers in Vietnam take enormous advantage of the drugs cheaply available from the opium-growing areas nearby, but for the first time in U.S. military history, there were incidents of "fragging," wherein soldiers forced to move under fire threw grenades that killed their own officers. One can take the instance of rotation as one more illustration of the sociological theorem of unintended consequences and of the sociological dilemmas for officers in an unpopular war.

27. No one knows what percentage of the students were radicals or how many were activitsts. But to focus on numbers alone misses the essential sociological point about the nature of cadre strength. It may be, as some have argued, that the percentage of student radicals did not greatly exceed that of the 1930—say 10 percent: but in a school with a thousand students, 10 percent numbers a hundred; in a school with ten thousand students, 10 percent numbers a thousand. Though the percentages are the same, a thousand becomes a more effective striking force within their cohort than a hundred within theirs. The change in scale is the key variable in understanding some of the activity of student radicalism, in addition to the more improved modes of communication (walkie-talkies) and the television publicity that becomes a thread of contagion.

The excitement and the frenzy, especially amid the obsessive attention of the media, and the impassioned nostalgia of old intellectuals reliving their youth (at Columbia, Norman Mailer threw a large fundraising party; Dwight Macdonald wrote a "begging" letter to his friends for money to support the SDS), made the participants feel that the world had shrunk to the circle of their delusions. Tom Hayden, who had entered one of the occupied buildings at Columbia, wrote an article in *Ramparts* entitled "Two, Three, Many Columbias," a self-conscious echo of a famous article by Guevera, calling for guerrilla action in Latin America and entitled "Two, Three, Many Vietnams."[28]

Eruptive fantasies of revolution lead, as Karl Mannheim wrote about earlier chiliastic movements, to the fantasy that the world can be transformed in a flash, that *die Tat,* the deed—a shooting, a bombing, a general strike—would turn the world upside down and usher in the new day. Yet any such romantic spasm could only pass, leaving the next, gray day of reality to be faced. A few would go on, as did the Weathermen, to a "day of rage" in Chicago, provoking the police to acts of violence, and to desperado tactics of bombing (though the explosion of a bomb factory in Greenwich Village killed a number of young Weathermen) or living in the underground for years, waiting for the revolutionary movement to arrive—again, a *parousia* promised by their eschatology. Living on the thin gruel of revolutionary rhetoric, the student movement (unlike the blacks) could not transform its inchoate ideology into a tangible program and was fated to sputter out.[29]

28. In the curious apocalyptic language that merges the posturing catechism of Nechayev with the practical instruction of Régis Debray, Hayden wrote: "Columbia opened a new tactical stage in the resistance movement . . . from overnnight occupation of buildings to permanent occupation; from mill-ins to the creation of revolutionhary committees; ffrom symbolic civil disobedience to barricades resistance. Not only arre these tactics being duplicated on other campuses, but they are sure to be surpassed by even more militant tactics . . . Many of the tactics learned can also be applied in smaller hit-and-run operations between strikes: raids on offices of professors doing weapons research could win substantial support among students while making the university more blatantly repressive."

29. As I wrote in 1969: "The SDS will be destroyed by its style. It lives on turbulence, but is incapable of transforming its chaotic impulses into the systematic responsible behavior that is necessary to effect broad societal change. In fact, its very style denies the desirability of such conduct, for like many chiliastic sects its ideological antinomianism carries over into a similar psychologiccal temper, or rather distemper. It is impelled not to innovation, but to destruction." From "Columbia and the New Left," *The Public Interest,* Fall 1968, reprinted in Daniel Bell and Irving Kristol, *Confrontations: The Universities* (New York: Basic Books, 1969), p. 106.

Did the upsurge of radicalism in the 1960s "disprove" the thesis of the end of ideology? I think not.[30] What one saw in the West was not a political but a cultural (and generational) phenomenon. If there was a single, symbolic pronunciamento that defined this phenomenon, it was the famous poster plastered onto the bolted door of the Sorbonne in May 1968, which declared: "The revolution that is beginning will call into question not only capitalist society but industrial society. The consumer society must perish a violent death. The society of alienation must disappear from history. We are inventing a new and original world—*Imagination au Pouvoir*."[31]

It was a utopian dream. But from a dream one awakens, or one continues into a nightmare. In all this turbulence there were no new socialist ideas, no ideologies, no programs. What one saw was an outburst of romantic yearning that restated the Arcadian visions of earlier generations. It was a reaction against rationality, against authority and hierarchy, and even against culture. There were real issues: the rationalization of life that Max Weber had deplored more than a half century before; the privileges of old elites (including university professors) who had not earned their authority; and the spread of a spurious and manufactured culture, the mass culture of the day, of which, ironically, the rock and heavy-metal music itself was an integral part.

30. As Aron has written, reflecting on these debates: "No one has refuted the diagnosis—that there is no ideological system extant to replace Marxist-Leninism if and when it dies out. What events have contradicted is the apparent if not explicit confusion among doctrinal systematization of ideology, fanaticism and chiliasm. At the same time, themes of social protest forgotten during the cold war or overshadowed by the economic success of the West have acquired new currency. Thus, the weakening of the last great ideological system did not promote a pragmatic approach to politics but, quite to the contrary, encouraged wide-spread social protest." Raymond Aron, "On the Proper Use of Ideologies," in *Culture and Its Creators,* Joseph Ben-David and Terry Nichols Clark, eds. (Chicago: University of Chicago Press, 1977), p. 3

31. One is reminded of the sardonic scene in Flaubert's *L'education sentimentale,* at the Club de l'Intelligence, whose chairman is the incorruptible pedagogue Senecal, during the revolution of 1848:

"It was the custom for figures of that period to model themselves after a pattern—some imitating Saint-Just, others Danton, others Marat. Senecal tried to resemble Blanqui, who was a follower of Robespierre . . . the air was thick with revolutionary proposals . . .

'Down with academics. Down with the Institute!'

'No more missions!'

'No more matriculations!'

'Down with university degrees!'

'No,' said Senecal, 'let us preserve them; but let them be conferred, by universal franchise, by the people, the only true judge.' "

But all this was a reaction, as I indicated, against the organizational harnesses that societies were imposing on individuals entering into the new bureaucracies of the world. With some hyperbole, yet with some truth, I described these as the first "class struggles" of postindustrial society, just as the Luddite machine breakers had reacted a hundred and fifty years earlier to the factory discipline of the first industrial revolution.[32] Yet without any hard-headed sociological analysis and understanding, it could, again, only errupt as a romantic protest.

What was left after the events of '68 was a generation in search of an ideology. As the philosopher Charles Frankel once observed: it is not that Marxism creates radicals; each new generation of radicals creates its own Marx. In this instance, the generation that began to find (tenured) places in the university, in publishing, in the media, discovered its ideology in a heretical Marxism: in the critical theory of the Frankfurt School, in the rediscovered writings of Georg Lukács, in the opening of the seals of Antonio Gramsci. What is striking about the use of all these writers (different as they are from each other) is the plane of criticism was *cultural* (the self-enclosed world of the intelligentsia) and not economic or programmatic. There were no positive proposals; the socialist ideal had become a ghost. And, equally true, none of those writers—and few of the acolytes who read them—openly confronted the nature of Stalinism or the tragic paradoxes posed by Niebuhr about the corruption of idealism in the use of total power to transform society and man—the corruption that reddened Cambodia in 1975 during the reign of the incorruptible Pol Pot.

* * *

Let me turn briefly to some other intellectual and political issues that are still relevant today. In the twenty-five years since this book was published, the concept of ideology has unraveled completely. What is not considered an ideology today? Ideas, ideals, beliefs, creeds, passions, values, *Weltanschauungen*,

32. The *first* (and most violent) student uprisings of the 1960s were in Japan, where the Zengakuren shut down the universities and fought violent battles with the police. But then the graduating students went quietly into the corporations, and only a tiny minority resorted to terrorism in the actions of the Red Army faction. In the United States, a decade later (behold Jerry Rubin), the change was from Yippies to Yuppies.

religions, political philosophies, moral systems, linguistic discourses—all have been pressed into service. One hears about "communism and capitalism as competing ideologies" and "the failure of the United States [before Reagan] to develop an ideology." In an essay in *Partisan Review*, ideology is defined as "fantasy cast in the form of assertion," a loose and associative form of thought "sharing qualities with pornography." A front-page essay in the *Times Literary Supplement* on pre-Christian religious thought talks of the effects of "hostile ideologies (i.e. early Epicureanism) on Christian apologists." And a book on military strategy is entitled *The Ideology of the Offensive: Military Decision Making and the Disaster of 1914*.[33]

And then there is the clotted verbiage of Marxian scholaticism. A book on "social representation in the cinema" defines ideology as that which "reproduces the existing relations of production." Ideology "uses the fabrication of images . . . to persuade us how things are, how they ought to be, and that the place provided for us is the place we ought to have. Such a definition stresses the interconnection of base and superstructure or of social existence and consciousness." Yet the Marxist historian George Rudé writes a book, *Ideology and Popular Protest*, which defines ideology "as the full range of ideas or beliefs that underlie social and political action, whether of old-style rulers, 'rising' bourgeois or of 'inferior' social groups."[34]

There is a singular reason for these contradictory usages. As is true with almost all his sociological concepts, Marx rarely clarified his terms or kept to a consistent usage. If one reads through his work, one finds a stupefying set of confusions and substitutions between the words *ideas, ideology, consciousness*, and *superstructure*—and in the latter instance we often do not know when *superstructure* applies to institutions or ideas. At times in *The German Ideology* the use of "ideological super-

33. What is striking is that certain words, by their lexical fluency, quickly achieve a linguistic universality, so one finds, with minor orthographic variation, the words *ideology, idéologie, Ideologie, ideologia* permeating virtually all European languages. Can one imagine what would have been the fate of the idea if Marx had used the term *ideationalism* as the counterpart to material practice? For a recent effort to establish some typologies for these diverse usages, see the papers of Dearthé, Bachelar, and von Leyden, at the colloquium in Florence of the European University Institute, *Ideology and Politics*, edited by Maurice Cranston and Peter Mair, published in 1980 by four publishers: Sijthoff (Alphen aan den Rijn), Klett-Cotta (Stuttgart), Bruylant (Brussels), and Le Monnier (Florence).

34. See Bill Nichols, *Ideology and the Image* (Bloomington: University of Indiana Press, 1981), p. 1, and George Rudé, *Ideology and Popular Protest* (New York: Pantheon Books, 1980), pp. 7–9.

structure'' suggests all forms of social consciousness that are determined by or vary from material practice. In another instance (*the 18th brumaire*), Marx uses the term superstructure to refer to the ''distinct and perculiarly formed sentiments, illusions, modes of thought and views of life *which the entire class* creates and forms . . . out of its material foundations.'' In the 1859 preface to the *Critique of Political Economy*, the *fons et origo* of all subsequent discussion of Marx's formulation, he writes about ''the economic *structure* of society—the real foundation, on which rise legal and political *superstructures* and to which *correspond* definite forms of social consciousness'' (emphasis added). But then are there two sets of parallel relations: the relation of structure to structure and of material practices to ideological ideas? And what of the relation of structure to ideas, and how does this come about; how does the material base or social location determine or shape the ideas? On these questions of ''micro'' social processes, Marx—and Marxists—have never given an answer.[35]

How does one make one's way through this bramble bush? Are there any boundaries that one can establish? One strategy has been to enlarge the term so as to include any and all beliefs that impose some obligations upon their adherents. Thus the philosopher Patrick Corbett writes:

> By ''ideology,'' therefore, is meant here any intellectual structure consisting of a set of beliefs about man's nature and the world in which he lives; a claim that the two sets are interdependent; and a demand that those beliefs should be professed . . . by anyone who is to be considered as a full member of a certain social group . . . On this usage, Ghandism, Catholicism, Leninism, Nazism, American Democracy, and the Divine Right of Kings are, or were ideologies; and so on a similar scale, are the myths of English Public Schools or Amazonian tribes. The Theory of Relativity is not, since it has no implications for conduct.[36]

But since almost all beliefs, from vegetarianism to monasticism, entail some consequences for conduct—in fact any creed to which the suffix *ism* can be added—a definition this broad simply blurs all distinctions. And even on the theory of relativity, Corbett was wrong, for to orthodox Leninists, relativity

35. See Jorge Larrain, *Marxism and Ideology* (London: Macmillan, 1983), especially pp. 170–171.

36. Patrick Corbett, *Ideology* (London: Hutcheson, 1965), p. 12.

theory (and quantum mechanics) contradicted the simply copy theory of knowledge and the strict determinism of Lenin's *Materialism and Empirio-Criticism*, and so constituted an "idealist cosmology"; thus for several decades, these theories were denounced as "bourgeois physics" and could not be taught openly in the physics curriculum in the Soviet Union.

In the efforts to stipulate a generic or formal definition, one forgets that the concept of ideology is an *historical* term to be understood contextually, to see how it emerged and how it has been used. As Reinhard Bendix has written:

> the term [ideology] is not properly applicable to Western civilization prior to the seventeenth or eighteenth centuries, somehow in the way that terms like "economy" or "society" or "intellectuals" do not fit the "premodern" period either. All these terms are applicable to the ways in which men think abouut their society. The shift is one of cultural patterns and intellectual perspective although relations between these levels are important also.[37]

In the perspective of culture, ideology is one of the dimensions of modernity. In the past several hundred years, the Western world has witnessed an extraordinary seachange in consciousness. Modernity, that great galvanizing force, is more than the emergence of science, the explosion of technology, the idea of Revolution, the entry of masses of people into society—though it is all of these. Modernity is the inchoate Promothean aspiration, now made flesh, of men to transform nature and transform themselves: to make man the master of change and the redesigner of the world to conscious plan and purpose.

In the Marxian and Mannheimian tradition, ideology is an epiphenomenon, the symbolic expression of economic interests, the fusion of class and politics. In the broader argument I have sought to elaborate, ideology is the interplay of culture and politics. In the great crossover that took place in the eighteenth century, ideology emerged with the breakup of chiliastic religious movements as a political force. The play of politics in *religious* terms that one saw in aspects of the wars of religion or the English Puritan revolution now became the *political* expression of eschatological creeds ("religions of virtue" and

37. Reinhard Bendix, "The Age of Ideology: Persistent and Changing," in David Apter, ed., *Ideology and Discontent* (Glencoe: The Free Press, 1964), p. 295.

"religions of humanity") played out in secular terms[38] Ideology, then, as I have used the term, deals with social movements that seek to mobilize men for the realization of such beliefs, and in this fusion of political formulas and passions, ideology provides a faith and a set of moral certitudes—in the case of Marxism, the view that History will judge—by which ends are used to justify immoral means. The disillusion of individuals with such movements results in the dissipation of ideology among the adherents; or, when such movements are in power, ideology becomes a coercive force used by the rulers to maintain conformity.

In respect to political consequences, *The End of Ideology*, secondly, has some resonance today because we are in a new cycle of disillusionment in the communist world. There were the Moscow trials and the Nazi-Soviet pact in the late thirties; the Khrushchev revelations and the Hungarian uprising in 1956; the Prague spring of 1968 and the smashing by the Brezhnev regime of Dubcek's effort to propose a "socialism with a human face." There is one startling difference in the present situation. The previous disillusionments were moral, intellectual, and political. The admitted failures this times are primarily *economic*.

Whatever the previous disenchantments, the overriding argument for the superiority of socialism was that the anarchy of the market is replaced by conscious social organization. As Engels wrote in *Socialism: Utopian and Scientific*: "The laws of society come under man's control, and men, for the first time, can make their own history." The justification for Stalin's forced industrialization and brutal collectivism in agriculture was that the Soviet Union could make the leap from a backward nation to a modern state only through the mechanisms of central planning and the primacy of heavy industry as the basis for

38. The theme of crossover, and the alternative responses to the breakup of religious beliefs in the eighteenth and nineteenth centuries, is taken up in my Hobhouse lecture (1977), "The Return of the Sacred?" and reprinted in *The Winding Passage*. The English edition (Heinemann Educational Books) is called, simply, *Sociological Essays and Journeys, 1960–1980*.

In this view of ideology, I would demur, too, from the influential formulation of Clifford Geertz. While Geertz is right, I believe, in emphasizing the primary cultural and symbolic nature of ideology, rather than seeing it as a reflection of social structure, he expands the term to encompass any set of world views that provide orientations and meanings for its adherents, but in doing so neglects the specific *political* dimension that has given ideology its emotional and mobilizing force. See Clifford Geertz, "Ideology as a Cultural System," in *The Interpretation of Cultures* (New York: Basic Books, 1973), chap. 8.

later differentiation of production and the expansion of consumption. After World War II, with the emergence of the Third World, the Soviet model was touted as the only workable model for "underdeveloped countries," whose economic expansion was being held back by unequal exchange and dependency on the capitalist societies.[39] But Deng Xiaoping and Mikhail Gorbachev have conceded that central planning has become cumbersome and inflexible, and that the economies of both countries have begun to stagnate. At the same time, the extraordinary economic successes of Japan, South Korea, the smaller East Asian countries, as well as Brazil, within a shorter period of time than in the Soviet Union, have provided a very different mixed market-state economic model for Third World countries.

In historical retrospect, it is quite clear that Soviet industrialization proceeded by the vast transfer of labor out of the country into the city and by the focus on a few primary targets—similar to what any country creating a war economy could do. But while *production* increased, productivity was always low and there were huge waste and inefficiencies in the industrial sector, as well as great deficiencies in housing, infrastructure, and consumption in the other sectors. But once a large industrial base had been created, the lack of capital accounting (say an interest rate to measure the costs of capital) and the rigid control of wages and prices, whereby Gosplan dictated the production quotas and "markups" of several hundred thousand products, added up to an inflexible system and a stagnant economy. What Gorbachev seems to be saying is that there is a contradiction between the social relations of production (the bureaucracy) and the forces of production.[40]

39. As Horowitz wrote, in the preface to a posthumous collection of the essays of Mills, the obsolescence of liberalism and conservatism mean that it is in the socialist countries that one will have to look for new roads. "It is now in the Soviet Union, China, Poland and Cuba that differential pluralistic responses to problems of social development are presented and fought out." I. L. Horowitz, ed., *Power, Politics and People: The Collected Essays of C. Wright Mills* (New York, Oxford University Press, 1963), p. 13. Horowitz subsequently changed his mind and became a fierce critic of those regimes.

40. Much of this was laid out in a remarkable document during the Brezhnev period, the Novosibirsk Report, prepared (one is told) under the direction of Abel Aganbegian and Tatiana Zaslavskaya, who are now advisers to Gorbachev. See *Survey* (London) 28.1 (1984). Probably the best and most sober analysis of the problems encountered by a socialist economy in adapting to market processes is the essay by Janòs Kornai, "The Hungarian Reform Process: Visions, Hopes and Reality," *Journal of Economic Literature,* 24 (December 1986), pp. 1687–1737.

In China, Mao Zedong's efforts to involve millions of persons in a great leap forward, by producing steel and machine tools in the small hearths and backyards of the communes, resulted in a disaster that led Mao's opponents to seek to push him aside. And this led, in turn, to the riposte of the Cultural Revolution and the even greater disaster, the destruction of intellectual institutions and the loss of an educated generation—apart from the purges and humiliations of hundreds of thousands of individuals—in the spasm of leveling that went on in China, applauded by so many European and American innocents, until the downfall of the Gang of Four.

In China and the Soviet Union, the new policies seek to provide material incentives geared to output, the introduction of market mechanisms, a large leeway for enterprise managers to make their own production and pricing decisions, and a degree of competition to weed out the inefficient firms even at the cost of bankrupticies and unemployment. What, then, is the economic meaning of "socialism"? In the 1920s, the journalist Lincoln Steffens returned from the Soviet Union and fashioned a phrase that for decades became the banner for all progressive-minded persons: "I have seen the future and it works." As a character in the satirical novel *Mother Russia* by Robert Littell (1978) remarks about Soviet life: "I have seen the future, and it needs work."

On the political level, the situation in Eastern Europe presents a mirthless paradox that completes the ideological reinversion of Marxism. On his road to discovering the materialist foundations of society, Marx had sought to show that Hegel's views of political life were "illusions" derived from a false relation between ideology and reality. In his *Critique of Hegel's Philosophy of Right* and *On the Jewish Question*, Marx argued that Hegel had inverted the relation of State to civil society by postulating a false autonomy to the former. And Engels, picking up that theme in his monograph on *Feuerbach and the Outcome of German Classical Philosophy* (1888), wrote: "The State presents itself to us as the first ideological power over mankind," for though it was created by society to safeguard the general interest, it "makes itself independent in regard to society; and indeed, the more so, the more it becomes the organ of a particular class, the more it directly enforces the supremacy of that class." This statement could be—it is—an adequate formulation of the relation of state to society in Poland, that is, of the regime to the working class; and, in the Soviet Union of the *nomenklatura,* the "new class" of privilege, to the remainder of the society.[41]

The ideology of Marsixm is the belief in the inevitable polarization in advanced Western society between capitalist and worker and the victory of the proletariat as the necessary outcome of the cunning of reason. This is the "philosophy of history" that replaced the Augustinian *parousia* as the faith system that prophesied the "leap from the kingdom of necessity into the kingdom of freedom."[42] Does anyone still believe those illusions?

But a different intellectual and theoretical issue is at stake. The fundamental theorem of Marxian sociology is that, *au fond,* all social structure is class structure, and class is the relevant unit of politics, even for the analysis of culture. What is striking in almost all societies, particularly in the West, is not only the rapid shrinking of the industrial working class but the breakup of economic class as the fundamental axis of social division. Every society (with the exception of Japan) is a "plural society" with large admixtures of minorities. And apart from the multiple identities of gender, age, religion, education, and occupation, ethnic identities seem to become more and more salient as a group attachment, and conflicts between groups on ethnic, linguistic, or religious lines seem to be the source of cultural/political identifications. Yet in the *Communist Manifesto,* Marx had written: "National differences and antagonisms between people are already tending to disappear more and more, owing to the development of the bourgeoisie, the growth of free trade and a world market, and the increasing uniformity of industrial processes and of the corresponding conditions of life. The rule of the proletariat will efface these differences and antagonisms even more."

Apart from the fact that there is less cooperation and solidarity within the international working class today than at any time in the past hundred years, what is striking is the rise of national tensions in almost every part of the world, as much in the communist world as anywhere else. How, on Marxist

41. Perhaps the neatest illustration of the situation in dystopia is the Polish story of General Jaruzelski going to Lenin in his tomb, in the dead of night, to plead for advice. "Comrade Lenin," he said, "we are facing a counterrevolution." "A counterrevolution?" Lenin replied: "Our answer is always clear: Arm the working class!"

42. The phrase occurs in Engels' *Anti-Dühring* (1877) where, citing the huge advances in wealth in the Western capitalist societies, he remarks that the possibilities of socialism are now *here* (emphasis in the original).

grounds, can one explain the rivalry between the Soviet Union and China; the smoldering war between China and Vietnam; the occupation of Cambodia by Vietnamese puppets; the armed wall between Albania and Yugoslavia; and the threatened breakup of Yugoslavia itself, as ancient antagonisms between Serb and Croat, Serb and Albanian, become visible? What is one to say of the large minority enclaves of Hungarian national groups in Rumania, of the Baltic peoples within the Soviet Union, of the Muslim nationalities in Central Asia whose demographic growth rates threaten to overwhelm the balance of nationalities within the Soviet Union?

As we approach the twenty-first century, the problems of color, of tribalism, of ethnic differences—in Southeast Asia, the Middle East, the fratricidal hatred in the Muslim world—all bespeak an agenda of issues that contemporary sociology, least of all Marxism, is ill prepared to understand. We see, particularly in Marxism, how much our sociological categories were framed within the context of Western society, and how the themes of the Enlightenment, rationality, industrialization, consciousness, class development, the idea of "historic nations" and social evolution, became our prisms of understanding. And how irrelevant Marx, and even Weber and Durkheim, may be. But that, too, is a long and different exploration.

There may be a third reason, twenty-five years later, for interest in this book. It was a product of the 1950s and deals with social changes of the postwar period. There is a tendency to think of that time as dull and sober, of little intellectual interest or excitement, as against the intensity of the 1930s and the depression period, and the fevered days and heady excitements (the liberation of eros, or at least its flaunting) in the 1960s. I disagree. If one thinks of the intellectual hallmarks of the time, it was not one of creativity but of rediscovery. It was a reading of Kierkegaard, the neo-orthodoxy and neo-Augustianian views of Karl Barth, Paul Tillich, and Reinhold Niebuhr. It was the discovery of Kafka, of the disordered and disoriented world that has bequeathed to the language the eponymous word "Kafkaesque." It was the reading of Simone Weil and her despair at not being able to find an adequate faith. It was a period in which the discussion of religion could again be taken seriously, as against the legacy of the "cultured despisers." It was an age of criticism and of great critics—Leavis and Empson, Ransom and Tate, Winters and Blackmur, Trilling and Wilson—and, as in the elucidation of the writer most discussed at the time, Henry James, it saw an emphasis on complexity, irony, ambiguity, and paradox. And it was a time of social criticism as well. As the radical historian Richard H. Pells wrote in *The Liberal Mind in a Conservative Age: American Intellectuals in the 1940s and 1950s,* reviewing the work of Hannah Arendt, David Riesman, William H. Whyte, John Kenneth Galbraith, Paul Goodman, Louis Hartz, Daniel Boorstin, Dwight Macdonald, C. Wright Mills, and myself:

> I also admire enormously much of what they said. I consider them neither complacent nor mean-spirited defenders of the status quo. On the contrary, because of their hostility to and liberation from the ideological dogmas of the prewar Left, their preference for asking questions instead of inventing answers, and their desire to act as free-floating intellectuals, rather than as spokesmen for a mass movement, I think they offered more provocative and imaginative criticism of their society than one can find in the manifestoes of either the 1930s or the 1960s. Indeed I regard [their work] as superior in quality to any comparable collection of works produced in America during other periods in the twentieth century. Consequently, those of us who came afterward remain in their debt even as we try to transcend their perspective.[43]

Let me close on a more personal note. In the last decade or so, there has been a large and growing curiosity about that cultural phenomenon called "the New York intellectuals" and the worlds of their fathers and sons. This is the group of writers and critics associated with such magazines as *Partisan Review, politics, Commentary, The New Leader, Dissent* and identified, in the first generation, with such figures as Lionel Trilling, Sidney Hook, Philip Rahv, William Phillips, and their younger siblings such as Saul Bellow, Alfred Kazin, Clement Green-

43. New York: Harper and Row, 1985, p. x. I might call attention also to a book by Paul Attewell, *Radical Political Economy since the Sixties: A Sociology of Knowledge Analysis* (Rutgers University Press, 1984). Attewell, reviewing the scholarly achievements of his compeers, regrets the break in continuity between the generations: "It is very difficult for the younger generation of left-wing academics in America to come to terms with scholars like Daniel Bell and his collaborators. If history had taken a slightly different course, his generation would have constituted the leading group of left intellectuals of the post-World War II era, for they are among the most important intellectual remnants of the last great upsurge of American leftism. They experienced the political turmoil of the thirties and forties and emerged from it as a left intelligentsia whose knowledge of socialist intellectual history, along with the practical concerns of political organization, has yet to be equalled in this country," (p. 1). Attewell regrets that we "quit the socialist left" and announced the end of ideology, since he still feels some strength in radical political economy. Is there? That, too, is another debate.

berg, Harold Rosenberg, and Mary McCarthy.[44] There has been a spate of personal memoirs, accounts by participants in the events of the times, and a flood of books by academic historians and sociologists about the careers and writings of individual figures and of the time and place.

What is striking is how the conflicts in the coteries during their youth and the family quarrels among the *fratelli* become played out in later years against the larger canvas of the culture. I was a product of this milieu and a participant in these sandbox wars. My intellectual interests and concerns were formed in the alcoves of the City College of New York and my mind tempered in the cauldron of those intellectual debates. As my friend and quondam colleague Irving Kristol wrote about those early days: "Daniel Bell . . . was at the opposite pole from Irving [Howe]. He was that rarity of the 1930s, an honest-to-goodness social-democratic intellectual who believed in 'mixed economy,' a two-party system based on the British model, and other liberal heresies . . . Over the years, his political views have probably changed less than those of the rest of us, with the result that, whereas his former classmates used to criticize him from the Left, they now criticize him from all points of the ideological compass."[45]

In 1965 I was the cofounder with Kristol of *The Public Interest,* a journal that sought to transcend ideology through reasoned public debate and disinterested inquiry into public policy. Disinterested inquiry is always a difficult matter. As we wrote in the first issue: "It goes without saying that human thought and action is impossible without *some kinds* of preconceptions—philosophical, religious, moral or whatever—since it is these that establish the purposes of all thought and action. But it is the essential peculiarity of ideologies that they do not simply prescribe ends but also insistently propose prefabricated interpretations of existing social realities—interpretations that bitterly resist all sensible revisions."

Ten years later, I resigned from the magazine because our intellectual paths had diverged. Kristol had begun to believe that all modern politics is inescapably ideological because these views are competitions to control the shape of the future, and

44. I have laid out a "genealogy" of the family in "The 'Intelligensia' in American Society," *The Winding Passage,* pp. 127–129.

45. "Memoirs of a Trotskyist" in *Reflections of a Neoconservative* (New York: Basic Books, 1983), p. 9. I have discussed my differences with the neo-conservatives in my article "Our Country—1984," in the Fiftieth Anniversary issue of *Partisan Review,* 1984.

that the liberal culture is a frail reed against the compulsions of the utopian or eschatological claims which drive Western culture to the destruction of liberty. I disagree on both counts. I think that liberalism—the liberalism of an Isaiah Berlin—is sufficiently tough-minded to resist those illusions. And I think that all ideology is bound to self-destruct. Ideology is a reification, a frozen mimicry of reality, a hypostatization of terms that gives false life to categories. And that it also its fatal flaw, its Achilles heel, which leaves it vulnerable in the end to other forms of cognition and faith.

In our time, we have seen two contrasting ideological modes in the politics of the past two hundred years. One is the mode that mobilizes what William James called "the will to believe," the "passional and volitional" tendencies that drive men to go beyond logic in order to satisfy emotional needs. The breakdown of religious attachments, the turn to this-worldly concerns, the spur of modernity all gave impetus to the ascent up the faith ladders of secular utopias. The desiccation of the older ideologies, however, has now been followed by a "revolt against modernity," by the return of the repressed, the surging impulses of religious fundamentalisms which invoke both traditional symbols as well as accommodations to the wealth of the world or, as in Islam, a martyrdom in the next one. The fusion of passion and ideology, of blood and race, which we saw first in the "reactionary modernism" of the National Socialist regime, now reappears in the new spasms of rage throughout the world, as in the Iran of the Ayatollah Khomeni, and we see again the same blood-chilling slogans and practices that result when such atavisms and technology are fused in the new "triumphs of the will."[46]

The second mode is the ideology in power, the totalitarian regimes that compel conformity by emphasizing, through posters and slogans, the "little red book" or the "cult of personality," the hammered repetitions of quotations from the founders or the obligatory visit to the tomb of Lenin ("Lenin Lives"), the participatory obedience to the system. This is ideology as ritualized code and ritualized communication, the ideological caul that envelops people and makes the rest of the

46. See Jeffrey Herf, *Reactionary Modernism: Technology, Culture and Politics in Weimar and the Third Reich* (Cambridge: University Press, 1984). It is an instructive lesson in how technology and modernist aesthetics can be harnassed to reactionary causes. See also my essay "The Revolt Against Modernity," *The Public Interest,* Fall 1985.

world opaque. As Vaclav Havel, the Czech playwright and one of the inspirers of the great document of dissent, Charter 77, writes of the deceits of belief: the facade of ideology "offers human beings the illusion of an identity . . . and of morality while making it easier for them to *part* with them," to be stripped of an individual identity within the casing of the system.[47] Yet such ideology, because it is used for an uneasy legitimacy, breaks down as well. One reason is that, at first recourse, the easiest mode of conformity is terror. Yet terror, as in the rampant executions in Stalin's day or the diffuse hysteria of the Red Guards, has its limits. People seek for a normalization in their lives, even if it is the normalization of the dull conformity of a gray everyday life, and overt terror cannot be resorted to again once its legitimacy has been destroyed, as in the instance of the 1956 revelations of Stalin's paranoia.

There is also the fact, which ideological discourse (left and right) tends to obscure, that few movements are monolithic or can sustain such uniformity for long. There are, first, the structural rigidities that breed pressure for change: the increasing inability to operate a large, complex modern society from a narrow base of power, either for economic management or political direction, so that widening the arena of decision making, providing for some decentralization and individual initiatives, becomes necessary if a society is not to sag or stagnate.[48] Whether such needs can be translated into institutional change is, of course, the crucial question.

More intangible may be the psychological elements that play a role in the transformation of such societies. It may be that the humiliation Khrushchev felt at being forced to play the clown at Stalin's whim, as well as the recognition of the structural problems, led to his reform efforts. Or the humiliation of Deng Xiaoping, forced to be a pig farmer during the Cultural Revolution, may have been a motivating element in his revision of Mao Zedong's thought. Nor should one underestimate the elements of idealism that often linger in the minds and hearts of old Communists, even those in power, which led Nagy and

47. Vaclav Havel et al., *The Power of the Powerless* (London: Hutchinson, 1985). I am grateful to Alan Montefiore, in a review in *Government and Opposition* (London, Spring 1987), for bringing the book to my attention.

48. For an instructive account of such pressures and a prescient view of the paths that the Soviet Union might have to take, see Zbigniew Brzezinski, *Between Two Eras* (New York: Viking, 1970), pp. 164–172.

the intellectuals in Hungary of Dubcek in Czechoslovakia a dozen years later to seek for a socialism with a human face.[49] Communism produces not only conformity, but ex-Communists as well (see in this volume the section "Myth and Monolith").

Beyond all these may be the most powerful solvent of all: the inescapable and immutable need of men for a moral justification for their acts, moral justifications that in the end encounter the test of rival beliefs and of some transcendental standards. Perhaps the most malevolent and self-defeating theorem in Marxist thought is the moral relativism that girds the theory of historical materialism. As Engels wrote in 1877:

> We . . . reject every presumptuous attempt to impose upon us any dogmatic morality whatever as eternal, final, immutable ethical laws under the pretext that also the moral world has its permanent principles which stand above history and national differences. We maintain, on the contrary, that all past theories of morality are the product, in the last instance, of the contemporary economic conditions of society. And just as society hitherto has moved in class antagonisms, so has morality always been a class morality.[50]

In the name of a higher morality, the Bolsheviks lied and cheated and executed hundreds of thousands of persons. In

49. One of the most instructive books in this respect is the neglected and fascinating memoir, *Nightfrost in Prague,* by Zdenek Mylnar (New York: Karz Publishers, 1980). Mylnar, a Czech, was trained in law and philosophy in Moscow, and after World War II returned to become a high party official and the theoretician in the Central Committee. Over the years, in alliance with Dubcek, he began to argue that communism could not work not only because of its rigidities but because it was betraying its original idealism. Mylnar drafted the plans for the "democratization" of the party and accompanied Dubcek to Moscow when the Czech leaders were summoned there to answer Brezhnev's charges of heresy. Mylnar's book is not only an important account of the unfolding of Czech revisionist thought but also one of the few first-hand accounts of the way the Russian leaders sought to cajole or bully the Czechs and finally sent in the tanks to end the Prague Spring.

To return to the individuals cited at the beginning of this essay: Sartre supported the Soviet Union until 1956, when he veered off in a Maoist direction; toward the end of his life, drugged, blind, and under the influence of a former disciple, he spoke religious babble. Merleau-Ponty repudiated his defense of terror, but his death in 1961 cut short his work in philosophy and politics. Brecht remained in East Berlin and, after a workers' uprising in 1953, reportedly said, in his sardonic way: "The people have revolted against the government; the government must change the people." To the end of his life he retained an Austrian passport, and his royalties were paid to his West German publisher. Bloch, having achieved a professorship in Leipzig after the war (he had not held a major academic post in Germany before), reluctantly came back to the West in 1961. Lukács joined the Nagy government in 1956 and was arrested when the revolution was crushed by the Russians, but he refused to surrender his Hegelian belief in the cunning of history and remained in Hungary until his death in 1971.

50. *Anti-Dühring* (Chicago: Kerr, 1935), pp. 93–94.

denouncing bourgeois democracy as a sham, the Communists worked with the Nazis to destroy the Weimar Republic in the 1930s. Painfully, painfully, socialists learned during World War II and after that democracy and legal rights are an inviolable condition for a decent society and that liberty, necessarily, has to be prior even to socialism.

As for culture and religion, it may be that, in their origins, they derive from the material conditions of their times, but once created they take on lives of their own, with the power to continue, if they can reach the wellsprings of moral beliefs that are renewed over time. The continuity of culture is the rebuttal to any historicism, and the recurrent impulse to seek truth is the insistent beat that erodes the stones of total power. No political system can exist outside the context of moral justifications. But a moral order, if it is to exist without coercion or deceit, has to transcend the parochialisms of interests and tame the appetites of passions. And that is the defeat of ideology.

But all this now is only one chain of ideological thought, in that larger domain of what Nietzsche called *Ketten-Denken,* the fetters of the chain-thinkers.[51] Today in the widening gyre of passional discourse, the links entangle and ideology has come to designate almost any creed held with the will to believe, held with dogmatism or stridency—the ideologies of Black Power, the New Right, Feminism. The historicity of the term has lost its context, and only the pejorative and invidious penumbra, but no conceptual clarity, remains. Ideology has become an irretrievably fallen word. And so is sin.

51. Aphorism 376 in *Human, All Too Human:* "Chain-Thinker—One who, so full of thoughts, hails each new idea that he hears or reads, and places them within the form of his chain" (my free translation; I owe the initial reference to Melvin J. Lasky).

Acknowledgment

THE ACKNOWLEDGMENT OF OBLIGATIONS is a pleasure for the writer but often a burden for the reader: I shall try to balance my responsibilities.

These essays were collated and revised while I was a Fellow at the Center for Advanced Study in the Behavioral Sciences, in 1958-59. No individual can ask for finer work surroundings—fittingly called "The Leisure of the Theory Class"—and the stimulation provided by so many different scholars. My obligations to the Center are indeed great. I have a particular debt to Mrs. Ruth Ohlin, for research help, and to Mrs. Dorothy Brothers, for secretarial assistance. A friend, Miss Pearl Kazin, undertook the arduous task of checking proofs.

These essays were written during the years I was labor editor of *Fortune* magazine. Only two of the essays, however, the one on longshoremen, and the one on crime waves, are based on *Fortune* articles. I have not included my articles on labor, in part because they stand outside the concerns of the text, and in part because I want to rework these materials into a more unified book on the labor movement. (A list of the major *Fortune* labor articles appears on page 461.) I want to thank Ralph D. Paine, Jr., and Hedley Donovan, the successive managing editors, for their encouragement and for their respect for intellectual differences, which made working on *Fortune* a valuable experience.

A number of these essays appeared first in the pages of *Commentary* and *Encounter,* and my most enduring obligation is to Irving Kristol, who, as an editor of the two magazines, prompted these articles, and, as friend, wrestled to bring order out of them.

Three of the longer essays were first presented as papers from conferences sponsored by the Congress for Cultural Freedom, an international organization of intellectuals opposed to totalitarianism. I was fortunate in being able to work for a year in Paris, in 1956-57 (while on leave from *Fortune*), as director of international seminars for the Congress. I learned much in discussion with the seminars planning committee—Raymond Aron, C. A. R. Crosland, Michael Polanyi, and Edward Shils—and several of the essays, particularly on the themes of ideology, reflect these talks. With Melvin Lasky, an old comrade, and with Herbert Passin, there was the stimulus of exhilarating, and exhausting, conversation in Paris and Tokyo. And, in equating obligation with pleasure, I owe much to Michael Josselson, administrative secretary of the Congress, whose practical political wisdom was often ballast for intellectual fancies.

I have on another occasion expressed my regard for Sol Levitas and for the *New Leader,* which he has directed for thirty years.

My earliest writings were for the *New Leader* and, whatever political differences existed, it has always been an intellectual home. Some of the shorter essays here appeared first in its pages.

Conversations and intermittent discussion about the subjects of a number of these essays with Nathan Glazer, Richard Hofstadter, S. M. Lipset, Robert Merton, and Elaine Graham have profited me in the intangible ways that find expression in a phrase, an illustration, and an idea.

In a personal and intellectual sense, I owe most, however, to Sidney Hook, who taught me the appreciation of ideas. While never, formally, his student, I learned from him in the more valuable ways of working together in common enterprises and in the informal, albeit argumentative, exchange of ideas. I share most of his intellectual concerns while disagreeing with some of his passions; but above all I admire his courage, personal and intellectual, which is expressed in his refusal to shirk a fight, however unpopular the cause, or to abandon a friend. He is, as all who have heard him know, one of the great teachers of the generation.

The author and the publisher acknowledge, with thanks, the permission granted by publishers and copyright holders to reprint papers included in this volume.

Chapter 1 was read as a paper at the conference on "The Future of Freedom," sponsored by the Congress for Cultural Freedom at Milan, Italy, September, 1955, and appeared, slightly shortened, in *Commentary,* July, 1956.

Chapter 2 was part of the original paper presented at the Milan Conference, and appeared in its present form in *Partisan Review,* Spring, 1957.

Chapter 3 is a revised version of a paper first presented before the Columbia University Faculty Colloquium in Sociology, and was printed in the *American Journal of Sociology,* November, 1958. The present chapter includes some pages from my essay, "America's Un-Marxist Revolution," which appeared first in *Commentary,* March, 1949, and was reprinted in Bendix and Lipset (eds.), *Class, Status and Power* (Glencoe, Ill.: The Free Press, 1953).

Chapter 4 appeared in *Commentary,* March, 1953. (In shortening and revising it, I want to thank Professor Gören Ohlin, of the Economics Department of Columbia University, for his comments.)

Chapter 5 is an expanded version of a two-part essay that appeared in the *New Republic,* March 10 and March 17, 1958.

Chapter 6 appeared first in *Encounter,* January, 1956, and was reprinted as the first chapter of *The New American Right,* edited by Daniel Bell (New York: Criterion Books, 1955). The present version contains some sections from a discussion of American populism in my essay, "The Grass-Roots of American Jew Hatred," in the *Jewish Frontier,* June, 1944.

Chapter 7 appeared originally in the *Antioch Review,* Summer, 1953.

Chapter 8 is based on research for an article, "What Crime Wave?" in *Fortune,* January, 1955. (I am indebted to Professor Thorstein Sellin of the University of Pennsylvania and Professor Herbert Wechsler of Columbia University Law School for many suggestions.)

Chapter 9 is based on research for a *Fortune* project. Some of the data appeared in my article on the longshoremen in *Fortune,* June, 1951.

Chapter 10 was given as a paper for the seminar of Professor Georges Friedmann, at the L'École Pratique des Hautes Études of the Sorbonne. It appeared in the February, 1958, issue of *Encounter.*

Chapter 11 was originally published as a small hard-covered book by Beacon Press, November, 1956. The present version contains a few pages from my essay "Adjusting Men to Machines," *Commentary,* January, 1947.

Chapter 12 appeared first in the *Antioch Review,* March, 1952, and in somewhat abridged form as the introductory section of my monograph. "The Background and Development of Marxian Socialism in America," included in the compendium, *Socialism and American Life,* edited by Donald Egbert and Stow Persons (Princeton: Princeton University Press, 1952).

Chapter 13: Section A appeared in the *New Leader,* April 1, 1957, as part of its symposium on the younger generation. Section B appeared in the *Saturday Review of Literature,* March 21, 1955; Section C, in the *New Leader,* December 9, 1957; Section D in *Encounter,* September, 1959.

Chapter 14 was presented as a paper at the conference on "Changes in Soviet Society," held at Oxford, England, June, 1957, under the auspices of St. Antony's College, Oxford, and the Congress for Cultural Freedom. It appeared in *World Politics,* April, 1958.

Chapter 15 was presented as a paper before the international seminar on "Workers' Participation in Management," at Vienna, September, 1958, under the auspices of the Congress for Cultural Freedom. Sections of the paper have appeared in *World Politics,* July, 1959; *Dissent,* Summer, 1959; while an expanded version of the section on Alienation was read at the Christmas 1959 meetings of the American Philosophical Association, Eastern Division, and printed in the *Journal of Philosophy,* containing the papers of that meeting.

Notes

1. For a neutral discussion of the idea of "mass" in "mass media," see, e.g., Paul F. Lazarsfeld and Patricia Kendall, "The Communication Behavior of the Average American," in *Mass Communication,* ed. Wilbur Schramm (Urbana, Ill., 1949).

2. Herbert Blumer, "Collective Behavior," in *New Outlines of the Principles of Sociology,* ed. A. M. Lee (New York, 1936). For a further discussion, see Eliot Friedsen, "Research and the Concept of the Mass," *American Sociological Review,* June, 1953.

3. José Ortega y Gasset, *The Revolt of the Masses* (New York, 1932), pp. 18-19, 39.

4. Friedrich George Juenger, *The Failure of Technology* (Chicago, 1948).

5. Karl Mannheim, *Man and Society in an Age of Reconstruction* (London, 1940), pp. 53-67. Mannheim uses several other terms to round out his analysis. Modern society, he says, is based on "fundamental democratization," a term that is fuzzy, but close to Ortega's idea of "massification." Because of "fundamental democratization," i.e., the idea that culture should belong to all and that each man's opinion is as good as the next man's, the "creative elites," through whom culture is sustained, have no means of functioning.

6. Emil Lederer, *The State of the Masses* (New York, 1940), pp. 23-40.

7. Hannah Arendt, *The Origins of Totalitarianism* (New York, 1951), pp. 305, 341-42.

8. Gabriel Marcel, *Man against Mass Society* (Chicago, 1952), pp. 101-3.

9. Karl Jaspers, *Man in the Modern Age* (London, 1951), p. 65.

10. Ortega, *op. cit.,* p. 124.

11. This antithesis, associated with the German sociologist Tonnies, is central to almost every major modern social theory: Weber's traditional-rational behavior, Durkheim's mechanical-organic solidarity, Redfield's folk-urban society, and so on. Sometimes this distinction is presumed to be a historical one, describing societies in some undefined past as against the present; sometimes it is used as an ahistorical, analytic distinction, setting up two

ideal types in contrast with each other. The result, however, is confusion.

12. For a discussion of the roots of the idea of the "mindless masses" in Western social theory, see my essay, "Notes on Authoritarian and Democratic Leaders," in *Studies in Leadership,* ed. Alvin Gouldner (New York, 1950).

13. In a brilliant essay, "Daydreams and Nightmares: Reflections on the Criticism of Mass Culture" (*Sewanee Review,* LXV, 1957), Edward Shils points to the curious convergence of both conservative and neo-Marxist critics in their attacks on mass culture. In this respect, the radical has taken over uncritically the aristocratic view that the past was dominated by a high culture that is now being debauched. In fact, as Shils points out, the lives of most people were brutalized by long hours of work at arduous labor, while the entry of the "mass" into society has resulted in the extension of culture—of art, music, and literature—to a degree hitherto undreamed of. This argument is elaborated by Professor Shils in a paper prepared for the Tamiment Conference on Mass Culture, June, 1959, which appears in *Daedalus,* Spring 1960.

14. Karl Mannheim, *Ideology and Utopia* (New York, 1936), pp. 190-97.

15. August Comte, *Cours de philosophie positive* (2d ed.; Paris, 1864), Books IV-V.

16. T. R. Malthus, *An Essay on Population* (in the University of Chicago readings) Book III, Chapter II.

17. Philip Selznick, *The Organizational Weapon* (New York, 1952), pp. 275-308.

18. Joseph Schumpeter, *Capitalism, Socialism and Democracy* (New York, 1942), pp. 145-56.

19. As Morris Watnick has pointed out in a pioneering study (in the University of Chicago symposium *The Progress of Underdeveloped Areas*), the Communist parties of Asia are completely the handiwork of native intellectuals. The history of the Chinese Communist party from Li Ta-Chao and Ch'en Tu-hsu, its founders, to Mao Tse-tung and Liu Shao-Chi, its present leaders, "is virtually an unbroken record of a party controlled by intellectuals." This is equally true of India, "where in 1943, 86 of 139 [Communist] delegates were members of professional and intellectual groups." The same pattern also holds true "for the Communist parties of Indo-china, Thailand, Burma, Malaya and Indonesia, all of which show a heavy preponderance of journalists, lawyers and teachers among the top leadership."

20. Between 30 and 40 million of the 80 million U.S. joiners work at their voluntary jobs. In 1950, 2 million volunteer workers pounded sidewalks for the Community Chests (the fund-raising and disbursing bodies in each community for local hospitals and social service agencies) and raised $200 million. Other thousands raised over $100 million for the United Jewish Appeal, $67 million for the Red Cross, $30 million for the National Foundation for Infantile Paralysis, $20 million for the National Tuberculosis Association, $13,600,000 for the American Cancer Society—in all about a billion dollars a year for philanthropy. In 1950 there were 17,000 conventions—national, regional, or state, but not counting district or local—held in the U.S., attended by 10 million persons. In Atlantic City, famed seaside resort, 244,000 individuals went to 272 conventions ranging from the American Academy of Periodontology to the Telephone Pioneers of America. (Figures compiled by *Fortune* magazine research staff.)

21. Gunnar Myrdal, *An American Dilemma* (New York, 1944).

22. In December, 1954, for example, when the issue of Cyprus was first placed before the United Nations, the Justice for Cyprus Committee, "an organization of American citizens," according to its statement, took a full-page advertisement in the New York *Times* (December 15) to plead the right of that small island to self-determination. Among the groups listed in the Justice for Cyprus Committee were: The Order of Ahepa, the Daughters of Penelope, the Pan-Laconian Federation, the Cretan Federation, the Pan-Messinian Federation, the Pan-Icarian Federation, the Pan-Epirotic Federation of America, the Pan-Elian Federation of America, the Dodecanesian League of America, the Pan-Macedonian Association of America, the Pan-Samian Association, the Federation of Sterea Ellas, the Cyprus Federation of America, the Pan-Arcadian Federation, the GAPA, and the Federation of Hellenic Organizations. We can be sure that if, in a free world, the question of the territorial affiliation of Ruthenia were to come up before the United Nations, dozens of Hungarian, Rumanian, Ukrainian, Slovakian, and Czech "organizations of American citizens" would rush eagerly into print to plead the justice of the claims of their respective homelands to Ruthenia.

23. Morris Janowitz, *The Community Press, in an Urban Setting* (Glencoe, Ill., 1952), pp. 17-18. More recent research, particularly by British sociologists, has questioned the idea that the modern society inevitably tears down primary ties. As Peter Willmott put it succinctly: "Stereotypes die hard, even among sociologists. Ever since Tonnies and Durkheim proclaimed the decline of the family, the notion has persisted that in urban industrial societies it is rootless and atomized, confined to parents and dependent children, isolated from relatives. Only in recent years has

this impression been challenged—by field inquiries in London and other English cities, even in such unlikely places (one would have thought) as Detroit and San Francisco. These have suggested that the kindred may be an important source of companionship and support in the heart of the modern city" ("Kinship and Social Legislation," *British Journal of Sociology,* June, 1958, p. 126). The chief British studies are those by Michael Young and Willmott, in Bethnal Green, entitled *Family and Kinship in East London* (London, 1957), and the researches of the Institute of Community Studies, headed by Michael Young, particularly Peter Townsend, *The Family Life of Old People* (London, 1957). Among the American studies, cited by Willmott, are: *A Social Profile of Detroit: 1955* (Ann Arbor, 1956); Morris Axelrod, "Urban Structure and Social Participation," *American Journal of Sociology,* February, 1956; Wendell Bell and M. D. Boar, "Urban Neighborhoods and Informal Social Relations," *American Journal of Sociology,* January, 1957.

24. For a scholarly summary on American living standards, see William Fielding Ogburn, "Technology and the Standard of Living in the United States," *American Journal of Sociology,* January, 1955, pp. 380-86. Data on cultural participation can be found in F. B. Turek, "The American Explosion," *Scientific Monthly,* September, 1952.

25. Malcolm Cowley, in his essay on "Cheap Books for the Millions," points out that there were few book clubs in 1931, when a broad survey of the book publishing industry was made, while in 1953 there were seventy-four clubs that recommended books for adults. "The fear had been," he writes, "that the clubs would encourage a general uniformity of taste in the American public, and instead they were, to some extent, encouraging a diversity" (*The Literary Situation* [New York, 1955], p. 101).

26. Delmore Schwartz, "The Present State of Poetry," in *American Poetry at Mid-Century* (The Whittall Lectures, Library of Congress, 1958), p. 26.

27. See David Landes, "French Business and the Businessman: A Social and Cultural Analysis," in Edward Mead Earle (ed.), *Modern France* (Princeton, 1951).

28. Bernard Bailyn, *The New England Merchants in the Seventeenth Century* (Cambridge, Mass., 1955).

29. Robert K. Lamb, "The Entrepreneur and the Community," in William Miller (ed.), *Men in Business* (Cambridge, Mass., 1952). For a somewhat different view from that developed in this essay, one which sees the fusion of family and enterprise under capitalism as a special case, see Talcott Parsons and Neal Smelser, *Economy and Society* (London, 1956), pp. 285-90.

30. V. I. Pareto, *The Mind and Society* (New York, 1935). The numbering follows the notation system used by Pareto for his paragraphs. The sections cited here can be found in Vol. III, pp. 1146-56.

31. Engels to Sorge, January 6, 1892, in Karl Marx and Friedrich Engels, *Letters to Americans: 1848-1895* (New York, 1953), p. 239. Italics in the original.

32. Among these actions: Taking the Attorney General's list of subversive organizations, which was originally drawn as a guide to security risks, as a blank checklist to deny not only government jobs but passports and even non-governmental jobs to individuals belonging to organizations on the list; an unfair loyalty program in which individuals could not even face their accusers; the prosecution of the Communist leaders under the Smith Act.

33. The essays by Hofstadter and Lipset, as well as others by Talcott Parsons, David Riesman, Nathan Glazer, and Peter Viereck, which independently converged on the concept of "status politics," are published in the volume *The New American Right*, edited by Daniel Bell (New York, 1955).

34. For an elaboration of the relation of Populism to anti-Semitism, see my essay, "The Grass-Roots of American Jew Hatred," *Jewish Frontier*, June, 1944; also Richard Hofstadter, *The Age of Reform* (New York, 1957).

35. Toward the end of his hearings, Senator Kefauver read a telegram from an indignant citizen of Italian descent, protesting against the impression the committee had created that organized crime in America was a distinctly Italian enterprise. The Senator took the occasion to state the obvious: that there are racketeers who are Italians does not mean that Italians are racketeers. However, it may be argued that to the extent the Kefauver Committee fell for the line about crime in America being organized and controlled by the Mafia, it did foster such a misunderstanding. Perhaps this is also the place to point out that insofar as the relation of ethnic groups and ethnic problems to illicit and quasi-legal activities is piously ignored, the field is left open to the kind of vicious sensationalism practiced by Mortimer and Lait.

36. A fact which should occasion little shock if one recalls that, in the nineteenth century, American railroads virtually stole 190,000,000 acres of land by bribing Congressmen, and that more recently such scandals at the Teapot Dome oil grabs during the Harding administration consummated, as the Supreme Court said, "by means of conspiracy, fraud and bribery," reached to the very doors of the White House.

37. Adonis, and associate Willie Moretti, moved across the river to Bergen County, New Jersey, where, together with the quondam

racketeer Abner "Longie" Zwillman, he became one of the political powers in the state. Gambling flourished in Bergen County for almost a decade, but after the Kefauver investigation the state was forced to act. A special inquiry in 1953, headed by Nelson Stamler, revealed that Moretti had paid $286,000 to an aide of Governor Driscoll for "protection" and that the Republican state committee had accepted a $25,000 "loan" from gambler Joseph Bozzo, an associate of Zwillman. Moretti was later murdered, and Adonis deported to Italy.

38. The role of ethnic pride in corralling minority groups is one of the oldest pieces of wisdom in American politics; but what is more remarkable is the persistence of this identification through second and third generation descendants, a fact which, as Samuel Lubell noted in his *Future of American Politics,* was one of the explanatory keys to political behavior in recent elections. Although the Irish bloc as a solid Democratic bloc is beginning to crack, particularly as middle-class status impels individuals to identify more strongly with the GOP, the nomination in Massachusetts of Jack Kennedy for the United States Senate created a tremendous solidarity among Irish voters, and Kennedy was elected over Lodge although Eisenhower swept the state.

39. In 1959, the Justice Department set up a special group to study the "crime syndicates." The group found in a preliminary report, that the old crime leaders have eschewed violence and "created the appearance of successful businessmen" by entering legitimate business. It is quite possible that in many of these areas (trucking, vending, restaurants, entertainment) these old mobsters are able, by various means, to gain competitive advantages. But the significant thing, sociologically, is that these new areas are legitimate business, and this may not mean, as the Justice Department construes it, the "infiltration" of mobsters into new crime areas, but their attempt to gain quasi-respectability. Significantly, when *Life* magazine, February 23, 1958, presented a large graphic demonstration of the Justice Department findings, the individuals singled out had all been in the rackets over thirty years—a point that *Life* and the Justice Department missed. There were relatively few new, younger men in crime. The original mobsters had won hegemony when they were in their early thirties and had held sway all this time. The problem of "generations" in crime has never been studied, and, in the U.S., would make a fascinating subject.

40. Says Thorstein Sellin, a top criminologist at the University of Pennsylvania, "The United States undoubtedly has the poorest statistics of any of the important nations of the free world. This is in part due to our form of government for no federal state such as ours has ever succeeded in developing systematic and comprehensive statistics on a national scale. But even our constituent

states, many of which outstrip from the point of view of population, wealth and criminality most of the European national states, have made only feeble attempts to develop criminal statistics. . . . Our judicial statistics are undoubtedly the poorest of the lot."

41. In October, 1951, a young Negro in Chicago, Harold Miller, noticed a white woman with a bruised face staring at him in a bus, and found himself accused by the woman of having raped her two nights before. Although the area in which the crime allegedly took place was densely populated, no one seems to have observed the woman, screaming, being dragged off into the side street. A lie-detector test showed Miller to be lying, and the judge, mindful of the newspaper attention, sentenced Miller to life imprisonment. Two years' investigation by a *Sun-Times* reporter disclosed that the medical report showed the woman had not been raped, that the prosecutor was sweating out a graft charge on letting another man go, and that the police, being indifferent, had not checked beyond the woman's story.

42. But if one sees assaults, robberies, and burglaries as lower-class crimes, one should also note that bank embezzlements, a middle-class crime, is booming. In 1948 there were 500 cases; last year, 1,103 cases. In his widely discussed book, misleadingly entitled *White Collar Crime,* the late Edwin Sutherland argues that persons in the upper socio-economic class engage in considerable criminal behavior which is masked by the different administrative procedures adopted by the law. Sutherland points out that 70 per cent of the largest 200 United States corporations have over their life spans committed a total of 980 "crimes." These included restraint of trade, misrepresentation in advertising, infringements, unfair labor practices, rebates, and others. If one adds company violation of wartime administrative regulations during the war, the unethical practices of loan companies, the citations of the FTC against companies for misrepresentation, infringements, and restraints of trade, then the financial cost of white-collar crime, including embezzlement, is "probably several times as great as the financial cost of all crimes which are customarily regarded as 'the crime problem.' "

Whatever the logical merit of Sutherland's argument, from the viewpoint of a person who has been held up or whose house has been burglarized, the result is a direct and immediate loss, whereas the defalcations and frauds of business are spread, like a tax, on the community at large. When an individual speaks of crime, he is thinking of something which affects him directly.

43. The comic fan, according to a study by Kathryn Wolf and Marjorie Fiske, is one, lacking self-confidence, who dreams of safety under the fantasied protection of the comic-book hero. As one index of the role of insecurity, the study noted that 52 per cent of the children who were below normal height were comic

fans, while only 16 per cent of children above normal height were fans.

44. Although income from loading was never as fancy as reported in several sensational accounts, it was quite substantial. Records from fifteen piers showed that in 1950 $1,807,000 was paid out in loading, at an average of $14,600 a loader. *These averages, however, are deceptive.* In theory, the loaders were workers who pooled their income and shared equally the fees received; such at least was the fiction maintained by the International Longshoremen's Association, which justified union membership on this ground. Actually, the loaders who did the heavy lift work were merely hired employees of the boss loader (who on many piers never comes to work), or the men behind him; and the income distribution was vastly different. If, as one might suppose, the working loader received $4,000 a year wages, the net income for the small controlling group at the Waterman pier would be $300,000 a year; at Luckenback $180,000 a year; at Cuba Mail $72,000 a year. Where a small syndicate controlled a few piers grouped closely together, the profits naturally were even higher. Thus, the Allied Stevedoring Company, dominated by the Bowers gang, controlled piers 84 to 92, the larger piers which berthed the big ocean-going liners. Although no figures are available, the income from these piers would be well over a million dollars a year.

45. In 1931, with the backing of Lucky Luciano, underworld leader of the Unione Siciliane, who controlled narcotics and prostitution in New York, Marinelli became the first Italian district leader in Tammany Hall. In 1937, Marinelli, who was the County Clerk, was blasted by District Attorney Dewey as a "political ally of thieves . . . and big-shot racketeers," and removed from office by Governor Lehman. Luciano, who was convicted of being vice overlord of the city and sentenced to jail for life, was mysteriously pardoned by Governor Dewey and deported to Italy, where he is the subject of an occasional lurid feature by tabloid writers.

46. The first collective bargaining agreement was signed in 1916 by the Deepwater Steamship Association with the ILA. But from 1917 to 1919, collective bargaining was regulated by the government's National Adjustment Commission.

47. Lording over it all, living like a pasha while the longshoremen toiled like fellahin below, was Joseph P. Ryan. In the five years before 1952, Joe Ryan had taken out of the union treasury a total of $241,097, of which $115,000 was salary and the remainder expenses. Among the expenses: $12,494 to buy Cadillacs, $460 for a cruise to Guatemala, $10,774 for insurance premiums, $1,332 in golf-club dues and charges, and $478 for the burial of his sister-in-law. But the union graft was only one side of the picture. In this Levantine atmosphere, business was deep in the muck

itself. Jarka, a stevedoring concern, had paid $89,582 in "petty cash" to steamship company officials over a five-year period to earn "good-will," $20,000 had gone to Walter Wells, the president of the Isthmian Lines (owned by U.S. Steel), another $34,000 to Adriaan Roggoveen of the Holland-American Lines, and so on. In the headlines, the union leaders alone figured as the villains, and the graft to the shipping lines was quickly forgotten. But the ship owners were part of the system, too. They had paid out dirty money for favors, and some of the dirty money had been returned to the top operating officials. This was the business method along the waterfront.

48. The research for this essay was first done in 1951 in conjunction with the article, "Last of the Business Rackets," which appeared in the June, 1951, issue of *Fortune.*

I owe a debt to Father John Corridan of the Xavier Labor School, and to William J. Keating, formerly Assistant District Attorney of the County of New York, for information.

The data on loading were taken from unpublished source material in the Kefauver Committee files. The economic data are from the report of the Sub-Committee on Cargo Handling and General Costs of the Mayor's Joint Committee Report on Port Industry, January 2, 1951.

Further material on labor conditions on the waterfront can be found in the Final Report to the President on the Labor Dispute Involving Longshoremen and Association Occupations in the Maritime Industry on the Atlantic Coast (the Taft-Hartley Board in the 1948 strike), October 21, 1948, and in the Final Report of the New York State Board of Inquiry on the Longshore Industry Work Stoppage, issued January 22, 1952.

A valuable assessment of racketeer influence is contained in Malcolm Johnson's "Crime on the Labor Front" (New York, 1950). The New York State Crime Commission hearings, running from December, 1952, to February, 1953, form the most comprehensive source of data on crime on the waterfront.

For early surveys of the New York waterfront, see Msgr. Edward Swanstrom's book, *The Waterfront Labor Problem,* and "The New York Waterfront," a report by the Citizen's Waterfront Committee, New York, 1946, headed by William Jay Schiefflein.

There is little published on the history of the union; an interesting source is the biography of Dick Butler, called *Dock Walloper,* by Joseph Driscoll. Some material on other early figures in the union, such as Paul (Kelly) Vacarelli, can be found in Herbert Asbury's *The Gangs of New York* and in Thompson and Raymond, *Gang Rule in New York.* An account of early longshore organization on the Greak Lakes appears in a chapter by John R. Commons in his *Labor and Administration* (New York, 1944).

49. The most succinct summary of the role of government in aiding the formation of unions can be found in two articles by

plications or break-downs. Management wants to produce 267 cars in an 8-hour day (i.e., 480 minutes). Each car is 18 feet long. The time-study men have calculated that it will take 147.48 minutes to assemble one car. Each worker has a fixed operation along the line. He stands at a work station, which is defined as the length of one car, plus the space to the next one. Since 267 cars are to be produced within 480 minutes, each car on the belt will pass a work station in 1.8 minutes. The length of the work station, in this instance, is 21 feet (the car length of 18 feet plus 3 feet for work space). We can now calculate the speed of the line. Since 21 feet of belt have to pass a point in 1.8 minutes, the line will run at 11.67 feet per minute. And, at this speed, a fully assembled car trundles off the line every 1.8 minutes during the day.

If the work space between the units is cut, and the line runs at the same speed as before, the worker has to "speed up" his operation in order to finish before the car passes his work station. If the work space remains the same, but the line is run faster, a man has to complete his work cycle in less than 1.8 minutes to keep up with the line.

A company can also "speed up" operations without running the line faster, or reducing work space, by cutting the number of men. Usually the number of men required depends upon the initial estimate of the amount of work, and therefore the time needed to assemble a complete car. In this illustration, the estimate was 147.48 working minutes. But since work cycles for each man cannot be evenly spaced (e.g., some operations may take only 1.6 minutes), there is an inherent delay which, in this instance, is computed at 7.32 minutes per car. The new total, 154.80 minutes, divided by the 1.8 minutes for the work cycle at each station, rounds out to 86 workers. But since each man is entitled to 30 minutes relief during a day (and the relief man is entitled to his 30 minutes off), one relief man, working 450 minutes, can spell 15 men during a day. For 86 workers, this would mean 6 relief men, or a total of 92 men, on the line to produce the 267 cars. (I am indebted to Robert Kanter, of the Engineering department of the United Auto Workers, for the computations.)

57. The relation between the mode of visualization by the engineer and the forms of expression of modern art have been compared vividly by Siegfried Giedion in his *Mechanization Takes Command* (New York, 1948).

58. Reported in *The Human Problems of an Industrial Civilization* (New York, 1933); republished by Harvard University Press, 1946).

59. T. North Whitehead, *The Industrial Worker* (Cambridge, Mass., 1938); F. L. Roethlisberger and W. L. Dickson, *Management and the Worker* (Cambridge, Mass., 1938). The latter vol-

ume describes the entire experiment, and draws its theoretical implications.

60. The explanation recalls an old folk tale: A peasant complains to his priest that his little hut is horribly overcrowded. The priest advises him to move his cow into the house, the next week to take in his sheep, and the next week his horse. The peasant now complains even more bitterly about his lot. Then the priest advises him to let out the cow, the next week the sheep, and the next week the horse. At the end the peasant gratefully thanks the priest for lightening his burdensome life.

61. Perhaps this is the place, then, to tell the untold story of a follow-up to the researches at the Harwood Manufacturing Company, researches which have been for so many years the foundation for some "fundamental principles" in social psychology.

Harwood Manufacturing, which makes pajamas and women's wear, was a family-owned enterprise headed by Alfred Marrow, a forward-looking young industrialist, who had taken a Ph.D. in social psychology under the late Kurt Lewin. The company, finding labor costs high in New York, had moved to West Virginia, where the problem was to train the untutored hill girls to perform the simple sewing skills. Marrow brought in Alex Bavelas, a student of Lewin, as the plant psychologist, and the second year, John R. P. French and Lester Coch. Careful records of all experiments were kept: learning curves were checked against aspiration levels to see that the young girls did not become too easily frustrated in mastering their tasks. Questions of who was to perform onerous tasks, or questions of changes in work pace, were settled by "group decision." Output kept increasing, the girls seemed happy, the psychologists were busy knitting teams, and the plant seemed well on its way to becoming the model solidary community that Robert Owen, or at least Elton Mayo, had sought.

Quietly, the psychologists began publishing their studies—though without mentioning Harwood as the place of experiment. (Lewin, who had kept a close eye on the plant, wrote several studies which were published in the posthumous volume *Resolving Social Conflicts.*) Marrow, feeling that this extraordinary social experiment should be widely celebrated—that it was perhaps as path-breaking as Hawthorne—obtained wide publicity in the business press, including *Fortune,* pointing out that by practicing group decisions and keeping close watch on the tensions, the plant had been able to increase output—and—*to escape unionization.* If workers are happy, was the theme, they will not want a union.

Seeing this claim, the International Ladies Garment Workers sent an organizer into West Virginia. He handed out a series of leaflets which reproduced the laudatory stories in the business press, and across these he wrote: *"To the Workers of Harwood Manufacturing: Do you know that you are being used as guinea pigs?"* The union signed the plant.

62. See my essay, "Advertising: Its Impact on Society," *Listener,* December 27, 1956.

63. So compelling was the old American myth, that Chrysler, who built the third largest auto empire in the United States, entitled his autobiography the *Life of an American Workman.* Would a European tycoon ever do likewise?

64. From a speech by Lenin in June, 1919, entitled "Scientific Management and the Dictatorship of the Proletariat," reprinted in J. R. Commons, *Trade Unionism and Labor Problems* (Second Series, 1921); also in Lenin's *Collected Works,* Vol. VII.

65. In reading Marx's description of modern industry it is striking to see how he grasped simple distinctions which have eluded generations of sociologists. His solution for the deadening effects of machine work was variety. "It becomes a question of life and death for society . . . to replace the detail worker of today, crippled by life-long repetition of one and the same trivial operation, and thus reduced to the mere fragment of a man, by the fully developed individual, fit for a variety of labours, ready to face any change of production, and to whom the different social functions he performs are but so many modes of giving free scope to his own natural and acquired powers." And, in a footnote, Marx quotes approvingly, as a model to be emulated, the account of a French workman who recounted his experiences in the "new world" of San Francisco: "I was firmly convinced that I was fit for nothing but letterpress printing. . . . Once in the midst of this world of adventurers who change their occupation as often as they do their shirt, egad, I did as the others. As mining did not turn out remunerative enough, I left for the town where in succession I became a typographer, slater, plumber, etc. In consequences of thus finding out that I am fit for any sort of work I feel less of a mollusk and more of a man." (See *Capital* [Chicago, 1906], I, 534.)

66. "The Experimental Change of a Major Organizational Variable," by Nancy C. Morse and Everett C. Riemer, *Journal of Abnormal and Social Psychology,* January, 1956. For a discussion of the value problem in the testing of executives and supervisors, see my essay, "Screening Leaders in a Democracy," *Commentary,* April, 1948.

67. One of the more imaginative explorations of alternative organization of work is that of Eric Trist and a group from the Tavistock Institute in London on the impact of mechanization in British coal mining. In traditional mining, control and regulation of work at the coal face was carried out autonomously by the work group, "which developed customs of self-regulation, task continuity and role rotation appropriate to the underground work situation." With the introduction of machines, new specialized

tasks were developed, the old work groups were broken up, and control of operations was extended "upward" along multiple layers of management. But, as Trist points out, these assumptions of organization themselves were made mechanically on the basis of engineering notions of work tasks. The research team carefully worked out proposals to return "autonomous control of work" to the face team itself (see "Work Organization at the Coal Face: A Comparative Study of Mining Systems," by E. L. Trist and H. Murray [The Tavistock Institute, mimeographed report, June, 1958]). Not surprisingly, perhaps, the proposals met with resistance from some of the Coal Board officials and even within the union.

68. Although some engineers never give up trying. The long Westinghouse strike of 1955-56 was precipitated when the company began time studies of so-called "day-rate" workers (i.e., material handlers, repairmen, sweepers) in an effort to set performance standards for these men. This was, in effect, the first "automation" strike in U.S. industrial history. Automation changes the "mix" in the industrial labor force, reducing the number of direct production workers and increasing the number of indirect production workers. In an effort to control the rising costs of this latter group, Westinghouse began measurement studies of jobs that hitherto had been considered unmeasurable.

69. Letter to Danielson, No. 169, in *Karl Marx and Friedrich Engels: Selected Correspondence, 1846-1895* (New York, 1934), p. 360.

70. Letter to Schleuter, No. 222, *op. cit.*, p. 497.

71. Quoted in Goetz A. Briefs, *The Proletariat* (New York, 1937), p. 193. Communist economists, embarrassed by this situation, have tried to deny this material gain. A statistician, Jurgen Kuczynski (now an official of the East German government), argued, in an effort to defend Marx's proposition of the growing impoverishment of the working class under capitalism, that the living conditions of the American workers in the nineteenth century had actually deteriorated. Confronted from his own evidence with the fact that real wages had increased from 1790 to 1900, Kuczynski fell back on the Leninist theory that capitalism divided the workers into a labor aristocracy that did benefit and that in effect was bribed by higher wages, and a larger group of exploited masses. But this was only a rhetorical rather than a statistical claim. See Jurgen Kuczynski, *A Short History of Labour Conditions under Industrial Capitalism* (Vol. II of *The United States of America, 1789 to the Present Day*) (London, 1943).

72. A general hypothesis, such as the one above, can, however, only suggest an answer. It states conditions; it sensitizes one to questions. But the empirical inquiry into the fate of a social move-

ment has to be pinned to the specific questions of time, place, and opportunity. A social movement, like an individual, defines its character in the choices it makes. Therefore, one has to locate the "crisis points," define the alternatives which confronted the movement, and understand the motives for the choices made. In my monograph, "The Background and Development of Marxian Socialism in the United States," I have tried to locate such turning points in American Socialism. (See Egbert and Persons [eds.], *Socialism and American Life* [Princeton, 1952], pp. 215-404.

73. Cited in Gertrude Himmelfarb, "The American Revolution in the Political Theory of Lord Acton," *Journal of Modern History,* December, 1949, p. 312.

74. "Politics As a Vocation," in *From Max Weber: Essays in Sociology,* ed. H. H. Gerth and C. W. Mills (New York, 1946), pp. 119 ff; also p. 9.

75. Karl Mannheim, *Ideology and Utopia* (New York, 1936), pp. 190-93.

76. Georges Sorel, *Reflections on Violence* (3d ed.; Glencoe, Ill., 1950).

77. In *The German Ideology* Marx poses the question of how self-interest becomes transformed into ideology. "How does it come about," he asks, "that personal interests continually grow, despite the persons, into class-interests, into common interests which win an independent existence over against individual persons, in this independence take on the shape of general interests, enter as such into opposition with the real individuals, and in this opposition, according to which they are defined as general interests, can be conceived by the consciousness as ideal, even as religious, sacred interests?" But Marx, exasperatingly, never goes on to answer the question. (See *The German Ideology* [New York, 1939], p. 203.) Sidney Hook, in his article on "Materialism" in the *Encyclopedia of the Social Sciences* (New York, 1933), X, 219, sought to rephrase the problem of consciousness in these terms: "What are the specific mechanisms by which the economic conditions influence the habits and motives of classes, granted that individuals are actuated by motives that are not always a function of individual self-interest? Since classes are composed of individuals, how are class interests furthered by the non-economic motives of individuals?" But having phrased it more sharply, he too left it as a question. So far no Marxist theoretician has yet detailed the crucial psychological and institutional nexuses which show how the "personifications" or masks of class role are donned by the individual as self-identity.

78. The question of how the proletariat achieves self-consciousness, and of the role of the intellectual, a person from another

class, as the leader of the proletariat, long bedeviled the radical movement. In Marx's writings there are three different conceptions of class. In the *Communist Manifesto* there is the eschatological view in which the Götterdämmerung of history polarizes society into two classes and awareness of class position rises from beholding the widening abyss. In the conclusion to *Das Kapital,* Marx begins a simplified analysis of "essential" class division (i.e., as ideal types, rather than as reality) on the basis of source of income; but the conversion of income groups into congruent categories still begs the question of what the mechanisms of self-awareness are. Marx's actual historical analyses, as in *The Eighteenth Brumaire,* shows a subtle awareness of the complex shadings of social divisions, which in action give rise to many varied social categories and diverse political interest groups. It is only, then, in "final" instances, rather than day-to-day politics, that class division and identity become crucial for Marxist politics. (For a discussion of Marx's theory of class, see Raymond Aron, "Social Structure and the Ruling Class," *British Journal of Sociology,* March, 1950.) The question of the relationship of the intellectual to the proletariat on the question of consciousness is explored at some length in the next chapter, "Two Roads from Marx."

79. It was in this statement, in the course of a debate with the Socialists, that Gompers first used the phrase, which later was to become the common description of the AFL, of unionism pure and simple. See Samuel Gompers, *Seventy Years of Labor,* I, 286-87.

80. *Ibid.,* II, 105.

81. Ray Ginger, *The Bending Cross* (New Brunswick, N. J., 1949).

82. Thomas has made some autobiographical references in his *As I See It* (New York, 1932). The above quotations, as well as some description of Thomas' beliefs, are from an unpublished memoir which Thomas wrote for his family in 1944 and to which this author had access.

83. A situation which provoked from Dwight Macdonald the comment: "This failure to split on the war issue has always seemed to me an indication of a certain lack of political seriousness in all the S. P. factions." (Why I Will Not Support Norman Thomas," *Politics,* October, 1944, p. 279).

84. "The believer in an ethic of ultimate ends," wrote Max Weber, "feels 'responsible' only for seeing to it that the flame of pure intention is not quenched."

85. V. I. Lenin, *What Is To Be Done* (New York, 1929), p. 116.

86. Leon Trotsky, *My Life* (New York, 1930), pp. 161-62.

87. V. I. Lenin, "On Slogans," in *Toward the Seizure of Power, Collected Works* (New York, 1932), XXI, Book I, 43-50.

88. *Pace* President Roosevelt, who wrote on the flyleaf of his personal copy of Joseph E. Davies' *Mission to Moscow,* a book which defended the authenticity of the Moscow Trials: "This book will last." Richard H. Ullman, "The Davies Mission and United States-Soviet Relations, 1937-1941," *World Politics,* IX, No. 2 (January, 1957), 220.

89. Margaret Mead, *Soviet Attitudes to Authority* (New York, 1951).

90. Geoffrey Gorer and John Rickman, *The People of Great Russia* (London, 1949).

91. Henry V. Dicks, "Observations on Contemporary Russian Behavior," *Human Relations,* V, No. 2 (1952), 111-75.

92. Dick's original research was done in conjunction with Edward A. Shils. Unfortunately Shils's larger work was never declassified by the RAND Corporation, its sponsor, and therefore was unavailable for discussion.

93. Dicks, *op. cit.,* p. 171.

94. *Ibid.*

95. Nathan Leites, *A Study of Bolshevism* (Glencoe, Ill., 1954).

96. Raymond A. Bauer, Alex Inkeles, and Clyde Kluckhohn, *How the Soviet System Works* (Cambridge, Mass., 1956).

97. Barrington Moore, Jr., *Terror and Progress—USSR* (Cambridge, Mass., 1954), and *Soviet Politics: The Dilemma of Power* (Cambridge, Mass., 1950).

98. "The Permanent Revolution Is on Again," *Commentary,* XXIV, No. 2 (August, 1957), 105-12.

99. *Ibid.,* p. 109.

100. See particularly E. H. Carr's *Socialism in One Country,* the fifth installment of his *History of Soviet Russia* (London, 1958).

101. Isaac Deutscher, *Russia: What Next?* (London, 1953).

102. Isaac Deutscher, *The Prophet Armed: Trotsky, 1879-1921* (New York, 1954).

103. *Russia: What Next?* pp. 123, 125.

104. Isaac Deutscher, "Russia in Transition," *Universities and Left Review*, I, No. 1 (Spring, 1957), 4-12.

105. *Ibid.*, p. 12.

106. The first book to insist that Russia was a new class state —calling it "bureaucratic collectivism"—was that of Bruno R., *La bureaucraticisation du monde* (Paris, 1939). The theme was debated in the Menshevik press in the early 1940's, with the late Theodor Dan arguing in *Novy Put* that Russia was still a workers' state, and Rudolf Hilferding and Solomon Schwarz arguing the contrary in *Vestnik*. (Dan, following the invasion of Russia, gave qualified support to the Russian regime.) Hilferding's argument, a classic statement of the neo-Marxist position, was printed in the *Modern Review*, I, No. 4 (June, 1947), 266-71, under the title, "State Capitalism or Totalitarian State Economy," while Schwarz's data appeared later in his article, "Heads of Russian Factories," in *Social Research*, IX, No. 3 (September, 1942), 315-33, and in his collaborative effort with Gregory Bienstock and Aaron Yugow, *Management in Russian Industry and Agriculture* (New York, 1944). The debate was carried over into the Trotskyite press in the 1940's, principally in the *New International* and the *Fourth International* in New York. Trotsky's last argument is contained in the collection entitled *In Defense of Marxism* (*Against the Petty-bourgeois Opposition*) (New York, 1942). The revisionist position can be found in James Burnham's *The Managerial Revolution* (New York, 1941) and in Max Schactman's introduction to the revised edition of Trotsky's *The New Course* (New York, 1943). A long discussion in the French periodical *Le contract social*, March, 1959, sheds interesting light on the career of Bruno R., an Italian named Bruno Rizzi, and on the origins of the theory of bureaucratic collectivism. For a further discussion see my essay "The Strange Tale of Bruno R," in *The New Leader*, Sept. 28, 1959.

107. Hannah Arendt, *The Origins of Totalitarianism* (New York, 1951; published in England as *The Burden of Our Times*).

108. Horst Jablonowski and Werner Philipp (eds.), *Forschungen zur ost-europäischen Geschichte*, Vol. I (Berlin, 1954).

109. Hans Kohn in the *Russian Review*, XIV, No. 4 (October, 1955), 373.

110. *A Study of Bolshevism*, p. 527.

111. *Ibid.*, p. 137.

112. *Ibid.*, pp. 135, 261.

113. *Ibid.*, pp. 403-4.

114. The effort to construct "social character" out of unconscious strivings is not limited to psychoanalysis. It is central, for example, to Pareto's sociology. For Pareto, the springs of social action were "interests" (or rational assessments), "derivations," (or rationalizations) and "residues" (or fundamental drives). As George Homans, a quondam follower of Pareto, once wrote: "American historians are given to discussing at length the 'Pioneer character,' the 'Pioneer spirit.' What they are talking about when they are not simply romancing is the prominence in the 'pioneers' of certain residues, notably those of the integrity of the individual."

115. *Hamlet . . . With a Psycho-analytic Study by Ernest Jones, M.D.* (London, 1947), p. 22. The argument is elaborated in Jones's *Hamlet and Oedipus* (New York, 1951), pp. 83-90.

116. The example has been adapted from Alex Inkeles, "Understanding a Foreign Society: A Sociologist's View," *World Politics,* III, No. 2 (January, 1951), 269-80.

117. Bauer, Inkeles, and Kluckhohn, *op. cit.,* p. 20.

118. The *Radio Liberation Daily Information Bulletin* of May 14, 1957, carried the following news item, headed "Andropov—Head of the Satellite Countries Department of the CC":

> "*Pravda* for May 12, 1957 twice mentions the former ambassador of the USSR in Hungary, Yu. V. Andropov, as 'head of a department of the Central Committee of the CPSU.' According to *Pravda,* Andropov was present at Khrushchev's reception for the government delegation from the Mongolian People's Republic and also at a lunch given by Bulganin in honor of the same delegation.
>
> "Although the Tass reports do not state precisely which department Andropov controls, it may be assumed that it is the fairly secret satellite countries department (even its official name is not known).
>
> "In the past, B. N. Ponomarev, who was invariably called 'a member of the Central Committee of the CPSU' usually took part in such receptions and banquets in honor of party and government delegations from the satellite countries. The position occupied by Ponomarev has never been mentioned anywhere. In this connection it is interesting to note that at the lunch given by Bulganin and Khrushchev in honor of the Albanian party and government delegation on April 12th this year (*Pravda,* 13th April 1957) the order of those who attended was as follows:
>
> ". . . Serov—Ponomarev—Palgunov—Nikitin . . .
>
> "At the lunch which was recently given by Bulganin for the Mongolian delegation, the order of protocol was as follows:

". . . Serov—Andropov—Nikitin—Palgunov. . . .* [Footnote: *The protocol order at the reception given by Khrushchev was as follows: Gromyko—Pisarev (ambassador in Mongolia)—Andropov; however, it should be remembered that according to protocol, at a reception for a foreign delegation, the Soviet ambassador of the country concerned is always given the place of honor, whether or not he actually merits it 'on the protocol ladder.']

"Despite all these facts, it would be premature to conclude that Ponomarev has been replaced by Andropov, because Ponomarev is also to some extent connected with the international communist movement. (For example, he was a member of the delegation of the CPSU to the Fourteenth Congress of the French Communist Party in July 1956). A more probable explanation is that an 'international division of labor' has been carried out in the Central Committee; Ponomarev will henceforth maintain contact only with those Communist parties outside the orbit, while Andropov deals with the satellites.

"Bearing in mind the fact that Andropov was released ('in connection with a transfer to other work'—Pravda 7 March 1957) in the course of a reshuffle of senior officials of the Ministry of Foreign Affairs which was begun by Shepilov immediately before his withdrawal from the post of Minister of Foreign Affairs, there can be no doubt to whom Andropov owes his promotion (on the 'protocol ladder' he is now several stages above his former chief—V. V. Kuznetzov, first deputy Minister of Foreign Affairs—see *Pravda,* 12 May, 1957)."

119. Immanuel Birnbaum, "Destalinization: Motives and Consequences," *Problems of Communism,* VI, No. 1 (January-February, 1957), 41.

120. Perhaps the most extraordinary attempt to trace Soviet elite maneuverings by means of "Kreminological" methods is the RAND study of Myron Rush, *The Rise of Khrushchev* (Washington, D.C., 1958.) In 1955, Rush observed that Khrushchev's title as first secretary of the party (*pervi sekretar*), which normally appeared in the Russian press in lower case, suddenly was given in *Pravda,* of May 25, 1955, as *Pervi Sekretar.* (The next day the capital S was diminished, but the capital P retained, and the title appeared thereafter as *Pervi sekretar.*) From a clue as slim as this, and from others which at first glance might seem to be equally tendentious (e.g., Khrushchev's emulation of Stalin's use of the word *otriskoi,* or "belching forth," to characterize Malenkov as a right deviationist), Rush argued, in a paper prepared for RAND at that time, that Khrushchev was beginning to make his bid for power, and that he would use Stalin's ladder, the party secretariat apparatus, in his ascent. For some detailed questioning of

Mr. Rush's reasoning, see my review of his book in *Problems of Communism,* Vol. VII, No. 2, March-April 1958.

121. Insufficient attention has been paid, for example, to the techniques of evasion practiced by Soviet scientists in carrying out their work in accordance with the common fund of scientific knowledge. Alexander Weissberg-Cybulski, who was an editor of the physics journal in the Soviet Union and later a director of an institute in Kharkov before being jailed in the 1937-38 purges, tells the highly amusing story of how, in the journal articles, research advances in Russia were attributed, out of political necessity, to the wisdom derived from dialectical materialism, and of the problems that confronted the editors when the German Academy of Science asked for the secret of the new method. (See *Science and Freedom,* Proceedings of the Hamburg Conference [London, 1955].)

More recently, Ivan D. London has noticed wholesale evasions of *partinost* in science: "For example, it is not difficult to show, on the basis of items abstracted from speeches, prefaces, introductory paragraphs, etc., that in the Soviet Union the whole development of physiology of the sense organs was prescribed by the Communist Party in order to provide a 'concrete basis for Lenin's theory of reflection' and to meet the 'demands of practice': industrial, medical, and military, the latter two in particular. Yet a detailed scrutiny of the technical literature, the published minutes of various meetings, conferences, etc., over the years reveals little to suggest that the serious programs of research in the field of sensory physiology in the Soviet Union have been really influenced in any respect, by either practical considerations or Party dicta. Of course, superficially there may seem to be a planned compliance with practical programmatic aims—after all, 'Soviet language' fulfills, besides communicative, also prophylactic functions —but any sensory physiologist who is alert to his subject will recognize the dust-in-the-eyes purpose of certain parts of research programs. . . ." ("Toward a Realistic Appraisal of Soviet Science," *Bulletin of the Atomic Scientists,* XIII, No. 5 [May, 1957], p. 170.)

122. Bauer, Inkeles, and Kluckhohn, *op. cit.,* p. 239; Rush, *op. cit.,* p. 21.

123. Vladimir Dedijer, *Tito* (New York, 1953), p. 327.

124. Robert W. Campbell, "Some Recent Changes in Soviet Economic Policy," *World Politics,* IX, No. 1 (October, 1956), p. 8.

125. In this connection, see the interesting study, *When Prophecy Fails* (Minneapolis, 1956), by Leon Festinger, Henry W. Riecken, and Stanley Schacter.

126. For a discussion of the background of this debate, see Leopold Haimson, *The Russian Marxists and the Origins of Bolshevism* (Cambridge, Mass., 1955), pp. 36-45.

127. Leon Trotsky, *My Life* (New York, 1931), pp. 129-43.

128. Only snippets of Machajski's works are available in English, in the anthology *The Making of Society*, edited by V. F. Calverton (New York, 1937). The fullest exposition of Machajski's ideas can be found in the article by Max Nomad, "White Collars and Horny Hands" (*Modern Quarterly*, Vol. VI, No. 3, Autumn, 1932), and I am indebted to this account. Nomad, Machajski's major disciple, used his theory as the frame of analysis for his own studies of revolutionary personalities in two books, *Rebels and Renegades* (New York, 1932), and *Apostles of Revolution* (New York, 1939). Machajski's ideas, through Nomad, explicitly influenced the writings of Harold Lasswell, a leading American political scientist. In a number of books, Lasswell expounded the theory that the revolutions of the twentieth century have been led by intellectuals who, in the name of the myths and symbols of socialism, used these revolutions to place themselves in power. See particularly, Harold Lasswell, *World Politics and Personal Insecurity* (New York, 1935), pp. 111-16, and *The World Revolution of Our Time* (Stanford, Calif., 1951). The theory of the double role of the intellectuals, perhaps a commonplace by now, can also be found in the writings of Robert Michels and Joseph Schumpeter, and received its most poignant expression in the dialogue between Pietro Spina and Uliva, in Ignazio Silone's memorable novel *Bread and Wine*. Machajski's name is almost completely unknown in the Soviet Union, and a cursory account of his life and ideas can be found in the larger *Soviet Encyclopedia* in the article on A. Wolski, the pen name Machajski first used.

129. The most interesting discussion of the thought of young Marx can be found in the recent study by Hannah Arendt, *The Human Condition* (Chicago, 1958). The most comprehensive exposition of the early views of Marx is in the unpublished Ph.D. dissertation (Harvard, 1957) by Robert W. Tucker, entitled *The Self and Revolution: A Moral Critique of Marx*. This study was published in 1960 by Cambridge University Press, as *The Alienated World of Karl Marx*. Mr. Tucker's work is the first to trace at length the transposition of Marx's philosophical thought to economic categories. I am indebted to him for many insights. A more orthodox discussion of the early manuscripts can be found in Herbert Marcuse's *Reason and Revolution* (New York, 1941). A useful, if overly simple exposition of Marx's writings before *The Communist Manifesto*, can be found in H. P. Adams, *Karl Marx in His Early Writings* (London, 1940). The most detailed study of Marx's relations with the young Hegelians is in Sidney Hook's *From Hegel to Marx* (New York, 1936), though

Hook neglects Marx's unfinished *Economic-Philosophical Manuscripts,* where the major discussion of alienation is to be found. The most ambitious attempt in recent years to reconstruct the works of the early Marx from a Communist point of view was made by August Cornu, *Karl Marx et Friedrich Engels* (Vol. I: *Les années d'enfance et de jeunesse: La gauche hégèlienne*) (Paris, 1955). There is also, from a Catholic point of view, the extraordinarily thorough work by Père Jean-Yves Calvez, *La pensée de Karl Marx* (Paris, 1956). One of the most lucid discussions of the ideas of the young Marx is by Jean Hippolyte, *Ètudes sur Hegel et Marx* (Paris, 1955), especially pp. 147-155.

130. The abolition of private property, however, it should be pointed out, does not, for the early Marx, usher in the state of human freedom. The abolition of private property produces only "unthinking" or "raw" communism.

Marx clearly drew much of his notions about communism from Proudhon's great study *What Is Property?* In his sketch of history, Proudhon drew a three-stage picture of evolution: in the first, man lived in primitive communism, sharing equally all women and all means of production; in the second, the stage of private property, powerful individuals were able, by theft, to appropriate communal property for private use; in the third, higher stage, there would be individual ownership but co-operative work.

In discussing Feuerbach, Marx points out that the negation of a negation is not, per se, an affirmation. Similarly, he said (in the *Manuscripts*) that the abolition of private property, the negation, would not produce human freedom but "raw communism." This type of communism, he said, "completely negates the personality of man." It expresses "envy and a desire to reduce all to a common level." It is "universal envy constituted as power." Raw communism, however, is to give way to true communism as a "positive transcendance of private property" and to a positive humanism in which "man recognizes himself in a world he has himself made." He returns, therefore, to his "species character." He is no longer partial man, bound by class behavior, but once again generic Man, transcending human self-alienation and "returning to himself."

Twenty-five years later, when Marx was again forced to confront the question of the nature of the future society, in the *Critique of the Gotha Programme,* the image of two stages of the future society was again invoked. It is clear, in this context, that when he spoke of the "dictatorship of the proletariat" as the "immediate transitional stage," it was "raw communism" that would be superseded by the idyllic world of true communism where each man would live "from each according to his means, and to each according to his needs." And it seems equally clear that Lenin, in his distinction of two phases of society, in *State and Revolution,* was aware of Marx's meanings. The transitional stage was, for Lenin, too, a distasteful phase. Chiding Edward Bernstein, who had called the action of the Paris Commune in reducing all wages to a common level as "naive, primitive, democracy," Lenin said, "[Bernstein] fails completely to understand that, first of all, the transition from capitalism to socialism is impossible without 'return,' in a measure, to 'primitive democracy.' "

From the criteria established by both Marx and Lenin, one would have to say that present-day Soviet society is one of the most misshapen products ever seen of "unthinking" or "raw communism."

131. Friedrich Engels, *Ludwig Feuerbach and the Outcome of German Classical Philosophy,* in Karl Marx, *Selected Works* (Moscow, 1953), I, 417.

132. Engels to Florence Kelley Wischnewetzky, February 25, 1886, in Karl Marx and Friedrich Engels, *Letters to Americans: 1848-1895* (New York, 1953), p. 151.

133. A. Voden, "Talks with Engels," in *Reminiscences of Marx and Engels* (Moscow, undated), pp. 330-31. Lewis Feuer, to whom I am indebted for this reference, has also pointed out to me that Engels, in a little-known essay, "On Authority," had, in a polemic against the anarchists, argued that modern technology imposes upon men "a veritable despotism independent of all social organization"; hence it was utopian to question the nature of authority in a factory. ("If man, by dint of his knowledge and inventive genius, has subdued the forces of nature, the latter avenge themselves upon him by subjecting him, in so far as he employs them, to a veritable despotism independent of all social organization. Wanting to abolish authority in large-scale industry is tantamount to wanting to abolish industry itself, to destroy the power loom in order to return to the spinning wheel.") Thus the "realism" of the scientific socialists, as it has even of contemporary sociology, turned Marx and Engels away from the *work process,* the source of alienation and to the formal social relations of employer and worker. For the Engels essay, see *Marx and Engels: Basic Writings on Politics and Philosophy,* ed. Lewis S. Feuer (Anchor Books; New York, 1959), pp. 481-85.

134. Addressing the philosophical section of the Communist Academy in 1934, Lukacs stated:

> "The mistakes into which I fell in my book *History and Class Consciousness* are completly in line with these deviations [i.e., those attacked in Lenin's *Materialism and Empiric-Criticism*] . . . I began as a student of Simmel and Max Weber. . . .
>
> "At the same time the philosophy of syndicalism (Sorel) had a great influence on my development; it strengthened my inclinations toward romantic anti-capitalism. . . . Thus

I entered the Communist Party of Hungary in 1918 with a world-outlook that was distinctly syndicalist and idealist. . . .

"The book I published in 1923 . . . was a philosophical summation of these tendencies. . . . In the course of my practical party work and in familiarizing myself with the works of Lenin and Stalin, these idealist props of my world-outlook lost more and more of their security. Although I did not permit a republication of my books (which was sold out by that time), nevertheless I first came to full appreciation of these philosophical problems during my visit to the Soviet Union in 1930-31, especially through the philosophical discussions in progress at that time.

"Practical work in the Communist Party of Germany, direct ideological struggle . . . against the Social Fascist and Fascist ideology have all the more strengthened my conviction that in the intellectual sphere, *the front of idealism is the front of Fascist counter-revolution and its accomplices, the Social Fascists.* Every concession to idealism, however significant, spells *danger* to the proletarian revolution. Thus, I understood not only the *theoretical falsity* but also the *practical danger* of the book I wrote twelve years ago. . . .

"With the help of the Comintern, of the All-Union Communist Party and of its leader, Comrade Stalin, the struggle . . . for that iron discipline, implacability and refusal to compromise with all deviations from Marxism-Leninism which the All-Union Communist Party . . . achieved long ago. . . ."

The statement is quoted by Morris Watnick in his study, "Georg Lukacs: An Intellectual Biography," sections of which have appeared in *Soviet Survey* (London) Nos. 23-25. (It is one of the best discussions of Marxist revisionism to appear in recent years.) Lukacs' book is generally unobtainable here. A chapter from it, under the title "What is Orthodox Marxism," appeared in *The New International,* Summer, 1957. Sections of the book have been translated into French, in the review *Arguments,* published by Les Editions de Minuit.

135. *The German Ideology,* particularly Part I, deals, in the main, with the problems of historical materialism, while the *Economic-Philosophical Manuscripts* take up the question of alienation. In fact, other than some short discussions in *The Holy Family,* the only sustained discussion of the concept of alienation is in the *Manuscripts.* The *Manuscripts* were written in 1844, *The Holy Family* in 1845, and *The German Ideology* in 1845-46.

The early philosophical writings, principally the uncompleted *Economic-Philosophical Manuscripts* and *The German Ideology,* were first published (with some small sections missing) in 1932 by S. Landshut and J. P. Mayer under the title of *Der historische Materialismus,* in two volumes. (Some small fragments of the third part of *The German Ideology*, on Stirner, had been published by Edward Bernstein in *Dokumente des Sozialismus*, in 1902-3.) A detailed description of the early manuscripts, particularly of *The German Ideology*, was published by D. Riazanov in Vol. I of the Marx-Engels Archiv, in 1927. The complete texts are available in the *Marx-Engels Gesamtausgabe*, under the direction of V. Adoratski (Berlin, 1932). Early papers of Marx were published in 1953 by S. Landshut, under the title of *Die Frühschriften von Karl Marx*, which include the 1932 edition. A complete guide to the works of Marx can be found in, Maximilien Rubel, *Bibliographie des oeuvres de Karl Marx*, (Paris, 1956).

136. *Capital* (Kerr ed.; Chicago, p. 12), emphasis added.

137. Leon Trotsky, *The Living Thoughts of Karl Marx* (New York, 1939), p. 6.

138. For a penetrating discussion of this question of rationality in the "apocalyptic economics" of Bolshevism, see Michael Polanyi, "The Foolishness of History," *Encounter*, October, 1957.

139. Karl Marx, *Selected Works* (Moscow, 1935), II, 474.

140. Charles Rihs, *La commune de Paris* (Geneva, 1955), pp. 70-72, 244; also Frank Jellinek, *The Paris Commune of 1871* (Oxford, 1937), pp. 398, 403.

141. Karl Marx, *Critique of the Gotha Programme* (London, 1943), esp. pp. 12-13, 26.

142. Karl Kautsky, *The Social Revolution* (Chicago, 1902), p. 112.

143. *Ibid.*, pp. 126-27.

144. All citations are from V. I. Lenin, *Collected Works*, Vol. XXI (New York, 1932); see esp. pp. 184-89. Unless otherwise indicated, emphases have been added.

145. For a discussion of the varying interpretations of this claim, see Alfred G. Meyer, *Leninism* (Cambridge, Mass., 1957), pp. 187-96. See also the footnote on pp. 371-72 in this book containing Lenin's statement on the greater ease of transition if Russia had been state capitalist.

146. For extracts from Lenin's notebooks, and his marginal comments on the *Critique*, see Appendix II, *Critique of the Gotha Programme*, the edition of the Marxist-Leninist Library, No. 15 (London, 1933), pp. 65-85.

147. For these crucial passages, see Lenin, *Collected Works*, XX, Book 1, 101, and XXI, Book 2, 28-29.

148. From: "Will the Bolsheviks Retain State Power?" *Collected Works,* XXI, Book 2, 34-35. The first systematic account of the history of the workers' councils in Russia and the theoretical controversies in the Russian movement on the problem, is Oskar Anweiler's *Die Rätebewegung in Russland: 1905-1921* (Leiden, 1958).

149. See Rosa Luxemburg, *Die russische Revolution,* in *Die Aktion,* Jhrg. 12 Heft, Vol. V, No. 6, February 4, 1922. Reprinted in English as *The Russian Revolution* (New York, 1940), Introduction by Bertram D. Wolfe.

150. See "Theses on the Basic Tasks of the C.I." and "Theses on the Role of the Communist Party in the Proletarian Revolution," in *Documents of the Communist International, 1919-1947,* Vol. I, 1919-1922, selected by Jane Degras (Oxford, 1956), pp. 113-27 (esp. p. 126), 128-36.

151. Cited in Manya Gordon, *Workers Before and After Lenin* (New York, 1941), p. 79.

152. For a discussion of this debate, see Leonard Schapiro, *The Origin of the Communist Autocracy* (London, 1955), pp. 254-55.

153. *Collected Works* (3d Russian ed.), XXVI, 101, 103.

154. *Ibid.,* p. 141.

155. Lenin, *Selected Works,* IX, 9. Lenin's "practical" awareness of the threat of bureaucracy as an immediate and ever present reality contrasts strangely with the "naive" notions one also finds expressed by him. In an essay written a few days after the seizure of power, called "Report on the Right to Recall," Lenin said that as long as *any* state exists, a Marxist has no right to speak of freedom. "The state is an instrument of coercion," he wrote; "Formerly this was oppression of the entire nation by a bunch of money bags . . . we want to organize coercion in the interests of the working people." What counted, for Lenin, was that the state would be under the *control* of the workers, and therefore be subject to check. "Report on the Right to Recall," *Collected Works,* XXII, 97.

156. I follow, here, the account by Leonard Schapiro, *op. cit.*

157. Lenin, *Selected Works,* XIV, 338, cited in Theodore Draper, *The Roots of American Communism* (New York, 1957), p. 249.

158. See Joseph Stalin, *Leninism,* Vol. II, "Tasks of Business Managers," February 4, 1931; "New Conditions—New Tasks," June 23, 1931.

159. See Alexander Vucinich, *Soviet Economic Institutions: The Social Structure of Production Units* (Stanford, 1952).

160. See, for example, the explicit statement by Trotsky, the 1931 letter entitled *Über Arbeiterkontrolle der Produktion,* reprinted in the *New International,* May-June, 1951, pp. 175-78. "For us," said Trotsky, "the concept of workers' control exists within the scope of a capitalist regime, under bourgeois domination . . . [it] means a kind of economic dual power in the factory, banks, business enterprises, etc. . . . Thus a workers' control regime, by its very nature, can only be thought of as a provisional, transitional regime during the period of the shattering of the bourgeois state. . . ."

161. Hannah Arendt, the keenest student of totalitarianism, and a sympathetic critic of the idea of workers' councils, writes apropos of the Hungarian and Polish experiences of 1957: ". . . it is quite doubtful whether the political principle of equality and self-rule can be applied to the economic sphere of life as well. It may be that ancient political theory, which held that economics, since it was bound up with the necessities of life, needed the rule of masters to function well, was not so wrong after all." For her extraordinary discussion of the meaning of the spontaneous emergence of workers' councils during the 1957 events, see her article, "Totalitarian Imperialism," *Journal of Politics,* XX (1958), 5-43.

162. Even joint consultation, it should be pointed out, runs the danger of being a catchword. One can point out, wryly, that in practice joint consultation may simply become a "buck-passing" mechanism whereby each of the parties, managers as well as workers' council representatives, evades its own responsibilities. For a revealing picture of this, particularly for those who fear the specter of "managerialism," see the study by Elliot Jaques, *The Changing Culture of a Factory* (London, 1951).

163. For an interesting attempt to set an "objective" standard of pay differentials, see the article by Elliot Jaques in the *New Scientist* (London, July 3, 1958), p. 313. Jaques believes that by measuring the "time-span" which an individual has to perform jobs on his own initiative, without review, he is able to elicit "an unrecognized system of norms of what constitutes fair payment for any given level of work," and that these norms are "intuitively recognized by the people at work themselves." This would lead, says Jaques, to "an empirical basis for a national wages and salary policy."

164. Karl Jaspers has assembled a fascinating collection of laments by philosophers of each age who see their own time as crisis and the past as a golden age. These — and the quotations from the Egyptian papyri as well as the remark of Talleyrand— can be found in his *Man in the Modern Age* (rev. ed., London,

Index